THE INDEX LIBRARY

NORTHAMPTONSHIRE ADMINISTRATIONS AND INVENTORIES

1711-1800

ISSUED BY
THE BRITISH RECORD SOCIETY, LIMITED
[92]

THE INDEX LIBRARY

ADMINISTRATIONS AND INVENTORIES

OF THE

ARCHDEACONRY OF NORTHAMPTON
Part II
1711-1800

(now preserved in the County Record Office at Northampton)

extracted by the late
REV. HENRY ISHAM LONGDEN, M.A., F.S.A.

Edited by
MRS. CLARE BAGGOTT, B.A.

Issued to Subscribers by
THE BRITISH RECORD SOCIETY
1980

Published by

The British Record Society, Limited
c/o Dr. Peter Spufford, Queens' College, Cambridge

ISBN 0 901505 08 0

in conjunction with
The Banbury Historical Society
Records Volume 17

ISBN 0 900129 18 2

This volume has been published with the aid of a legacy from the Reverend Henry Isham Longden which is most gratefully acknowledged.

The generous assistance of the British Academy with the publishing programme of the British Record Society is also gratefully recorded.

Printed by Parchment (Oxford) Ltd., Oxford

CONTENTS

Pre-1858 testamentary jurisdictions in Northamptonshire, the Soke of Peterborough and Rutland

This map showing Northamptonshire and Rutland probate jurisdictions is based on that published by the Institute of Heraldic and Genealogical Studies, Canterbury, and is reproduced from *Wills and Where to Find Them*, compiled by J. S. W. Gibson, British Record Society, 1974, by kind permission of the compiler.

The Archdeaconry Court of Northampton had jurisdiction over the southern part of Northamptonshire, except for the parish of Kings Sutton (marked '7' on the map) and Grimsbury, the Northamptonshire part of the parish of Banbury, of which the rest was in Oxfordshire. These places were in the Peculiar of Banbury, an index to whose probate records, 1542-1857, has been published by the Oxfordshire Record Society, vol. 40, and the Banbury Historical Society, vol. 1, 1959. The records themselves are in the Oxford Diocesan Record Office, Department of Western Manuscripts, Bodleian Library, Oxford.

The Consistory Court of Peterborough had jurisdiction over the northern part of Northamptonshire, including the Soke of Peterborough, and over Rutland. Records of both the Consistory Court of Peterborough and the Archdeaconry Court of Northampton are at the Northamptonshire Record Office.

Records of the Northamptonshire Peculiars of Gretton and Nassington, and the Rutland Peculiars of Empingham, Ketton and Liddington, are at the Lincolnshire Archives Office, The Castle, Lincoln. Indexes to wills and administrations in all of them have been published in the Index Library, vol. 57.

Further details of the probate records of Northamptonshire and Rutland are given in *Wills and Where to Find Them,* pages 96-99.

KEY

(places in Northamptonshire and Rutland outside the jurisdictions of the Bishop of Peterborough and the Archdeacon of Northampton)

1 Empingham and Hardwick in the Peculiar of Empingham

2 Ketton, Geeston and Tixover in the Peculiar of Ketton

3 Duddington in the Peculiar of Gretton

4 Liddington, Caldecott and Thorpe by Water (in the parish of Seaton) in the Peculiar of Liddington

5 Gretton in the Peculiar of Gretton

6 Nassington, Apethorpe, Woodnewton and Yarwell in the Peculiar of Nassington

7 Kings Sutton in the Peculiar of Banbury; Grimsbury, parish of Banbury, not marked on the map, is slightly to the north of Kings Sutton.

INTRODUCTION

It is unusual to publish a volume 38 years after the death of its compiler. The Reverend Henry Isham Longden (1859—1942), the well known Northamptonshire antiquary, left a legacy in his will for the publication of some of his calendars of Northamptonshire probate material. Long ago the unfortunate decision was taken to begin by publishing his calendars of administrations and inventories rather than the far more useful calendars of wills. In 1947 the first volume of his calendar of administrations and inventories was published by the British Record Society and appeared in the Index Library as volume 70. The present volume, begins in 1711, where that volume left off, and its publication exhausts the legacy left by Mr. Isham Longden. This means that no more of his numerous calendars to Northampton probate records can be published in the foreseeable future.

From the 1590's until its abolition in 1857 the probate jurisdiction of the archdeaconry court of Northampton covered the deaneries of Brackley, Daventry, Haddon, Higham, Northampton, Preston and Rothwell, in other words the larger part both of the administrative county of Northamptonshire and of the diocese of Peterborough (see map). After being moved from Northampton to Birmingham the records of this court are now again back in Northampton in the care of the county's chief archivist in the record office at Delapré Abbey. The principal documents of the archdeaconry court are the wills from 1469 to 1857 and the administrations from 1510 to 1857. Of the wills only those proved between 1510 and 1652 have a published calendar, *Index Library* I (1888). Mr. Isham Longden compiled manuscript calendars of the wills from 1469 to 1504 and from 1660 to 1857. For the administrations and associated documents much more has been published.

In his lifetime Mr. Isham Longden contributed abstracts of some 700 Administrations, granted in the Archdeaconry Court of Northampton, to *Miscellanea Genealogica et Heraldica* and these, with an index, were subsequently reprinted as a separate book (1939). These covered the years 1545-6; 1638-1641, 1660-1676. Volume 70 of the *Index Library*, edited for the British Record Society by Miss Lucy Drucker, contained an alphabetical calendar, arranged by year, of some 4000 administrations granted by the same court from 1677 to 1710. Inventories frequently survive and were calendared with the administrations. In addition two bundles of some three hundred separated inventories, from the period 1660 to 1710, were calendared at the end of the volume, and the whole indexed for *all* the names given: deceased, administrators, sureties, appraisers, and guardians.

Similar full calendars were made by Mr. Isham Longden for the later administrations and inventories. If this full format had been published in the present volume it would not have been possible to include the 6,500 or so remaining eighteenth century administrations within the scope of such a volume as the Society can afford to publish at the present level of prices. Mrs. Clare Baggott has therefore edited Mr. Isham Longden's calendars for the Society into a single much more succinct index.

The material covered by the present volume covers:

1. Administrations from 1711 to 1724 inclusive, including also the inventories, wills, accounts and letters of guardianship which are

bundled up in the annual bundles of administrations. Of these inventories are by far the most common.

2. Administrations from 1725 to 1800 inclusive, including related inventories, accounts and letters of guardianship, excerpted by Mr. Isham Longden from the mixed annual bundles of wills and administrations.
3. Inventories from 1711 to 1797, from the separate bundle of inventories.
4. Administrators' Accounts from 1665 to 1685, from the separate bundle of accounts.

Mr. Isham Longden's full original notes on these documents are to be found in volumes XXIV and XXVII of the Isham Longden MSS bequeathed to the Northamptonshire Record Society and kept at Delapré Abbey, Northampton. In cutting down Mr. Isham Longden's notes, Mrs. Baggott left out the sureties for the administrators, since it is highly unlikely that any user of these documents will want to approach them from the point of view of these sureties, especially as many of them were patently irrelevant, such as the mythical 'John Doe' or Edward Scriven, maltster of Northampton who was repeatedly brought into court as a nominal surety. He appeared as such 127 times between 1677 and 1706, occasionally twice in one day. Mrs. Baggott also left out the appraisers of the inventories, whom Mr. Isham Longden had assiduously noted down, since it again seemed unlikely that any user of the documents would want to approach them from the appraisers point of view. The appraisers were most frequently drawn from the leading men of the local community in which the dead man or woman had been living.

The entries are, however, a very great deal fuller than is now normal in a British Record Society publication. As in other volumes of the *Index Library* the entries begin with the surname and christian name of the deceased, and the parish within which he or she lived, together with his or her occupational designation. In most volumes of the *Index Library* this would be followed directly by a document reference. However in this volume details of the deceased are followed by the christian name of the Administrator, together with his or her surname if different from the deceased's, the occupation of the administrator and his or her relationship to the deceased. In addition wills are mentioned if applicable. Where letters of guardianship are involved the name or names of the minor(s) have been retained. Where inventories are available, the total values of goods appraised have also been retained in the index for the benefit of social historians to provide an easily accessible standard against which the wealth of individuals may be compared.

The index is arranged continuously for all categories of documents. The entries are grouped under the most common spelling for the surname. Under each surname the entries are arranged chronologically rather than alphabetically by christian name.

For the benefit of local historians a supplementary index of place names is provided. Various places have been identified with the aid of the Northamptonshire volume of the English Place Name Society's Publications, and the spelling of Northamptonshire place names standardised in accordance with it. However the spelling of places outside the county is that of Mr. Isham Longden's notes, which is presumably that of the documents themselves. For the benefit of social historians a supplementary index of trades and conditions has been provided, and there is, in addition, a supplementary index of other personal names, for administrators, minors for whom letters of guardianship survive, and any others of a different surname from the deceased.

How to use the volume

To find an administration.

Look under the surname of the deceased. From 1711 to 1725 the references are to the year bundle of administrations and to the document numbers within the bundles.

After 1725 the references are to the combined year bundles of wills and administrations, followed by the day and month.

To find an inventory *without administration*.

Look under the surname of the deceased. The entry will specify 'Inv. Only'.

If the inventory is in the bundle of some four hundred separate inventories the reference gives the year followed by the document number. Ask for the inventory bundle 1700-97 and give the document number. If the inventory is to be found in the *a*dministration bundles, the reference is to the year bundle, followed, up to 1725, by the document number and the letter *A*. Ask for the administration bundle for the year and give the document number. After 1725, if in the mixed bundles, the reference is in the same form as for administrations, the year bundle followed by day and month.

Letters of guardianship are normally found with other probate documents under the name of the deceased. However occasionally they are to be found alone. They are indexed under the name of the person whose death gave rise to the need for a guardian, not by the name of the child or children. The index of 'other persons' must therefore be used to find the children. The documents themselves can be found in the same way as administrations.

Administrators' Accounts are relatively rare, and a bundle of 170 separate accounts is quite unusual. They cover the period from 1665 to 1685 and have been separated from their letters of administration, many of which will be found to have already been indexed by Mr. Isham Longden in his earlier indexes of administrations and inventories. They should, properly, have been put into Volume 70 of the *Index Library*, but since they were omitted then, are included now. The entry makes clear that only an account is involved, and the reference is to the year followed by the document number. Ask for the accounts bundle for 1665—85 and give the document number.

The Society's thanks are due to the late Sir Gyles Isham, Bart. for his encouragement in taking up the work again after so long a lapse of time; to Mrs. Clare Baggott for reducing Mr. Isham Longden's calendars to index form; and to Mr. Patrick King, the chief archivist of Northamptonshire, for his forbearance and assistance in the lengthy gestation of this volume.

Queens' College
Cambridge
1980

Peter Spufford
for the Editorial Committee,
British Record Society

Of the residue of Mr. Isham Longden's legacy and accrued interest, £191 was expended on the editorial work of reducing his manuscript calendars to a single consolidated index, and £1430 was used as a contribution towards printing costs.

LIST OF ABBREVIATIONS

admin.	administrator
decd.	deceased
exor.	executor
gent.	gentleman
guard.	letters of guardianship
husb.	husbandman
Inv.	inventory
lab.	labourer
spin.	spinster
wid.	widow
yeo.	yeoman

ABBEY, Mary, wid., Inv.only £70.14.9 1714/42A
Charles, Stoke Bruerne, to William, mason, son, 1784/12 Mar.
William, Stoke Bruerne, lab., to William, mason, 1786/27 Feb.
ABBOTT, Mary, Raunds, wid., Inv.only £105.12.0 1713/11A
Elizabeth, Spratton, Inv.only £2.18.6 1714/18A
John, Wellingborough, fuller, to William Hensman, Pytchley, gent., principal creditor, Inv. £17.19.10 1714/60
William, Weston Favell, mason, to Anne, wid., Inv. £6.1.0 1715/16
Sarah, Little Addington, wid., to William, husb., son, 1719/90
Thomas, Little Addington, to Thomas Kennell, Wimington, Beds., yeo., principal creditor, 1719/136
Thomas, Little Addington, Account of Thomas Kennell, principal creditor and admin., £26.8.2 1720/143
Henry, Kislingbury, husb., to Elizabeth, wid., 1727/4 Mar
Henry, Kislingbury, Inv.only £226.15.0 1727/151
Henry, Cranford St. Andrew, to Penelope Harvey Abbott, w[illegible] '61/22 June
Abraham, Weston Favell, to John, mason, son, 1762/14 Aug.
Abbot, John, Raunds, victualler, to Hannah, wid., 1783/10 Jul.
John, Welford, farmer, to John, farmer, son, 1785/15 Oct.
ABEARNE, Bridget, Irchester, spin., to William, Kimbolton, Hunts., tanner, brother. 1728/12 Nov.
ABELL, William, Weedon Beck, to Anne, wid., Inv., £32.13.6 1721/67
ABET, John, Sulgrave, butcher, to Susanna, wid., Inv. £37.11.3 1718/98
ABORNE, John, Chelveston cum Caldecott, husb., to Elizabeth, wid., 1727/10 Oct.
John, Chelveston cum Caldecott, Inv.only £247.10.0 1727/194
John, Chelveston, yeo., Guardonly of Elizabeth and Mary, minors, daughters. 1739/31 Aug.
Aburn, Mark, Towcester, to Elizabeth, wid., 1759/24 Mar.
Aburn, Mark, Towcester, cordwainer, to Sarah, Cockspur St., Middx., spin., daughter, 1799/31 Dec.
ACAM, Mary, Weedon Beck, wid., to Robert, Aynho, gent., son, 1720/158
ACHURCH, Samuel, Wellingborough, tanner, Inv.only £127.4.6 1714/105A
ADAMS, Nathaniel, Towcester, to Mary, wid., Inv. £14.10.0 1712/86
Adams, Anne, Kettering, to Hannah Good, spin., niece, 1725/28 Apr.
Knightley John, Charwelton, gent., to William, clerk, father, 1728/25 Oct.
Fitzherbert, Charwelton, gent., to Grace, wid., Inv. £791.19.6 1747/5 Oct.
Joseph, Chalcombe, to William, lab., son, Elizabeth, wid., renounced, 1762/28 June
Thomas, West Haddon, to Anne, wid., 1769/18 Mar.
Alice, Abthorpe, wid., to Robert Barford, yeo., principal creditor, Thomas Willifer, yeo., father, renounced, 1776/15 Nov.
Samuel, Brampton, farmer, to John, farmer, son, and John Walton, Harlstone, victualler, Mary, spin., daughter, Henry Miller, farmer, son-in-law, Henry Crutchley, cordwainer, and Esthuc, his wife, daughter, William and Elizabeth Bucker, tailor, Kingsthorpe, daughter, renounced. 1777/14 July
John, Northampton, tailor, to William, Daventry, cordwainer, brother, 1782/29 July
als. Cockerill, Mary, Wappenham, to Thomas, tallow chandler, husband, 1782/Aug. or Sept.
Thomas, Farthinghoe, turner, to Elizabeth, wid., 1783/2 Jan.
Aimer, Daventry, whipmaker, to Samuel Judkins, cordwainer, brother-in-law. 1785/26 Apr.
Thomas, Holdenby, lab., to Leah, wid., Will, 1794/8 Aug.
John, Castle Ashby, victualler, to Elizabeth, wife of Jonathan Howkins, Hackleton, butcher, daughter, 1800/21 Oct.
ADAMSON, Thomas, Floore, to Mary, wid., 1726/20 Apr.
ADCOCK, James, Paulerspury, carpenter, Inv.only £77.4.0 1717/144A
James, Paulerspury, weaver, Inv.only £5.10.10 1721/117A
John, Brackley, victualler, to Anne, wid., 1754/10 May
ADDERSON, Robert, Clipston, lab., to Robert, yeo., son, Inv. £12.12.8 Alice, wid., renounced. 1720/91
Adderston, Edward, Braybrooke, to Elizabeth, wid., Inv. £38.16.6 1729/9 June
ADDIS, Richard, Grendon, gent., to Robert, Ingatestone, co. Essex, and Jane, wife of Richard Petit, son and daughter, 1746/3 May

ADDIS continued
Robert, Bozeat, to Ann, wid., 1755/29 Dec.
Ann, Bozeat, wid., to Sophia, wife of John Estal, and Jane, wife of Thomas Toms, daughters, 1757/18 Feb.
ADKINS see ATKINS
ADSON, Mary, Daventry, wid., to Samuel, carpenter, son, 1735/1 Dec.
Francis, Wellingborough, to Joseph Tester, pipemaker, 1797/8 Aug.
AGER, Mary, Northampton, wid., to Joseph Cooper, butcher, Elizabeth, Uppingham, co. Rutland, daughter-in-law, renounced, 1775/20 Nov.
AGUTTER, John, Wollaston, Inv.only £20.6.4 1719/29A
Mary, Northampton, wid., to Mary, wife of George Reynolds, horse dealer, daughter, 1761/28 Feb.
Guy, Northampton, woolstapler, to John, draper, brother, Dinah, wid., renounced. 1768/24 May
ALDERMAN, Francis, Little Harrowden, to Thomas, yeo., brother, 1711/32
Francis, Rothwell, tailor, to John, yeo., son, Inv. £114.9.0 1732/15 June
Mary, Little Harrowden, spin., to Thomas, gent., and Martha, wife of William Langley, gent., brother and sister, 1737/10 Sept.
Jane, Rothwell, to John, junior, husband, 1760/6 May
Mary, Irthlingborough, wid., to John, victualler, exor. of Benjamin, husb., decd., and guardian of Anne Groome, grandaughter 1763/13 July
George, Rothwell, weaver, to Elizabeth, wife of John Foster, and Sarah, wife of Richard Cook, daughters, Elizabeth, wife, exor., decd., Will. 1770/4 Aug.
ALDRIDGE, John, Guilsborough, bachelor, to Elizabeth, wife of Edward Clarke, West Haddon, tailor, sister, 1724/105
William, Braunston, to Sarah, spin., sister, 1735/3 Jan.
ALLAM, Andrew, Bradden, to Jane, spin., sister, 1721/111
ALLARD, William, senior, East Farndon, Inv.only £352.5.0 1719/12A
John, Great Oxendon, yeo., to Elizabeth, wid., Inv. £18.14.0 1740/31 May
Martha, Haselbech, wid., to William, grazier, son, 1754/13 Apr.
Esther, Ashby Ledgers, spin., to Thomas, Long Buckby, lab., John, Hockbrooke, co. Derby, lab., Richard, Hinckley, co. Leic., lab., and Elizabeth Birch, wid., brothers and sister, Will, 1796/23 Aug.
ALLEN, Nicholas, Towcester, to Thomas, cobbler, son, Inv. £40.10.6 1712/91
Allin, Alleyn, Thomas, Lilbourne, weaver, Inv.only £72.17.6 1722/34A
John, Ravensthorpe (late of London), to Joan, London, wid., 1723/35
Oliver, Irthlingborough, blacksmith, to Rebecca, wid., Inv. £8.17.6 1723/46
Allin, John, Weedon Beck, yeo., Inv.only £28.10.6 1724/131
Richard, Brackley, to Anne, wid., 1725/30 Apr.
Alice, Weedon Beck, wid., to Samuel, husb., son, Inv. £8.8.0 1727/8 July
Clement, Grendon, Inv.only £197.10.0 1727/157
Joseph, Yardley Hastings, lab., Inv.only £17.7.0 1729/242
Thomas, Norton, yeo., to Elizabeth, wid., 1730/9 Apr.
Anne, Finedon, wid., to John, innholder, son, 1741/26 Feb.
Clement, Wollaston, baker, to Elizabeth, wid., 1750/28 Dec.
John, Abthorpe, to Hannah, wid., 1751/25 May
Anne, Brixworth, wid., to William, yeo., son, 1770/22 May
William, Brixworth, yeo., to William, yeo., son, admin. of Ann, wid., exor., decd., Will, 1770/22 May
William, Newbold Grounds, to Anne, wid., 1775/20 Mar.
William, Boughton, papermaker, to Mary, spin., daughter, 1777/9 Dec.
Anne, Stowe Nine Churches, to Elizabeth Linnen, sister, 1779/31 May
Richard, Lilbourne, grazier, to Anne, wid., 1780/28 Jan.
Allin, Elizabeth, Barby, to Thomas, cordwainer, son, 1782/19 Jan.
William, Boughton, dealer, to Ann, wid., 1783/17 Mar.
Richard, Boughton, baker, to Sarah, wid., 1784/2 Aug.
John, Boughton, papermaker, to William, shopkeeper, son, 1786/15 July
ALLGOOD see HAWGOOD
ALLIBONE, Elizabeth, Stowe Nine Churches, wid., to John, carpenter, uncle and guardian of John, minor, son, 1739/12 June
Mary, Helmdon, wid., to Elizabeth, spin., daughter, 1765/8 Jan.
Job, Helmdon, yeo., to Elizabeth, spin., daughter, Ann, wid., renounced. 1765/6 Feb.
ALLICOCKE, Caroline, Loddington, spin., to Mary, Elizabeth and Dorothy, spins., sisters, 1759/29 Dec.
ALLISON, Alliston, Elizabeth, Wilby, wid., to John Worley, principal creditor, Inv. £11.4.5 1732/24 July

ALLISON continued
Alliston, Thomas, Northampton, innholder, to Obrien, gent., brother, Mary, wid., renounced. 1740/4 Aug.
John, Ringstead, gent., to Elizabeth, wid., 1765/25 Sept.
John, Ringstead, to Christopher Hobson, Cliffords Inn, London, gent., nephew, of goods unadministered by Elizabeth, wid., decd., 1770/23 July
ALSOP, Hannah, to Rebecca, wife of Abraham Parkins, Astwell, lab. 1712/9
ALTHORPE, Daniel, Kettering, to Anne, wid., 1728/15 Feb.
George, Kettering, to Hannah, wid., Inv. £59.12.6 1730/8 Sept.
Mark, Moulton, yeo., husb., to Elizabeth, wid., Inv. £349.8.6 1742/4 Sept.
Thomas, Northampton, victualler, to Sarah, wid., 1767/4 Apr.
AMAN, William, Northampton, to Ruth, wife of Charles Bason, staymaker, daughter, 1775/27 July
AMOS, Amoz, Susanna, Byfield, wid., to Thomas Webb, Sulgrave, husb., son, 1723/72
Edward, Silverstone, lab., to Edward, woodman, son, 1753/6 Oct.
ANCELL, William, Hartwell, to Jane, wife of John Green, sister, Inv. £23.9.6 1722/122
ANDREWS, Andrew, Robert, Long Buckby, yeo., Inv.only £456.11.8 1722/139A
Andrew, Sarah, Mears Ashby, wid., to James Guetier, clerk, vicar, widower of Anne, decd., daughter and exor. of Sarah, Will, 1729/22 Mar.
Anne, Overstone, wid., to Richard Gaudern, Earl's Barton, gent., principal creditor, 1730/17 Jan.
John, Thorpe Malsor, to John, 1750/1 Dec.
Ann, Quinton, to Richard Welford, Brill, Bucks., yeo., nephew, Will, 1756/23 June
Richard, Yardley Hastings, to Mary, wid., 1760/5 Aug.
John, Little Billing, to Martha, wid., 1769/10 June
Elizabeth, Cransley, spin., to John, Thorpe Malsor, cordwainer, and Joseph, cordwainer, brothers, Inv. £33.6.1 1777/26 Nov.
John, Thorpe Malsor, to John, cordwainer, son, 1783/27 Oct.
ANGEL, Thomas, younger, Potterspury, to Sarah Downing and Ann Hindes, 1784/26 Feb.
ANNIS, James, Loddington, Inv.only £28.1.0 1711/113A
William, Great Oxendon, shepherd, to Constance, wid., Inv. £33.14.3 1714/9
Thomas, Oxendon, to John, weaver, son, 1741/15 Jan.
Benjamin, Slapton, carpenter, to Mary, wid., 1770/12 June
ANTROBUS, William, Everdon, clerk, to Elizabeth, wid., 1742/19 June
APPLETON, Elizabeth, Northampton, wid., to Elizabeth, spin., daughter, 1784/22 Mar.
ARCH, Joseph, Broughton, to Anne, wid., Inv. £150.0.0 1718/85
Susanna, Broughton, spin., to Joseph, farmer, nephew, 1789/4 July
ARCHBOLD, Alice, Cold Higham, wid., to Thomas Robinson, John, son, exor., renounced, 1717/29
Richard, Grimscote, Cold Higham, Inv.only £159.5.0 1726/178
ARCHER, Mary, Northampton, St. Peter's, spin., to Ferdinando, gent., and Rebecca, spin., brother and sister, Inv. £5.12.0 1711/145
Edmund, Rothwell, weaver, to Thomas, father, Inv. £27.14.2 1714/168
Ambrose, Rothwell, baker, Inv.only £16.2.0 1715/85A
Thomas, Rothwell, to Anne, wid., Inv. £5.16.4 1720/80
William, Cranford St. Andrew, Inv.only £23.15.6 1723/102A
John, Thorpe Malsor, to Joseph Fox, yeo., 1724/10
Charles, Kettering, to Tingles, uncle and guardian of Charles and Ann, minors, children, 1752/31 Aug.
William, Cranford, to Mary, wid., Will, 1773/9 June
Joseph, marine, to Emma, wife of Thomas Roughton, Kettering, mother, 1782/19 Jan.
ARDEN als. Watworth, James, Silverstone, lab., Inv.only £22.0.0 1721/78A
ARIES, ARIS see AYRES
ARMITT, George, Middleton Cheney, wheelwright, Inv.only £30.10.5 1723/114A
John, Chalcombe, carpenter, to Mary, wid., Inv. £10.5.0 1728/19 July
Armit, William, Middleton Cheney, to Sarah, wife of Edward Chester, Marston St. Lawrence, sister, 1741/1 Sept.
Mary, Chalcombe, wid., to John, wheelwright, son, 1746/20 Dec.
ARMSTRONG, Eleanor, Welton, wid., to Mary Sumerland, Rugby, co. Warwick, wid., sister, 1750/28 Apr.
ARNOLD, Anne, Daventry, wid., Inv.only £1042.13.7 1711/82A
John, Cottesbrooke, to Sarah, wid., 1725/9 Nov.
Mary, Boddington, wid., to Henry, wheelwright, son, 1786/4 May

ARNSBY, John, Raunds, mason, to Hannah, wid., Inv. £298.14.6 1781/27 Nov.
ARRINGTON see ERRINGTON
ARUNDELL, Charles, Ashton, to Elizabeth, Courtenhall, wid., 1723/25
Rev. Edward, Courtenhall, clerk, to Samuel Lancaster, Newbold Pacey, co. Warwick, clerk, principal creditor, Inv. £111.19.2 Francis, father, renounced. 1731/30 Mar.
ASBEY see ASHBY
ASBYLAND, John, Northampton, to William, weaver, son, Will, 1722/99
ASDELL see ASTELL
ASH, John, Sulgrave, yeo., to Henry, yeo., son, Inv. £69.6.6 1725/22 May
Thomas, Sulgrave, bachelor, shepherd, to Henry, yeo., brother, Inv. £27.18.0 1743/25 Mar.
Henry, Sulgrave, to William Mayo, tailor, 1767/26 Feb.
ASHBRIDGE, Robert, Courtenhall, to Mary, Northampton, wid., 1720/69
ASHBY, Thomas, Yelvertoft, carpenter, Inv.only £14.12.0 1712/14A
Thomas, Yelvertoft, yeo., Inv.only £120.4.0 1712/49A
John, Kislingbury, Inv.only £146.15.0 1713/10A
Thomas, Yelvertoft, Guard.only of John, minor, son, 1714/28
John, Yelvertoft, to Benjamin, yeo., son, 1714/44
Thomas, Yelvertoft, carpenter, to John Miles, husb., principal creditor, Inv. £14.8.6 Benjamin, and John Sawbridge, renounced, 1715/77
Asbey, John, Northampton, to Anne, wid., Inv. £39.3.0 1726/6 Dec.
William, Newnham, to Mary, wid., Inv. £11.7.0 1727/15 July
Ashbye, Ann, Inv.only £38.9.9 1736/333
Edward, marine, to William, Litchborough, lab., father, 1760/5 May
Richard, Gayton, yeo., to Martha, wid., 1778/9 May
John, Yelvertoft, blacksmith, to John, Daventry, blacksmith, son, 1782/28 Jan.
Lamb, Bugbrooke, grazier, to Sarah, wid., and Richard Pinckney, Northampton, clogmaker, Will, 1782/26 Feb.
William, Lower Heyford, grazier, to William Court, Shottery, co. Warwick, farmer, grandson, William, grazier, renounced, Will, 1785/20 June
Ann, Northampton, wid., to Mary, wife of Edward Wood, glazier, and Sarah, wife of Francis Osborn, innholder, daughters, 1786/3 Apr.
Saul, Northampton, saddler, to Sarah, wid., and William, saddler, son, 1788/29 Mar.
John, Kislingbury, grazier, to Thomas, Bugbrooke, yeo., brother, 1792/11 Feb.
Sarah, Northampton, wid., to John Wilkinson, gent., cousin, 1796/6 May
ASHER, Edward, Desborough, to Jane, wid., 1766/24 Nov.
ASHLEY, Henry, Barford Lodge, Glendon, to Henry, son, Will, 1717/135
ASHTON, Philip, Higham Ferrers, to Alice, wid., 1722/90
ASKEW, Thomas, Cranford, Account of Thomas White, principal creditor, admin. £20. 1681/4
Samuel, Broughton, to Hannah, wid., 1742/22 Jan.
John, Cranford St. Andrew, woolcomber, to Rebecca, wid., Inv. £440.13.0 1748/12 Nov.
ASKHAM, John, Raunds, butcher, to Elizabeth, wid., Inv. £76.2.6 1729/22 July
Askam, Thomas, Stanwick, Account of Elizabeth, wid., £88.10.0 undated/117
ASPINAL, Elizabeth, Kingsthorpe, to John, farmer, brother, 1775/30 Jan.
ASTELL, Asdell, William, Barton Seagrave, Inv.only £4.15.8½ 1723/143A
Edward, Claycoton, yeo., to Thomas, yeo., brother, 1736/29 Apr.
ATHEY, William, Northampton, innholder, to Jane, wid., 1733/1 Aug.
ATKINS, Adkins, Henry, Towcester, to Mary, wid., Inv. £171.18.10 1712/45
Adkins, William, Wappenham, Inv.only £28.5.0 1717/68A
Richard, Welton, hempdresser, to Mary, wid., Inv. £15.19.5 1719/114
John, Blisworth, yeo., Inv.only £191.3.0 1719/119A
Adkins, William, Floore, lab., to Richard, son, 1719/128
John, Desborough, yeo., Inv.only £209.14.0 1722/10A
Adkins, Sarah, Blakesley, spin., to Moses, servant, brother, 1732/8 Jan.
Adkins, Joseph, Wellingborough, shepherd, to William, mealman, cousin, Inv. £39.5.4 1737/4 Jan.
William, Wellingborough, to Mary Fisher, daughter, Inv. £17.15.0 1758/7 Apr.
Ann, Welton, spin., to Anne Gupwell, Kilsby, spin., 1766/19 Feb.
Adkins, John, Denton, to John, woolcomber, son, 1768/3 Aug.
Adkins, Isaac, Wicken, to Ann, wid., 1774/10 Aug.
Adkins, George, Maidford, lab., to Elizabeth, wid., 1796/23 June

ATTERBURY, William, Northampton, tanner, to Frances, wid., Inv. £37.7.0 1716/59
Laurence, Little Houghton, yeo., Inv.only £1040.10.0 1719/118 A
Alice, Milton, spin., to Martha Hopkins, wid., sister, 1727/10 Nov.
James, Little Houghton, chandler, to Elizabeth, Hollowell, spin., sister, 1749/17 Nov.
Ann, Little Bowden, to Sarah, wife of James Whitny, Northampton, plumber glazier, 1777/5 July
Sarah, Little Houghton, spin., to William Collier, Thorpe Malsor, yeo., nephew, 1782/22 July
Elizabeth, Crick, wid., to Thomas Pittam, 1793/1 July
ATTHEY, Abigail, Sywell, Inv.only £17.15.0 1743/387
ATWELL, Edward, Daventry, schoolmaster, Inv.only £8.10.11 1738/358
Henry, Earl's Barton, to John, yeo., brother, 1744/10 Apr.
Attwell, Henry, Earl's Barton, yeo., to Thomas Dalley, Dingley, gent., nephew, 1785/27 Dec.
Attwell, Joseph, Weston Favell, shopkeeper, to William King, Northampton, grocer, creditor, Elizabeth, wid., renounced, 1789/15 July
AUSTIN, Thomas, Little Harrowden, husb., Inv.only £55.1.6 1712/126 A
William, Thenford, yeo., Inv.only £260.7.9 1721/100 A
Thomas, Rothwell, Inv.only £89.8.4 1724/127
William, Thenford, farmer, to Mary, wid., 1755/11 Apr.
AWBERY, Awbrey, William, Higham Ferrers, currier, Inv.only £14.8.7 1720/102 A
Aubury, Awbury, William, Brackley, hatter, to Sarah, wid., 1741/1 June
AYRES, Eyre, William, Kilsby, husb., to Alice and Hannah, spins., sisters, Will, 1711/27
Eyre, James, elder, Murcott, Watford, yeo., Inv.only £422.18.0 1713/104 A
Eyre, Air, Ayre, Abraham, Kettering (Wellingborough), shoemaker, to John, senior, brother, Inv. £17.13.4 1714/153
Aris, Earis, Joyce, West Haddon, wid., Inv. £75. Guard.of Jane, minor, 1715/51 and 52
Aris, William, Hellidon, to Mary, wid., Inv. £19.2.0 1715/100
Eayre, Thomas, Kettering, blacksmith, to Thomas, clockmaker, son, Sarah, wid., renounced, 1716/62
Eyre, Eyare, Robert, Raunds, glover, Inv.only £50.0.0 1718/90 A
Henry, Isham, to Sarah, wid., 1720/43
Eyre, Ayres, John, Murcott, Watford, to Elizabeth, wid., 1725/9 Jan.
Ayer, Elizabeth, Wellingborough, wid., to Richard, weaver, brother and guardian of Henry, minor, son, 1741/28 Feb.
Eyre, Thomas, Maidford, yeo., to Anne, wid., 1755/29 Apr.
Eyre, Grace, Long Buckby, to Thomas, yeo., husband, 1755/25 Oct.
William, Brackley, to Elizabeth, wid., 1763/26 Feb.
Ayer, Ayres, Joseph, Finedon, to Ann, wid., Inv. £490.11.6½ 1766/10 Mar.
Eayre, Thomas, Kettering, bellfounder, to Sarah, wife of Joseph Pettifer, shoemaker, and Frances, wife of John Bates, watchmaker, daughters, Will, 1770/6 Sept.
Eyre, John, Murcott, Watford, to Sarah, wid., 1777/3 May
Aries, Ayries, William, Blakesley, farmer, to Mary, wid., 1779/4 Feb.
Eyre, Thomas, Helmdon, to Edward Barnett, Wappenham, victualler, creditor, 1780/26 Sept.
Ayer, Elizabeth, Abthorpe, wid., to Anne, wife of Valentine Barford, Foscote, Abthorpe, grazier, daughter, 1785/14 Feb.
Thomas, Badby, victualler, to Mary, wid., 1785/26 Apr.
Eayrs, Samuel, Kilsby, weaver, to Samuel, son, Elizabeth, exor., decd., Will, 1796/12 May

B

BABBINGTON, Rebecca, Isham, wid., to Margery Shrieve, daughter, Will, 1722/19
BADBY, Elizabeth, Brackley Hatch, innholder, Inv.only £25.5.6 1726/159
John, Syresham, higler, to Ann, wid., 1790/28 Dec.
BAGGOTT, John, Wellingborough, Inv.only £77.15.2 1714/50 A
Baggitt, Rebecca, Wellingborough, wid., Inv.only £85.4.10 1720/3 A
BAGLEY, Baggerly, Mary, Finedon, wid., Inv.only £10.14.6 1717/81 A
Elizabeth, Ecton, wid., to Sara, wife of John Maule, gent., daughter, 1723/36
Joseph, Towcester, joiner, to Hannah, wid., Will, 1773/8 June
BAGSHAW, Henry, Brixworth, Inv.only £3.10.0 undated/408

BAILES, Anne, Northampton, wid., to Sara, wife of Giles Twigden, hatter, daughter, 1720/5
Bayls, Richard, Irthlingborough, lab., to Hanna, wid., 1727/11 Nov.
Anne, Northampton, wid., to Francis Twigden, victualler, son-in-law, of goods unadministered by Sarah, daughter, decd., 1745/10 Sept.
BAILEY, Bayley, John, Gayton, Inv.only £206.2.8 1713/75A
Bayly, Richard, Broughton, to Susanna, wid., Inv. £5.4.10 1715/111
Bayley, John, Inv.only £63.3.6 1717/101A
Bayly, William, West Haddon, husb., to Sarah, wid., Inv. £81.14.10 1718/100
James, Finedon, Inv.only £101.16.6 1721/18A
Baily, John, Kingsthorpe, to Anne, wid., 1721/24
Baily, John, Pattishall, Inv.only £25.10.0 1721/72A
Baily, Anne, Collingtree, Inv.only £9.0.8 1721/116A
Bayley, Philip, Rushden, mason, Inv.only £34.3.6 1724/48A
Baily, Francis, Finedon, poulterer, to Mary, wid., Inv. £140.18.6 1724/155
Bayley, Thomas, Whilton, Inv.only £49.11.6 1727/192
Thomas, junior, Sywell, to Dorothy, wid., 1727/14 Jan.
Bayley, Thomas, junior, Sywell, husb., Inv.only £48.0.0 1727/149
Bayley, Thomas, Whilton, husb., to Sarah, wid., 1727/11 Nov.
Elizabeth, Finedon, wid., to William, husb., son, 1728/4 July
John, Irthlingborough, mason, to John, mason, son. Frances, wid., renounced, 1728/3 Sept.
John, Passenham, victualler, to Anne, wid., now wife of Thomas Smith, blacksmith, 1733/13 Oct.
James, Denford, fellmonger, to Matthew, fellmonger, son, Inv. £373.5.0 Mary, wid., renounced, 1754/4 May
Bayley, William, Middleton Cheney, to Thomas, King's Sutton, yeo., son, Sarah, Souldern, co. Oxford, wid., renounced, 1755/11 Apr.
Bayly, George, Northampton, to Richard Kent, Gayton, nephew, 1764/14 July
John, Rothersthorpe, yeo., to Elizabeth, wife of John Hutt, Cosgrave, miller, daughter, Grace, exor., wid., decd., Will, 1768/25 Aug.
Bayley, Elizabeth, Navesby, to Lydia and Hannah, spins., sisters, 1769/8 July
Mary, Everdon, to Thomas, lab., son, 1772/29 Oct.
Thomas, elder, Wollaston, to Mary, wid., 1780/19 June
Sarah, Mears Ashby, wid., to Elizabeth, spin., daughter in law 1782/19 Aug.
BAINES, Nicholas, Inv.only £39.14.6 1713/123A
BAKER, Sarah, Kettering, wid., to Daniel, ironmonger, son, 1712/96
John, Nobottle, Great Brington, Inv.only £4.6.8 1712/139A
Dorothy, Chipping Warden, wid., Inv.only £10.19.7 1714/87
William, Chipping Warden, to John, Finnycomb, co. Warwick, lab., uncle and guardian of William and Anne, minors, children, Inv. £10.19.7 1714/189
John, Newbottle, Inv.only £209.17.0 1717/12A
John, senior, Kettering, Inv.only £35.19.0 1720/131A
John, Aynho, Inv.only £17.12.6 1724/123A
John, Potterspury, Inv.only £14.12.8 1735/327
John, Potterspury, victualler, to Mary, wid., 1736/28 Aug.
Joseph, Kettering, to Sarah, wid., mother, 1743/6 Jan.
Thomas, Crick, yeo., to Alice, wid., 1744/17 Mar.
Francis, Barton Seagrave, yeo., to Frances, wid., Inv. £684.3.5 1746/19 July
Samuel, Crick, farmer, to James, farmer, son, Inv. £98.5.6 Elizabeth, wid., renounced, 1752/10 Feb.
BALDWIN, James, Newnham, dealer, to Elizabeth, wid., 1741/24 Aug.
John, Newnham, blacksmith, to Elizabeth, wid., 1756/21 June
John, Whitfield, to Anne, wid., 1758/19 Oct.
BALL, Mary, Ashby St. Ledgers, to William, carpenter, husband, 1745/25 July
Ann, Northampton, spin., to Richard, coachmaker, father, 1754/25 Nov.
Mary, Wellingborough, spin., to John, Astcote, Pattishall, lab., grandfather, 1764/1 Dec.
Thomas, Desborough, husb., to Ruth, wid., William Gutteridge, exor., decd. Will, 1786/24 Oct.
BAMFORD, Henry, Old, yeo., to Elizabeth, wid., 1735/2 Aug.
John, Little Billing, to Thomas Groome, grazier, son-in-law, of goods unadministered by Elizabeth, wife, and Elizabeth, daughter, Margaret, wid. of John, grazier, son, renounced, Will, 1771/13 Apr.

BAMFORD continued
John, Spratton, yeo., to Henry, Southwark, co. Surrey, yeo., and John, yeo., sons, Ann, wid., exor., decd., Will, 1789/28 Feb.
John, Kettering, to Sarah, wife of Thomas Jackson, sergemaker, sister, 1792/22 Feb.
BANBURY, Thomas, Newnham, to Lucy, wid., 1727/7 Nov.
Thomas, Newnham, Account of Lucy, wid., 1727/183
Lucie, Newnham, wid., to William Muscott, Floore, gent., principal creditor, 1750/22 Aug.
Thomas, Newnham, Inv.only £44.0.0 undated/222
BANKES, William, Arthingworth, Account of Cicilie als. Clarke, wid., admin., £221.16.0 1672/104
Banks, Joyce, Newnham, to William, son, clerk, and George Watkin, Northampton, clerk, 1775/23 May
Banks, William, Newnham, clerk, to John, Wootton, co. Oxford, clerk, brother, 1776/7 Mar.
Banks, Henry, Pottespury, shopkeeper, to Anne, wid., 1785/22 Jan.
Banks, John, Wood End, Blakesley, to Hannah, 1791/22 July
Banks, William, Northampton, Guard.only of Elizabeth, minor, 1791/23 Aug.
BANNISTER, Benjamin, Lilbourne, to Grace, wid., Inv. £9.2.0 1711/137
Jonathan, Barby, cordwainer, Inv.only £37.3.0 1715/66A
Banister, Benjamin, Northampton, to Martha, wid., 1726/27 Sept.
als. Wade, Ann, see Wade
BANWELL, John, Brackley, victualler, to Vade, wid., 1748/22 Apr.
BARBER, Barbor, John, senior, Moulton, Inv.only £287.11.5½ 1715/165A
Mary, Moulton, minor, to John, farmer, uncle, 1760/24 Nov.
Chapman, Moulton, to John, farmer, uncle and admin. of Mary, spin., daughter, decd., of goods unadministered by Thomas Pell and William Smith, Will, 1761/10 Mar.
Susanna, Moulton, to Robert, farmer, husband, 1766/8 Nov.
Mary, Moulton, spin., to Mary, wife of Thomas Fennell, Harpole, woolcomber, 1766/22 Nov.
Daniel, Moulton, to John, son, 1773/7 Aug.
Chapman, Moulton, yeo., to John, Thrapston, draper, nephew, Will, 1777/7 June
John Clarke, Moulton, yeo., to Elizabeth, wid., 1797/24 Jan.
BARFORD, Barfoot, Richard, Ringstead, sandman, to Thomas, shepherd, son, Mary, wid., renounced, Inv. £36.5.0 1758/8 Aug.
Robert, Abthorpe, yeo., to Sarah, wid., 1773/12 May
Sarah, Foscote, Abthorpe, wid., to Sarah, wife of Thomas Higham, yeo., and Elizabeth, wife of Winckles Cleaver, Greens Norton, miller, daughters, Inv. £400.13.6 1787/27 Nov.
Robert, Foscote, Abthorpe, yeo., to Elizabeth, wid., 1788/14 Feb.
Sarah, Abthorpe, wid., Guard.only of Mary Dover, minor, granddaughter, 1795/29 Dec.
BARINGHAM, Mary, Wollaston, wid., Inv.only £22.18.0 1717/138A
BARKER, John, Rushden, Account of William and Hannah Child, £123.6.6 1671/123
Robert, West Haddon, to Anne, wid., Inv. £52.6.2 1711/25
Joseph, Welton, Inv.only £3.12.6 1712/24A
Thomas, Earl's Barton, servant, Inv.only £22.1.6 1720/19A
Richard, Stanford, to Jane, wid., Rev. James Bond, vicar, exor., decd., Will, 1721/131
William, Finedon, Inv.only £88.11.0 1723/132A
Anne, Northampton, spin., to Thomas Greenrough, cordwainer, 1724/82
Thomas, Earl's Barton, Guard.only of George, minor, son, 1724/97
Jane, Inv.only £34.11.0 1724/132
Joseph, Brafield, to Thomas Morris, Whiston, husb., father in law, 1728/17 Feb.
William, Cransley, to Anne, wid., Inv. £74.1.6 1729/3 Jan.
Richard, Earl's Barton, yeo., to Susannah, wid., 1736/20 Mar.
Richard, Earl's Barton, yeo., Inv.only £91.18.0 1736/326
William, Walgrave, lab., to Jane, wid., Inv. £15.11.6 1740/9 Feb.
Joseph, Kettering, victualler, to Elizabeth, wid., Inv. £16.15.3 1745/10 Aug.
Samuel, Cottesbrooke, servant, to Mary, wid., 1748/27 Feb.
Sarah, Bugbrooke, wid., to Hannah, wife of John Ingram, younger, tailor, daughter, Inv. £17.9.9 1748/15 Mar.
Elizabeth, Earl's Barton, wid., to Vincent, son, 1755/1 Feb.

BARKER continued
William, Ecton, yeo., to Mary, wid., 1755/1 Mar.
William, Pisford, to Anne, wid., 1773/10 July
BARNARD, William, Kingsthorpe, to Grace, wid., 1773/12 Aug.
William, Northampton, victualler, to Ann, wid., 1790/23 Mar.
BARNES, William, Whittlebury, yeo., to Anne, wid., Inv. £67.10.0 1711/141
Edward, Northampton, tailor, Inv.only £9.13.0 1713/32A
John, senior, Radstone, yeo., to Richard, father and guardian of John, minor, exor., Inv. £500.1.6 John, son, exor., renounced, 1717/78
James, Hargrave, to Anne, wid., 1723/106
James, Hargrave, lab., Inv.only £29.16.4 1723/117
Anne, Whittlebury, wid., Inv.only £5.6.6 1739/369
Joseph, Blakesley, cordwainer, to Elizabeth, wife of David Higham, butcher, sister, 1743/18 Apr.
Lucy, Bugbrooke, to John, carpenter, husband, 1764/16 June
John, Doddington, farmer, to Ruth, Ampthill, co. Bedford, wid., 1790/20 Oct.
BARNETT, Thomas, Evenley, to Frances, spin., daughter, 1739/9 May
Barnet, Jane, Kilsby, to Richard, lab., husband, 1758/25 Feb.
Elizabeth, Kilsby, spin., to Richard, lab., brother, 1771/5 June
Anne, Crick, wid., to Joseph Roe, Floore, lab., brother, 1795/18 Feb.
BARRETT, George, Ringstead, blacksmith, to Keziah, wid., Inv. £19.14.6 1744/21 June
Barratt, John, Northampton, coachmaker, to William Morhall, Houghton on the Hill, co. Leic., farmer, nephew, 1776/8 Feb.
John, Sulgrave, to Persis, wid., 1779/29 July
Thomas, Wellingborough, to Thomas, son, 1795/27 July
BARRINGER, William, Kettering, to Khazoah, wid., Inv. £369.11.1 1714/147
BARROW, Thomas, Potterspury, Account of Mary, wid., admin., £30.6.4 1685/24
Mary, Potterspury, wid., to John, husb., son, 1727/10 June
BARRY, William, Rushden, to William Campion, principal creditor, Alice, wid., renounced, Inv. £46.12.6 1718/12
BARTLETT, William, Chapel Brampton, to Robert Caswell, Thrupp, father and admin. of Ann, wid., exor., decd., Inv. £121.18.2 Will, 1718/37 and 38
Anne, Chapel Brampton, wid., to Robert Caswell, Thrupp, yeo., father, 1718/43
Oday, Kilsby, shoemaker, to Sarah, wid., 1770/19 May
John, Brackley, apothecary, to William Moore, Sulgrave, grocer, brother in law, Ann, daughter, renounced, 1771/19 Jan.
Elizabeth, East Haddon, wid., to Mary, wife of Thomas Sargent, Floore, baker, daughter, 1789/19 Dec.
Richard, East Haddon, cordwainer, to Mary Sargent, Floore, wid., daughter, Elizabeth, wid., exor., decd., Will, 1791/29 Jan.
Richard, East Haddon, to John, lab., son, 1792/19 May
BARTON, James, Brackley, apothecary, to Elizabeth, wid., Inv. 1712/84
BARWELL, John, Helmdon, Inv.only £33.18.2 1717/95 A
BARWICK, John, Towcester, to Phebe, wid., 1719/51
John, Scaldwell, mason, to Thomas, Old, mason, brother, Frances, wid., renounced, 1773/20 Mar.
John, Moulton, mason, to Susanna, wid., 1728/11 May
BASELEY, John, Duston, Account of Mary, wid., now wife of Richard Rogers, £143.4.10 1674/44
John, Hellidon, to Andrew Hinde, Daventry, chandler, 1711/33
Basely, John, Hellidon, to Thomas Andrews, Daventry, tailor, of goods not fully administered by Andrew Hind, principal creditor, decd.,1712/120
Elizabeth, Farthingstone, spin., Inv.only £16.16.0 1714/79
Edmund, Charwelton, to John Maud, yeo., principal creditor, Inv. £64.16.8 1722/1
Laurence, Northampton, tailor, to Elizabeth, wid., 1728/18 May
Richard, Upton, farmer, to Elizabeth, wife of William Follett, Great Houghton, gent., daughter, Elizabeth, wid., renounced, 1730/18 Mar.
Euseby, Woodford cum Membris, yeo., to Richard Fifield, Boddington, yeo., 1730/31 Aug.
Bazlee, Elizabeth, Newbold, Catesby, wid., to William, yeo., son, 1737/8 Mar.
Bazley, John, Farthingstone, yeo., to Rebecca, wid., 1738/10 Jan.
Samuel, Whittlebury, baker, to Anne, wid., 1738/9 Sept.
Bazelee, William, Daventry, gent., to Ann, Northampton, wid., 1782/8 Oct.
Bazelee, Ann, Northampton, wid., to Elizabeth, wife of Cardwell Wills, carrier, granddaughter, 1784/24 Mar.

BASON, William, Potterspury, lab., Inv.only £4.13.0 1727/185
William, Potterspury, mason, to Joshua, mason, son, 1795/12 Oct.
BASS, William, Whittlebury, Inv.only £55.12.8 1713/128A
Thomas, Shutlanger, Stoke Bruerne, yeo., to Sarah, wid., Inv. £227.7.0 1722/89
Elizabeth, Shutlanger, wid., to Barbara, wife of William Rogers, Kislingbury, woolcomber, daughter, 1799/9 Mar.
BASSETT, Daniel, Sibbertoft, to Mary, wid., 1753/20 Oct.
BATELY, Ann, Daventry, wid., to Prudence, wife of Samuel White, Thorpe Mandeville, carpenter, sister, 1751/28 Oct.
BATEMAN, Nicholas, Culworth, grazier, to William Moor, Sulgrave, yeo., and Edward Howse, yeo., guardians of Nicholas, minor, son, exor., Inv. £327.1.6 Will, 1712/137
Edward, Culworth, yeo., Inv.only £498.16.6 1729/221
Batman, Elizabeth, Barby, to Edward, elder, lab., husband, 1758/18 Oct.
Elizabeth, Braunston, spin., to Samuel Shaw, lab., 1760/8 July
John, Culworth, cordwainer, to Edward, Wardington, Oxon., baker, brother, 1763/22 July
Bridget, Sibbertoft, to Samuel Sturgis, gent., cousin, 1764/22 May
Edward, Barby, lab., to Edward, weaver, son, 1762/3 Nov.
Michael, marine, to Mary, Oundle, wid., 1782/13 Oct.
BATES, Emanuel, Grendon, yeo., to Innocence, wid., Inv. £342.8.9 1712/30
Bate, John, Hackleton, Piddington, to Francis, brother, 1715/116a
Battes, Thomas, Hackleton, yeo., Inv.only £93.0.0 1716/96A
Beates, Wardner, Raunds, husb., Inv.only £9.3.4 1718/71A
Francis, Hackleton, Inv.only £186.0.0 1720/138A
Thomas, Welford, lab., Inv.only £51.9.0 1722/4aA
Francis, Rushden, Inv.only £31.12.3 1722/114A
John, Raunds, husb., to Mary, wid., 1727/9 Sept.
Martha, Daventry, to Robert, turner, husband, 1776/16 Mar.
Robert, Hellidon, farmer, to William, lab., son, Mary, wid., renounced, Will, 1784/28 Jan.
William, Brixworth, farmer, to John Ekins, farmer, son-in-law, 1787/6 Feb.
BATSON, Badson, Thomas, Inv.only £18.10.0 1717/98A
BATTIN, Francis, Northampton, glazier, to Elizabeth, wid., 1744/3 Dec.
Ann, Northampton, to Nicholas, glazier, husband, 1764/8 May
BATTISON, William, West Haddon, grazier, to Alice, wife of William Gore, Dallington, carpenter, daughter, 1742/26 May
John, Brafield, lab., to Sarah, wife of Thomas Morris, Denton, lab., daughter, 1795/26 Sept.
Thomas, Little Houghton, schoolmaster, to Elizabeth, wife of Daniel Higgins, victualler, daughter, 1800/23 Aug.
BATTLE, James, Cranford St. Andrew, farmer, to Margaret, wid., and James, 1795/27 July
BAWCUTT, John, Ashby St. Ledgers, husb., Inv.only £921.17.6 1724/101A
Bawcott, Edward, Daventry, lab., to Edward, servant, son, 1730/21 Nov.
John, West Haddon, to Jane, daughter, 1735/20 Jan.
John, Sywell Mill, miller, to Mary, wid., Inv. £207.9.0 1769/18 Mar.
Bawcott, Mary, Sywell Mill, to William, miller, husband, 1788/14 Apr.
Richard, Grafton Regis, to John, grazier, son, John Elliott, Towcester, grocer, and John Plowman, Caldecote, grazier, exors., renounced, Will, 1794/15 Aug.
BAXTER, Matthew, Little Bowden, blacksmith, Inv.only £69.15.0 1713/84A
John, Little Bowden, Inv.only £83.10.0 1727/208
John, Little Bowden, to Anne, wid., 1728/18 Apr.
Edward, Little Bowden, blacksmith, to Mary, wid., 1731/27 June
William, Daventry, victualler, to Mary, wid., 1767/16 July
BAYES, William, Rushden, carpenter, Inv.only £38.7.4 1716/54A
Nicholas, Mears Ashby, mason, Inv.only £29.19.6 1728/201
Nathaniel, Wollaston, carpenter, to Joseph, husb., son, Inv. £31.7.6 1729/7 Oct.
Elizabeth, Wollaston, wid., to Elizabeth, wife of Lucas Smart, Bozeat, husb., daughter, 1778/3 June
BAYLEY, BAYLY see BAILEY
BAYLIS, Bayliss, James, Wappenham, to Elizabeth, wid., Inv. £131.15.0 1729/9 Oct.
William, Grimsbury, yeo., to William West, Sulgrave, yeo., brother-in-law, Anne, wid., decd., Will, 1758/24 June
Richard, Eydon, to Richard Newcomb, Charlton, son-in-law, 1778/11 Mar.

BAYNARD, William, Hinton, Inv.only £132.15.0 1714/38A
BAYNHAM, Edward, Brackley, cooper, to Joyce, wid., 1752/1 Nov.
BEADLES, Bettles, Thomas, Kettering, wheelwright, to William, Kimbolton, Hunts., tailor, and Thomas Easton, same, husb., Inv. £57.19.6 1715/1
BEAL, Beall, Thomas, Isham, husb., to Rebecca, wid., Inv. £45.12.0 1728/8 June
Thomas, Isham, to Susannah, wid., Inv. £237.7.0 1757/7 Dec.
Henry, Northampton, grocer, to Susannah, wid., 1763/25 Nov.
John, Weedon Beck, widower, to Robert Warr, Everdon, uncle and guardian of Mary, Elizabeth, William, Sarah, and John, minors, children, Guard., 1782/4 Dec.
William, Wellingborough, innholder, to Anne, wife of Joseph Rose, victualler, daughter, Mary, exor., wife, decd., Will, 1783/17 Mar.
BEARDWELL, Allen, Northampton, gent., to Grace, wid., mother, 1736/30 Oct.
BEASELY, William, Wollaston, horsecourser, to Martha, wid., Inv. £38.15.6 1722/16
BEAUFOY, Charles, Kettering, excise officer, to Mary, wid., 1793/20 Feb.
BEAUMONT, Beamount, William, Culworth, to Thomas, Adstone, 1719/76
Beamont, William, Moreton Pinkeney, to Elizabeth Carrier, Bishopsgate, London, spin., daughter of William Carryer, legatee, decd., Will, 1720/150
Elizabeth, Adstone, to Thomas, tailor, husband, 1751/9 Apr.
BECK, Mary, Kilsby, Inv.only £87.5.6 1797/423
BECKETT, John, Wootton, Account of Mary, wid., admin., £76.17.10 1684/71
John, Thomas, Northampton, barber, to Anne, wid., 1729/9 Sept.
BEDFORD, Anne, Cogenhoe, Inv.only £120.19.0 1727/170
BEEBY, Thomas, East Farndon, to Elizabeth, wid., 1726/26 Nov.
BEECH, Anne, Farndon, Woodford cum Membris, Account of John Buckerfield, brother, £41.2.0 1680/8
BELCHER, Belshur, William, Inv.only £6.5.6 1727/402
William, Newbottle, to Keziah, wid., 1799/1 Oct.
BELL, Thomas, Cottesbrook, lab., to Anne, wid., Inv. £13.5.0 1718/41
Thomas, Thorpe Malsor, to Olive, wid., Inv. £21.2.6 1722/21
BENBOW, Mary, Weedon Pinkeney, spin., to Susannah Watts, wid., sister, 1760/21 Mar.
BENNETT, Bennit, Hugh, Burton Latimer, Inv.only £22.19.3 1718/82A
William, senior, Welford, weaver, Inv.only £9.7.0 1719/8A
John, Crick, cooper, Inv.only £64.8.0 1720/92A
Bennet, Michael, Chalcombe, Inv.only £203.10.0 1727/186
Thomas, Whittlebury, Inv.only £17.3.7 1728/260
Thomas, West Haddon, to Thomas Johnson, Braybrooke, felmonger, 1729/27 Dec.
als. Heritage, Hannah, Chalcombe, to John, yeo., husband, 1744/24 Mar.
Thomas Gery, Earl's Barton, clerk, to Thomas, Southwark, London, gent., son, 1787/19 Dec.
Benjamin, Welford, currier, to Elizabeth, wid., 1800/25 June
BENSON, Anne, Lower Boddington, Inv.only £11.10.6 1723/54A
George, Towcester, gent., to William, gent., and Anne, wife of William Clarke, gent., son and daughter, 1727/29 Dec.
BENT, Anne, Moulton, wid., to Anne, wife of Francis Blunt, wheelwright, daughter, Will, 1763/13 June
BENTLY, Hugh, Irchester, lab., Inv.only £40.6.6 1718/59A
BERRILL, Berril, Thomas, Wellingborough, farmer, to Mary, wid., Inv. £141.16.6 1766/19 Sept.
Samuel, Earl's Barton, to Sarah, wid., 1781/7 Feb.
Judith, Yardley Hastings, to Joseph, son, Will, 1787/13 Oct.
BERRY, William, Northampton, All Saints, plasterer, to Robert, plasterer, son, Inv. £5.3.3 1714/184
John, Northampton, plasterer, to Anne, wid., Inv. £46.19.0 Will, 1715/117
Anne, Blakesley, spin., Inv.only £34.0.0 1722/80A
Francis, Northampton, to Robert, Hitchin, co. Hertford, clockmaker, brother and guardian of Mary, Frances and Francis, minors, children, 1726/30 June
Daniel, Little Harrowden, to Anne, wid., Inv. £61.0.0 1771/3 Apr.
BESSANT, Bessand, Thomas, Chipping Warden, husb., Inv.only £188.17.6 1711/53A
BETSON, Judah, Wellingborough, Guard.only of Mary, minor, daughter, 1724/157
BETTLE, William, Bozeat, farmer, to Mary, wid., Inv. £295.17.0 1714/73
William, Bozeat, Commission to John Lettice, clerk, Rector of Strixton, to swear Susanna, wid. and exor., 1714/197

BETTLE continued
Jonathan, Wollaston, yeo., to Anne, wid., 1740/25 Mar.
Thomas, Ringstead, carpenter, to Susannah, wid., 1754/18 Dec.
Elizabeth, Wollaston, lacemaker, to William, brother, Will, 1796/4 Jan.
John, Wollaston, shepherd, to Thomas, son, Will, 1798/6 Feb.
BETTS, Mary, wid., Inv.only £10.2.0 1722/105
Mary, Aynho, wid., to Thomas, Banbury, co. Oxford, son, 1723/30
Bett, Elizabeth, Ringstead, wid., Inv.only £51.10.0 1733/297
John, Towcester, blacksmith, to Mary, wid., 1745/7 Dec.
John, Ringstead, baker, to Mary, wid., 1779/19 Oct.
BICKNELL, William, Northampton, gunsmith, to Mary, spin., daughter, 1753/4 Aug.
Elizabeth, Northampton, to Mary, spin., daughter in law, William, gunsmith, husband, exor., decd., Will, 1755/20 Jan.
BIDDLE, Charles, Desborough, lab., to Sarah, spin., daughter, Inv. £4.10.0 1728/30 Aug.
BIGGS, William, Coton, Ravensthorpe, to William and Richard, farmers, sons, 1761/8 July
William, elder, Welford, grazier, to Joseph, farmer, son, Mary, exor., decd., 1793/15 Oct.
BIGNELL, Robert, Passenham, to Elizabeth Hopcraft, Denshanger, Passenham, sister, 1715/69
Anne, Eydon, spin., to John, husb., brother, 1716/3
BIKER, Kezia, Bourton, co. Warwick, to Thomas, clerk, husband, 1771/10 Dec.
BILLING, Sarah, Weedon Beck, wid., Inv.only £150.1.0 1711/102 A
Dorothy, Weedon Beck, Inv.only £38.0.0 1715/139 A
Philippa, wid., Inv.only £2.10.0 1716/95
Thomas, Weedon Beck, to Hannah, wid., Inv. £283.15.0 1718/115
John, Raunds, grocer, to Elizabeth, wid., Inv. £147.14.0 1721/46
Elizabeth, Weedon Beck, wid., to Anne, wife of Christopher Sheppard, sister, Inv. £11.6.6 1731/8 July
William, Duston, lab., to Mary, wid., 1734/30 Mar.
Elizabeth, Weedon Beck, wid., to Thomas, Floore, shoemaker, son, 1736/6 Aug.
Samuel, Kettering, to Jude, wid., 1737/9 Apr.
Mary, Bugbrooke, wid., to Thomas, farmer, son, Inv. £39.13.0 1749/28 Jan.
Thomas, Weedon Beck, carpenter, to Thomas Butlin, baker, creditor, Elizabeth, wid., renounced, 1769/27 May
John, Ringstead, butcher, to Mary, wid., 1771/4 Jan.
George, Yelvertoft, yeo., to Mary, wife of William Matthew, Guilsborough, grazier, daughter, Elizabeth, wife, decd., Will, 1782/15 Oct.
BILLINGHAM, John, Blisworth, Guard.only of William, minor, son, 1714/180
Richard, Blisworth, lab., to Elizabeth, wid., 1730/9 May
Richard, Blisworth, Inv.only £11.11.6 1730/280
Dorothy, Kingsthorpe, wid., to Ann, wid., daughter in law, Will, 1749/7 Jan.
Elizabeth, Kingsthorpe, to John, servant, husband, 1749/18 Aug.
BILSON, William, Abington, to Sarah, wid., 1747/18 June
BILTON, John, Rushton, All Saints, to Susanna, wid., 1744/13 Feb.
BINDLEY, Robert, Braybrooke, wheelwright, to Anne, wid., mother, 1785/2 Sept.
BINYON, William, Holcot, Inv.only £186.12.1 1712/100 A
Thomas, Overstone, to William, husb., son, 1716/82
Thomas, Great Billing, to Margaret, wid., Inv. £16.12.6 1718/16
Bynyon, William, Moulton, to Elizabeth, wid., 1724/85
Thomas, Great Billing, Guard.only of John, son, 1726/12 Apr.
BIRD, Samuel, Everdon, Inv.only £15.1.0 1713/110 A
Richard, Great Everdon, Inv.only £18.2.8 1721/7 A
Hugh, Everdon, Inv.only £49.11.0 1724/143 A
William, Everdon, yeo., to Mary, wid., Inv. £200.0.0 1730/9 Apr.
Thomas, Everdon, yeo., to Mary, wid., Inv. £57.11.0 1738/19 May
Thomas, Everdon, husb., to Mary, wid., Inv. £123.2.0 1747/5 Oct.
Richard, Great Everdon, yeo., to Anne, wid., 1763/11 Mar.
Elizabeth, Everdon, wid., to Dorothy, wife of John Elmes, wheelwright, daughter, 1763/5 Apr.
Thomas, Great Everdon, yeo., to William Brumwich, Little Everdon, yeo., and William Brown, blacksmith, Anne, wid., renounced, Guard. of Sarah and Thomas, children, 1764/11 Dec.
Samuel, Everdon, lab., to Mary, wid., 1772/17 July

BIRD continued
George, Everdon, servant, to Richard and John, farmers, brothers, 1778/18 Apr.
Thomas, Guard.only of Sarah, minor, daughter, 1779/9 Aug.
James, Mears Ashby, schoolmaster, to Margaret, wid., 1782/24 Aug.
John, Everdon, dairyman, to Robert Marriott, Newnham, gent., and Henry Wright, gent., Eleanor, wid., renounced, Will, 1787/7 Feb.
Samuel, Everdon, tailor, to Richard, farmer, and Thomas, tailor, Anne, wid., exor., decd., Will, 1789/28 Feb.
BISHOP, Thomas, Plumpton, yeo., to Susanna, wid., 1733/7 July
Hawley, Crick, clerk, to Hannah, wid., 1757/20 Dec.
BISSELL als. Marlow, Elizabeth, Braunston, to Richard, wheelwright, husband, 1740/11 Sept.
BITHERY, John, Irthlingborough, St. Peters, Account of Anne, wid., admin., £154.19.4 1672/107
Bithray, John, Irthlingborough, husb., Inv.only £98.10.0 1724/113A
BLACK, John, West Haddon, lab., to Sarah, wid., 1729/15 July
BLACKABY, Edward, Cottesbrooke, lab., to Rebecca, wid., Inv. £40.9.4 1733/3 Feb.
BLACKBOURN, John, Dr. in Divinity, Rector of Stoke Bruerne, to Catherine, wife of Henry Abbott, sister, Inv. £752.8.4 1719/50
BLACKWELL, Thomas, Syresham, to Dorothy, wid., 1725/30 Apr.
Thomas, Lilbourne, to Elizabeth, wife of Thomas Whitmell, Crick, yeo., sister, 1750/20 Oct.
BLAND, George, Shutlanger, Stoke Bruerne, yeo., Account of Charles, yeo., £147.3.0 1669/133
Richard, senior, Northampton, plumber, Inv.only £13. 1716/8A
William, Long Buckby, junior, to Elizabeth, wid., Inv. £245.5.0 1718/31
Francis, Thorpe Malsor, to Judith, wid., Inv. £147.13.6 1724/102
Lydia, Northampton, wid., to John, Lombard St., London, goldsmith, 1728/29 Apr.
William, Braunston, farmer, to John, farmer, brother, 1749/18 Aug.
John, Long Buckby, to Joseph Fraunces, Daventry, apothecary, principal creditor, 1759/13 Feb.
John, Braunston, farmer, to Ann, wid., 1759/5 Oct.
Thomas, Yardley Gobion, Potterspury, lab., to Richard, carpenter, brother, 1791/14 Jan.
John, Crick, yeo., to Mary, wid., 1796/26 Oct.
John, Crick, yeo., Inv.only £366.4.3 1796/422
BLAXLEY, Samuel, Towcester, carpenter, to Sophia, wife of Edward Grubb, Holcot, yeo., daughter, 1742/15 Apr.
Anna Maria, Towcester, to Fletcher, carpenter, son, 1778/25 Nov.
BLEEKE, George, Weston, Weedon Pinkney, farmer, to Elizabeth, wid., 1775/10 Jan.
BLENCOWE, Blencow, Blincow, William, Whilton, to Elizabeth, wid., 1712/72
Francis, Eydon, to Sarah Churchill, sister, 1713/143
James, Farthinghoe, Inv.only £14.10.0 1730/272
William, Whilton, shoemaker, Inv.only £15.11.6 1735/324
John, Halse, Brackley, gent., to Francis, ironmonger, and Timothy, grazier, sons, Temperance, wid., decd., Will, 1761/24 Dec.
Blencoe, Cato, Brington, victualler, to John Wye, Northampton, wine merchant, creditor, Martha, wid., renounced, 1777/17 Jan.
James, Charwelton, to Nathaniel, lab., son, 1781/1 May
John, Marston St. Lawrence, yeo., to Thomas, farmer, nephew, Frances, exor., decd., Will, 1788/26 Mar.
BLETSOE, Joan, Rushden, wid., Inv.only £166.11.0 1711/9A
Francis, Irchester, farmer, Inv.only £549.3.0 1714/136A
Thomas, Irchester, to Edward Kempton, yeo., nephew, 1714/166
William, Wellingborough, tanner, Guard.only of John, minor, son, 1739/2 May
Thomas, Irchester, to Elizabeth, wid., 1777/29 Apr.
John, Northampton, gent., to Anne Chesser, wid., principal creditor, 1795/12 Sept.
BLEWITT, Blewit, Susanna, Earl's Barton, Inv.only £26.14.6 1728/246
Mary, Duston, spin., to Mary, wid., mother, 1733/27 Oct.
Sarah, Northampton, minor, to Thomas Easton, plasterer, uncle and guardian, 1790/25 Nov.
Catherine, Duston, wid., to Robert, farmer, son, 1796/13 Aug.

BLICK, John, Weston, Weedon Lois, Guard.only of George, minor, 1715/94
William, Barby, to William, Houghton, co. Bedford, farmer, son, 1782/28 Dec.
BLISS, Elizabeth, Kislingbury, to John, husb., husband, 1721/76
Blisse, Jonas, Barby, to Mary, wife of Edward Marriott, Granborough, co. Warwick, maltster, daughter, 1728/1 Apr.
John, Floore, to Grace, wid., 1737/8 Dec.
John, Welton, yeo., to William, yeo., son, Elizabeth, wid., renounced, 1738/7 Jan.
John, Kislingbury, yeo., to Elizabeth, wife of Thomas Tomkins, farmer, daughter, 1751/4 Jan.
John, Farthingstone, yeo., to Elizabeth, wid., 1751/19 Oct.
James, Blakesley, miller, to Thomas, Whitfield, miller, son, 1754/25 May
Joseph, Preston Capes, grazier, to Ruth, wid., 1777/5 Mar.
Thomas, Whitfield, miller, Guard.only of John, minor, son, 1785/20 Oct.
Philip, Welford, innholder, to William Wood, grazier, and John Briggs, grazier, guardians of George, John, Elizabeth, Margaret, minors, children, Guard., 1791/25 June
William, Welford, cordwainer, to Sarah, wid., 1800/31 Jan.
BLOCKLEY, Joseph, Welford, shoemaker, Inv.only £17.12.0 1717/59A
William, Welford, lab., Inv.only £4.8.6 1736/336
BLOFIELD, Matthew, Raunds, maltster, to William, son, Inv. £19.10.6 1714/48
Blowfield, Thomas, Wellingborough, blacksmith, to Martha, wid., Inv. £10.5.4 1720/115
Humphrey, Burton Latimer, to John, St. Martins in the Fields, Westminster, son, 1777/19 July
Humphrey, Burton Latimer, to Richard, carpenter, son, of goods unadministered by John, son, 1778/7 May
Blowfield, John, Wollaston, blacksmith, to Andrew Willson, Wellingborough, grocer, principal creditor, 1782/5 June
BLONDELL, John, Hannington, to Elizabeth, wid., 1763/15 Jan.
BLOSSOM, Edward, Higham Ferrers, to Elianor, wid., 1722/74
BLOXHAM, Edward, Towcester, baker, to Elizabeth, wid., 1717/53
BLUNDELL, John, Maidford, farmer, to Richard, Lichborough, yeo., brother, Elizabeth, wid., renounced in favour Henry, brother, 1725/22 May
John, Maidford, Inv.only £50.2.6 1725/144
William, Long Buckby, baker, to John, Drayton, Daventry, baker, grandson, 1785/11 Nov.
BLUNDON, Sarah, Long Buckby, wid., to John, lab., son, 1712/37
BLUNSOM, Blumsum, William, Wellingborough, to Mary, wid., Inv. £17.8.8 1725/15 May
John, Rushton, blacksmith, to John Squire, Islip, merchant, 1763/30 Mar.
Frances, Rushton, to John, St. Peter's, Rushton, brother, 1775/2 May
BLUNT, William, Roade, Inv.only £682.9.6 1715/38A
Anne, Roade, wid., to Elizabeth, wife of William Stoakes, Inv. £26.16.0 Will, 1716/126
Richard, Little Houghton, Inv.only £9.1.8 1722/2A
David, Ashton, lab., to Mary, wid., 1729/1 Feb.
Francis, Ashton, husb., to Alice, wid., 1734/4 May
Alice, Ashton, to Francis, yeo., son, 1744/24 Nov.
John, Old, farmer, to William, Weedon Beck, brother, Elizabeth, wid., mother, renounced, 1781/28 Nov.
William, Moulton, to Anne, wid., 1788/6 Sept.
William, Ashton, farmer, to Mary, wid., 1791/1 Oct.
BODDINGTON, William, Holcot, Inv.only £336.0.6 1715/2A
Edward, Great Harrowden, butcher, to Mary, wid., Inv. £83.16.6 1717/46
John, Rothwell, weaver, Inv.only £71.5.6 1719/23A
Hannah, Wellingborough, wid., to John Ellington, upholsterer, son in law, 1727/17 Nov.
John, Finedon, butcher, to Edward, yeo., butcher, son, Dorothy, wid., renounced, 1755/3 Mar.
BODFISH, Thomas, Arthingworth, shepherd, to John, shepherd, brother, Inv. £18.15.4 1746/19 July
BOGVILLE, James, Northampton, painter, to Ann, wid., Inv. £555.0.0 1762/23 Mar.
BOLLARD, Samuel, Rothwell, to Mary, wid., 1721/127
Isaac, Yelvertoft, victualler, to William, victualler, brother, 1729/12 July
William, Raunds, yeo., to Elizabeth, wid., 1731/2 Nov.

BOLLARD continued
Thomas, Easton Maudit, shepherd, to Hannah, wid., 1733/31 Jan.
John, Cold Ashby, Inv.only £4.0.0 1736/334
BOLNEY, James, senior, Great Addington, to Margaret, wid., Inv. £79.4.2 1724/141
Thomas, Great Addington, woolcomber, to Thomas, woolcomber, son, Inv. £11.10.0 1746/20 Dec.
BOLTON, William, Hartwell, yeo., Inv.only £142.11.0 1718/44A
John, Helmdon, husb., to Elizabeth, wid., 1729/17 Apr.
John, Helmdon, Inv.only £130.0.0 1729/244
Boulton, William, Yelvertoft, lab., to Mary, wid., 1729/27 Dec.
Thomas, Chelveston, to Henry, Poddington, Beds., husb., brother, 1777/4 July
Thomas, Chelveston, farmer, Inv.only 1777/417
BOND, James, Stanford on Avon, vicar, to Catherine, wid., 1720/137
Elizabeth, Knuston, Irchester, wid., to Thomas Angrave, grazier, guardian of William Francis, minor, son, Guard., 1786/24 Jan.
William, Knuston, Irchester, grazier, to Thomas Angrave, grazier, and Edward Wood, Irthlingborough, farmer, guardians of William Francis, son in law, and William, Elizabeth, Mary, Lydia, James, minors, children, Elizabeth, wid., exor., decd., Will, Guard., 1786/24 Jan. and 5 Apr.
BONNER, Mark, Hackleton, to Thomas, son, 1718/107
BONNICASTLE, Bonnycastle, John, Chipping Warden, Inv.only £23.15.0 1714/43A
John, Maidford, yeo., to Elizabeth, wid., 1722/22
BONO, Nathaniel, Ringstead, Account of Rebecca, wid., admin., £82.6.6 1674/146
BOOKER, Thomas, Towcester, victualler, Inv.only £30.15.0 1722/85A
BOONE, John, Old, husb., to Mary, wid., Inv. £178.7.8 1720/56
Boon, Daniel, Piddington, Inv.only £257.12.6 1730/269
BOOT, William, Sulgrave, husb., Inv.only £180.8.6 1715/35A
Elizabeth, Sulgrave, Inv.only £167.2.6 1715/71A
Boote, Anthony, Byfield, yeo., Inv.only £96.4.0 1721/52A
Crescent, Westhorpe, Byfield, Inv.only £19.10.0 1723/75A
Zachary, Westhorpe, Byfield, to John, yeo., brother, Crescens, brother, exor., decd., Inv. £18.15.6 Will, 1723/77
John, Byfield, Inv.only £35.6.0 1724/61A
John, Westhorpe, Byfield, Inv.only £184.16.6 1724/96A
John, Byfield, farmer, to Crescens, farmer, son, 1750/7 May
Boote, Alice, Westhorpe, Byfield, wid., to John, Northampton, innholder, son, Inv. £82.18.0 1759/19 Nov.
BOOTH, Thomas, Kettering, to Elizabeth, wid., Inv. £13.7.0 1722/104
BORDRIGGE, James, Northampton, innholder, to Elizabeth, wid., Inv. £1045.13.6½ 1743/16 July
Elizabeth, Northampton, wid., to Judith, daughter, 1744/9 Mar.
BOREMAN, Joseph, Little Brington, husb., Inv.only £126.11.2 1722/56A
Bourman, Sarah, Wootton, wid., to William Harris, junior, Little Houghton, lab., brother, 1730/14 Sept.
William, Whilton, yeo., to Ann, wid., Inv. £212.4.8 1756/4 Oct.
BOSDEN, William, Braybrooke, to Susanna, wid., Inv. £72.17.6 1720/73
William, Braybrooke, to Alice, wid., 1758/7 Jan.
BOSTOCK, John, Braunston, bachelor, to Thomas, husb., brother, 1722/38
BOSWELL, Thomas, Higham Ferrers, to William Errington, Carlton, co. Bedford, blacksmith, husband of Mary, sister, 1711/72
Buswell, Samuel, Duston, yeo., to Mary, wid., Inv. £330.2.0 1748/8 Oct.
BOSWORTH, Nedham, Findeon, to Susanna, wid., Inv. £493.0.0 1718/97
Susanna, Finedon, wid., to Martha Hall, wid., daughter, Inv. £57.1.6 1722/46
William, farmer, Inv.only £168.0.0 1727/400
John, Cottesbrooke, shepherd, to Mary, wid., and William, shepherd, son, 1728/10 Aug.
John, Inv.only £171.9.2 1728/265
Mary, Cottesbrooke, to William, shepherd, son, and Anne, daughter, 1734/12 Jan.
Benjamin, Broughton, to Benjamin, yeo., son, Inv. £37.15.6 1740/23 July
William, Brampton, to Nathaniel Ingram, Lubenham, co. Leic., blacksmith, brother, 1744/27 Oct.
John, Haslebech, grazier, to Mary, wid., 1755/6 Dec.
Richard, Draughton, yeo., to Richard, farmer, son, Jane, wife, exor., decd., Will, 1762/1 May

BOSWORTH continued
William, Barby, to Mary, wid., 1779/17 Mar.
William, Brington, lab., Guard.only of Elizabeth, minor, daughter, 1798/1 May
BOTHEY, Robert , Knuston, Irchester, to William, Wollaston, gent., Inv. £10.16.6 1714/167
BOTT, Mary, Guilsborough, spin., to Lydia, wife of William Crann, Northampton, gent., sister, 1740/29 July
BOTTERILL, Botterell, Jonathan, Grendon, shepherd, to Alice, wid., Inv. £12.14.6 1727/7 Jan.
Botterell, Roger, Broughton, servant, to John, Scaldwell, carpenter, father, 1732/11 Mar.
Sarah, Duston, to John Abarns, Moulton, shepherd, Will, 1745/27 July
Elizabeth, Paulerspury, wid., to William, Barnett, co. Middx., lab., son, 1783/13 Oct.
BOTTOLD, Borrold, Joseph, Brockhole, to Mary Manning, wid., daughter, 1716/140
BOULTON, Samuel, Yelvertoft, yeo., Inv.only £32.9.6 1723/3A
See also BOLTON
BOUNDY, Anne, Wellingborough, to John, joiner, husband, Will, 1757/8 Dec.
BOX, James, Aston le Walls, grazier, to Emme, wife of William Yates, Culworth, mason, sister, 1735/18 Aug.
BOYER, Jane, Farndon, to John, farmer, husband, 1772/27 Feb.
BOYES, William, Guilsborough, shepherd, Inv.only £38.10.10 undated/360
Boyce, John, elder, Ashby St. Ledgers, Account of Mary, wid., admin., £29.13.4 1676/48
Boys, John, Ashby St. Ledgers, Account of Anne, wid., admin., £284.11.6 1680/15
Boyce, Anne, Courtenhall, wid., to George Tompson, All Saints, Northampton, grocer, principal creditor, Mary, wife of William Roberts, sister, renounced, 1720/58
Sarah, Little Harrowden, spin., to Joseph Wright, Moulton, baker, 1747/24 Oct.
Elizabeth, West Haddon, to William, shepherd, husband, 1751/30 Nov.
Boys, Ralph, Braunston, lab., to Ralph, servant, son, 1769/20 June
Thomas, Braunston, yeo., to John, yeo., brother, Will, 1796/7 Oct.
Mary, Long Buckby, wid., to Richard Devonshire, son in law, woolcomber, 1796/19 Dec.
BOYFIELD, Robert, Inv.only £17.3.4 1727/187
BRACEGIRDLE, Justinian, Holcot, Inv.only £178.12.2 1717/96A
BRADFORD, John, Wilby, to Frances, wid., 1716/85
BRADGATE, William, Hellidon, Inv.only £14.10.6 undated/134
William, Hellidon, to Thomas Prestidge, Byfield, gent., Sarah, wid., William and Thomas, sons, and Sarah, daughter, renounced, 1724/121
BRADLEY, John, Inv.only £22.8.11 undated/91
John, Rothwell, to Hannah, wid., Inv. £70.11.6 1715/70
George, East Farndon, Inv.only £48.2.0 1717/52A
Elizabeth, Bozeat, wid., to Robert Taylor, lacemaker, 1728/12 June
Elizabeth, East Farndon, wid., to Mary, spin., daughter, 1737/3 Dec.
Richard, Long Buckby, to Esther, spin., niece, 1742/17 Mar.
Richard, Long Buckby, gent., to Simeon Jones, Rugby, co. Warwick, of goods unadministered by Esther, his wife, niece, 1745/6 Sept.
Anne, Wellingborough, to Lewis, husb., husband, 1776/19 June
BRADSHAW, John, Northampton, to Susanna, wid., Inv. £6.0.0 1714/190
Andrew, Old, to Elizabeth, wid., 1721/122
William, Northampton, cooper, Guard.only of Elizabeth Kinning, minor, 1734/16 July
Mary, Wilby, to William, farmer, husband, 1761/31 Jan.
Thomas, Wellingborough, to Mary, wid., 1764/3 Nov.
William, Mears Ashby, to Elizabeth, wid., 1775/25 Feb.
Elizabeth, Mears Ashby, wid., to Mary, spin., daughter, 1778/21 Mar.
BRAFIELD, Thomas, Northampton, to Mary, wid., 1726/7 Oct.
Thomas, Inv.only £18.15.0 1726/174
John, Barwick, Daventry, to Catherine, wid., 1777/13 June
Catherine, Daventry, wid., to John Smith, Newnham, yeo., Guard. of Anne, Jemima, Jane, minors, daughters, 1778/18 Mar.
BRAINE, Robert, Rothwell, husb., Inv.only £234.16.0 1715/62A
Joseph, Rothwell, to William Fitch, grocer, guardian of Joseph, Susannah, Mary, and Samuel, minors, children, 1742/9 Jan.

BRAINE continued
Anthony, Heyford, gent., to Anne, wife of William Davis, Farthingstone, yeo., and Grace, wife of Richard Adams, gent., daughters, 1743/12 Mar.
Brain, Robert, Rothwell, to Elizabeth, wid., 1767/8 Oct.
BRAMLEY, Nicholas, Harlestone, to Thomas, tailor, son, 1712/74
Robert, Holdenby, miller, to Catherine, wid., Inv. £35.3.0 1729/2 Aug.
Richard, Holdenby, miller, to Mary, wife of Richard Seale, Cold Ashby, drover and salesman, daughter, 1750/10 Feb.
William, Holdenby, miller, to Mary, wife of Richard Seale, Cold Ashby, drover, sister, 1750/10 Feb.
BRAMPTON, Anne, Kettering, Inv.only £26.18.0 1713/125A
Samuel, Warkton, yeo., Inv.only £200.19.0 1714/115A
Samuel, Cranford St. Andrew, to Samuel, husb., son, Inv. £19.3.0 1719/105
Elizabeth, Warkton, to Thomas, yeo., son, 1722/117
Edward, Little Harrowden, to Elizabeth, wid., 1764/30 July
BRANGUIN, Elizabeth, to Mary Gorstelow, Brackley, sister, 1760/22 Dec.
BRANSOM, Elizabeth, Floore, wid., to William Bliss, farmer, Will, 1782/14 Sept.
BRANSTON, Joan, Towcester, spin., Inv.only £6.5.0 1713/28A
Branson, Jeremiah, Elkington, shepherd, Inv.only £30.0.0 1719/47A
Braunston, Thomas, Staverton, yeo., to Thomas, yeo., son, Anne, wid., renounced, 1729/13 Sept.
BRAY, John, Brixworth, Guard.only of John Page, minor, 1714/176
Henry, Spratton, yeo., Inv.only £57.4.0 1723/131A
Thomas, Brixworth, to Hesther, wid., 1731/3 Nov.
Richard, Spratton, lab., to Mary, wid., 1734/6 Apr.
BRAYBROOK, James, Burton Latimer, shepherd, Inv.only £4.17.6 1734/301
BREARLY, Edward, Northampton, jersey comber, to Mary Tebbutt, Milton, sister, 1745/1 Apr.
BREARS, Breears, John, Northampton, to Jane, wid., 1745/6 Apr.
BREE, William, Long Buckby, bachelor, to William Archer, Preston Capes, servant, nephew, 1743/26 Oct.
BREEN, James, Great Billing, to Sarah, wid., 1773/2 Feb.
BRETT, Thomas, Wollaston, cordwainer, Inv.only £75.1.0 1711/120A
Thomas, elder, Desborough, yeo., Inv.only £14.1.0 1714/45A
Richard, senior, Thornby, cordwainer, to Richard, yeo., son, Elizabeth, wid., renounced, Will, 1721/106
John, Rothersthorpe, blacksmith, to Elizabeth, wife of George Nicholls, Upton, lab., sister, 1753/11 Dec.
Jane, Thornby, wid., to Richard, farmer, son, Will, 1766/8 Feb.
BRICE, William, Quinton, Account of John, son, £313.10.8 1679/138
Joseph, Hardingstone, husb., to Elizabeth, wid., Inv. £136.16.2 1717/151
William, Weston Favell, to George, tailor, nephew, 1728/14 Sept.
Robert, Hartwell, yeo., to William, brother, yeo., Inv. £25.8.4 1730/11 Apr.
Richard, Alderton, shepherd, to Mary, wid., 1744/12 May
Thomas, Piddington, victualler, to Jane, wid., 1751/6 June
BRICKETT, William, Floore, to Richard Adams, farmer, and William Bliss, farmer, exors. of Mary, wid., decd., Will, 1771/9 Nov.
William, Floore, Guard.only of John, minor, son, 1774/4 May
BRICKNELL, John, Aynho, yeo., to Thomas, farmer, son, Martha, wid., exor., decd., Will, 1764/2 Oct.
BRIGGS, John, Rothwell, to John, Inv. £62.12.10 1713/33
Edward, Irthlingborough, to Martha, wid., 1727/7 Apr.
Edward, Irthlingborough, Inv.only £16.7.2 1727/188
John, Kettering, to Mary, wid., 1734/21 Oct.
Benjamin, Welford, innholder, to William Hill, Theddingworth, co. Leic., grazier, creditor, Elizabeth, wid., renounced, Will, 1770/18 May
William, Northampton, butcher, to Jane, wid., 1784/8 Nov.
BRIGHTMAN, Thomas, senior, Northampton, Inv.only £67.0.0 1723/73A
BRIGHTWELL, John, Byfield, to John, yeo., son, 1741/1 June
Thomas, Eydon, yeo., to Thomas, farmer, son, 1754/5 Apr.
Thomas, Eydon, to Devereux, brother, farmer, 1776/26 Nov.
BRIMLEY, Edward, Cotton End, Hardingstone, blacksmith, Account of Abigail, wid., admin., £15.17.3 1679/137
Richard, Newnham, to Mary, wid., 1781/7 Apr.

BRINGEST, William, Loddington, Inv.only £78.4.0 1713/53A
Thomas, Faxton, Lamport, Inv.only £125.19.0 1723/57A
Bringhurst, William, yeo., to Elizabeth Bamford, Old, wid., sister, Guard. of Elizabeth and Mary, minors, daughters, 1744/3 Apr.
BRITTEN, Brittain, Joseph, Perry Park, Potterspury, to Susannah, wid., Inv. £85.11.3 1713/86
Robert, Pisford, to Anne, wid., and Joseph, husb., son, Inv. £435.10.0 1720/157
Bernard, Irthlingborough, lab., Inv.only £6.18.8 1724/51A
Edward, Sywell, Inv.only £370.2.0 1727/190
Frances, Sywell, wid., to Mary and Anne, spins., daughters, 1729/28 June
Frances, Sywell, wid., Inv.only £273.15.0 1729/226
Elizabeth, Irthlingborough, wid., to Bernard, tailor, son, 1743/11 Jan.
John, Milton, yeo., to Catherine, wid., Inv. £379.8.0 1746/14 June
William, Pisford, to Richard, yeo., brother, 1775/1 July
John, elder, yeo., Collingtree, farmer, to John and Thomas, farmers, sons, Guard. of Mary, minor, daughter, 1783/28 June and 13 Sept.
BROCKLIS, William, Moreton Pinkeney, yeo., to Ann, wife of William Smith, Preston Capes, yeo., sister, Inv. £41.11.6 1723/7
BRODIE, Broodie, Bryan, Earl's Barton, Account of Elizabeth, wid., admin., £161.9.7 1674/142
BROMLEY, Richard, Weedon Beck, to Grace, wid., 1739/9 Apr.
BROMWICH, Edward, Daventry, cordwainer, to Elizabeth, wid., 1751/14 Feb.
William, Badby, maltster, to John, gent., father, and John, farmer, brother, 1796/14 Apr.
John, Badby, yeo., to John, maltster, son, 1797/11 Nov.
William, Hardwick, farmer, to Sarah, wid., 1800/10 June
BROOKS, Thomas, Moreton Pinkney, lab., to Elizabeth, wid., Inv. £18.18.6 1712/81
Brooke, Elizabeth, Daventry, wid., to Alice, Brockhole, spin., daughter, 1713/87
Brooke, John, Daventry, to Anne, wid., 1726/27 Aug.
Brookes, Thomas, Pisford, victualler, to Elizabeth, wid., Inv. £11.11.11 1728/9 Nov.
Thomas, Chalcombe, to Mary, wid., 1735/3 May
Thomas, Chalcombe, Inv.only £27.13.6 1735/323
Mary, Chalcombe, wid., to John Handes, elder, carpenter, father, 1738/27 Mar.
Samuel, Yardley Chase, keeper, to Benjamin, Loughborough, co. Leic., grazier, brother, 1750/23 Aug.
John, Sibbertoft, to Anne, wid., 1776/20 Jan.
Elizabeth, Lois Weedon, wid., to Mary, wife of William Ivens, Moreton Pinkney, farmer, daughter, Will, 1800/27 Mar.
BROOME als. Hicks, see Hicks
BROTHERS, Samuel, Boddington, yeo., to Mary, wid., 1711/54
Robert, Upper Boddington, to Catherine, wid., 1723/53
Robert, Upper Boddington, butcher, Inv.only £38.8.2 1723/114
Thomas, Boddington, shoemaker, cordwainer, to Charles, shoemaker, son, Inv. £18.2.0 1725/17 Apr.
Edward, Boddington, butcher, to Catherine, wid., mother, 1727/5 May
Jonas, Boddington, to Anne, wid., 1766/3 Feb.
Ann, Upper Boddington, wid., to Mary, wife of Thomas Wimbush, aunt and guardian of Mary, minor, daughter, Inv. £42.18.11½, Guard., 1767/10 Mar.
BROUGHTON, Anne, Inv.only £13.0.0 1719/95A
John, Cosgrave, lab., shopkeeper, to Mary, wid., Inv. £29.16.2 1731/6 Nov.
BROWNE, Thomas, Lilbourne, Account of Francis Collins, guardian of Henry, undated/158
Thomas, Grafton Underwood, Account of Henry, brother, admin., £37.0.0 1680/16
Brown, Giles, senior, Kettering, to Giles, sergemaker, son, 1712/110
Brown, Alexander, Towcester, Inv.only £65.6.8 1712/143A
John, Holcot, Inv.only £8.16.0 1713/38A
William, Paulerspury, husb., Inv.only £72.15.6 1714/54A
Richard, Gayton, yeo., Inv.only £35.11.0 1714/86A
William, Potterspury, to Jane, wid., Will, Inv. £311.19.8 1714/121
Daniel, Earl's Barton, fellmonger, to Elizabeth, wid., Inv. £38.7.1 1715/23
Nathaniel, Dallington, to Elizabeth, wid., 1715/42

BROWNE continued
John, West Haddon, lab., Inv.only £11.11.6 1715/47 A
John, Inv.only £64.10.8 1716/99 A
als. Miller, William, Great Creaton, husb., Inv.only £152.10.0 1716/143 A
Brown, Thomas, Raunds, to Mary, wid., 1717/85
Samuel, Grafton Underwood, yeo., to Sarah, wid., Inv. £529.15.0 1717/91
William, Chipping Warden, Inv.only £21.17.4 1717/118 A
Brown, Elizabeth, Great Billing, wid., Inv.only £15.14.4 1717/137 A
Brown, Mary, Raunds, wid., Inv.only, £40.6.0 1718/45 A
Sarah, Kettering, wid., to Thomas, Kettering, carrier, grandfather and guardian of William and Hanna, minors, children, Inv. £63.1.4 1718/118
Richard, Yardley Gobion, Potterspury, to Jane, wid., Inv. £84.15.0 1719/64
Thomas, Northampton, to John, carpenter, father, 1721/15
Thomas, Great Houghton, yeo., Inv.only £28.5.0 1721/145 A
Richard, Green's Norton, yeo., to Mary, wid., Inv. £59.12.6 1722/81
Brown, Anne, Chipping Warden, to John, mason, son, 1722/103
William, Westhorpe, Byfield, Inv.only £18.2.0 1723/115
Brown, Mary, Wellingborough, wid., to Joseph, draper, son, 1724/30
Jane, Potterspury, Inv.only £118.5.0 1724/127 A
Brown, George, Charwelton, to Elizabeth, wid., 1725/30 Apr.
Brown, Joyce, Paulerspury, to John Cooke and Samuel Cross, yeos., sons in law, 1726/28 Apr.
Brown, Joyce, Paulerspury, Inv.only £18.6.0 1726/166
John, Northampton, to Anne, wid., 1727/14 Feb.
William, Yardley Gobion, farmer, to Anne, wid., 1727/8 Dec.
Mary, Green's Norton, wid., to Susannah, wife of Samuel Osmond, Towcester, butcher, sister, 1728/26 Feb.
Richard, Green's Norton, Guard.only of Anna Maria, minor, daughter, 1728/24 May
Anne, Lilbourne, wid., to Anne, spin., daughter, 1729/16 Apr.
Thomas, Hollowell, Guilsborough, yeo., to Eleanor, wid., 1729/20 Sept.
Mary, Towcester, spin., to John, maltster, 1730/24 Oct.
Thomas, Boddington, lab., to John, servant, son, 1731/4 Jan.
Anne, Eastcote, Pattishall, wid., to John Winckles, yeo., church warden, 1731/7 July
Brown, Tobias, Helpston, Inv.only £39.16.6 1733/302
Richard, Little Addington, Inv.only £32.7.0 1734/317
Samuel, Kettering, to Mary, wid., 1735/30 May
William, Clipston, miller, to Mary, wid., 1738/19 Aug.
Broome, William, Clipston, Inv.only £18.2.0 1738/354
Mary, Spratton, wid., to Ann, wife of Samuel Shelton, daughter, Inv. £11.9.6 1738/3 Oct.
Samuel, Northampton, baker, to Anne, wid., 1739/19 Jan.
William, Holcote, Inv.only £169.7.6 1741/380
James, Little Addington, to Mary, wid., Inv. £23.18.0 1743/20 Apr.
Stephen, Coton Mill, Ravensthorpe, miller, to Elizabeth, spin., daughter, 1743/14 May
Andrew, Eydon, to Mary, wid., 1743/24 June
Brown, Rev. John, Brackley, clerk, to Keziah, wid., Will, 1745/25 Oct.
Brown, John, Paulerspury, gent., to Mary, wid., 1746/27 Aug.
Thomas, Grafton Underwood, yeo., to Samuel, yeo., brother, 1748/1 Feb.
Joseph, Clipston, farmer, to Ann, wid., 1748/27 Aug.
Jonathan, Wappenham, mason, to Elizabeth, wid., Inv. £11.0.0 1754/19 Oct.
William, Yardley Gobion, butcher, to Mary, wid., 1755/15 Mar.
Brown, Mary, Northampton, spin., to Hannah, wife of Henry Knight, Spratton, weaver, 1762/5 Jan.
Brown, William, Yardley Gobion, yeo., to Elizabeth, wid., and Thomas, yeo., and Mary, spin., grandchildren, 1764/2 Feb.
Brown, Thomas, Yardley Gobion, to Joyce, wid., 1764/28 Apr.
Brown, John, Northampton, parchment maker, to Mary, wid., Mary, spin., daughter, exor., renounced, Will, 1765/28 Aug.
Brown, John, Boddington, widower, to William, Great Everdon, blacksmith, cousin, 1765/20 Nov.
Brown, Sarah, Badby, to Jonathan, gardener, husband, 1767/20 July
Brown, Thomas, Wootton, servant, to Daniel Evans, shepherd, brother in law, 1777/15 Mar.
Samuel, Sudborough, farmer, Inv.only £208.6.0 1790/420
Brawn, Abraham, Irchester, farmer, to Elizabeth, wid., 1791/9 Nov.

BROWNE continued
Mary, Knotting Green, co. Bedford, spin., to Anne, wife of John Hine, grazier, mother, 1795/27 June
Samuel, Holcot, carpenter, to Ann, wid., and William, Scaldwell, son, 1798/29 Nov.
BROWNSELL, Edward, Maidford, to Elizabeth, wid., and Comfort Downing, daughter, Inv. £58.16.8 1719/7
John, Eydon, Inv.only £72.1.6 1723/118 A
BROWNSGRAVE, Mary, Northampton, to William, butcher, husband, 1767/5 Sept.
BROWNSWORD, William, Denton, to Jemima, spin., daughter, 1723/14
BRUCE, Giles, Kettering, to Susannah, wid., 1740/26 July
BRUDENELL, Edward, Barton Seagrave, to Elizabeth, wid., 1717/112
BRUNTON, Francis, Northampton, servant, to Ellen Waddington, Scriven, co. York, wid., aunt, 1757/8 Mar.
BRYAN, Thomas, Westhorpe, Byfield, yeo., to John, yeo., son, Anne, wid., renounced, 1730/9 Apr.
Thomas, Westhorpe, Byfield, Inv.only £207.0.5 1730/278
William, junior, Orton, to Rebecca, wid., 1753/20 Mar.
Robert, Westhorpe, Byfield, yeo., to Edmund Burton, Daventry, gent., Hannah, wid., exor., decd., Will, 1782/25 Jan.
BRYANT, Lewis, Little Harrowden, Inv.only £21.5.0 1735/3 Oct.
BUCKBY, William, Desborough, Inv.only £140.16.0 1722/82 A
John, Rothwell, weaver, Inv.only £566.8.6 1724/108 A
William, Desborough, to Elizabeth, wid., 1775/29 Dec.
BUCKINGHAM, William, Middleton Cheney, framework knitter, to William, framework knitter, son, Inv. £38.0.0 1767/11 Dec.
Elizabeth, Middleton Cheney, wid., to William, son, 1768/30 July
BUCKLAND, Edward, Welford, Inv.only £84.5.6 1713/23A
BUCKLER, Sarah, Brampton, wid., to Mary, wife of John Camp, tailor, daughter, Inv. £45.10.10 1763/10 Aug.
BUGBY, Thomas, Great Oxendon, weaver, Inv.only £71.4.4 1712/38A
Bukby, Hugh, Great Oxendon, lab., to Michael, Inv. £3.18.6 1715/127
BULL, Edward, Lois Weedon, to Henry, husb., son, 1712/25
Ann, Eydon, Inv.only £2.9.6 1714/80
Henry, Marston Trussell, Inv.only £168.17.0 1714/112A
Benjamin, Brackley, plumber, Inv.only £17.15.0 1720/105A
Richard, Wootton, to Anne, spin., sister, Inv. £90.0.0 Richard, father, renounced, 1721/33
Bridget, Brackley, wid., Inv.only £47.5.0 1724/139A
Thomas, Middleton Cheney, butcher, to Anne, wid., Inv. £29.5.2 1733/24 Oct.
Hannah, Eydon, wid., to Thomas, lab., son, 1734/9 Mar.
Timothy, Helmdon, Inv.only £14.7.0 1739/372
William, Aston le Walls, to Alban, Chalcombe, grazier, son, 1741/31 Jan.
James, Helmdon, to Jane, wid., 1750/7 May
John, Northampton, saddler, Guard.only of Benjamin, minor, son, 1751/21 Sept.
Benjamin, Rothwell, to John, son, 1751/23 Sept.
John, Weston, Weedon Lois, yeo., to Hannah, wid., Inv. £487.2.6 1752/14 July
Ann, Helmdon, wid., to Ann, wife of Edward Bayliss, victualler, daughter, 1758/19 Oct.
Edward, Eydon, to Mary, wid., 1769/25 Nov.
John, Rothwell, to Benjamin, son, 1770/28 May
Susannah, Weston, Weedon Lois, to Benjamin, butcher, son, 1771/22 Feb.
Elizabeth, Eydon, to Anthony, 1771/21 Mar.
John, Kingsthorpe, to Judith, wid., 1777/30 Dec.
Benjamin, Rothwell, to Elizabeth, wid., 1778/22 Jan.
Lionell, Brington, to Benjamin, Wappenham, wheelwright, brother, 1781/14 Aug.
BULLIMORE, Thomas, Hardingstone, blacksmith, to Elizabeth, wid., Guard. of Hannah, minor, daughter, 1783/9 and 16 Sept.
BULLIVANT, John, Cransley, to Elizabeth, wid., 1715/134
John, Rushton, to Elizabeth, wid., 1741/21 Jan.
Mary, Guilsborough, to John, clerk, husband, 1759/27 June
Thomas, Great Harrowden, to John, Finedon, baker, brother, Inv. £162.18.11 1763/15 Oct.
BULLOCK, William, Little Oakley, clerk, to Gervase, sergemaker, brother, 1712/105

BULLOCK continued
Hannah, Floore, to John, yeo., husband, 1716/142
Thomas, Kilsby, husb., to Millicent, wid., Inv. £78.11.6 1722/31
Hannah, Heyford, wid., to Mary, wife of Robert Collett, miller, daughter, 1728/13 Apr.
James, Higham Ferrers, miller, to Elizabeth, wid., 1731/17 July
BUNCHER, William, Paulerspury, to John Wickens, yeo., guardian of Robert, minor, Will, 1714/111
BUNTING, John, East Haddon, woolcomber, to Mary, wid., Inv. £85.8.1 1756/28 Aug.
Richard, Long Buckby, to John, Richard, John Porter and William Porter, woolcombers, nephews, Will, 1797/27 Feb.
BURBIDGE, William, elder, Long Buckby, yeo., Inv.only £18.1.4 1714/27A
William, Maidford, to Ursula, wid., 1723/109
Elizabeth, Long Buckby, spin., to John, woolcomber, brother, Mary, wid., mother, renounced, 1723/128
Robert, Sywell, lab., to Sarah, wid., 1735/28 Jan.
Henry, Maidford, yeo., to Mary, wid., 1753/14 July
Robert, Staverton, gent., to Catherine, wid., 1756/8 Nov.
William, West Haddon, to Mary, wid., 1757/10 Dec.
BURBOROW, Timothy, Aynho, Inv.only £14.2.10 1719/70A
BURBURY, William, Clipston, to Anne, wid., 1712/66
BURCH, Edward, Wellingborough, victualler, to Anne, wid., Inv. £85.0.0 1735/22 Feb.
BURDEN, Rev. Richard, Rector of Braunston, clerk, to Euseby Slater, yeo., principal creditor, William, brother, renounced, Inv. £168.4.0 1724/151
William, Braunston, gent., to John Welchman, junior, Banbury, gent., Mary Iliffe, Lutterworth, co. Leic., spin., niece, renounced, 1729/10 June
BURDITT, Henry, Rushton, shepherd, to Elizabeth, wid., Will, 1748/10 Oct.
Burdett, William, Warkton, to Elizabeth, 1771/1 July
Burdett, Moses, Navesby, farmer, to Elizabeth, wid., 1792/22 Nov.
William, Staverton, shoemaker, to Henry, yeo., and William Dickins, carpenter, Will, 1800/1 Jan.
BURGES, Anne, Blisworth, wid., to Anne Millington, daughter, and Anne Clarke, spin., granddaughter, 1729/8 Oct.
Mary, Higham Ferrers, wid., to Robert, farmer, son, 1783/22 Apr.
BURKITT, Sarah, Northampton, wid., to Mary, spin., daughter, 1739/18 Aug.
BURNBY, John, Kettering, to Elizabeth, wid., 1720/57
BURNHAM, Burman, William, Milton, to Dorothy, wid., Inv. £9.5.0 1720/107
Thomas, Staverton, to Mary, wid., Inv. £39.13.0 1722/27
Burnman, John, Long Buckby, to John Parsons, Draughton, tanner, and Joseph Woolston, Northampton, gent., principal creditors, 1725/4 Sept.
Robert, Staverton, to Robert, farmer, son, 1776/21 Oct.
BURNILL, Thomas, Wappenham, yeo., to Thomas, lab., son, 1759/12 Dec.
Burnhill, Robert, Abthorpe, husb., to Mary, wid., 1790/21 July
BURROWS, Burrow, John, Brington, Account of Jane Jayes als. Burrow, wid., admin., £38.4.4 1678/63
John, Braunston, to Mary, wid., 1720/81
Thomas, Cransley, weaver, to Mary, wid., 1734/24 July
William, Braunston, lab., to Sarah Rennard, Willoughby, co. Warwick, wid., sister, 1763/12 Nov.
BURT, Elizabeth, Northampton, wid., to Elizabeth, spin., daughter, 1736/1 Oct.
BURTON, John, Newnham, mason, yeo., to Elizabeth, wid., Inv. £321.2.6 1723/88
Thomas, Paulerspury, Guard.only of John, minor, exor., 1725/6 Feb.
John, Paulerspury, yeo., to Sarah, wid., 1741/13 July
Richard, Fawsley, bachelor, to Thomas, Newnham, mason, nephew, 1742/8 Jan.
Robert, Daventry, servant, to Martha, wid., Inv. £64.4.6 1776/4 Nov.
Elizabeth, Helmdon, to Benjamin, cordwainer, husband, 1796/25 June
BURY, Robert, Helmdon, Account of Martha, wid., admin., £130.5.10 1680/26
BUSH, Matthew, Woodford, to Elizabeth, wid., 1772/4 Nov.
BUSWELL, George, Marston Trussell, yeo., Inv.only £128.15.6 1720/2A
Anne, Marston Trussell, wid., Inv.only £117.0.10 1723/111
Daniel, East Farndon, to Alice, wid., 1726/2 Sept.
Mary, Wappenham, wid., to Richard, miller, son, 1729/11 Oct.
Thomas, Astwell Mills, Wappenham, to Richard, miller, brother, 1729/11 Oct.

BUSWELL continued
William, Marston Trussell, yeo., Inv.only £148.3.6 1729/267
John, Mears Ashby, Inv.only £501.2.0 1738/363
John, Mears Ashby, yeo., to Mary, wid., 1740/5 Jan.
Daniel, Duston, to Rebecca, wid., 1755/25 Apr.
John, Grimscote, Cold Higham, miller, to Mary, wife of John Tomkins, miller, daughter, 1755/6 Dec.
John, Kettering, to Ann, wid., now wife of Luke Elkins, junior, 1764/19 Sept.
Richard, Marston Trussell, to Walter, 1774/5 July
John, Kettering, weaver, to Jonathan, weaver, brother, of goods unadministered by Ann Elkin, wid. of John 1779/15 Apr.
Matthew, Clipston, to Mary, wid., 1781/14 May
Thomas, Farndon, Woodford, to Susanna, Plumpton, wid., 1786/3 June
Edward, Thenford, to John, Marston St. Lawrence, brother, baker, 1793/20 Apr.
BUTCHER, Benjamin, Whitfield, to Anne, wid., Inv. £51.11.0 1712/93
Thomas, Evenly, yeo., Inv.only £17.5.6 1714/26A
Anne, Whitfield, wid., Inv.only £405.8.0 1717/115A
Rose, Wappenham, to Richard, yeo., husb., 1724/99
Mary, Wappenham, to Richard, husb., husband, 1729/15 Feb.
BUTLIN, Thomas, Ravensthorpe, to John, yeo., father, 1715/79
William, Spratton, Inv.only £12.12.0 1721/41A
Joseph, Nortoft, Guilsborough, yeo., Inv.only £133.10.0 1722/108A
James, Welton, Inv.only £297.5.0 1723/138A
Sarah, Yelvertoft, wid., to Benjamin Vice, yeo., 1728/14 Sept.
William Langton, Whilton, yeo., to Frances Barker, relict, 1745/18 May
William Langton, Whilton, Inv.only £194.2.0 1745/398
William, Teeton, miller, to William, miller, son, 1747/12 Nov.
Mary, Creaton, wid., to Elizabeth, wife of John Tarry, farmer, daughter, 1752/18 July
John, Nobottle, to Elizabeth, wid., 1768/17 Dec.
William, Creaton, to Benjamin, woolcomber, son, 1772/30 Jan.
John, Watford, cordwainer, to Joseph, cordwainer, son, Hannah, wife, exor., decd., Will, 1775/27 Sept.
Lucas, Althorp, keeper, to Anne, wid., Guard.of Elizabeth, and Anne, minors, children, 1780/8 Mar.
John, Ravensthorpe, farmer, to Mary, wid., 1797/5 Sept.
BUTLING, William, Ravensthorpe, mason, to Anne, wid., 1726/29 Oct.
BUTTON, Francis, Abthorpe, Account of Francis, son, £276.11.0 1676/147
Francis, junior, Abthorpe, to Anne, wid., Inv. £40.0.0 1712/107
Thomas, junior, Abthorpe, Towcester, Inv.only £53.13.0 1714/64A
Francis, Abthorpe, Towcester, Inv.only £29.0.0 1723/21A
Richard, Preston Capes, to Elizabeth, wid., Inv. £284.13.6 1740/29 Apr.
BYARD, John, Wellingborough, to Elizabeth, wid., 1752/8 Dec.

C

CABLE, Mary, Rothwell, wid., Account of Elizabeth, wife of Nathaniel Beeby, daughter, admin., £170.5.2 1676/153
CADE, Martha, Whitfield, spin., to Mary Wood, London, sister, 1715/128
CADWELL, Robert, Tiffield, to Elizabeth, wid., 1722/96
CALCOTT, William, Cotton End, Hardingstone, woolstapler, to Ann, wid., Mary Holmes, exor., renounced, Will, 1778/25 Sept.
CALVERT, John, Bradden, Guard.only of Mary and Eleanor, daughters,1712/142
CAMFIELD, Samuel, Kislingbury, to Richard, London, upholsterer, 1720/23
CAMPION, William, East Farndon, miller, Inv.only £26.13.2 1711/26A
John, Walgrave, Inv.only £24.18.4 1714/6A
William, Denton, blacksmith, to William, son, 1728/5 Oct.
John, Heathencote, Paulerspury, husb., to Susanna, wid., Inv. £209.15.0 1728/11 Oct.
William, Holcot, yeo., to Margery, wid., 1732/18 Mar.
Edward, Holcot, yeo., to William, yeo., brother, 1751/29 June
William, Holcot, gent., to Sarah, wid., 1752/29 Feb.
William, Holcot, gent., Guard.only of Elizabeth, minor, daughter, 1761/28 Nov.
William, soldier, to Jane, East Farndon, wid., 1763/24 Mar.
Jane, Stanwick, spin., to Anne, wife of Edward Woodroofe, Wellingborough, mother, Inv. £24.10.6 1766/21 Apr.

CANNELL, Grace, Northampton, wid., Inv.only £13.2.0 1713/71 A
Mary, Kingsthorpe, wid., to Richard Parr, Northampton, grocer, 1715/89
Ann, Great Doddington, wid., Inv.only £101.8.1 1715/123 A
Robert, Old, yeo., to Elizabeth, wid., Inv. £664.0.0 1730/13 June
John, Old, to Elizabeth, wid., 1738/28 Jan.
Elizabeth, Old, spin., to John, yeo., nephew, 1742/23 Jan.
Elizabeth, Old, spin., to George, woolcomber, nephew, 1743/2 Dec.
John, Old, yeo., to George, grazier, brother, 1783/16 May
CANNON, William, Kelmarsh, grazier, to Nicholas, grazier, and William, sons, 1733/2 June
Cannan, William, Kelmarsh, Inv.only £180.0.0 1733/313
CANWARDEN, Joseph, Hardwick, gent., to Elizabeth, wid., Inv. £771.10.7 1719/4
Elizabeth, Hardwick, to John, yeo., son, 1724/56
CAPELL, Thomas, Brington, Account of Margaret, wid., admin., £151.16.8 1672/96
George, West Haddon, Account of Katherine, wid., admin., £136.19.0 1675/62
William, Watford, Inv.only £33.7.8 1717/107 A
Thomas, Daventry, butcher, to Humphrey Baisley, Charwelton, grazier, principal creditor, Jane, wid., and Samuel, yeo., father, renounced, 1721/13
Joseph, Yelvertoft, lab., to Mary, wid., 1727/2 Sept.
Joseph, Yelvertoft, Inv.only £19.8.0 1727/211
Elizabeth, Watford, wid., to William, Yelvertoft, lab., son, 1736/8 Dec.
Elizabeth, Brington, spin., to Elizabeth, wid., mother, 1744/19 Apr.
Archbold, Cold Higham, farmer, to Elizabeth, wid., 1782/4 Nov.
John, Dodford, grazier, to Elizabeth, wid., 1783/10 Oct.
CAPORNE, als. Fitzhugh, William, Roade, yeo., Inv.only £54.10.0 1714/114 A
Caporn als. Fitzhugh, Sarah, Roade, spin., Inv.only £24.10.0 1722/84 A
Caporn, Thomas, Preston Capes, grazier, to Elizabeth, daughter, Elizabeth, wid., renounced, 1765/12 Mar.
CARDWELL, Rev. Richard, Raunds, clerk, to Mary Pinder, daughter, Inv. £74.3.7 1724/117
CAREY, John, Brackley, Inv.only £138.11.0 1720/29 A
CARMAN, Thomas, Daventry, fishmonger, glassman, to William Adams, Daventry, carrier, principal creditor, Eliza, wid., renounced, 1800/28 June
CARPENTER, Thomas, Adstone, Inv.only £153.10.0 1730/274
Thomas, Adstone, Canons Ashby, yeo., to Eleanor, wid., 1731/20 Feb.
Joseph, Wellingborough, attorney at law, to Ann Page, wid., principal creditor, 1747/27 July
Rebecca, to Charles, St. Margaret, Westminster, co. Middlesex, carpenter, husband, 1754/24 Apr.
George, Braunston, to Thomas, yeo., son, 1775/11 Feb.
John, Stowe, yeo., to Sarah, wid., and Mary, wife of John Manning, Harpole, yeo., 1795/10 Dec.
CARR, Susan, Blakesley, Inv.only £8.12.0 1715/112A
Robert, Sulgrave, Inv.only £79.11.0 1719/113A
Robert, Whilton, to Hannah, wid., 1723/69
Thomas, Hanging Houghton, to Sarah, wid., 1724/130
Thomas, Whilton, to William, husb., 1728/10 Aug.
Francis, Brixworth, to John Walker, Brampton, mason, John Cherry, exor., renounced, Will, 1736/21 Aug.
William, Whilton, yeo., to Thomas, farmer, brother, 1745/12 Apr.
William, Cold Ashby, to Mary, wid., 1769/25 Oct.
Elizabeth, Brampton, wid., to Wayte, farmer, son, 1778/21 Dec.
CARTER, Sarah, Daventry, spin., to John Humfreys, Welton, carpenter, uncle, Inv. £2.9.6, Roger and Elizabeth Moore, sister, renounced, 1720/40
Judah, East Farndon, to Dorothy, wid., 1729/22 Mar.
Thomas, West Haddon, yeo., to Elizabeth, wife of John Marson, Coventry, co. Warwick, miller, niece, Will, 1732/29 Apr.
Samuel, Towcester, barber, to Thomas, shopkeeper, Samuel, barber, and Anne, spin., sons and daughter, 1732/28 June
Dorothy, Yardley Hastings, wid., to Mary, spin., daughter, 1778/30 Apr.
CARTWRIGHT, Thomas, Long Buckby, clerk, Inv.only £459.4.0 1744/392
CARVELL, William, Desborough, butcher, to William, husb., son, Inv. £1.17.0 Will, 1715/160
Carwell, Bridget, Northampton, wid., to James, barber, son, 1724/158
Carvill, Francis, Catesby, tailor, to Elizabeth, Shugburgh, co. Warwick, spin., daughter, 1734/26 Apr.

CASTLE, Castell, Richard, Cold Ashby, gent., to Elizabeth Markham, spin., of goods unadministered by Elizabeth, wid., exor., decd., Will, 1749/18 May
William, Northampton, to John, perukemaker, son, 1775/6 June
CASWELL, William, Rothersthorpe, Account of Anne, admin., £143.9.6 1680/36
William, Milton, to Mary, wid., 1773/24 Apr.
CATTELL, John, Elkington, to Samuel Watlington, Redding, co. Berks., gent., Inv. £237.17.0, Anne, wid., renounced, 1715/105
Joseph, Rothwell, clerk, to Elizabeth, wid., Inv. £300.13.0 1720/37
John, Ravensthorpe, to Grace, wid., 1721/51
John, Broughton, yeo., Inv.only £155.10.0 1724/150A
Susanna, Irthlingborough, spin., to Dina Bell, wid., sister, 1725/19 Oct.
Cattle, William, Broughton, to Mary, wid., 1752/18 Apr.
Cattel, William, Braunston, yeo., to Sarah, wid., Inv. £90.3.4 1768/2 Sept.
William, Yelvertoft, yeo., to John, farmer, son, 1786/4 May
Richard, Yelvertoft, woolwinder, to Robert, woolcomber, son, 1791/4 May
CAUSEBY, Thomas, Chapel Brampton, yeo., to Martha, wid., Inv. £103.5.6 1735/25 Oct.
William, Croughton, to Thomas, King's End, Bicester, co. Oxford, 1799/6 July
CAVE, Elizabeth, West Haddon, wid., Inv.only £8.2.6 1711/22A
Samuel, Welton, yeo., Inv.only £7.17.1 1712/113A
William, Desborough, to Bryan Hull, Rushton, gent., principal creditor, 1713/134
Anne, Thorpe Malsor, wid., to Robert, yeo., son, 1716/20
Thomas, Duston, to Elizabeth, wid., 1720/26
John, Northampton, to Anne, wife of Francis Willson, plasterer, daughter, 1725/20 Mar.
William, Daventry, carpenter, to John, Hilmorton, co. Warwick, carpenter, brother, 1732/27 Jan.
George, Piddington, yeo., to John, yeo., son, Judith, wid., renounced, 1745/9 Nov.
Edward, Kingsthorpe, clerk, to Mary, wid., 1750/17 Feb.
Caves, William, Cheney House, Cogenhoe, yeo., to John, Horton, grazier, son, Elizabeth, exor., decd., Will, 1763/11 June
Shepherd, Roade, to John Bliss, Stoke Goldington, Bucks., innholder, and William, Cheney House, Cogenhoe, farmer, uncles and guardians of Elizabeth, Sarah, Mary, Ann, Frances and Susannah, minors, daughters, Inv. £67.0.0 1766/20 Oct.
Martha, Kettering, wid., to William Fenton, victualler, son, 1773/9 Mar.
Kezia, Roade, wid., to Ann, spin., daughter, 1777/24 Apr.
Thomas, Staverton, victualler, to Mary, wid., 1787/5 Oct.
George, Desborough, to Ann, wid., 1799/29 Aug.
Susanna, Harlestone, spin., to Elizabeth, wife of Joseph Vialls, yeo., sister, 1800/6 Feb.
William, Harlestone, farmer, to Elizabeth, wife of Joseph Vialls, yeo., daughter, Susannah, exor., decd., Will, 1800/6 Feb.
CHADWICK, John, Inv.only £25.0.6 undated/290
CHALLONER, Samuel, Wellingborough, gent., to William, Doddington, clerk, brother, 1753/24 Nov.
CHAMBERLIN, Chamberline, Henry, Cransley, Inv.only £49.10.6 1719/43A
John, Northampton, hatter, to Alice, wid., 1733/7 June
Robert, Welford, yeo., to Lydia, wid., 1736/26 Oct.
Chamberlayne, John, Overthorpe, Middleton Cheney, to Elizabeth, wid., 1743/19 Sept.
Chamberlain, Rebecca, Welton, to John, lab., brother, 1778/30 Oct.
Charles, Northampton, hatter, to Elizabeth, wife of Edward Dunkly, butcher, daughter, of goods unadministered by Mary Driver, Joseph Robinson, innholder, and James Williamson, draper, Will, 1781/18 Sept.
CHAMBERS, John, Castle Ashby, innkeeper, to Mary, wid., Inv. £60. 1714/92
Frances, Little Bowden, wid., to John, yeo., son, 1728/14 Sept.
Frances, Little Bowden, wid., Inv.only £102.0.0 1728/261
Sarah, Inv.only £21.10.0 1728/252
Benjamin, Wellingborough, pewterer, to Elizabeth, wid., Inv. £75.5.6 1743/20 Apr.
John, Lower Boddington, farmer, to Mary, wid., Inv. £418.15.0 1746/26 Apr.
William, Braybrooke, to Eleanor, wid., 1751/31 Jan.
John, Boddington, farmer, to John, lab., son, of goods unadministered by Mary, wid., decd., 1757/23 June

CHAMBERS continued
Joseph, Litchborough, to Elizabeth, wid., 1770/20 Feb.
William, Northampton, baker, to Sarah, wid., 1793/20 Dec.
CHANDLER, William, Brackley, gent., Inv.only £297.6.0 1718/33A
CHAPMAN, Thomas, Old, Inv.only £286.10.6 1712/44 A
Elizabeth, Barton Seagrave, wid., Inv.only £142.16.3 1713/102 A
John, Kettering, to Sarah, wid., Inv. £73.6.7 1713/103
Thomas, Old, yeo., Inv.only £377.7.0 1716/39 A
Thomas, Old, senior, yeo., Inv.only £377.7.0 1716/93
Richard, Old, gent., Inv.only £212.10.0 1719/6 A
Alice, Walgrave, to William, yeo., son, 1720/98
David, Walgrave, to William, yeo., son of Alice, exor., decd., Will, 1720/114
Edward, Draughton, to Mary, wid., 1721/124
John, Inv.only £22.11.0 1723/107
John, Wollaston, Inv.only £22.11.0 1723/123 A
John, Irchester, yeo., to Sarah, wid., Inv. £750.7.0 1731/10 May
John, Denton, carpenter, to John, lab., father, 1733/7 July
Stephen, Old, to Rebecca, wid., 1734/29 June
als. Warwick, Catherine, to Benjamin, All Saints, Northampton, baker, husband, 1735/27 May
John, Thorpe Malsor, to Mary, wid., 1735/7 June
Samuel, Cottingham, Inv.only £124.10.0 1737/340
William, Old, yeo., Inv.only £173.15.0 1739/367
Edward, Rothwell, clerk, to Elizabeth, wid., 1741/11 May
Elizabeth, Old, spin., to Tresham, gent., brother, Anne, wife of Thomas Kerton (Kirton), Harlestone, mother, renounced, 1743/22 Oct.
Thomas, Brafield on the Green, shepherd, to Sarah, wid., 1747/24 Oct.
Thomas, Kettering, joiner, to John Hinkley, senior, principal creditor, Elizabeth, wid., renounced, 1764/14 Mar.
Elizabeth, Higham Ferrers, to Elizabeth Wagstaffe, wid., mother, 1768/18 Feb.
John, Harrowden, co. Bedford, to Thomas, Puddington, co. Bedford, servant, brother, 1772/3 Oct.
Edward, East Haddon, to Edward, carpenter, son, 1773/27 Apr.
Bet, Brackley, to Richard, apothecary, husband, 1778/28 Dec.
Edward, Kettering, to Ann, wid., now wife of Thomas Warner, victualler, 1781/23 Apr.
William, Rothwell, to Mary, wid., 1782/19 Dec.
John, Marston Trussell, gent., to Joseph, gent., brother, 1786/3 Oct.
Mary, Thorpe Malsor, wid., to Richard Garratt, elder, farmer, nephew, Samuel Meadows, farmer, renounced, Will, 1791/12 Jan.
John, Irthlingborough, dealer, to William Bradshaw, Mears Ashby, seedsman, principal creditor, 1796/24 Dec.
William, Newton Bromswold, to John Bollard, farmer, 1797/14 Feb.
Mary, Barham, Hunts., to Thomas, farmer, husband, 1797/2 Mar.
Robert, Braybrooke, clerk, to John Everett, butcher, creditor, 1800/27 May
CHARLES, Thomas, Pisford, grazier, to Elizabeth, wid., 1751/13 July
CHARLTON, Bartholomew, Northampton, to Elizabeth, wid., 1755/28 Mar.
George, Northampton, cooper, to Mary, wid., Inv. £16.3.8 1769/20 Mar.
Martha, Northampton, to George, cooper, husband, 1774/22 Aug.
CHARMAN, John, Daventry, to William Clarke, innholder, principal creditor, 1773/27 Dec.
CHATER, Usher, Kislingbury, tailor, to Anne, wid., 1727/23 Dec.
John, Moulton, maltster, to Mary, wid., 1751/11 May
CHECKLEY, William, Preston Capes, Account of Rebecca, wid., admin., £244.3.0 1672/105
Thomas, Hinton, Woodford cum Membris, Account of Mary, wid., admin., £122.0.0 1674/77
Thomas, Litchborough, shepherd, Inv.only £11.1.6 1711/112A
Elizabeth, Hinton, Woodford, wid., to John, yeo., son, 1719/56
Mary, Hinton, spin., to John, yeo., brother, 1719/57
Elizabeth, Hinton, spin., to John, yeo., brother, 1719/58
Edward, Sulgrave, yeo., Inv.only £49.3.6 1720/38A
William, Welford, shepherd, to William, shepherd, son, Grace, wid., renounced, 1729/24 May
als. Hickman, Sarah, Hinton, Woodford, to Edward, yeo., husband, 1736/23 Feb.
Judith, Woodford, to Edward, yeo., husband, 1737/14 Oct.

CHECKLEY continued
Comfort, Northampton, wid., to John Hollis, baker, brother in law, guardian of Catherine, daughter, minor, Guard., 1782/25 Jan.
William, Sulgrave, farmer, to Jane, wid., 1782/9 July
John, Daventry, wheelwright, to Robert Gibbs, plumber and glazier, and James Knibb, butcher, principal creditors, Elizabeth, wid., renounced, Guard. of William, George, Philippa, minors, children, 1786/16 Mar.
Comfort, Northampton, wid., to Catherine, spin., daughter, 1790/20 Dec.
Thomas, Moreton Pinkney, to Thomas, lab., son, 1791/30 Nov.
William, Preston Capes, dealer in pigs, to William Hands, yeo., principal creditor, Catherine, wid., renounced, Will, Inv. £54.11.9 1794/13 Aug.
CHENELL, William, Blakesley, husb., Inv.only £18.10.6 1711/74A
CHENEY, William, Woodford, tailor, to William, Thorpe Malsor, tailor, son, 1783/19 July
Edward, Navesby, innholder, to Roger, weaver, brother, Mary, wife, exor., decd., Will, 1793/20 July
CHERRY, Mary, Grendon, wid., Inv.only £14.5.0 1712/109A
Philip, Blakesly, to Thomas Lovell, Weston, Weedon Lois, principal creditor, Elizabeth, wid., renounced, 1718/63
John, Little Houghton, Inv.only £113.0.0 1724/106A
Catherine, Boddington, wid., to Valentine Orton, Byfield, yeo., 1729/29 July
Mary, Grendon, wid., to Thomas, Little Harrowden, farmer, and Francis, farmer, sons, Inv. £183.3.3 1754/30 May
Mary, Grendon, to Andrew Wilson, Wellingborough, merchant, William Bateman, father, exor., decd., Will, 1784/28 July
Thomas, Grendon, to Rebecca Lawton, wid., daughter, 1784/4 Oct.
Sarah, Wellingborough, to George Wakeman, clerk, nephew, 1786/4 June
John, Westhorpe, Marston St. Lawrence, blacksmith, to Honour Shepard, spin., niece, Will, 1787/18 Oct.
Anne, Northampton, to Joseph, carpenter, husband, 1800/9 Aug.
CHESTER, Mary, Alderton, to William, lab., husband, 1725/31 Aug.
Edward, Marston St. Lawrence, yeo., Inv.only £121.12.0 1726/164
Esther, Ashby St. Ledgers, to William, lab., husband, 1741/12 May
Augustine, Austin, Hargrave, lab., to Elizabeth, wid., Inv. £11.8.6 1750/10 Oct.
John, Sulgrave, wheelwright, to Anne, Inv. £200.0.0 1775/4 July
John, Sulgrave, wheelwright, Guard.only of Elizabeth, Susannah, Edward, minors, children, 1775/8 Oct.
John, Guilsborough, lab., to John, private in the Northants Regiment of Militia, Brighthelmston, Sussex, son, 1798/8 Dec.
CHESTERTON, Thomas, Wellingborough, tailor, to Benjamin, yeo., son, Alice, wid., renounced, 1711/59
Benjamin, Wellingborough, to Alice, wid., 1736/30 Apr.
CHETTLE, Henry, Chelveston cum Caldecott, Account of Anne, wid., admin., now wife of George Carter, Rushden, £231.5.0 1668/124
John, Chelveston cum Caldecott, yeo., Inv.only £1522.10.0 1711/144A
Henry, Higham Ferrars, to Frances, Wellingborough, wid., 1726/29 Oct.
CHILDS, Dorothy, Braunston, Inv.only £18.18.11 1721/54A
John, senior, Ecton, Inv.only £111.12.6 1721/119A
John, Raunds, Inv.only £148.0.0 1724/136
Childes, Richard, Raunds, yeo., to Susannah, wid., 1736/11 Sept.
John, Ecton, to John, yeo., son, Inv. £261.0.0 1761/28 Mar.
Stephen, Eydon, mason, to John Pratt, Helmdon, gent., Martha and Mary, spins., daughters, renounced, 1771/26 Aug.
CHINNER, Henry, Chalcombe, to Mary, wid., 1735/3 Oct.
Henry, Chalcombe, Inv.only £19.14.6 1735/329
William, Chalcombe, to Mary, wid., 1763/22 Apr.
Charles, Chalcombe, victualler, to Amos, farmer, son, 1764/23 May
CHOWN, Thomas, Doddington, miller, to Elizabeth, wid., Inv. £55.1.9 1753/8 Sept.
Elizabeth, Stoke Bruerne, to Frances, wife of William Goodman, Hackleton, lacemaker, sister, 1768/16 Apr.
Mary, Stoke Bruerne, to Frances, wife of William Goodman, Hackleton, lacemaker, sister, 1768/16 Apr.
CHURCH, Thomas, Hartwell, Account of Margaret, wid., admin., £185.19.0 1671/122
Richard, Potterspury, tailor, Inv.only £90.19.8 1717/104A

CHURCH continued
Elizabeth, Potterspury, wid., Inv.only £32.7.6 1718/51A
Jane, Hartwell, wid., Inv.only £55.10.0 1720/61 A
Thomas, Hartwell, Inv.only £165.5.0 1729/268
Thomas, Collingtree, yeo., to Mary, wid., Inv. £137.15.0 1747/29 Dec.
Elizabeth, Maidwell, spin., to Edward, lab., brother, 1756/10 Jan.
Thomas, Great Billing, farmer, to Sarah, wid., Guard. of Martha, minor, daughter, 1774/20 Aug.
Thomas, Great Billing, farmer, Guard.only of Martha, minor, daughter, 1776/24 Feb.
John, Brington, farmer, to Elizabeth, wife of John Elliott, farmer, aunt and guardian of Elizabeth, minor, daughter, Guard., 1787/22 Oct.
William, Bozeat, shepherd, to William, farmer, son, Susanna, exor., decd., Will, 1798/25 July
CHURCHILL, Penelope, Northampton, to Joseph, elder, gent., husband, 1750/14 June
CHURCHMAN, Thomas, Kettering, to Elizabeth, wid., 1746/3 May
CLAPHAM, Richard, Orlingbury, to William, shepherd, son, Inv. £9.15.0, Rachel, wid., renounced, 1725/17 Nov.
John, Pytchley, tailor, to Mary, wid., Inv. £7.10.0 1726/12 Nov.
Joseph, Finedon, tailor, to John, Little Harrowden, shepherd, 1741/14 Mar.
William, Orlingbury, to Anne, wid., Will, 1754/3 Aug.
John, Wellingborough, to Elizabeth, wid., 1777/26 May
CLARE, John, Spratton, to Daniel, grocer, son, Inv. £66.19.2 1725/2 Jan.
Daniel, Spratton, grocer, to Martha, wife of Thomas Goodliff, Belton, co. Rutland, and Hannah, spin., sisters, 1727/9 Dec.
CLARIDGE, Clarridge, Jeremiah, Higham Ferrers, Inv.only £99.4.6 1723/91A
William, senior, Great Brington, blacksmith, Inv.only £48.13.8 1733/303
John, Towcester, chandler, to Sarah, wid., 1751/6 Apr.
William, Brington, blacksmith and grocer, to Rose, wid., Inv. £141.12.1¼ 1755/10 Mar.
Thomas, Northampton, victualler, to Mary, wid., 1770/15 Oct.
Elizabeth, Brington, wid., to John, Ravensthorpe, farmer, son, 1776/9 Oct.
Thomas, Ravensthorpe, farmer, to Sarah, wid., 1786/7 Oct.
Richard, Northampton, shopkeeper, to Mary, spin., daughter, 1788/1 Dec.
William, Northampton, blacksmith, to Sarah, wid., 1792/21 Apr.
John, Duston, victualler, to Rebecca, wid., John Pickering and John Hilliard, yeos., exors., renounced, Will, 1793/8 Jan.
CLARKE, Samuel, Chelveston cum Caldecote, Account of Edward, admin., £200.0.0 1669/90 and 139
William, Courtenhall, Account of John, £155.8.6 1671/115
Robert, Braunston, yeo., Account of Mary, wid., £152.18.8 1673/151
Clerke, Joseph, Towcester, Account of Elizabeth, wid., admin., £419.15.4 1682/21
Clerke, George, Braunston, Account of Anne, wid., admin., £84.18.0 1685/25
Mary, Braunston, wid., Inv.only £19.13.0 1711/5A
Clerke, Thomas, Silverstone, to Martha, wid., Inv. £106.9.6 1711/28
John, Kettering, to Elizabeth, 1711/42
Catherine, Hardingstone, Inv.only £102.7.8 1712/47A
Henry, Wootton, Inv.only £25.3.6 1712/95A
Abraham, Bugbrooke, yeo., Inv.only £474.1.0 1713/36A
George, Braunston, Guard.only of George and Mary, minors, children 1713/51
Elizabeth, Blakesley, Inv.only £4.5.0 1713/74A
Anne, Crick, wid., Inv.only £72.11.0 1713/98A
Henry, Marston Trussell, Inv.only £108.5.0 1713/118A
John, Denshanger, Passenham, to Anne, wid., Inv. £500.2.6 1714/33
James, Brafield on the Green, Inv.only £27.0.0 1714/65A
Christopher, Crick, cordwainer, Inv.only £179.4.7 1714/74A
Henry, Knuston, Irchester, to Elizabeth, wid., Inv. £10.8.6 1714/138
Clark, Mary, Winwick, Inv.only £7.0.10 1715/96A
Clark, Edward, West Haddon, Inv.only £45.9.0 1716/66A
Thomas, Brington, Inv.only £87.11.6 1716/69A
Joseph, Welton, to William, husb., brother, 1716/74
Clark, William, Hargrave, lab., Inv.only £15.0.0 1716/118A
Thomas, West Haddon, yeo., Inv.only £145.0.8 1716/125A
Clark, John, Moulton, to John, son, 1717/146
Clark, Samuel, Rushden, to Sarah, wid., 1719/19
Mary, Cold Ashby, wid., Inv.only £27.10.6 1720/16a A

CLARKE continued
Richard, Charwelton, to George Horne, Weedon Beck, yeo., principal creditor, Inv. £7.15.6 1720/51
John, Sywell, yeo., to Elizabeth, wid., Inv. £661.3.2 1720/54
Clark, George, Rothwell, lab., to Elizabeth, wid., Inv. £49.14.9 1721/91
William, Little Bowden, to Elizabeth, wife of John Elson, Oxendon, baker, daughter, Inv. £11.11.0 1721/110
John, Ringstead, husb., to Mary, wife of William Smith, daughter, Inv. £66.9.4 1723/11
Clark, Robert, Pytchley, weaver, to Elizabeth, spin., daughter, Inv. £9.10.0 Elizabeth, wid., renounced, 1723/13
Margaret, Barby, wid., Inv.only £18.12.6 1724/69A
Thomas, Chelveston cum Caldecote, to Elizabeth, wid., Inv. £180.9.6 1724/92
William, Tiffield, yeo., to Anne, wid., Inv. £23.0.0 1725/30 Sept.
John, Sywell, Guard.only of Elizabeth, daughter, 1725/13 Nov.
John, Northampton, baker, to Sarah, wid., Inv. £40.10.6 1726/6 Aug.
William, Northampton, victualler, to Elizabeth, wid., Inv. £107.17.6 1729/15 Jan.
Richard, Ravensthorpe, cooper, to Mary, wid., 1729/24 May
Samuel, Brackley, to Sarah, wid., 1730/9 Apr.
Joseph, Welton, to John French, senior, Wardington, co. Oxford, yeo., of goods not fully administered by William, brother, 1731/4 Nov.
Frances, Nortoft, Guilsborough, to Richard, gent., husband, 1732/2 Mar.
Moses, West Haddon, grazier, to Moses, grazier, son, Inv. £1628.0.0 1732/3 June
Mary, Ravensthorpe, wid., to Elizabeth, wife of Joseph Frost, lab., niece, 1735/25 Oct.
Richard, Kettering, to Frances, wid., 1737/18 Feb.
Clerke, Mary, Watford, to Edward, husband, 1737/15 Apr.
Joseph, Hardingstone, to John, gent., son, Inv. £378.7.0 1737/9 July
Elizabeth, Northampton, spin., to Lucy, spin., sister, 1740/23 Dec.
John, Hardingstone, to John, Courtenhall, gent., son, 1741/19 Dec.
Elizabeth, Northampton, wid., to William, innholder, son, 1742/23 Feb.
John, Great Billing, lab., to John, lab., son, 1743/1 Mar.
John, Hardingstone, gent., to Elizabeth, wife of John Murray, Northampton, surgeon, daughter, 1743/10 Aug.
William, West Haddon, farmer, to Mary, spin., sister, Inv. £56.12.6 1747/15 Jan.
Martha, Bosenham Mill, Roade, to Edward, yeo., father, 1749/12 Feb.
Clerk, George, Watford, to Joseph Fraunces, Daventry, apothecary, principal creditor, Penelope, spin., renounced, Will, 1750/17 Feb.
Clark, Charles, Denshanger, Passenham, farmer, to Richard Joseph, yeo., principal creditor, Hannah, wid., renounced, 1750/8 May
Frances, Raunds, wid., to Sarah, wife of William Flawn, Irthlingborough, attorney, daughter, Robert Bates, exor., renounced, Will, 1751/8 Aug.
Frances, Watford, to Domitilla, spin., sister, 1754/9 May
Richard, Wootton, to Mary, wid., 1755/20 Dec.
Thomas, Cottesbrooke, yeo., to Ann, wid., 1756/18 Feb.
Joseph, Brixworth, grazier, to Joseph, yeo., son, Will, 1756/23 Feb.
William, Murcot, Watford, yeo., to Mary, wid., Inv. £733.0.0 1756/29 May
Joseph, Brixworth, to Lucy, spin., sister, 1757/9 Nov.
Elizabeth, Yelvertoft, spin., to Clamont, wife of William Dove, carpenter, mother, 1759/20 Oct.
Clark, Thomas, Barby, yeo., to John, yeo., son, Rebecca, wid., renounced, 1760/7 Feb.
Clark, John, Stanwick, to Elizabeth, wid., Inv. £272.1.6 1763/4 Feb.
Thomas, Wollaston, blacksmith, to John Morris, Cogenhoe, lab., exor. of Elizabeth, wid., decd., Inv. £8.15.0 1765/16 July
Clark, John, Claycoton, miller, to Thomas Chamberlain, Hillmorton, co. Warwick, bricklayer, creditor, John Chambelain, Hillmorton, bricklayer, grandson, renounced, 1766/15 Apr.
Elizabeth, Hardingstone, wid., to Mary, spin., daughter, Will, 1766/24 Sept.
Cheney, Stanwick, butcher, to Jane, wid., Inv. £18.13.6 1766/16 Dec.
Clark, John, Milton, to John, lab., son, 1769/21 Jan.
Robert, Blisworth, to John, mason, son, 1769/14 Oct.
William, Northampton, Will, 1771/28 Jan.

CLARKE continued
John, Northampton, to Anne, Brixworth, spin., daughter, 1772/3 Nov.
Edward, Daventry, to Mary, wife of John, Drayton, Daventry, farmer, sister, 1774/13 Apr.
Henry, Daventry, victualler, to Hannah, victualler, wid., 1776/30 Jan.
Elizabeth, Daventry, to Mary, wife of John, Drayton, Daventry, farmer, 1776/6 June
Hannah, Daventry, wid., to Peter Handsley, brother, 1777/1 Aug.
Clerk, Timothy, Dallington, to Charles Ward, Lincoln's Inn, co. Middx., gent., John Vernon, younger, same, gent., and Joseph Cunningham, same, gent., Will, 1777/10 Oct.
John, Hardingstone, yeo., to Mary, wid., 1778/20 July
Alice, Brington, spin., to Richard, grazier, brother, 1778/25 July
Ruth, Helmdon, wid., to Ruth, spin., daughter, 1780/16 Aug.
Sarah, Roade, wid., to Keziah Wesley, daughter, Will, 1782/22 July
Hannah, Marston Trussell, wid., to Judd Randle, uncle and guardian of George, minor, son, Guard., 1783/15 Mar.
Elizabeth, Daventry, wid., to Edward and John, farmers, sons, 1783/11 Oct.
John, Wootton, farmer, to Elizabeth, wid., 1784/7 Feb.
William, East Haddon, to Penelope, wid., 1784/22 May
William, Milton, gardener, to Mary, wid., 1786/28 Oct.
Ruth, Marston Trussell, wid., to John, carpenter, son, 1788/6 Dec.
William, Stoke Bruerne, farmer, to Elizabeth, wid., 1790/14 Aug.
Thomas, Daventry, to Mary Skinner, Braunston, wid., sister, 1792/4 Oct.
Clark, Richard, Braunston, blacksmith, to Robert Rowell, Rugby, grocer and ironmonger, principal creditor, Sarah, wid., renounced, 1793/7 Oct.
John, Northampton, draper, to Robert Rowell, Rugby, grocer and ironmonger, of goods unadministered by Catherine Alsager, daughter, 1793/25 Nov.
Clark, Edward, Yelvertoft, victualler, Inv.only £94.1.11 1794/421
Elizabeth, Kettering, to John, glover, husband, 1799/19 Mar.

CLASON, Nathaniel, Brafield on the Green, mason, to Edward, mason, brother, Inv. £127.7.1 1712/108
James, Hackleton, Piddington, to Elizabeth, wid., 1771/31 Jan.
John, Cogenhoe, tailor, to John, son, Sarah, wid., exor., decd., Will, 1771/22 July
Edward, Wellingborough, to Sarah, wid., 1781/6 Dec.
Clayson, Thomas, Wellingborough, to Samuel, St. Botolph Aldgate, co. Middx., woollen draper, son, 1797/30 May

CLAY, Thomas, Daventry, bookseller, to Samuel, Rugby, co. Warwick, grocer and ironmonger, brother, 1781/23 July

CLEADEN, Edward, Guilsborough, to Sarah, wid., 1732/16 May
William, Heyford, woadman, to William, woadman, son, 1738/25 Nov.
Cleadon, Sarah, Guilsborough, wid., to William Wills, butcher, principal creditor, 1767/25 Mar.

CLEAVELEY, John, senior, Weedon Beck, Inv.only £31.0.0 1714/22A
Thomas, Paulerspury, maltster, Inv.only £2.17.6 1718/104A
Cleavely, Elizabeth, Weedon Beck, wid., Inv.only £26.15.0 1723/93A
Thomas, Weedon Beck, farmer, to Sarah, wid., 1751/14 Sept.

CLEAVER, Thomas, Hellidon, clerk, Account of Mary, wid., admin., £75.2.8 1677/170
Andrew, Hellidon, yeo., Will only 1712/64
Richard, Little Preston, Inv.only £22.5.0 1714/162A
Thomas, Towcester, to Susanna, wid., 1716/53
Anne, Kislingbury, wid., to John Aylworth, Cold Higham, gent., and Elizabeth Stuart, same, spin., William Bland, exor., lunatic, Will, 1716/91
Anne, Kislingbury, wid., Inv.only £27.18.6 1716/94
Esther, Hellidon, wid., to Edward Rawbone, Ladbrooke, co. Warwick, carpenter, nephew, Anne Rawbone, sister, renounced, 1720/31
Clever, Thomas, Spratton, baker, to Mary, wid., Inv. £19.13.0 1721/30
John, Yelvertoft, yeo., to Richard, yeo., Inv. £112.15.6 1721/70
Sarah, Yelvertoft, to Richard, yeo., husband, 1722/50
Edward, Hellidon, yeo., Inv.only £37.11.7 1733/315
Joseph, Handley, Towcester, grazier, Inv.only £21.17.6 1738/357
Thomas, Upper Boddington, gent., to William, farmer, Thomas Theede, Daventry, and William Weston, Aston le Walls, gents., renounced, Will, 1749/13 May
Thomas, Hellidon, yeo., to Comfort, wid., Will, 1753/28 Apr.

CLEAVER continued
Clever, Thomas, Staverton, yeo., to Catherine Marriott, wid., daughter, 1756/19 Feb.
Clever, William, Hellidon, yeo., to Richard, yeo., son, of goods unadministered by Mary, wid., 1760/22 Oct.
Thomas, Caldecote, Towcester, yeo., to Ann, wife of William Gray, Whittlebury, carpenter, sister, 1778/12 Feb.
John, Moreton Pinkney, yeo., to Thomas, yeo., brother, 1792/31 Oct.
Richard, Preston Capes, to Thomas, son, 1799/19 Sept.
Sarah, Green's Norton, wid., to Winckles, baker, son, 1800/5 July
CLEMENTS, George, Stanwick, Account of Elianor, wid., admin., £63.13.4 1679/128
CLENDON, Eleanor, Ringstead, spin., to Elizabeth Cox, sister, 1782/11 Apr.
William, Lamport, yeo., to John, West Haddon, yeo., son, Will, 1788/27 Dec.
CLIFF, Thomas, Braunston, victualler, to Elizabeth, wid., 1789/24 Sept.
CLIFFORD, Mary, Northampton, wid., to Mary, wife of John Gibson, innholder, and Elizabeth Martin, spin., John Cowper and John Cooke, exors., renounced, Inv. £530.5.4 Will, 1715/108
CLIFTON, William, Heathencote, Paulerspury, gent., Inv.only £232.18.10 1716/132A
William, Maidford, yeo., to Elizabeth, wid., 1737/29 Mar.
Christopher, Northampton, barber, to James, barber, son, Inv. £153.11.5 1743/8 Aug.
Samuel, Guilsborough, shepherd, to Thomas Comfield, schoolmaster, guardian of Samuel and John, minors, sons, 1778/11 July
Elizabeth, Hardingstone, wid., to Thomas Sargent, Northampton, baker, nephew, Will, 1782/25 Sept.
William, Byfield, yeo., to John Bliss, farmer, nephew, 1784/13 May
CLIPSHAM, William, Braybrooke, husb., Inv.only £345.1.4 1729/229
Sarah, Market Harborough, to Dennis, hosier, husband, 1795/6 Oct.
COACH, George, Denton, husb., to James Rose, Great Billing, cousin, Elizabeth, wid., exor., renounced, Will, 1773/24 Apr.
COATES, Timothy, Aynho, baker, to James, baker, son, 1777/4 July
COBB, Samuel, Warkton, to John, son, Inv. £23.18.0 1719/129
Thomas, Horton, to Alice, wid., 1725/29 Apr.
COCKBOLE, Cockbould, Nicholas, Wappenham, Account of Jane, wid., £130.13.8 1676/61 and 81
COCKERILL, als. Adams, Mary, see Adams
John, Wappenham, to Anne, wid., Inv. £992.0.0 1718/64
Henry, Hanly, Towcester, gent., to Mary, wid., 1735/30 Apr.
John, Wappenham, to John, gent., son, of goods not fully administered by Anne, wid., 1735/27 Sept.
Daniel, Collingtree, yeo., to Sarah, wid., 1741/27 July
Walter, Northampton, to Mary Bradshaw, daughter, 1742/30 Mar.
Richard, Woodend, Blakesley, to Joan Gubbins, wid., sister, 1743/14 July
John, Hellidon, weaver, to William, weaver, son, 1746/9 May
Daniel, Collingtree, yeo., to Rebecca, wid., 1753/16 Apr.
COCKINGTON, John, Roade, to Edward Abby, of goods not fully administered by Anne, wid., decd., 1717/7
COCKMAN, Mary, Wollaston, spin., to Jane, wife of Thomas Foster, Uppingham, Rutland, pharmacopolist, sister, 1720/13
COCKRAINE, Elizabeth, Northampton, spin., to Mary Goodwin, wid., and Margaret, spin., sisters, 1719/111
COE, Francis, Grendon, to Sarah, wid., Inv. £561.13.3 1780/10 Nov.
COFFLEY, William, Kingsthorpe, to Mary, wid., Inv. £19.19.0 1718/65
COGAN, Thomas, Rothwell, apothecary, Inv.only £258.5.0 1713/109A
COLDWELL, Margaret, Kilsby, Inv.only £1.18.1 1712/119A
Colewell, Thomas, Holcot, to Hannah, wid., 1770/5 Apr.
Francis, Overstone, farmer, to Alice, wid., 1783/14 May
COLE, John, Weedon Beck, Account of Richard, admin., £219.12.6 1680/18
Richard, Long Buckby, yeo., Inv.only £161.9.8 1711/52A
Coles, Bartholomew, Little Houghton, yeo., Inv.only £25.3.0 1711/140A
Coles, William, Long Buckby, to Mary, wid., 1715/97
William, Northampton, to Hannah, wid., 1716/50
Coales, Peter, Wellingborough, to Peter, son, Inv. £19.4.4 1716/95
John, Weedon Beck, Inv.only £87.10.6 1716/114A
Richard, Inv.only £102.10.0 1718/116A
Coales, Thomas, Isham, to Rose, wid., 1720/63

COLE continued
Coales, Coale, Thomas, Brackley, baker, to Elizabeth, wid., Inv. £17.19.10 1721/55
Coles, William, Badby, tailor, to Thomas, tailor, brother, Inv. £8.11.0 1721/71
Coles, Coals, Robert, Navesby, farmer, Inv.only £102.1.0 1722/35A
Coles, Richard, Rothwell, Inv.only £199.2.6 1724/95A
James, Inv.only £90.0.0 1726/169
Joseph, Ashby St. Ledgers, husb., to Ruth, wid., Inv. £169.10.0 1727/28 Sept.
Coles, Thomas, Wellingborough, butcher, to Alice, wid., Inv. £18.7.0 1729/14 Oct.
Coles, William, Wellingborough, shepherd, to Anne, wid., Inv. £189.17.9 Guard. of William, minor, son, 1741/4 and 7 Nov.
Coles, William, Ecton, minor, to William Thompson, gardener, uncle and guardian, 1744/21 June
Coles, William, Ecton, Inv.only £76.16.0 1744/395
Coles, Coales, William, Asthorpe, Newbottle, yeo., to Jane, spin., daughter, Will, 1746/7 Apr.
John, Wellingborough, tailor, to Elizabeth, wid., Inv. £19.2.0 1746/8 Nov.
James, Wellingborough, to Sarah, wife of Henry Page, innholder, principal creditor, 1750/8 Mar.
Coles, Francis, Rothwell, to Joanna, wid., 1751/1 Oct.
William, Ashby St. Ledgers, yeo., to Elizabeth, wid., 1756/30 Aug.
Coles, John, elder, Desborough, to Grace, wid., John, and Robert, farmers, sons, Will, 1775/15 Mar.
John, Northampton, innholder, to John, gent., son, of goods unadministered by Ann, wid., exor., Will, 1779/20 Dec.
William, Northampton, cordwainer, to Rachel, wid., mother, 1785/25 Jan.
Coles, William, Wellingborough, yeo., to Charles Robinson, son in law, Inv. £3.1.5 1789/7 Feb.
Coles, William, Bozeat, grazier, to John, Buckingham, carpenter, 1794/6 Feb.
Coles, William, Whiston, yeo., to Thomas, yeo., brother, 1795/26 Sept.
COLEMAN, Edward, Long Buckby, Account of Thomas, admin., £40.0.0 1681/69
Thomas, Slapton, Inv.only £102.5.0 1711/48A
Thomas, Long Buckby, to Richard Bland, yeo., Inv. £19.5.0 1713/25
George, Northampton, sailor, to William, weaver, 1753/1 Feb.
John, Watford, blacksmith, to Robert, Long Buckby, blacksmith, brother, Rebecca, wid., renounced, 1787/20 Jan.
William, Kingsthorpe, weaver, to Alice, wid., 1791/19 May
COLLETT, Collitt, John, St. James End, Dallington, gent., to Samuel Clay, maltster, husband and exor. of Sarah Clay als. Collitt, decd., wid. and exor. of John, Will, 1732/13 Jan.
Grace, Stowe Nine Churches, wid., to William Bliss, Floore, farmer, nephew, 1770/28 July
Ruth, Braunston, to Robert, yeo., husband, 1790/14 Apr.
COLLIER, Henry, Brafield on the Green, yeo., Inv.only £27.19.0 1712/2A
Elizabeth, Brafield on the Green, wid., Inv. only £28.17.0 1714/71A
Elizabeth, Thorpe Malsor, wid., to Thomas, yeo., son, 1722/128
Mary, Little Houghton, wid., Guard.only of William, minor, son, 1757/20 Apr.
Richard, Hardingstone, farmer, to Anne, wid., mother and guardian of William, son, Thomas Vinter and John Kilpin, farmers, exors., renounced, Will, 1771/5 Mar.
Sarah, Little Houghton, spin., to Simon, farmer, brother, 1793/27 Apr.
COLLINS, Edmund, Oundle, gent., Guard.only of Cesar Hunt, minor, son of Edmund Hunt, and legatee of Edmund Collins, 1711/109
John, Daventry, servant, to Anne, Hillmorton, co. Warwick, spin., and Ruth, wid., sisters, Inv. £66.10.0 1713/37
John, Upper Heyford, lab., to Lydia, wid., Inv. £5.10.3 1715/14
William, Badby, to Elizabeth, wid., 1721/109
William, Northampton, to Edward, Little Billing, lab., father, 1725/14 Dec.
Henry, Woodford, to Mary, wid., 1741/3 June
William, Brixworth, horse dealer, to Thomas, Northampton, innholder, son, Inv. £47.12.8 1770/11 June
Susanna, Broughton, wid., to William, Walgrave, lab., nephew, Inv. £17.1.0 1778/13 July

COLLINS continued
William, Great Billing, farmer, to Anne, wid., Inv. £632.12.6 Will, 1781/25 Aug.
William, Brixworth, cutter, to Thomas, Northampton, innholder, brother, 1791/11 Jan.
COLLIS, William, Wellingborough, husb., Account of Isabell, wid., admin., £196.14.10 1672/101
Thomas, Wellingborough, yeo., Inv.only £301.19.10 1711/119A
George, Wellingborough, Inv.only £197.3.6 1712/101A
John, elder, Wellingborough, Inv.only £34.6.10 1714/101A
Samuel, East Haddon, to Elizabeth, wid., 1718/25
Thomas, West Haddon, yeo., Inv.only £267.19.3 1719/79A
William, Teeton, Ravensthorpe, to Jane, spin., daughter, Thomas Lucas, and Thomas Ward, exors., renounced, Will, 1724/148
William, East Haddon, to Mary, wid., 1726/11 Aug.
John, Wellingborough, husb., to William, husb., and Elizabeth, wife of Joseph Mee, brother and sister, Inv. £180.12.10 1730/9 May
Thomas, Charlton, clerk, to Robert, West Haddon, gent., brother, 1752/29 Feb.
Fisher, Great Billing, victualler, to Elizabeth, wid., 1756/22 May
William, Brixworth, clerk, to Robert, West Haddon, farmer and maltster, brother, 1761/7 Sept.
Samuel, East Haddon, to Elizabeth, wid., 1776/13 Apr.
Elizabeth, West Haddon, wid., to Thomas, farmer, son, 1783/15 Mar.
Elizabeth, Wellingborough, to Keziah, wife of James Mee, Harrold, Bucks., baker, niece, 1784/20 July
John, Harpole, land surveyor, to Sarah, wife of Benjamin Dillow, Green's Norton, lab., daughter, 1789/11 Apr.
John, Northampton, shopkeeper, to Hannah, wid., 1793/15 Oct.
COLLISON, Collyson, Mary, wid., Towcester, to Richard, son, 1716/111
Collyson, Mary, Towcester, wid., to Mary, spin., 1716/121
John, Northampton, pinmaker, to Mary, wid., 1729/30 Dec.
Stephen, Potterspury, lab., to Richard Hall, Chicheley, Bucks., yeo., brother in law, Martha, wid., renounced, Will, 1752/25 Mar.
COLSON, Joseph, Raunds, cordwainer, Inv.only £26.12.0 1724/136A
Daniel, Rothwell, to Mary, wid., 1763/11 July
Joseph, Raunds, widower, butcher, to William Pentelow, maltster, principal creditor, Inv. £38.10.0 1782/26 Mar.
COMFIELD, Jane, Sywell, wid., to Abigail, wife of Thomas Athey, daughter, 1719/72
Confield, George, Moulton, to Mary, wid., 1722/71
Elizabeth, Abington, wid., to Thomas, blacksmith, son, 1722/136
CONEY, Thomas, Silverstone, yeo., to William, yeo., son, 1773/18 Oct.
CONQUEST, John, Wellingborough, to Sara, wid., 1728/28 May
John, Wellingborough, Inv.only £18.15.6 1728/209
COOCH, John, Kingsthorpe, yeo., to Thomas, elder, yeo., son, 1740/4 Aug.
Sarah, Harlestone, to Thomas, farmer, husband, 1791/26 Nov.
COOK, Cooke, Richard, Chipping Warden, Account of Dorothy, admin., £165.4.10 1678/60
Cooke, James, Brafield, Account of Elizabeth, wife of Henry Burnham, sister, admin., £37.14.0 1680/30
Elizabeth, Newnham, wid., Inv.only £19.2.6 1711/20A
Cooke, William, Braunston, clerk, to John Champante, Oakham, co. Rutland, gent., Thomas Peet, mercer, and William Buning, Glaston, co. Rutland, grazier, 1711/68
Cooke, John, Great Doddington, yeo., Inv.only £55.11.2 1711/95A
William, Sulgrave, to Joyce, wid., Inv. £91.10.0 1714/31
Cooke, Sarah, Harpole, to Richard, son, 1715/27
James, Finedon, to Thomas, lab., brother, 1715/161
Anne, Sywell, spin., to William, Preston, husb., brother, 1716/113
John, Moulton, servant, to Robert, Spratton, Inv. £41.12.4 1716/134
Joyce, Sulgrave, wid., to Jane Brocklis, daughter, Inv. £26.4.9 1717/76
Anne, Sywell, spin., to Thomas, Preston, husb., nephew, of goods not fully administered by William, brother, 1717/125
Richard, Pytchley, to Mary, wid., Inv. £568.3.6 1718/132
Mary, Lilbourne, wid., to Mary, wife of Francis Bannister, husb., daughter, 1719/46
Cooke, Thomas, Weedon Lois, Inv.only £45.10.11 1720/155A

COOK continued
Cooke, John, Kettering, to Elizabeth, wid., Inv. £19.2.0 1720/147
Thomas, Marston St. Lawrence, to Thomas Whitton, butcher, 1722/97
John, Badby, bachelor, to Elizabeth, Braunston, wid., mother, 1723/84
Robert, Shutlanger, yeo., Inv.only £649.10.0 1724/135A
Cooke, Robert, Syresham, to Robert, lab., son, 1725/22 Oct.
John, Sulgrave, husb., to John, husb., son, Elizabeth, wid., renounced, 1727/30 Sept.
John, Sulgrave, Inv.only £359.14.0 1727/206
John, Blisworth, lab., to Alice, wid., 1729/3 May
John, Rothwell, weaver, to Sarah, wid., Inv. £34.10.6 1731/2 June
Cooke, Anne, Paulerspury, wid., to John Williams, lab., nephew, Edward Gray, yeo., brother, renounced, 1735/3 May
John, Hardingstone, to William, carrier, 1735/15 July
Thomas, Desborough, to Elizabeth, wid., 1737/1 Feb.
Elizabeth, Desborough, wid., to Elizabeth, wid., mother, 1737/26 Aug.
Elizabeth, Kettering, to Elizabeth, spin., daughter, 1740/11 Feb.
Richard, Rothwell, to Sarah Williams, daughter, 1744/25 Apr.
als. Orm, Sophia, Great Houghton, to James, weaver, husband, 1744/8 May
Cooke, Jane, Dodford, spin., to Joseph, grazier, brother, 1774/15 Dec.
Martha, Northampton, wid., to John Potter, whipmaker, nephew, 1778/31 Mar.
John, Blisworth, to Sarah, Collingtree, wid., Will, 1780/10 June
William, Great Houghton, to Ann, wid., 1782/3 Aug.
Cooke, Elizabeth, Northampton, wid., to Mary, wife of Joseph Ekins Lewis, joiner, and Elizabeth Dawkes, wid., 1793/11 July
Mark, Great Houghton, yeo., to Elizabeth Samson, city of London, wid., sister, 1797/22 May
Anne, Highfield, Adstone, wid., to William and Thomas, yeos., sons, 1798/6 Mar.
Cooke, Mary, Harpole, wid., to John Blackwell, baker, son in law, 1800/29 Mar.

COOPER, John, Gretworth, carpenter, Inv.only £12.16.11 1714/163A
John, senior, Newnham, to Mary, wid., Inv. £13.2.6 1715/19
Cowper, William, Roade, shepherd, Inv.only £151.2.6 1715/159 A
Samuel, Northampton, barber, Inv.only £17.19.0 1716/88A
Anne, Northampton, spin., to Thomas, cobbler, brother, Inv. £14.2.6 1716/133
William, Braybrooke, Inv.only £16.2.0 1717/38A
Edward, Rothwell, to Rebecca, wid., Inv. £11.16.0 1727/14 Oct.
John, Wellingborough, lab., to Keziah, wid., Inv. £9.0.4 1728/9 Nov.
Penelope, Northampton, wid., to Penelope, wife of Thomas Miller, gent., daughter, 1736/26 Nov.
Berijah, Northampton, carpenter, to Sarah, wid., 1740/16 Apr.
William, Wood Burcote, Towcester, to Mary, wid., Joseph Wilkes and Samuel Wood, elder, exors., renounced, Will, 1740/30 Sept.
Richard, Brackley, schoolmaster, to Alice, wid., and Elizabeth, spin., daughter, 1753/11 May
John, Wellingborough, shoemaker, to John, St. Bartholomew the Less, London, watchmaker, son, Inv. £19.8.0 1756/1 Apr.
John, Maidford, to John, lab., son, 1762/23 Nov.
Martha, Northampton, wid., to Thomas, butcher, son, 1783/14 Oct.
Cowper, Francis, Northampton, to Robert Cane, Medmenham, Bucks., yeo., brother in law, Elizabeth, exor., decd., Will, 1786/28 Oct.
Anthony, Green's Norton, farmer, to Stephen, Whitfield, farmer, brother, 1792/4 May
Rachel, Northampton, to John, cordwainer, husband, 1796/6 Dec.
James, Northampton, maltster, to Amy, wid., Inv. £16.18.0 1799/31 Aug.

COPE, Michael, Stanford, grazier, to Thomas Miles, North Kilworth, co. Leic., yeo., grandfather and guardian of Thomas, minor, son, Inv. £256.2.6 1732/10 June

CORBETT, Robert, Cosgrave, husb., Inv.only £113.6.5 1722/86A
William, Isham, to Elizabeth, wid., 1742/17 Sept.
James, Northampton, victualler, to Ann, wid., 1786/13 Dec.

CORBY, Edward, junior, Welford, innkeeper, to Mary, wid., Inv. £73.7.0 1715/31
William, Draughton, to Elizabeth, wid., Inv. £48.15.0 1715/119
Alice, Cranford St. John, wid., to Mary, wife of John Stackhouse, Wellingborough, gent., niece, Will, 1721/6
John, Rushden, to Elizabeth, wid., 1732/5 Oct.

CORBY continued
Elizabeth, Doddington, wid., to William, blacksmith, son, 1787/20 Apr.
William, Bozeat, blacksmith, to Andrew Willson, Wellingborough, merchant, principal creditor, 1791/17 Jan.
CORNFIELD, George, Holdenby, to Elizabeth, wid., Inv. £166.2.0 1761/21 Mar.
George, Abington, blacksmith, to John, Wellingborough, blacksmith, brother, and Anne, spin., 1797/10 Feb.
CORNISH, Thomas, elder, Yelvertoft, yeo., Inv.only £215.12.4 1721/35A
Thomas, Yelvertoft, yeo., to Mary, wid., 1737/30 Apr.
Thomas, Yelvertoft, Inv.only £171.19.0 1737/347
Mary, Yelvertoft, wid., to Thomas, yeo., son, 1739/21 Apr.
Mary, Yelvertoft, wid., Inv.only £234.19.6 1739/359
John, Northampton, victualler, to Martha, wid., 1794/6 Mar.
Sarah, Earl's Barton, to Charles, matmaker, husband, 1800/19 Sept.
COREY, Samuel, Harpole, Account of Susan, admin., £131.18.8 1682/52
Cory, Nicholas, Harpole, yeo., to Mary, wid., Inv. £23.3.2 1711/49
Cory, John, Harpole, lab., Inv.only £23.10.0 1721/57A
John, Harpole, Inv.only £16.8.0 1728/262
John, Floore, to Alice, wid., 1729/29 Nov.
Cory, Thomas Mutton, Harpole, gent., to John, yeo., son, Will, 1731/4 Sept.
John, Harpole, yeo., to Eleanor, wid., 1744/3 Jan.
Cory, John, Harpole, farmer, to Susannah, wid., 1764/5 May
Cory, Samuel, Kislingbury, to Joseph, Duston, woolcomber, brother, 1768/5 Apr.
Cory, Anne, Bugbrooke, to Nathaniel, yeo., husband, 1771/7 Sept.
Cory, Richard, Chapel Brampton, to Mary, wid., 1775/31 May
Cory, John, Harpole, gent., to John, Fulbrooke, co. Warwick, farmer, son, 1794/22 Jan.
COSBY, George, Long Buckby, yeo., Inv.only £89.4.2 1718/29A
Edward, Woodend, Blakesley, to Jane, wid., Will, 1719/137
COTTON, Thomas, All Saints, Northampton, Account of Alice, wid., admin., £206.3.6 undated/86
Samuel, Northampton, to Anne, wid., mother, 1713/82
John, Wootton, yeo.,Inv.only £60.1.0 1723/137A
Mary, Tingewick, Bucks., to Charles, clerk, husband, 1781/3 Apr.
COURTMAN, Rev. John, Rector of Thorpe Malsor, Inv.only £472.6.8 1719/38A
Gibbon, Thorpe Malsor, to Anna Maria, sister, 1728/4 Dec.
COWLEY, John, Kilsby, yeo., Inv.only £442.17.0 1714/187A
Robert, Harpole, to William, husb., son, 1721/65
Anne, Yelvertoft, spin., to Nicholas, husb., father, Inv. £104.3.6 1729/18 Mar.
Mary, Yelvertoft, wid., to William, yeo., son, 1763/25 Jan.
John, Kilsby, to Anne, wid., 1783/8 Oct.
William, Braunston, to John, Kilsby, grazier, nephew, 1787/26 Dec.
COWPER see COOPER
COX, Anne, Northampton, wid., to Jeremy Wright, Harborough, butcher, brother, 1711/130
Thomas, Hellidon, woolman, Inv.only £14.7.0 1713/76A
John, Mears Ashby, to Samuel Reynolds, Wellingborough, gent., 1714/41
William, Ringstead, yeo., Inv.only £88.0.0 1716/56A
William, Byfield, Inv.only £18.8.1 1716/77A
Samuel, Woodford, to Ruth, wid., 1717/84
Richard, Denton, lab., Inv.only £10.18.6 1719/121A
Henry, Thorpe Malsor, to Susannah, wife of Benjamin Archer, cordwainer, daughter, 1723/141
Mary, Pytchley, wid., Inv.only £75.15.0 1724/16A
John, Irthlingborough, to William Groome, yeo., 1724/75
Elizabeth, Pytchley, spin., to Anne Hobey, wid., aunt, 1724/134
John, Sywell, to John, lab., son, 1726/9 Apr.
John, Northampton, gent., Inv.only £58.5.6 1729/248
William, elder, Irthlingborough, yeo., Inv.only £3.0.6 1730/276
Thomas, Kettering, to Judith, wid., Inv. £19.11.0 1733/5 July
William, Walgrave, lab., Inv.only £19.19.0 1736/338
William, Great Billing, to Mary, wid., 1742/31 July
William, Byfield, tanner, to Penelope, wid., 1742/11 Oct.
Samuel, Northampton, stonecutter, to Ann, wid., 1750/8 May
Thomas, Pytchley, yeo., to Thomas, Isham, farmer, son, 1752/2 Dec.
William, Byfield, to Thomas, grocer, 1761/15 Aug.

COX continued
William, Desborough, to John and Robert, sons, 1764/11 Feb.
Daniel, Cold Ashby, to William, farmer, son, 1765/2 Oct.
Samuel, Daventry, to Martha, Northampton, wid., 1772/7 Mar.
Robert, Northampton, to Mary, wid., Will, 1777/4 Apr.
Francis, Northampton, chandler, to Richard, Barrowden, co. Rutland, farmer, brother, 1783/24 Nov.
John, Northampton, servant, to Martha, spin., sister, Will, 1784/31 July
CRADDOCK, John, Overstone, to Anne, wid., 1719/132
William, Kingsthorpe, miller, to Christian, wid., 1729/26 Mar.
Samuel, Cotton End, Hardingstone, miller, to Sarah, wid., 1730/29 May
Christian, Kingsthorpe, wid., to William, miller, son, 1731/9 June
Cradock, Peter, Earl's Barton, miller, to Eve, wid., Inv. £234.17.0 1746/28 Oct.
William, Overstone, yeo., to Frances, wid., 1787/28 Sept.
Cradock, William, Overstone, yeo., to Thomas Wareing, Moulton, maltster, and William Litchfield, yeo., exors. of Frances, wid., admin., decd., 1788/12 Apr.
Frances, wid., Guard.only of Elizabeth, minor, niece, 1798/27 Sept.
CRAFTS, Robert, Braunston, to Sarah, wid., Will, 1768/16 June
CRANE, Thomas, Barton Seagrave, Inv.only £13.1.0 1713/100A
Craine, Samuel, Northampton, saddler, to Maria, wid., mother, 1748/10 Feb.
CRANWELL, Henry, Northampton, to Sarah, wid., 1774/23 July
CRASHAW, Richard, Little Addington, clerk, to Mary, wid., 1719/52
CRASS, Richard, Little Houghton, to Thomas, Northampton, schoolmaster, nephew, John, Milton, lab., brother, renounced, 1763/19 Oct.
CREAMER, Cremer, Robert, Helmdon, to Mary, wid., 1742/14 Dec.
CREATON, Thomas, Great Brington, to Anne, wid., Inv. £151.7.7 Will, 1712/115
William, Spratton, to Elizabeth, wid., 1714/53
William, Norton, yeo., to William, lab., son, Inv. £143.13.6 1742/25 Oct.
CREED, Robert, Northampton, brewer, to Elizabeth, wife of John Smith, Birmingham, cutler, 1780/23 Sept.
CRICKE, Robert, Sywell, Account of Elizabeth, wid., admin., £166.10.0 1682/53
CRIPPS, Anne, Blakesley, wid., Inv.only £5.0.0 1721/25
CRISP, Anne, wid., Inv.only £64.6.0 1741/382
Mary, Lilbourne, wid., to Joseph, weaver, son, 1746/8 Apr.
CROFTS, Robert, Inv.only £12.0.6 1718/119A
CROOK, Alice, Falcutt, wid., to John Tims, Syresham, shoemaker, 1731/20 May
CROSS, Bridget, Ardley on the Hill, co. Oxford, Inv.only £19.19.5 1716/80 A
Crosse, Robert, Astcote, Pattishall, Inv.only £18.13.8 1717/120A
Nathaniel, Helmdon, to Mary, wid., 1719/107
William, Long Buckby, to Edward, Kilsby, yeo., father, 1723/67
Richard, Middleton Cheney, carpenter, to Sarah, spin., daughter, Inv. £91.3.6 Will, 1724/74
John, Long Buckby, to Mary, wid., 1755/7 Jan.
Hannah, Hardingstone, wid., to Thomas, Northampton, weaver, and Richard, weaver, sons, 1787/1 Jan.
James, Harpole, lab., to Ann Jeyes, spin., granddaughter, Sarah, wid., exor., renounced, Will, 1788/29 Mar.
CROSSMAN, Samuel, Kettering, to Thomas, son, 1715/7
CROUCH, Richard, Wellingborough, gent., to John Kesting, innholder, principal creditor, Elizabeth, wid., renounced, 1764/6 Jan.
CROXON, Benjamin, Burton Latimer, to Anne Smith, wid., daughter, Elizabeth, wife, decd., Will, Inv. £9.6.6 1762/25 Oct.
CRUMP, William, Canons Ashby, yeo., to Mary, wid., Inv. £192.7.6 1713/8
Thomas, Brackley, innholder, to Elizabeth, wid., 1792/10 Oct.
CRUTCHLEY, William, Northampton, victualler, to Catherine, wid., Samuel Stanton, yeo., and John Potter, whipmaker, exors., renounced, Will 1780/2 Aug.
Elizabeth, Creaton, wid., to Edward, farmer, son, 1781/11 Apr.
CRYER, Thomas, Lilbourne, butcher, to Sarah, wid., 1734/4 May
Sarah, Lilbourne, to Thomas, farmer, son, 1773/29 Nov.
CUFFLEY, Joseph, Kingsthorpe, wheelwright, to Martha, wid., 1792/28 July
Daniel, Kingsthorpe, carpenter, to Elizabeth, spin., aunt and guardian of Martha and Benjamin, minors, children, Guard., 1793/21 Jan.
CULCHETH, Frances, Daventry, to John, innholder, husband, 1749/24 June

CULL, William, Yardley Gobion, to Jane, wid., 1728/7 Sept.
CUNNINGTON, Edward, Kettering, to Mary, Seaton, co. Rutland, wid., and Ann, spin., 1783/10 Feb.
CURE, John, Ashby St. Ledgers, husb., Inv.only £83.17.0 1713/142A
John, Ashby St. Ledgers, yeo., Inv.only £143.10.0 1715/124A
Elizabeth, Yelvertoft, to Thomas Cornish, farmer, uncle and guardian of Joseph, Ann, Mary, minors, children, 1769/2 Sept.
Ann, Kilsby, spin., to Thomas Usher, gent., 1788/12 Mar.
CURRIN, John, Kettering, Guard.only of Samuel, Mary, Elizabeth, minors, children, 1738/11 Feb.
Samuel, Kettering, to Mary Gibson, spin., sister, 1742/2 Apr.
Currens, Martha, Kettering, wid., to Martha, wife of Edward Bellamy, daughter, 1751/18 Apr.
CURTIS, John, Barby, lab., Inv.only £10.0.0 1722/83A
William, Irthlingborough, to John, yeo., son, 1723/105
John, Catesby, to Catherine, wid., 1730/17 Feb.
William, Irthlingborough, to Hannah, wid., 1772/17 June
CUTHBERT, John, Finedon, butcher, to Eliza Mary Anna, wid., Inv. £19.9.. 1713/99
Leonard, Irthlingborough, Inv.only £157.10.0 1718/74A

D

DADSON, Elizabeth, Kettering, wid., to John Burnby, son, Inv. £7.8.0 1716/119
DAGLEY, James, senior, Inv.only £276.2.10 1729/227
James, Halse, Brackley, farmer, to Thomas Bannard, farmer, 1789/25 Nov.
DAINTY, Deanty, John, Barton Seagrave, Inv.only £145.10.0 1715/26A
Giles, Orton, husb., to Anne, wid., 1728/28 Sept.
Giles, Orton, Inv.only £63.17.0 1728/235
Robert, Barton Seagrave, yeo., to Elizabeth, wid., 1740/15 Nov.
William, Orton, to Elizabeth, wid., 1776/18 Apr.
William, senior, Broughton, to Mary, wid., and William, junior, farmer, 1780/27 May
DAKIN, Thomas, Northampton, tailor, to Martha, wid., 1784/26 Oct.
DALLY, Mary, Earl's Barton, wid., Inv.only £39.6.10 1712/53A
Dalley, Thomas, Tobias, senior, Wellingborough, ironmonger, Inv.only £183.1.2 1716/123A
William, Earl's Barton, shopkeeper, Inv.only £278.0.0 1722/30A
Elizabeth, Earl's Barton, spin., Guard.only of Mark Griggs, minor, 1731/8 May
Tobias, Wellingborough, ironmonger, to John, yeo., son, Will, Inv. £28.5.6 1768/20 Apr.
DANCER, Jacob, Syresham, gent., to Jane, wife of Robert Styles, Northampton, clerk, daughter, 1716/92
Henry, Wicken, to Mary, wid., Inv. £74.10.0 1719/2
Rev. Jacob, Rector of Syresham, to Mary, wid., 1724/1
DANES, Anne, Kingsthorpe, spin., to Charles, yeo., son, 1799/22 June
DANIEL, Joseph, Northampton, joiner, to Joseph, joiner, son, 1730/24 July
William, Caldecote, Towcester, to Richard, Long Crendon, Bucks., shepherd, and Valentine Barford, yeo., 1734/16 Mar.
Daniels, Joseph, Burton Latimer, to Joseph, farmer, son, Inv. £32.19.0 1747/25 May
Mary, Woodford, wid., to Crescent, Knapton on the Hill, co. Warwick, butcher, son, 1764/11 Sept.
Abigail, Hinton, Woodford, to Thomas Stanton, farmer, and John Stanton, lab., nephews, 1775/20 Apr.
Jeremiah, Northampton, to Elizabeth, wid., 1780/26 Sept.
Bridget, Northampton, spin., to Ann, wife of Edward Kerby, plumber, and Elizabeth, wife of William Gibson, maltster, sisters, 1788/17 Dec.
D'ANVERS, Sir John, Culworth, bart., to Mary, wid., Will, 1745/5 Oct.
DARBY, Derby, Richard, Staverton, gent., to Elizabeth, spin., sister, 1751/22 Oct.
Edward, Piddington, lab., to Sarah, wid., Will, 1788/1 Feb.
DARKER, Thomas, Sywell, tailor, to Mary, wid., 1760/5 May
DARLING, Henry, Inv.only £268.2.0 1714/151A
DARLOW, Clement, Kingsthorpe, Inv.only £37.2.6 1719/126A
DARNELL, William, Daventry, to Anne, wid., 1733/24 Oct.
Jane, Dodford, to Ann Bradshaw, Wilby, wid., sister, 1767/26 Dec.

DARNELL continued
William, Long Buckby, widower, baker, to John, yeo., brother, 1773/15 July
Anne, Daventry, to Jane, spin., sister, 1775/10 Jan.
DAULBY, John, Rothwell, to Mary, wid., 1722/63
John, Rothwell, Guard.only of Anne, minor, daughter, 1725/28 Apr.
DAUNT, William, Northampton, to Mary, wid., 1774/25 Mar.
DAVIS, John, Maidford, woolwinder, Inv.only £17.14.6 1712/42A
Davies, Thomas, Yardley Hastings, weaver, Inv.only £17.1.6 1714/91A
Richard, Rothwell, Inv.only £124.7.6 1714/148A
Edward, Hinton, Inv.only £6.11.0 1714/157A
Luke, Rothwell, barber, to Mary, wid., 1715/72
Thomas, Brington, shoemaker, Inv.only £11.16.2 1715/109A
Thomas and Sarah, wife, Guard.only of James, Jane, Sarah, minors, children, 1719/34
Henry, Towcester, grocer and tobacconist, to Anne, wid., Inv. £154.19.1$\frac{3}{4}$ 1720/88
William, Welford, servant, Inv.only £39.12.0 1723/144A
Francis, Great Oxendon, butcher, Inv.only £151.3.0 1727/202
Francis, Oxendon, butcher, to Anne, wid., Inv. £150.13.9 1732/1 Mar.
George, Towcester, baker, to Elizabeth, wife of George Shackleton, glover, daughter, 1734/14 Nov.
Peter, Towcester, pipemaker, to Elizabeth, 1735/6 Dec.
Thomas, Newnham, to Elizabeth, wid., 1737/7 Oct.
Thomas, Stanford, butcher, to Mary, wid., 1746/24 June
William, Dodford Heath, Farthingstone, to Anne, wid., 1746/5 July
Thomas, Glasthorpe, Brington, yeo., to Elizabeth, wid., Inv. £185.1.0 1747/18 Apr.
William, Brington, yeo., to Elizabeth, wife of William Manning, tailor, daughter, 1747/24 Nov.
Ann, Tiffield, wid., to John, lab., son, 1749/9 Sept.
Thomas, Stanford, butcher, to Mary, wid., mother, 1751/22 Oct.
Eden, Paulerspury, shepherd, to Hannah, wid., 1755/19 Sept.
Elizabeth, Brackley, wid., to Hannah Parker, daughter, Inv. £14.10.0 1762/10 Mar.
Joseph, Harpole, to Mary, wid., 1770/22 Sept.
John, Welford, to Elizabeth, wid., 1778/4 Apr.
Joseph, Harpole Mills, miller, to Joseph, miller, son, of goods unadministered by Mary, wid., decd., 1785/15 Nov.
Davies, Mary, Brington, wid., to Elizabeth, wife of William Kenning, farmer, daughter, 1790/13 May
Richard, Towcester, innholder, to Eliena Clarke, wid., aunt and guardian of Ann, Eliena, William, Elizabeth, Mary, Jane, Rebecca, minors, children, Guard., 1794/14 Jan.
DAVY, John, Bugbrooke, lab., to Sarah, wife of John Muscott, husb., daughter, 1728/9 Sept.
DAWES, als. Dorr, Andrew, Rothwell, weaver, Inv.only £218.7.0 1713/70A
Thomas, Finedon, yeo., Inv.only £34.4.6 1717/150A
Daws, John, Finedon, yeo., to Elizabeth, wid., mother and guardian of Thomas, minor, exor., Inv. £216.16.6 Guard., Will, 1719/83
Thomas, Finedon, to Elizabeth, wife of Valentine Sibley, mother, 1740/3 June
John, Finedon, to Elizabeth, wid., wife of Valentine Sibley, mother, Will, 1740/3 June
Thomas, Northampton, watchmaker, to Francis Eck, watchmaker, son in law, Francis Beynon, Spratton, exor., renounced, Will, 1775/13 Sept.
DAWKES, Robert, Holcot, Inv.only £172 1714/11A
Robert, Little Billing, Guard.only of Alice, minor, daughter, 1722/26
DAWKINS, George, Desborough, to Susanna, wid., 1742/18 Feb.
John, Chipping Warden, yeo., to Elizabeth, wid., 1747/29 Apr.
George, Rothwell, to Jane, wid., 1794/16 May
DAWSON, Thomas, Faxton, widower, to Henry White, Pytchley, lab., half brother, 1750/27 Oct.
DAY, John, Towcester, Inv.only £53.4.10 1712/148A
John, Inv.only £31.12.6 1718/89A
Thomas, Higham Ferrers, mason, to Elizabeth, wid., Inv. £36.16.0 1725/11 Sept.
Peter, Finedon, miller, to Mary, wid., 1734/23 Nov.
John, Raunds, flax and hempdresser, to Anne, wid., Inv. £28.19.6 1735/5 May

DAY continued
Henry, Cottesbrooke, to Henry, London, joiner, 1738/7 Oct.
Henry, Cottesbrooke, Inv.only £89.0.0 1738/349
John, Northampton, to Richard, blacksmith, son, 1740/23 July
Samuel, Dallington Mill, miller, to Samuel, miller, son, Inv. £254.3.6 Mary, wid., renounced, 1768/30 July
Samuel, Dallington, miller, to Elizabeth, wid., 1783/20 June
Thomas, Ravensthorpe, farmer, to Elizabeth, wid., 1790/11 Dec.
DEACON, Philip, Walgrave, blacksmith, to Hannah, wid., Inv. £8.16.0 1715/131
Elizabeth, Hanging Houghton, Lamport, wid., to Elizabeth, spin., daughter, 1723/142
John, Fawsley, Inv.only £373.16.6 1725/30 Apr.
Priscilla, wid., Inv.only £82.11.10 1726/168
John, Hardingstone, shepherd, to Elizabeth, wid., 1727/22 Apr.
Easter, Northampton, spin., to William, barber, father, 1743/9 June
Thomas, Whittlebury, to Elizabeth, wid., 1785/24 June
Mary, Towcester, to Thomas Propert, Stony Stratford, Bucks., clerk, exor. of Samuel, surgeon, husband, decd., 1794/8 Oct.
Thomas, Spratton, carpenter, to Stephen, carpenter, son, 1795/10 Oct.
DEAN, Dennes, Thomas, Orlingbury, Inv.only £492.16.0 1725/130
Deans, Daines, John, Litchborough, lab., to Thomas, lab., brother, 1729/9 Oct.
Deans, John, Litchborough, lab., Inv.only £25.8.0 1729/232
James, Towcester, apothecary, to Elizabeth, wid., mother, George Doddington Manning, Little Houghton, and Samuel Stanton, Northampton, yeo., exors., renounced, Will, 1776/4 May
James, Towcester, apothecary, Guard.only of Jeremiah and James, minors, sons, 1779/2 Apr.
DELAVALL, John, Northampton, innholder, to Sarah, wid., 1734/30 Apr.
DELL, Francis, Stanwick, miller, to Sarah, wid., 1729/7 Oct.
DELLAMORE, Elizabeth, Floore, wid., to Samuel Rowledge, yeo., brother, 1720/96
DENNY, Henry, Dodford, to Hester, wid., 1716/136
Esther, Hester, Gayton, wid., to John Capell, Stowe, yeo., and Robert Capell, London, gent., guardians of Elizabeth, Robert and Esther, minors, children, Inv. £263.5.0, Guard., Will, 2 grants, 1723/32 and 33
Henry, Whilton, lab., to Elizabeth, wid., 1785/9 Nov.
DENT, Mary, Northampton, wid., to John, Blisworth, yeo., son, Inv. £10.16.0 1715/68
Thomas, Harlestone, Inv.only £88.2.4 1718/10A
John, Blisworth, miller, to Thomas, miller, son, Inv. £15.6.4 1730/3 Dec.
John, Harlestone, yeo., to Thomas, yeo., brother, Elizabeth, wid., renounced, 1738/13 May
Mary, Ecton, wid., to Pratt, weaver, son, 1754/9 Mar.
DENTON, Henry, Great Doddington, yeo., Inv.only £272.7.10 1711/124A
George, Great Houghton, yeo., Inv.only £414.16.0 1711/125A
Thomas, Hardingstone, blacksmith, Inv.only £61.14.4 1715/20A
Elizabeth, Great Houghton, wid., Inv.only £651.12.0 1718/108A
Thomas, Towcester, to Mary, wid., Inv. £33.16.2 1726/23 Apr.
John, Doddington, to Henry, farmer, son, Mary, wid., renounced, 1768/29 Sept.
Thomas, Hartwell, yeo., to John, farmer, son, Joan, wid., William, farmer, Robert, Hanslop, Bucks., farmer, exors., renounced, Will, 1776/19 May
DESBOROUGH, Desborow, Elizabeth, Northampton, spin., to John, shoemaker, brother, 1730/11 Apr.
Mary, Finedon, spin., to William, Oundle, innholder, brother, 1756/19 July
Ann, Wellingborough, spin., to Thomas, Finedon, matmaker, father, 1797/31 July
DEWBURY, Dewberry, John, Clipston, bachelor, to Thomas Thustian, senior, Hargrave, yeo., guardian of Thomas Thustian, minor, nephew, Guard., 1723/38 and 39
Lucy, Little Addington, wid., to Richard Whiteman, dealer, guardian of Martha and William Batley, grandchildren, Will, 1724/67
DEXTER, Stephen, Old, Inv.only £357.10.0 1723/92A
Mary, Old, wid., to Gregory, gent., son, 1741/17 Oct.
Thomas, Kettering, to Sarah, wid., 1768/11 Oct.
John, Kettering, gent., to Anna Grace, Loddington, wid., 1798/5 Jan.
Robert Edward, Loddington, gent., to Sarah, wid., 1799/19 July

DICKENS, Dickings, Henry, Pytchley, matmaker, Inv.only £7.5.0 1712/52 A
Richard, Coton, Ravensthorpe, butcher, to Alice, wid., Inv. £35.8.6 1717/109
Dickins, Elizabeth, Walgrave, Inv.only £37.8.8 1722/69 A
Anne, Woodford, wid., to William, yeo., son, 1724/114
Francis, Long Buckby, to John, lab., son, 1726/3 Jan.
John, Holcot, blacksmith, to Anne, wid., 1730/8 July
Dickins, John, Woodford, Thrapston, blacksmith, to William, blacksmith, brother, 1736/18 Mar.
William, Holcot, servant, to Stephen, yeo., brother, 1747/17 Oct.
Henry, Paulerspury, victualler, to Sarah, wid., 1752/15 Feb.
Dickins, Thomas, Denshanger, Passenham, yeo., to William, yeo., uncle and guardian of John, Thomas, Elizabeth, Ann, Mary, minors, children, Inv. £292.6.6 Guard., 1752/20 June
Thomas, Wellingborough, to Susannah, spin., 1757/21 Oct.
John, Hannington, to Elizabeth, wid., 1759/21 Apr.
Sarah, Long Buckby, to John, cordwainer, son, 1760/28 Jan.
John, Puxley Green, Passenham, to Elizabeth, wid., Inv. £78.19.1 1766/15 Apr.
John, Crick, maltster, to Thomas, weaver, son, 1774/29 June
Dickins, Daniel, Holcot, blacksmith, to John, Wellingborough, blacksmith, son, 1797/17 June
DICKENSON, Richard, Kingsthorpe, to Mary, wid., 1738/12 Aug.
DICKER, Thomas, Barby, to Rebecca, wid., 1715/118
als. Humfres, Rebecca, Barby, wid., Inv.only £10.19.7 1718/102 A
DIGHTON, John, Earl's Barton, gent., to William Royce, Rouce, Oakham, co. Rutland, farmer, Inv. £28.8.9 1754/4 May
DILLINGHAM, Anne, Little Addington, wid., to Elizabeth, wife of Henry Harris, yeo., 1769/4 May
DIMBLEBY, Rains, Loddington, servant, to Samuel, son, 1797/23 May
DING, Henry, Oundle, Inv.only £55.13.8 1743/388
DINGLEY, Alice, Floore, Inv.only £5.16.0 1711/127 A
Edward, Easton Neston, to Elizabeth, wid., Inv. £17.11.0 1712/70
William, Northampton, carpenter, to Jane, wid., 1770/19 May
DIPPLE, John, Isham, Account of Elizabeth, wid., admin., £218.0.0 1671/126
DITCHFIELD, William, Northampton, victualler, Inv.only £83.17.0 1716/105
DIX, John, Green's Norton, yeo., Inv.only £11.14.0 1714/78 A
William, Walgrave, to Arthur, brother, Elizabeth, wid., mother, renounced, 1717/8
Elizabeth, Walgrave, wid., Inv.only £318.15.0 1719/77 A
Thomas, Wellingborough, to Elizabeth, wid., 1744/26 Mar.
Elizabeth, Great Doddington, wid., to William, Knuston, Irchester, yeo., and Arthur, Will, 1747/28 Nov.
Thomas, Green's Norton, lab., to John, brother, 1770/13 May
DIXON, Dison, William, Irchester, lab., Inv.only £6.7.6 1730/263
Elizabeth, Northampton, wid., to Hannah, spin., daughter, 1778/10 Mar.
DOBBS, John, Rothwell, husb., to Thomas, husb., brother, 1727/7 July
William, Mears Ashby, Inv.only £11.3.6 1734/318
Thomas, Rothwell, yeo., to Elizabeth, wid., Inv. £244.17.4 1764/10 Feb.
DODD, Dod, Anne, Bugbrooke, to John, Litchborough, yeo., 1714/89
Dod, John, Bugbrooke, to John, Litchborough, husb., son, Inv. £17.2.10 Will, 1714/108
Dod, William, Eydon, to Hannah, wid., 1762/13 May
William, Byfield, yeo., to William, yeo., son, 1798/5 Mar.
DODFORD, John, Greatworth, lab., Inv.only £11.7.6 1714/152 A
DOLBIN, Thomas, Potterspury, servant, to Dorothy, wid., Inv. £49.3.5 Will, 1721/104
DONN, Thomas, Inv.only £14.11.0 undated/264
DORMER, Henry, principal of Rothwell Hospital, Inv.only £45.2.0 1727/401
DORR see DAWES
DORRELL, John, Northampton, innholder, to Elizabeth, wid., Inv. £191.14.4 1768/8 Feb.
DOUGLAS, Douglis, Elizabeth, Chipping Warden, Account of Anne, mother, admin., £75.0.0 1680/7
Thomas, Chipping Warden, to George, yeo., son, Elizabeth, wid., renounced, 1720/141
Duglas, Joseph, Grendon, yeo., grazier, to Barbara, wid. and exor. of John, son, Elizabeth, wife of John Stear, Steere, grazier, and Barbara, wife of John Lewis, drover, exors., renounced, Will, 1729/30 Nov.

DOUGLAS continued
Duglas, Thomas, Easton Maudit, butcher, to Sarah, wid., Inv. £268.17.0 1730/17 Mar.
Owen, Bugbrooke, tallow chandler, to George, Dallington, lab., son, 1759/10 Oct.
John, Daventry, innholder and victualler, to Bridget, wid., 1763/18 Aug.
Thomas, Chipping Warden, to Elizabeth, Inv. £760.5.0 1773/17 May
Ann, Greatworth, wid., to George, Culworth, lab., son, 1774/14 May
William, Daventry, grocer, to Anne, wife of William Waite, Pattishall, farmer, sister, 1778/10 June
DOWLEY, James, Daventry, hatter, to Susanna, wid., 1774/13 Apr.
DOWNING, William, Yardley Hastings, to Francis, yeo., son, Inv. £67.0.0 Will, 1712/19
Hannah, Guard.only of William, Samuel and Elizabeth, minors, children, 1723/94
DOWSE, John, Wollaston, victualler, to Lydia, wife of Jeremiah Partridge, wheelwright, daughter, 1753/2 Feb.
DRAKE, Thomas, Weston, Weedon Lois, Inv.only £4. 1714/72A
Anne, Helmdon, spin., to Anthony, weaver, brother, Elizabeth, mother, renounced, 1766/14 Apr.
DRAPER, Robert, Brixworth, Inv.only £10.8.0 1722/3A
John, Rushden, Inv.only £16.14.3 1724/50A
Thomas, Pytchley, to Hannah Coles, spin., niece, Inv. £10.4.6 1729/7 Oct.
John, Castle Ashby, grazier and blacksmith, to Alice, wid., Inv. £675.5.9 1753/24 Mar.
Marriott, Denton, baker, to James, baker, brother, 1760/1 Mar.
James, Denton, to Mary, wid., 1760/12 July
Mary, Wellingborough, spin., to Jerimiah Garratt, lab., Will, 1789/15 Sept.
DRICER, John, Byfield, to John Hitchcock, farmer, principal creditor, 1771/3 Jan.
DRIDEN, Mary, West Farndon, Woodford cum Membris, Account of William, gent., admin., £147.5.0 1677/45
DRIVER, Samuel, Harrington, yeo., Inv.only £313.11.0 1715/99A
Hannah, Rothwell, wid., to Lewis, son, Inv. £262.2.6 1721/121
Daniel, Broughton, husb., to Daniel, husb., son, Mary, wid., renounced, 1728/2 Mar.
DRURY, John, Sywell, husb., Inv.only £492.18.0 1718/20A
DUCKET, Francis, Haselbech, clerk, to Zacheus, Gedling, co. Nottingham, clerk, brother, 1749/9 Nov.
DUGLAS see DOUGLAS
DUKE, Joseph, Northampton, wine cooper, to Hannah, wid., 1750/15 May
DUMBLETON, James, Middleton Cheney, weaver, Inv.only £21.19.0 1719/39A
DUNBAR, James, Wellingborough, linendraper, to Anne, wid., guardian of John, minor, son, exor., Inv. £373.16.7 Will, 1719/24 and 25
DUNCOMBE, Peter, Syresham, gent., to Peter, gent., son, 1731/7 Jan.
DUNDASS, Elizabeth, Aynho, wid., to Elizabeth, wife of Joseph Arrowsmith, gent., daughter, 1741/1 June
DUNKLEY, Thomas, Northampton, wheelwright, Inv.only £15.0.6 1711/79A
John, Brington, to John, son, Will, 1713/43
Dunckley, Richard, Grendon, husb., Inv.only £899.4.10 1713/137A
James, Charwelton, Inv.only £1054.5.0 1714/37A
Dunckley, Thomas, Towcester, to Margaret, wid., 1721/84
Dunckley, William, Harpole, yeo., Inv.only £154.2.0 1724/33A
Dunckley, William, Weedon Beck, to Hester, wid., Inv. £14.11.6 1727/3 June
Robert, Weston Favell, carpenter, to Elizabeth, wid., 1729/3 May
Richard, Milton, carpenter, to Anne, wid., 1729/30 Aug.
Samuel, Northampton, butcher, to Mary, wid., 1730/16 Jan.
William, Moulton, yeo., to Thomas, yeo., brother, Inv. £128.6.6 1737/6 Aug.
James, Charwelton, grazier, to Sarah, wid., 1738/15 May
John, Courtenhall, tailor, to Elizabeth, wid., 1741/28 Feb.
John, Dodford, yeo., to Bridget, wid., Inv. £91.7.0 1742/5 Jan.
William, Weston Favell, to Rebecca, wid., 1742/6 Apr.
Elizabeth, Ravensthorpe, to Francis, yeo., son, 1742/15 May
Henry, Northampton, to Ann, wid., 1744/2 Aug.
John, Ashton, yeo., to Anne, wid., Inv. £136.2.6 1749/12 Feb.

DUNKLEY continued
Dunckley, John, Ashby St. Ledgers, farmer, to Elizabeth, wid., Inv. £68.5.6 1749/12 Oct.
Dunckley, Lydia, Gayton, spin., to Thomas, carpenter, father, 1755/4 Jan.
John, Northampton, to Sarah, wid., 1757/25 Apr.
Thomas, elder, Northampton, cordwainer, to Thomas, cordwainer, son, of goods unadministered by Elizabeth, wid., decd., 1757/25 Apr.
Dunkly, Anne, Ravensthorpe, wid., to Mary, wife of Thomas Towers, West Haddon, flax dresser, daughter, 1759/12 Jan.
John, Welton, to Ann, wid., 1761/21 Nov.
William, Crick, farmer, to Edward, farmer, son, 1764/8 Nov.
Mary, Crick, wid., to Edward, farmer, son, 1764/8 Nov.
William, Cold Ashby, to Elizabeth, wife of James Martin, weaver, daughter, 1769/18 Mar.
John, Ashton, to John, servant, son, of goods unadministered by Ann, wid., 1769/14 Oct.
Thomas, Moulton, farmer, to Mary, spin., sister, 1780/11 Nov.
Thomas, Staverton, innholder, to Mary, wid., 1785/7 Feb.
William, Braunston, grazier, to Sarah, wid., 1785/29 Sept.
Mary, Rothersthorpe, wid., to Ann, wife of Richard Gleed, gent., daughter, 1785/1 Oct.
Thomas, Whilton, maltster, to Elizabeth, wife of William Barker, maltster, daughter, Elizabeth, wife, exor., decd., Will, 1793/19 Sept.
Henry, Northampton, butcher, to Sarah, wid., and James, butcher, son, 1794/1 Sept.
Edward, Whilton, woolcomber, to Mary, wid., 1794/6 Dec.
Francis, Orlingbury, carpenter, to William Thomson, Wellingborough, creditor, 1794/8 Dec.

DUNMORE, John, Hannington, to Deborah, wid., 1763/12 Jan.
Susanna, Walgrave, to William, farmer, husband, 1788/24 Oct.

DUNN, Elizabeth, Stanford, wid., Inv.only £11.5.2 1715/126A
Thomas, Stanford, lab., to Anne, wid., 1732/13 May
John, Northampton, cordwainer, to Elizabeth, wife of Joseph Althrop, soldier, daughter, 1797/14 Mar.

DUNSBY, Henry, Badby, to William, Rudborne, husb., son, Joan, wid., renounced, 1712/89
Robert, Fawsley (Braunston), to John, Braunston, brother, husb., Inv. £50.0.0 Joan, mother, renounced, 1717/33

DURDIN, Dorothy, Holcot, wid., to John Lambley, Sibbertoft, weaver, brother, and Anne, wife of William Clarke, Spratton, sister, 1729/19 July
John, Holcot, to John Lambley, Sibbertoft, weaver, and Anne Clarke, brother and sister in law, of goods unadministered by Dorothy, wid., decd., 1729/19 July

DURHAM, George, Silverstone, lab., to John Webb, Towcester, brazier, and Robert Wilcox, stationer, Will, 1798/19 Dec.

DURNFORD, John, Preston, yeo., to William Tully, Great Stanmore, co. Middx., gardener, principal creditor, Will, 1747/23 Sept.

DURRANT, Thomas, Brackley, to William, gardener, brother, 1799/12 Apr.

DUST, Thomas, Northampton, to Elizabeth, wid., 1727/4 Feb.

DYE, Thomas, Kettering, to Abia, wid., Inv. £12.15.0 1714/40
Joseph, Kettering, to Anne, wid., 1735/25 Jan.

DYER, Arthur, Northampton, supervisor of excise, to William, Wootton Bassett, Wilts., gent., brother, 1790/10 Feb.

E

EAGLE, Thomas, East Farndon, to Mary, wid., 1791/8 Oct.

EALES, Joseph, Byfield, to Benjamin, lab., father, 1734/4 Jan.
John, Northampton, plasterer, to Catherine, wid., 1743/3 Feb.

EALEY, John, Daventry, chapman, to Hester, wid., Inv. £109.9.0 1719/103

EAMES, John, Clipston, farmer, to Jane, wid., 1765/1 Apr.

EARIS, see AYRES

EARLE, Nathaniel, Preston Capes, innkeeper, widower, to John, servant, Inv. £19.5.0 1720/20

EARNSBY, Robert, Winwick, Inv.only £69.17.0 1721/19A

EASON, EASONN, see EASTON

EAST, Edward, Orton, yeo., Inv.only £60.10.0 1711/142A
Benjamin, Orton, Inv.only £299.19.6 1724/128

EAST continued
Benjamin, West Haddon, to Mary, wid., 1757/3 Nov.
EASTON, Richard, Drayton, Daventry, Inv. only £206.14.0 1712/88A
Esson, Ellen, Sibbertoft, spin., Inv.only £15.7.3 1718/130A
Anne, Cogenhoe, spin., to Joyce, wid., mother 1720/95
Joyce, West Haddon, Inv.only £91.6.6 1728/219
Easson, William, Daventry, cordwainer, to Joseph, Coventry, woolcomber, son, Francis Gunn, Coventry, exor, decd., Will, 1775/16 Nov.
Eason, Thomas, Brafield, yeo., to William, farmer, son, Sarah, wid., renounced, 1799/5 Aug.
EATON, Thomas, Earl's Barton, to William Hudson, shoemaker, guardian of Anne, sister, Inv. £19.14.0, Will. 1711/103
Thomas, younger, Grendon, to William Pettit, lacebuyer, and Charles Narborow, husb., guardians of Thomas and Elizabeth, minors, children, 1712/73
Eatton, Anne, Woodford, wid., Inv.only £102.13.6 1714/109A
Richard, Woodford, yeo., Inv.only £171.15.6 1718/73A
John, Kelmarsh, elder, innkeeper, to Mary, wid., Inv. £168.9.1 1725/20 Feb.
Francis, Woodford, husb., to Francis, husb., son, Inv. £493.12.6 1732/8 Sept.
Mary, Ringstead, spin., to John, Fen Stanton, co. Huntingdon, merchant, 1765/3 Aug.
William, Walgrave, yeo., farmer, to Peter and William, farmers, sons, Rose, wid., renounced, Will. 1777/15 Mar.
John, Great Addington, to Simon Bland, Grafton Underwood, farmer, and Joseph Bland, farmer, brothers, 1783/31 Jan.
Samuel, Scaldwell, grazier, to Elizabeth, wid., 1784/7 Jan.
Thomas, Northampton, innholder, to Elizabeth, wid., 1784/15 Jun.
EAYRES see AYRES
ECCLES, John, Stoke Bruerne, clerk, to Betty, wid., and John, clerk, son, 1790/9 Feb.
ECTON, Ann, Northampton, spin., to Lydia, wife of Thomas Smith, butcher, sister, 1794/22 Aug.
EDEN, Aaron, Boddington, to Samuel Knight, Chalcombe, staymaker, Elizabeth, wid., renounced. Will. 1745/8 Jun.
Aaron, Inv.only £10.4.0 1745/407
Joseph, Finedon, maltster, to Martha, Thomas Odell, Leighton Buzzard, Beds., and John Odell, maltster, 1797/24 Jun.
EDGAR, Mary, Brackley, wid., to Henrietta Maria, spin., daughter, 1756/17 Jun.
EDGLEY, Jane, Rothwell, spin., to Nathaniel Latimer, Stoke Albany, Inv. £15.0.0 1713/49
EDIS, William, Woodford, cooper, to William, Ellington, co. Huntingdon, cooper, nephew, 1783/16 Sept.
EDMUNDS, Emma, Kilsby, wid., Inv.only £37.13.6 1721/93A
Edmund, William, Pytchley, gardener, to Elizabeth, wid., Inv. £15.17.0 1721/94
Thomas, Wollaston, to Mary, wid., Inv. £172.18.6 1723/78
Edmonds, Henry, Braunston, collarmaker, to John, collarmaker, son, Inv. £59.11.0 1725/21 Aug.
Samuel, Kingsthorpe, to Sarah, wid., 1741/29 Aug.
Edmonds, Samuel, Kingsthorpe, Inv.only £174.3.0 1741/381
Edmonds, Edward, Crick, yeo., to Mary, wid., Inv. £23.13.0 1747/13 Jan.
Robert, Braunston, yeo., to Hannah, wid., 1769/21 Jan.
John, Stuchbury, to Mary, wid., 1782/22 Oct.
John, Northampton, mariner, to Robert, victualler, father, 1792/30 July
EDWARDS, John, Newnham, Inv.only £39.2.6 1722/68A
Elizabeth, Helmdon, wid., to Anne, wife of John Sharpe, lab., daughter, 1733/16 Nov.
William, Braunston, yeo., to Humphrey, farmer, and Thomas, Upper Catesby, grazier, brother and nephew, guardians of William, son, Will. 1755/2 Dec.
James, Northampton, victualler, to Mary, wid., 1784/2 Feb.
John, Blakesley, coachman, to Mary, wid., now wife of John Cooper, shopkeeper, 1786/11 May
William, Byfield, grazier, to William, son, 1786/21 Oct.
EGLESTON, Richard, Long Buckby, to Susanna, wid., Will. 1717/34
EKINS, Thomas, Raunds, Inv.only £571.10.0 1713/16A
Robert, Raunds, yeo., to Elizabeth, wid., Inv. £183.7.2 1726/18 Oct.
Thomas, Moulton, farmer, to Catherine, wid., Inv. £314.0.0 1730/7 Feb.

EKINS continued
Mary, Rushden, spin., to George, Wellingborough, and Thomas, gents., sons, exors. of Mary, elder, decd., Will, 1730/14 July
Thomas, Moulton, yeo., to Thomas, yeo., son, 1746/16 Apr.
Sarah, Raunds, wid., to William, Islip, servant, son, Inv. £58.15.0 1771/14 May
James, Brixworth, to Elizabeth, wid., 1773/27 Feb.
John, Chelveston, yeo., to Anne, wife of John Harrison, Raunds, yeo., daughter, 1796/26 Feb.
Samuel, Raunds, farmer, to Robert, yeo., brother, 1797/1 Sept.
ELDERSHAW, John, Raunds, yeo., Inv.only £94.6.2 1718/91A
ELEY, Edward, Litchborough, yeo., Inv.only £87.18.0 1727/213
ELKINGTON, Elizabeth, Towcester, wid., to Elizabeth, wife of Thomas Lawton, daughter, 1718/8
John, Catesby, yeo., to Anne, wid., 1763/18 May
Elkinton, Thomas, Byfield, to Thomas, grazier, nephew, 1780/3 Nov.
ELLARD, Anne, Blisworth, Inv.only £64.8.0 1714/88A
ELLINGTON, Martha, Wellingborough, spin., to Samuel Richardson, gent., and Benjamin Middleton, draper, creditors, 1750/15 Dec.
Samuel, Wellingborough, yeo., husb., to Samuel, son, Inv. £20.6.5 1755/4 Dec.
John, Wellingborough, upholsterer, to Ephraim Pattison, younger, yeo., son in law, of goods unadministered by Mary Pattison, wife, decd., Will, 1756/18 May
ELLIOTT, Martha, Green's Norton, to Frances, wid., mother, 1712/138
William, Green's Norton, yeo., Inv.only £822.6.2 1721/73A
Benjamin, Navesby, to Grace, wid., 1723/19
Thomas, Dodford, blacksmith, Inv.only £49.7.6 1724/7A
Samuel, Hardwick, to Richard, brother, Will, 1724/115
John, Earl's Barton, Inv.only £14.12.0 1724/138
John, Earl's Barton, to Elizabeth, wid., 1725/25 Mar.
Edward, Brington, mason, to Mary, wid., 1729/12 Apr.
John, Cold Ashby, to William, exor. of Samuel, yeo., decd., Will, 1770/19 May
ELLIS, Thomas, Oxendon, yeo., to Elizabeth, wid., 1729/6 Sept.
Anne, Creaton, wid., to Clement, Hanging Houghton, shepherd, 1738/10 Apr.
Thomas, Welford, to Ann, wid., 1768/1 Mar.
ELMES, John, Alderton, Inv.only £3.14.6 1728/230
John, senior, Stowe Nine Churches, Inv.only £120.15.0 1733/309
ELSON, Samuel, Northampton, tailor, to Sarah, wid., 1789/21 Dec.
ELSTOW, Joseph, Orlingbury, husb., to Mary, wife of John Bland, Aldwinkle, All Saints, blacksmith, sister, aunt and guardian of Joseph and Elizabeth, minors, children, Guard., Inv. £346.19.10 1755/26 June
ELTON, William, Northampton, cordwainer, to Anne, wid., 1783/6 Aug.
ELWARD, Edward, Blisworth, yeo., Inv.only £66.0.0 1717/9A
EMBERY, Thomas, Northampton, to Rebecca, wid., 1769/23 Jan.
EMERLEY, Thomas, Helmdon, to Ann Townsend, Biddlesden, Bucks., spin., 1765/10 Sept.
EMERTON, Elinor, Great Houghton, wid., Inv.only £27.11.4 1723/119A
Jane, Thurnby, to Richard, gent., husband, 1764/2 Jan.
EMERY, Thomas, Scaldwell, to Elizabeth, wid., Inv. £49.18.0 1711/134
Joseph, Weedon, Inv.only £316.11.8 1722/61A
Joseph, Slapton, framework knitter, to Judith, wid., 1755/2 June
Elizabeth, Duston, to Jonathan, maltster, husband, 1799/26 Jan.
ENGLAND, Peter, Overstone, blacksmith, to Rebecca, wid., 1798/24 May
Dorothy, Mears Ashby, spin., to Rebecca, Overstone, wid., mother, 1799/27 May
ERRINGTON, Samuel, Harlestone, to Mary, wid., 1719/41
Arrington, Mary, Harlestone, wid., Inv.only £10.4.6 1723/61A
ESOM, Bartholomew, Woodford, Inv.only £13.16.6 1739/374
EVANS, John, Hinton, shepherd, to Edward, lab., brother, Inv. £5.10.0 1711/15
John, Middleton Cheney, to Thomas, roper, Thomas Bull, butcher, Nicholas Buttery, tailor, and Thomas Williams, lab., guardians of John, minor, son, Inv. £185.17.5 Will, Guard., 1711/99
John, Middleton Cheney, to John, tailor, son, Account of Thomas Bull and Thomas, guardians of John's children, £10.0.0 Will, 1713/89 and 91
Thomas, Brackley, wheelwright, Inv.only £93.1.6 1722/55A
John, Fawsley, servant, to William, Preston, shoemaker, father, 1728/8 June

EVANS continued
Edward, Ravensthorpe, husb., to Elizabeth, wid., 1728/12 Oct.
William, Brackley, lab., to Mary, wid., 1731/6 May
William, Brackley, innholder, Inv.only £18.13.6 1731/284
Thomas, Middleton Cheney, ropemaker, to Thomas, ropemaker, son, Keziah, wid., renounced, 1747/19 June
Charles, Helmdon, yeo., to John Mobbs, Weedon Pinkney, yeo., and Edward Harriot, clerk, of goods unadministered by Mary, wid., decd., William Wills, weaver, father in law, and Elizabeth, wife of Thomas Baker, Adstone, yeo., aunt, renounced, 1768/8 Feb.
Jane, Wappenham, wid., to William, lab., son, 1769/11 Feb.
Mary, Wootton, to Francis, Northampton, farmer, husband, 1791/6 June
EVERARD, George, Naseby, Account of Rebecca, wid., admin., £171.13.4 1677/54 and 58
EVINS, Ivins, Francis, Collingtree, farmer, to Elizabeth, wid., 1748/26 Apr.
EXTON, Elizabeth, Brington, wid., to Bernard Dunkley, weaver, brother, 1728/2 Mar.
EYETT, Robert, Grafton Underwood, to Mary, wid., 1750/14 Nov.
EYLE, John, Hardingstone, Inv.only £1001.15.8 1721/96A
EYRE, EYRES see AYRES

F

FABIAN, Mary, Northampton, to William, surgeon, husband, 1758/19 Dec.
Martha, to William, Northampton, surgeon, husband, 1762/11 Mar.
FACER, John, Yelvertoft, yeo., Inv.only £37.15.1 1714/76A
Benjamin, Inv.only £7.15.0 1715/22aA
Edward, Norton, to Edward, lab., son, 1715/39
George, Chapel Brampton, to John, husb., Inv. £114.19.0 1717/142
William, Yelvertoft, Inv.only £141.12.6 1723/90A
Joseph, Little Houghton, husb., to Jane, wid., Inv. £197.6.8 1728/19 May
John, East Haddon, blacksmith, to Catherine, wid., Inv. £88.17.0 1753/24 Nov.
William, Yelvertoft, farmer, to Anne, wid., 1783/27 May
Thomas, Hardingstone, lab., to Elizabeth, wid., 1784/30 Oct.
Elizabeth, Little Houghton, wid., to John Collier, elder, farmer, son in law, 1790/16 Mar.
John, Little Houghton, yeo., to Alice Perkins, wid., granddaughter, 1791/9 July
FANCOURT, Ann, Alderton, to Thomas, lab., husband, 1785/26 Apr.
FARDEN, Richard, Barby, Account of Anne, wid., admin., £63.11.8 1683/20
FAREBROTHER, Richard, Chipping Warden, Inv.only £95.16.0 1713/39A
Richard, Chipping Warden, Inv.only £248.8.4 1719/130A
FAREY, Thomas, Overstone, to Elizabeth, wid., 1720/17
Fary, Jane, Raunds, wid., Inv.only £36.17.6 1723/82A
FARMAN, William, Culworth, cordwainer, Inv.only £33.19.0 1714/13A
FARMER, William, Ravensthorpe, yeo., Inv.only £15.17.7 1719/26A
Moses, Wellingborough, to Mary, wid., 1778/21 Mar.
FARN, John, Crick, yeo., to Thomas, maltster, son, Inv. £232.4.10 1735/23 Apr.
Thomas, Crick, to Thomas, maltster, son, 1768/4 May
FARNDON, Elizabeth, Northampton, wid., to Frances Bond, Wollaston, wid., sister, 1797/5 Aug.
FARREN, Sarah, Floore, wid., to Francis, husb., principal creditor, 1711/81
Farring, Joseph, Northampton, to William, husb., son, Inv. £118.8.0 1715/133
Joseph, Northampton, yeo., to Margaret, wid., 1742/13 Jan.
FARROW, Alice, Wollaston, wid., Inv.only £9.7.6 1717/17A
Robert, Earl's Barton, bachelor, felmonger, to Anne Slater, wid., mother, and William, yeo., brother, Inv. £76.9.6 1722/24
Benjamin, senior, Cranford, Inv.only £197.5.0 1733/312
FASCUTT, William, Raunds, lab., to Elizabeth, wid., Inv. £35.1.8 1720/145
FAULKNER, John, Norton, to Judith, mother, Inv. £16.10.0 1712/85
Falkner, William, Isham, to Samuel, son, Inv. £28.19.6 1713/129
John, Tiffield, Inv.only £39.13.0 1717/117A
Falkner, John, elder, Daventry, shepherd, Inv.only £6.13.6 1720/32A
Robert, Walgrave, husb., to Elizabeth, wid., 1728/9 Mar.
Falkner, Edward, Clipston, baker, to William, baker, son, Esther, wid., renounced, 1784/15 Nov.

FAULKNER continued
Jeremiah, Sywell, farmer, to Mary, wid., daughter in law, 1785/6 Aug.
William, Sywell, yeo., farmer, to Mary, wid., 1785/6 Aug.
John, Boughton, yeo., to Elizabeth, wid., 1787/15 May
John, Wellingborough, butcher, soldier, to Edward, shoemaker, and John Green, Northampton, shoemaker, Susannah, wid., renounced, 1798/5 Nov.
FAWSITT, John, Northampton, leatherseller, to Thomas Barriff, currier, London, father and guardian of Thomas, minor, grandson, Will, 1769/20 May
Mary, Northampton, spin., to Thomas, tailor, brother, 1788/31 Oct.
FAWSON, Thomas, Lois Weedon, to Elizabeth, sister, 1735/3 Oct.
Richard, Hartwell, shepherd, to Esther, wid., 1784/13 Sept.
FEARY, John, Great Doddington, shepherd, Inv.only £4.10.0 1713/108A
Mary, Great Doddington, wid., Inv.only £1.11.0 1719/99 A
William, Inv.only 1771/416
FEAVER, Edmond, Kettering, Account of Marie, wid., now wife of Joseph Brampton, £105.16.0 1671/119
Fever, Daniel, Moulton, yeo., to William, farmer, exor. of Jane, wid., decd., Will, 1776/17 June
FELLNUES, James, Kettering, grocer, to Goodith, Inv. £55.13.2 1711/29
FELLOWS, Bridget, Welton, wid., Inv.only £20.7.0 1718/83A
Fellowes, William, Holcot, butcher, to Christopher, Scaldwell, grazier, uncle and guardian of Edward, minor, son, Guard., 1795/28 Mar.
Fellowes, Christopher, Scaldwell, grazier, to Elizabeth, wid., 1795/12 Dec.
FENNIMORE, Joseph, Brackley, to Joyce, wid., Inv. £14.15.6 1743/18 Apr.
FENSHAM, William, Northampton, victualler, to Sarah, wid., 1793/15 Jan.
FENTON, Thomas, Kettering, innholder, to Martha, wid., 1748/6 Feb.
FESSEY, Henry, Earl's Barton, yeo., Inv.only £75.6.2 1712/133A
FERRY, William, Hardingstone, gent., to Martha, wid., 1785/12 Aug.
Martha, Northampton, wid., to Martin Lucas, brother, Martha, wid., mother, renounced, 1797/23 Nov.
FETCH, Elizabeth, Grafton Underwood, wid., to John, lab., son, Will, Inv. £5.5.6 1784/28 Feb.
FIFIELD, Richard, Lower Boddington, mason, Inv.only £1.18.6 1723/111A
FILKES, Parker, Northampton, innholder, to Anne, wid., 1743/3 Jan.
Jonathan, Northampton, to Richard, Wooburn, Beds., gent., and John Fox, cooper, guardians of Sarah, Mary, Susannah, and Anne, daughters, Guard., 1774/11 Nov.
Susanna, Northampton, spin., to Sarah, spin., sister, 1797/11 Mar.
FINALL, Henry, Grafton Regis, innholder, to Anne, wid., 1730/30 May
FINDING, Richard, Ringstead, butcher, to Anne, wid., Inv. £274.14.0 1733/4 Aug.
FINDON, Anne, Ringstead, wid., to Elizabeth, spin., and Anne, spin., daughters, Inv. £329.19.0 1735/25 Jan.
FISH, Augustine, Sywell, clerk, to George, Northampton, watchmaker, son, 1795/30 May
FISHER, Richard, Wellingborough, gent., Inv.only £143.2.7 1711/87A
Mary, Cranford, Inv.only £7.17.0 1714/127A
William, Wellingborough, yeo., to Mary, wife of William Collis, and Elizabeth, daughters, Inv. £84.10.4 1716/102
Francis, Bugbrooke, Inv.only £197.8.0 1716/127A
Francis, Bugbrooke, Guard.only of Susanna, minor, 1717/35
Jeffery, Irchester, Inv.only £399.0.0 1718/60A
Priscilla, Easton Maudit, wid., to Thomas, husb., son, 1724/100
Rev. George, clerk, Vicar of Sulgrave, to James, gent., son, Dorothy, wid., exor., renounced, Inv. £305.18.6 Will 1725/4 Mar.
Nathaniel, Little Houghton, to John, husb., brother, 1727/23 Oct.
Elizabeth, Denton, to Samuel, lab., husband, 1732/30 Dec.
John, Milton, farmer, to Beatrice, spin., and Sarah, spin., daughters, Inv. £55.4.0 Sarah, wid., renounced, 1733/14 Apr.
Dorothy, Thorpe Mandeville, wid., to James, gent., son, 1734/14 Nov.
Hannah, Brington, wid., to Joseph, Duston, shoemaker, son, 1743/25 Jan.
William, Wellingborough, blacksmith, to Anne, wife of John Packwood, Smithfield, London, horse dealer, daughter, Will, 1748/20 Apr.
James, Milton, shepherd, to Alice, spin., daughter, 1749/14 Jan.
Mary, Wellingborough, wid., to Ann Farrow, Castlethorpe, Bucks., wid., 1758/29 Dec.
Joseph, Wellingborough, to Elizabeth, wid., Inv. £91.3.1 1767/21 Mar.

FISHER continued
John, Milton, to Susannah, wid., 1767/17 Nov.
Simon, Little Houghton, to John, brother, 1777/1 Feb.
FITZHUGH, Edward, Kingsthorpe, to Elizabeth, wid., 1718/35
Priscilla, Piddington, victualler, to Alice, spin., daughter, Will, 1781/12 July
als. Caporne, see Caporne
FITZPATRICK, Sarah, Lilbourne, wid., to William Nicholls, butcher, nephew, 1758/10 Nov.
FLAWN, Thomas, Irthlingborough, to William Wallis, husb., guardian of Thomas, minor, exor., Inv. £22.4.0 Will, Guard., 1725/20 Feb.
William, Irchester, to John, Irthlingborough, weaver, brother, 1788/22 Dec.
FLEMING, Robert, Kettering, to Ann, wid., 1750/19 Oct.
FLETCHER, Frances, Ringstead, wid., Inv.only £9.5.2 1724/15A
John, Northampton, victualler, to Mary, wid., 1759/2 Nov.
Thomas, Rushden, gent., to Thomas, yeo., son, Sarah, wid., renounced, 1786/1 Feb.
FLINT, Elizabeth, Weedon Beck, wid., to Elizabeth Billing, wid., daughter, Inv. £7.18.0 1719/62
Timothy, Weedon Beck, yeo., to Mary, wid., Inv. £7.15.0 1729/12 Sept.
William, St. James' End, Duston, to Sarah, wid., Inv. £137.3.2 1761/5 Oct.
FLINTHAM, William, Raunds, Inv.only £8.13.6 1723/110
William, Raunds, to Alice, wid., 1724/116
Thomas, Raunds, weaver, to Christian, wid., Inv. £13.12.0 1728/12 June
William, Raunds, to Lewis, Stanwick, yeo., 1792/24 Apr.
FLOOD, Rebecca, Grendon, wid., to Thomas Cherry, yeo., son of Jane, decd., sister and exor., Will, 1748/20 Apr.
FLOWERS, Thomas, Hinton in the Hedges, husb., Inv.only £638.15.0 1719/82A
Edward, Potterspury, to Jane, Buckingham, wid., 1723/9
Flowres, Henry, Whitfield, Inv.only £107.0.6 1729/233
George, Croughton, baker, to Martha, Brackley, spin., daughter, Martha, wid., decd., Will, 1764/28 Apr.
Thomas, Hinton, yeo., to George, son, 1766/10 Nov.
FODEN, Edward, Daventry, innholder, to Samuel Coles, brazier, and Robert Skinner, maltster, principal creditors, Inv. £27.7.8½ Mary, wid., renounced, 1714/123
FODEY, Richard, Alderton, Inv.only £38.5 1715/58A
FOLWELL, Richard, Kislingbury, Inv.only £412.15.0 1726/154
FOSBURY, Thomas, Bozeat, yeo., Account of Thomas, son, admin., £99.13.0 1676/113
James, Hardingstone, yeo., gent., to John Rose, Northampton, gent., principal creditor, William Hervey, clerk, and Elizabeth, his wife, daughter, renounced, 1715/107
FOSTER, Benjamin, Whittlebury, Guard.only of Edward, son, 1711/43
John, Roade, Inv.only £64.10.0 1712/145A
Nathaniel, Higham Ferrers, to Elizabeth, wife of John Hance, 1719/44
Zachariah, Kilsby, husb., Inv.only £112.10.0 1719/68A
Forster, Robert, Desborough, grazier, Inv.only £64.16.6 1719/131A
Judith, Roade, wid., to William Conn, St. Giles, Cripplegate, Middx., mealman, Inv. £12.14.0 1719/139
Robert, Braunston, yeo., Inv.only £61.10.6 1724/90A
Alice, Grafton Regis, wid., to Catherine Reade, spin., sister, and Elizabeth Finall, spin., niece, 1727/15 July
John, Denton, lab., to Elizabeth, wid., 1729/17 Jan.
Forster, James, Kingsthorpe, servant, to Anthony, Loddington, lab., Inv., 1731/8 Jan.
Rev. William, Woodford, clerk, to William, Thrapston, father, Inv. £82.0.0 1749/26 Jan.
George, Irthlingborough, cordwainer, to Sarah, wid., Inv. £217.3.0 1781/8 Mar.
FOWKES, Robert, Braybrooke, to Anne, wid., 1726/21 Aug.
Hesther, Whittlebury, wid., to John Tredwell, husb., son, 1728/12 June
Frances, Hulcot, spin., to Joseph Lucas, elder, lab., husband of Anne, niece, decd., 1736/2 Oct.
Foukes, Farmer, Towcester, butcher, to Mary, wife of Hopcroft Bloxham, baker, daughter, 1749/23 Oct.
Foulkes, William, Mears Ashby, farmer, to Ann, wid., Inv. £70.16.6 1775/7 Feb.

FOWLER, William, Cranford St. Andrew, clerk, to Sarah, wid., 1715/43
Sarah, Cranford St. John, Inv.only £10.13.6 1720/151A
FOX, Margaret, Ringstead, wid., Inv.only £58.5.6 1719/101A
John, Knuston, Irchester, yeo., Inv.only £515.19.0 1723/60A
Francis, Hardingstone, to Alice, Northampton, wid., mother, 1743/23 July
Samuel, Wellingborough, cordwainer, to Joseph, Wollaston, currier, principal creditor, Anne, wid., renounced, 1746/19 Feb.
Thomas, Wellingborough, shoemaker, to Samuel, cordwainer, son, Martha, wid., decd., Will, 1760/17 May
John, Northampton, cooper, to John, cooper, grandfather and guardian of Catherine, Eleanor, Sarah and Jane, minors, children, 1774/1 Aug.
Abel, Irthlingborough, shoemaker, to John, Sudborough, Inv. £59.5.0 1784/29 Apr.
Sarah, Northampton, wid., to Sarah Filkes, spin., and Eleanor, spin., granddaughters, Will, 1785/21 June
John, Hargrave, lab., to Richard Shinfield, yeo., husband and admin. of Elizabeth, wid. and exor. of John, decd., Will, 1786/15 Nov.
John, Northampton, innholder, to Rebecca, wife of Thomas Linnell, innholder, daughter, 1796/28 Dec.
FOXLEY, John, Syresham, to Charles, son, Elizabeth, wid., exor., renounced in favour Charles and Joseph, sons, Will, 1719/100
Charles, Syresham, carpenter, to Ruth, wid., 1735/14 Oct.
Joseph, Syresham, yeo., to Joseph, lab., son, and Allin Wooten, lab., son in law, Will, 1750/3 Apr.
James, Potterspury, forest keeper, to Mary, wid., 1793/10 May
FRAME, Thomas, senior, Northampton, Inv.only £18.17.0 1720/35A
FRANCIS, James, Great Harrowden, grazier, to Elizabeth, wid., Inv. £634.19.8 1711/97
John, Wellingborough, staymaker, to Mary, wife of Thomas Checkley, Daventry, baker, daughter, Inv. £38.13.6 1770/3 Feb.
Thomas, Hanging Houghton, Lamport, to William Palmer, husb., brother in law, and Thomas, gent., nephew, Will, 1784/23 July
Ann, Creaton, spin., to William Palmer, Houghton, Lamport, husb., and Thomas, Lamport, gent., of goods unadministered by Thomas, gent., brother, exor., decd., 1784/24 July
William, Bugbrooke, grazier, to Anne, Thorpe Malsor, wid., 1794/1 Mar.
FRANKLIN, John, Cosgrave, to Elizabeth, wid., Inv. £121.3.0 1716/61
Nicholas, Blakesley, baker, to Mary, wid., Inv. £44.13.0 1723/134
Nicholas, Blakesley, baker, to Laurence Bainton, yeo., of goods not fully administered by Mary, wid., decd., 1724/9
Franklyn, Bernard, Gayton, yeo., Guard.only of Mary, minor, 1734/30 Nov.
Thomas, Lois Weedon, cooper, to Elizabeth, wid., 1743/18 Feb.
FREEMAN, Anne, Cranford, wid., to Elizabeth Weaver, daughter, Will, 1718/96
John, carpenter, Inv.only £24.12.6 1727/147
Jane, Whilton, spin., to Elizabeth, wid., mother, 1754/16 Aug.
William, Daventry, minor, to Joseph, draper, brother, of goods unadministered by Joseph, father, 1779/9 Oct.
Edward, Faxton, shepherd, to Mary, wid., 1783/15 Mar.
Samuel, Brafield on the Green, shopkeeper, to Mary, wid., 1786/11 Feb.
als. Reader, Anne, see Reader
FREESTON, John, Great Harrowden, to Jane, wid., 1791/21 May
FREMANTLE, Bridget, Moreton Pinkney, wid., Inv.only £293.10.6 1714/83A
Rebecca, Moreton Pinkney, to Thomas, grazier, husband, 1748/8 Sept.
Thomas, Adstone, to Thomas Cox, Byfield, butcher, principal creditor, Walgrave, Moreton Pinkney, Samuel, yeo., John Orton, yeo., and his wife Mary, brothers and sister, renounced, 1768/7 May
FRENCH, George, Whitfield, yeo., to Susanna, wid., Inv. £383.10.6 1711/51
Martha, Kilsby, Inv.only £11.10.0 1714/25A
William, Brington, yeo., to Richard, lab., brother, 1748/18 Jan.
William, Little Billing, lab., to Jane, Wellingborough, wid., 1756/5 Apr.
Stephen, Kilsby, woolcomber, to Mary, wid., 1795/14 Oct.
Anne, Badby, to George, Newnham, farmer, 1797/3 Oct.
FRETTER, Thomas, All Saints, Northampton, Inv.only £3.5.0 1713/120A
George, Stowe, yeo., Inv.only £209.10.0 1722/112A
Richard, Newnham, weaver, to Thomas, weaver, son, Inv. £18.17.6 1735/11 Jan.
Mary, Towcester, wid., to Johnson, lab., son, 1754/16 Jan.

FRIEND, William, Northampton, to Margaret, wid., 1718/34
Anne, Chipping Warden, Inv.only £45.15.8 1718/49A
William, Chipping Warden, Inv.only £102.1.8 1723/50A
Thomas, Chipping Warden, to Anne, wid., Inv. £38.17.6 1729/16 Sept.
FRISBY, Robert, Maidwell, to Elizabeth, wid., 1722/102
FRITH, Elizabeth, Earl's Barton, spin., to James, St. George, Hanover Square, Middx., grocer, nephew, Will, 1788/18 Apr.
FRONE, Richard, Yelvertoft, yeo., Inv.only £78.11.0 1715/106A
John, Yelvertoft, cordwainer, Inv.only £34.10.6 1715/138A
FROST, John, Harpole, to John, son, 1721/139
Thomas, Guilsborough, butcher, to Thomas Lucas, Hollowell, Guilsborough, gent., principal creditor, Anne, wife of William Hopkins, Northampton, wheelwright, and Elizabeth, wife of John Long, London, sisters, renounced, 1729/17 May
Joseph, Rothwell, to Elizabeth, wid., Inv. £131.16.0 1731/17 Dec.
Richard, Sulgrave, butcher, to Richard, butcher, son, Inv. £63 1.6 Elizabeth, wid., renounced, 1732/3 Oct.
Thomas, Norton, to John, Priors Marston, woolcomber, son, 1744/14 Jan.
Christopher, Culworth, to Mary, wid., 1761/19 Aug.
John, Paulerspury, dairyman, to Thomas, dairyman, son, 1780/28 Nov.
Edward, Hardingstone, farmer, to Mary, wid., 1786/29 Mar.
Thomas, Northampton, cordwainer, to Frances, wid., Will, 1795/3 Nov.
FRYER, Thomas, Ringstead, bonesetter, to Elizabeth, wid., 1769/21 Feb.
FURNISS, Furnis, Richard, Grimscote, Cold Higham, Inv.only £59.15.0 1726/177
Furness, Elizabeth, Grimscote, wid., to John Archbold, Cold Higham, yeo., brother, 1729/7 July
Richard, Green's Norton, to William, shoemaker, son, Inv. £18.3.0 1763/19 July
William, Collingtree, to Thomas, Astcote, Pattishall, carpenter, father, Inv. £23.7.11¾ 1763/22 Oct.
Jonathan, Moreton Pinkney, to Hephzibah, wid., 1782/15 Oct.

G

GABELL, Mary, Edgcote, wid., Inv.only £33.17.9 1724/140A
GADD, Elizabeth, Great Houghton, wid., to Thomas Pell, tailor, son, 1761/15 Aug.
GADSBY, John, Wellingborough, apothecary, to Elizabeth, wid., 1746/9 Apr.
GALE, Hesther, Towcester, wid., to Elizabeth Jaunary, spin., niece, 1729/17 Apr.
GALLARD, Samuel, Grafton Regis, grazier, to Lydia, wid., 1758/11 Nov.
GALLAWAY, Thomas, Kettering, to Thomas, Hadleigh, co. Suffolk, father and guardian of Charles, minor, exor., Will, 1718/27
GAMAGE, Gammage, William, Harlestone, miller, to Mary, wid., Inv. £18.5.8 1713/131
Richard, Brington, tailor, to Elizabeth, wid., 1736/16 Feb.
Joseph, Brington, to Anne, wid., 1741/3 Jan.
Mary, Brington, wid., to Henry, Duston, yeo., son, 1741/6 July
Edward, Great Brington, yeo., victualler, to George Fisher, East Haddon, yeo., grandfather and guardian of Lucy and Mary, daughters, minors, Inv. £10.9.0 Guard., 1753/17 Mar.
Thomas, Lamport, to Ann, wid., 1769/11 Nov.
GAMBELL, George, Inv.only £184.8.6 undated/339
George, Northampton, to Elizabeth, wid., 1737/12 Jan.
Frances, St. Giles, Northampton, spin., to Hannah, spin., sister, Will, 1779/26 May
GANDERN, John, Collingtree, to Elizabeth, wid., 1777/15 Feb.
GARDNER, Rebecca, Nortoft, wid., to Elizabeth Muxloe, Guilsborough, wid., daughter, 1732/9 Sept.
Mary, Badby, to John, Safforn Hill, St. Anne's, Holborne, co. Middx., button maker, husband, 1742/3 Sept.
Gardiner, John, Marston St. Lawrence, farmer, to John, yeo., son, Inv. £55.17.0 Elizabeth, wid., renounced, 1751/4 May
Elizabeth, Marston St. Lawrence, wid., to John, son, Inv. £36.16.0 1751/21 Oct.
Gardiner, Richard, Silverstone, gent., to John, farmer, brother, 1758/14 Apr.
John, Kislingbury, victualler, to William, Harpole, farmer, son, Mary, wid., exor., decd., Will, 1776/21 Sept.

GARDNER continued
Mary, Duston, wid., to William, Harpole, farmer, son, 1776/21 Sept.
Thomas, Daventry, to Elizabeth, wid., 1791/21 Sept.
Gardiner, John, Silverstone, to Emma, wid., mother, 1793/2 Apr.
GARE, John, Weedon Beck, shepherd, to John, husb., son, Inv. £13.5.0 1713/114
John, Weedon Beck, to Deborah, wid., Inv. £97.10.0 1721/129
Samuel, Farthingstone, shepherd, to Elizabeth, wife of Edward Cox, lab., daughter, 1729/4 Jan.
John, Weedon Beck, yeo., to William Muscott, Floore, gent., principal creditor, 1743/28 Jan.
Deborah, Weedon Beck, to Martha, spin., daughter, 1743/26 Apr.
GARLAND, Humphrey, Helmdon, to Richard, lab., 1714/104
Mary, Brackley, wid., to Charles, gent., son, 1736/18 Mar.
GARLICK, Richard, Pytchley, Inv.only £29.0.0 1711/24A
Richard, Pytchley, grazier, Inv.only £199.15.0 1712/23A
John, Moulton, yeo., to Mary, wid., Inv. £379.0.0 1720/15
Alexander, Braunston, Inv.only £8.1.0 1724/133
Richard, Abington, yeo., to Elizabeth, wid., 1756/3 Aug.
Thomas, Bugbrooke, farmer, to Mary, wid., 1787/26 Jan.
GARNER, James, Isham, maltster, Account of Dennis, wid., £70.7.6 1671/100
Mark, Creaton, to Anne, wid., 1720/77
Richard, Long Buckby, blacksmith, to Anne, wid., 1721/133
Richard, Moreton Pinkney, to Jane, wife of Thomas Smith, yeo., daughter, 1721/141
Nathaniel, Edgcote, Inv.only £46.13.0 1724/119A
Henry, Wappenham, lab., to John, Croughton, lab., son, 1729/15 July
als. Smith, William, Long Buckby, to John Coleman, grocer, and John Wynn, Northampton, gent., 1745/28 Jan.
Moses, Lilbourne, framework knitter, to John, framework knitter, son, 1780/22 July
GARNETT, Thomas, Farthingstone, rector, to Samuel Pennington, Northampton, gent., and John Matthews, Everton, gent., principal creditors, Elizabeth, wid., renounced, 1714/175
Garnit, Rev., Fawsley, Inv.only £35.15.0 1738/351
GARNEY, Henry, Courtenhall, to Ezekiel, Harborough, co. Leic., gardener, uncle and guardian of Ann and Margaret, minors, daughters, Inv. £82.16.7 1734/17 Jan.
GARRATT, Richard, Thorpe Malsor, Inv.only £29.15.0 1713/63A
Richard, Wellingborough, carpenter, Inv.only £9.6.11 1714/159A
Francis, Crick, to Elizabeth, wid., 1718/113
Garrett, Thomas, Spratton, yeo., Inv.only £29.7.6 1719/67A
Garrett, Joseph, Spratton, to Elizabeth, wid., 1719/123
Thomas, West Haddon, yeo., Inv.only £3.7.0 1724/126A
Samuel, Burton Latimer, to Margaret, wid., Inv. £21.4.6 Account of Margaret, admin., £21.5.6 1726/9 Aug.
Margaret, Burton Latimer, wid., to Samuel, Weekly, miller, father in law, Inv. £41.6.6 1731/11 Sept.
Elizabeth, Watford, wid., to Mary Stevenson, wid., niece, 1731/16 Oct.
John, Staples Mill, Wellingborough, to Esther, wid., Inv. £156.19.7 1755/18 Apr.
Garret, Thomas, Helmdon, to Ann, wid., 1767/12 Jan.
Garrett, James, East Haddon, farmer, to John and William, butchers, brothers, 1781/28 Sept.
Garrett, Catherine, Ravensthorpe, wid., to William Hall, Welton, maltster, uncle and guardian of Elizabeth and William, minors, children, 1785/21 June
Garrett, John, Navesby, farmer, to Thomas, farmer, son, Hannah, wid., renounced, 1789/10 July
GAUDERN, Edward, Sywell, clerk, to Richard, Earl's Barton, yeo., brother, 1738/6 May
Stephen, Northampton, innholder, to Mary, wid., 1793/23 Dec.
GAWTHARNE, Elizabeth, Wellingborough, wid., to John, gent., son, 1715/29
GAYBELL, William, Heyford, grazier, to Elizabeth, wid., 1748/23 Jan.
GAYTON, John, Passenham, to Elizabeth, wid., 1756/21 May
Nathaniel, Brafield on the Green, woolcomber, to Stephen, woolcomber, and William, farmer, brothers, 1786/11 Feb.
GENT, Thomas, Brington, collarmaker, to Nicholas, Little Brington, husb., brother, Inv. £74.9.4 1714/195

GEORGE, John, Staverton, Inv.only £8.7.6 1713/135A
John, Newnham, yeo., to Benjamin, yeo., brother, 1740/10 Dec.
Thomas, Drayton, servant, to Samuel, Newnham, lab., father, 1753/10 Nov.
Benjamin, Newnham, to Elizabeth, wid., 1778/12 Feb.
GERRARD, Jerrard, William, Helmdon, Inv.only £101.13.6 1720/159A
GERY, Gerey, Thomas, Rushden, husb., to Elizabeth, wid., Inv. £139.10.10 1714/62
Thomas, Hartwell, Inv.only £5.2.6 1718/18A
Geary, Charles, Ringstead, farmer, to Charan Happuch Geary, wid., 1781/20 Mar.
GIBBINS, Thomas, Welton, to Thomas, husb., son, 1728/12 June
John, Cold Ashby, to Elizabeth, wid., 1757/18 Apr.
Thomas, Green's Park, Blakesley, to Elizabeth, wid., 1784/22 June
John, Kilsby, woolcomber, to John, woolcomber, son, 1786/10 May
GIBBS, William, Blisworth, Account of Anne, wid., admin., £487.12.0 1680/41
Gibbes, Rev. William, Rector of Gayton, Inv.only £595.15.0 1716/108A
William, Whiston, to John, South Kilworth, co. Leic., brother, 1716/139
Hanna, Wellingborough, wid., Inv.only £28.9.8 1718/40A
Samuel, Chipping Warden, husb., Inv.only £500.0.0 1722/25A
Thomas, Brackley, to William, gent., son, 1723/129
Alice, Whittlebury, wid., to ---, Inv. £23.15.0 1728/23 Oct.
Francis, Middleton Cheney, yeo., to James, glazier, son, 1747/16 Feb.
Gibbes, Susanna, Wellingborough, to William Cherry, gent., brother, 1753/1 May
Gibbes, Richard, Milton, baker, to William Tebbutt, Duston, miller, father in law and guardian of Richard, minor, and William, minor, sons, Guard., 1754/15 Feb.
William, Gayton, clerk, to Richard Pancoust, Ravenstone, Bucks., farmer and grazier, nephew in law, and William Kerby, Northampton, whittawer, of goods unadministered by John Gooday, brother in law, decd., 1764/24 July
John, Milton, yeo., to John Allen, farmer, uncle and guardian of Elizabeth, Gaffield, John, Samuel, Thomas, Francis, Joseph and Mary, minors, children, Inv. £400.0.6 1766/20 Sept.
Isaac, Welton, to Susanna, wid., 1773/1 Oct.
Sarah, Kettering, to John Rowlatt, gent., Will, 1776/15 May
John, Blisworth, farmer, to Anne, wid., 1783/19 Sept.
GIBSON, George, Sibbertoft, to Richard, shepherd, son, Hannah, wid., renounced, 1726/5 Nov.
GIDDING, Mary, Thorpe Malsor, wid., Inv.only £28.8.8 1716/13A
GILBERT, Nathaniel, Watford, to James, yeo., brother, 1721/135
Joseph, Watford, to Hannah, wid., 1722/59
Thomas, Grendon, lab., to John, lab., son, 1730/31 Jan.
William, Watford, yeo., to James, yeo., brother, Inv. £266.9.6 1732/27 May
Richard, Northampton, to Anne, wid., 1738/29 Apr.
Susannah, Tiffield, spin., to Elizabeth, spin., sister, Frances, wid., mother, renounced, 1739/20 Oct.
Edward, Sibbertoft, dealer, to Jane, wid., 1740/4 Mar.
Charles, Tiffield, to Frances, wid., mother, 1741/30 Nov.
John, Silverstone, yeo., to Mary, spin., sister, 1742/17 Apr.
Robert, Northampton, to Elizabeth, wid., 1761/3 Feb.
Richard, Floore, victualler, to Betty, wid., 1782/8 May
Roger, Sibbertoft, grazier, to Mary Neale, Lubbenham, co. Leic., wid., sister, and William Hill, Harborough, co. Leic., grocer, nephew, 1792/14 Feb.
GILES, John, Hackleton, to Thomas Smith, Preston Deanery, and Thomas Wills, Northampton, cordwainer, principal creditors, Mary, wid., renounced, Will, 1780/23 Mar.
Thomas, Hackleton, butcher, to Elizabeth, wid., 1796/22 Oct.
GILKES, Stephen, Gretworth, to Thomas, junior, blacksmith, son, Will, 1714/164
Alice, Lois Weedon, wid., to Laurence Bainton, Blakesley, shepherd, next of kin, 1734/22 Nov.
William, Byfield, lab., to Elizabeth, wid., Inv. £16.0.0 1735/6 Oct.
Gilks, John, Helmdon, to Margaret, wid., 1782/24 June

GILL, Sarah, Inv.only £15.7.0 undated/275
Thomas, Ecton, tailor, Inv.only £16.15.0 1718/19A
Thomas, Moulton, husb., Inv.only £234.14.0 1722/39A
Edward, Kettering, Inv.only £132.19.0 1723/127A
John, Syresham, husb., to John, husb., son, 1730/12 Oct.
Samuel, Navesby, weaver, to Mary, wid., 1748/23 July
Joseph, Welford, farmer, to Elizabeth, wid., 1777/14 July
GILLITT, John, Cogenhoe, Inv.only £18.16.2 1722/113A
Gillet, Richard, Mears Ashby, farmer, to Ruth, wid., 1748/24 Dec.
Gillit, Thomas, Mears Ashby, to Alice, wid., 1764/9 June
Gillit, William, Mears Ashby, farmer, to Thomas, farmer, son, Sarah, wid., renounced, 1766/22 Nov.
GILLOWAY, John, Yardley Hastings, keeper, to Susanna Faber, Taber, and Anne Foster, daughters, Inv. £84.17.6 1730/31 Oct.
GILPIN, John, Slapton, yeo., to Anne, wid., 1731/19 June
GINNS, John, Desborough, shoemaker, to Thomas, son, Elizabeth, wid., decd., Will, 1751/25 Nov.
Ginn, Edward, Burton Latimer, to Henry, Thorpe Malsor, grazier, grandson, 1790/25 June
GLASBROOK, John, Higham Ferrers, clerk, to William Simpson, draper, principal creditor, Susannah, wid., renounced, 1731/19 Jan.
GLEED, Edmund, Kingsthorpe, gent., to John, yeo., son, Mary, wid., and Mary, spin., daughter, renounced, 1726/31 May
Richard, Milton, farmer, to Elizabeth, wid., 1728/26 Apr.
Mary, Milton, spin., to John, Kingsthorpe, husb., nephew, 1728/24 Oct.
Elizabeth, Milton, wid., to Elizabeth Dodwell, wid., daughter, 1742/9 Sept.
Edmund, Milton, yeo., to Tomkins, yeo., son, Inv. £671.16.11 1755/17 Mar.
GLENN, Nathaniel, Daventry, elder, to Anne, wid., 1743/22 Dec.
GLOUCESTER, als. Warkman, Mark, Inv.only £6.8.5 1721/69A
GLOVER, John, Kettering, Account of Mary, wid., admin., £18.10.0 1680/1
John, Finedon, to Anne, wid., Deed of Gift or Will, 1717/83
Richard, Hellidon, to William, yeo., son, 1721/113
Richard, Wellingborough, butcher, Inv.only £24.1.0 1724/125A
William, Finedon, lab., to Elizabeth, wid., 1733/16 June
GOBEY, William, Moulton, yeo., Inv.only £6.3.0 1713/127A
Goobey, Gobby, Edward, Hannington, yeo., to Hannah, wid., 1729/10 Feb.
GODFREY, William, Old Stratford, Cosgrave, to Elizabeth, wid., 1717/73
GOFFE, William, Floore, Inv.only £76.19.0 1712/32A
William, Floore, Guard.only of Mary, minor, daughter, 1715/156
William, Floore, Guard.only of Mary, minor, daughter, 1716/104
Christiana, Milton, spin., to Sarah, wife of John Phipps, baker, mother, 1798/19 May
GOLDBY, Golbey, Nicholas, younger, Middleton Cheney, mason, to Nicholas, Westbury, Bucks., lab., son, Renunciation of Anne, wid., now wife of Fulk Denzie 1726/148
Nicholas, Middleton Cheney, to Nicholas, husb., son, 1727/21 Jan.
Nicholas, Sulgrave, lab., to Mary, wid., 1754/30 Nov.
William, Eydon, to Elizabeth, 1781/2 Apr.
Golby, George, Northampton, gardener, to John, yeo., father, 1792/7 Aug.
GOODE, John, Byfield, cordwainer, to Mary, wid., Inv. £16.8. 1713/96
Thomas, Ringstead, yeo., Inv.only £308.0.0 1722/43A
John, Brington, lab., to John, lab., son, 1733/24 Feb.
Good, John, Little Brington, Inv.only £14.5.0 1733/289
Henry, Byfield, to Elizabeth, wid., 1739/9 May
William, Barby, lab., to William, West Haddon, woolcomber, son, 1777/4 June
Edward, Brixworth, yeo., to Ann, wid., 1792/11 Aug.
GOODFELLOW, Sarah, Kettering, to John, plumber, husband, 1757/4 May
GOODMAN, William, Hackleton, Piddington, husb., to Anne, wid., Inv. £116.13.0 1711/58
Robert, Inv.only £34.11.8 1711/133A
Thomas, Maidwell, to John Bryan, senior, grazier, and John Bryan, junior, yeo., guardians of two children of Thomas, 1713/139
Joseph, Badby, Inv.only £27.12.6 1714/179A
John, Wollaston, Guard.only of Henry, Thomas, Anne, minors, children, 1714/188
William, junior, Staverton, to Anne, wid., Guard. of Catherine, minor, daughter, exor., Inv. £483.0.0 Will, 1717/19

GOODMAN continued
Joseph, Bradden, Inv.only £220.10.0 1717/22A
Thomas, Harpole, Inv.only £64.15.10 1717/45A
John, Wollaston, Account of Henry, admin., 1717/82
William, Everdon, Inv.only £9.6.4 1717/87A
James, Staverton, Inv.only £554.8.3 1720/83A
John, Newnham, yeo., Inv.only £36.14.10 1720/156A
Anne, Great Brington, wid., Renunciation of John, son, exor., in favour of Alice or Jane, daughters, 1721/99
Henry, Wollaston, Inv.only £15.7.9 1724/129
Elizabeth, Staverton, wid., Inv.only £15.7.0 1725/145
William, Quinton, to Jane, wid., Will, 1727/15 July
Elizabeth, Staverton, to Jonathan, husb., son, 1728/6 Apr.
Samuel, Newnham, Guard.only of Elizabeth, James, Samuel and Hannah Ansell, minors, 1728/29 Nov.
Hannah, Badby, wid., to Edward, husb., son, 1733/6 July
Susannah, Newnham, wid., to John Smith, Badby, yeo., and Thomas Smith, yeo., brothers, Inv. £17.16.6 1735/13 Nov.
William, Long Buckby, to Sarah, wid., 1739/14 July
William, Rothwell, butcher, to Elizabeth, wid., 1744/23 June
Elizabeth, Badby, spin., to Mary, wid., mother, 1747/6 Mar.
John, Everdon, farmer, to Richard, yeo., son, Mary, wid., renounced, 1757/19 Sept.
Ann, Staverton, to Ann Burbidge, wid., daughter, 1761/9 Apr.
Thomas, Badby, to Hannah, wid., 1778/2 July
Samuel, Long Buckby, to Eleanor, wid., 1780/21 June
Robert, Newnham, farmer, to Hannah, wid., 1786/6 May
John, Cosgrave, lab., to John, lab., son, Inv. £6.13.9 1787/17 Nov.
Elizabeth, Towcester, wid., to John and Job, curriers, sons, 1787/22 Nov.
Benjamin, Northampton, brazier, to Elizabeth, wid., 1796/23 Dec.
GOODRIDGE, Robert, Hartwell, to William, husb., son, 1726/30 June
William, Hartwell, to Susannah, wid., and William, yeo., son, 1739/8 May
GOODROOD, Anne, Northampton, to Thomas, blacksmith, son, 1712/90
GOODWIN, Thomas, Evenly, to Elizabeth, spin., sister, Inv. £319.0.0 1713/9
John, Northampton, gardener, Guard.only of Elizabeth Middleton, minor, granddaughter, 1721/2
Mary, Northampton, wid., to Margaret Cockraine, spin., sister, 1724/84
James, Northampton, merchant, to Elizabeth, wid., 1787/21 Feb.
GOOSEY, Richard, Holcot, to Mary, wid., Inv. £8.19.0 1718/62
Thomas, Rushden, yeo., husb., to Mary, wid., Inv. £261.0.0 1738/11 Oct.
Thomas, Irchester, to Mary, wid., 1746/9 Apr.
Thomas, Little Brington, tailor, to Elizabeth, wid., Inv. £113.12.0 1749/16 Feb.
GORE, Jane, Northampton, wid., to Charles, son, 1713/80
James, Northampton, to Charles, brother, 1714/139
Isabella, Northampton, spin., to Charles, brother, 1717/126
Mary, Northampton, spin., to Charles, brother, 1717/127
William, Dallington, carpenter, to Alice, wid., 1754/29 May
GOSTELOW, Richard, Middleton Cheney, lab., to Grace, wid., 1731/4 Nov.
Gostelo, Richard, Middleton Cheney, Inv.only £15.0.0 1731/283
Gostellow, Thomas, Brackley, carpenter and joiner, to Elizabeth Clarke, Tingewick, Bucks., spin., Will, 1758/30 June
Kirton, Adstone, to Mary, wid., 1761/5 Aug.
Mary, Adstone, wid., to William, Blakesley, yeo., and Thomas, Ampthill, Beds., surveyor, sons, 1791/28 Feb.
GOWEN, William, Newnham, to Elizabeth, wid., 1740/26 July
GRACE, Daniel, Stoke Bruerne, to Anne, wid., Inv. £271.4.4 1717/139
GRAHAM, John, Langham's Mill, Duston, miller, Inv.only £60.6.6 1722/13A
GRANDBOROW, Richard, Whilton, to Sarah, wid., 1712/29
Granborow, Francis, Inv.only £99.15.0 1719/140A
GRANT, Martha, Wellingborough, wid., to Milcha, wife of William Hawley, shoemaker, daughter, John Carver, minister of the gospel, renounced, Will, 1791/31 May
William, Hannington, husb., to William, Walgrave, yeo., and Thomas, yeo., sons, Samuel Fox, exor., decd., Will, 1793/1 June
GRAVES, Mary, Abington, wid., to Ann, wife of William Standen, victualler, sister, 1781/20 Aug.

GRAY, John, Paulerspury, grazier, Inv.only £69.17.6 1712/13A
Mary, Paulerspury, wid., Inv.only £36.6.0 1714/36A
Grey, Matthew, Grafton Underwood, to Mary, wid., mother, Inv. £290.19.0 1714/171
Mary, Grafton Underwood, wid., Inv.only £340.12.2 1716/106A
William, Grafton Underwood, to Elizabeth, wid., Inv. £30.0.0 Will, 1718/133
John, Finedon, to Sarah, wid., Inv. £8.8.0 1720/14
Thomas, Preston, to Mary, wid., 1721/37
Grey, John, Irchester, to Anne, wid., Inv. £18.12.0 1725/22 Jan.
Anne, Irchester, wid., to Henry Bull, farmer, principal creditor, 1725/3 Apr.
Edward, Grafton Underwood, yeo., to Sarah, wid., Inv. £423.13.6 1733/24 Mar.
Charles, Grafton Underwood, to Henry Fox, Woolley, co. Hunts., gent., of goods not fully administered by Mary and Matthew, exors., 1737/13 Sept.
Ann, Boddington, wid., to Henry, yeo., son, 1751/21 Oct.
GREEN, Greene, John, Warkton, bachelor, Account of Abreham, brother, admin., £55.15.0 1671/99
Thomas, Braunston, weaver, Inv.only £21.10.11 1712/26A
Richard, Wootton, Inv.only £19.3.6 1712/48A
John, Hardingstone, yeo., Inv.only £326.17.0 1713/50A
Greene, Edward, Eydon, shepherd, Inv.only £15.12.0 1713/75
Arthur, Bugbrooke, yeo., to Mary, wid., Inv. £7.18.1 1715/154
Joseph, Marston Trussell, to Mary, wid., Will, 1716/52
Richard, Wicken, Inv.only £52.12.0 1716/124A
Hannah, Eydon, wid., Inv.only £88.5.3½ 1718/92A
Joseph, Kettering, to Mary, wid., Inv. £19.3.6 1719/36
Joan, Overthorpe, Middleton Cheney, wid., Inv.only £132.10.6 1719/84A
William, Northampton, to Mary, wid., 1720/97
Greene, Christopher, Raunds, blacksmith, Inv.only £39.1.11 1721/48A
Thomas, Vicar of Lilbourne, to James, Northampton, draper, father, 1722/121
Judith, Wicken, wid., to Edward, yeo., son, Inv. £5.9.0 1722/140
William, Northampton, carpenter, Inv.only over £300. 1724/138A
Mary, Warkton, wid., Inv.only £30.0.0 1726/172
John, Rothwell, to Anne, wid., 1732/21 Apr.
Thomas, Milton, yeo., to Susanna, wid., 1733/24 Feb.
Adkins, Paulerspury, tailor, Inv.only £14.4.6 1735/328
Richard, Crick, butcher, to Katherine, wid., 1736/9 Apr.
Jane, Northampton, spin., to Rowland, Ravensthorpe, yeo., brother, 1738/7 Jan.
Jane, Northampton, Inv.only undated/391
Francis, Kilsby, gent., to John, butcher, brother, 1753/4 May
Richard, Harlestone, cordwainer, to John, cordwainer, brother, 1754/12 Jan.
Ann, Kilsby, spin., to Mary, wife of Joseph Sleath, sister, 1765/3 Oct.
Elizabeth, Kingsthorpe, wid., to William, farmer, son, 1766/5 July
James, Brixworth, yeo., to Dorcas, wid., 1769/17 May
James, Brixworth, farmer, Guard.only of Anthony, minor, son, 1774/13 Apr.
Thomas, Weedon Beck, to Alice, wid., 1774/27 June
Thomas, Clipston, cordwainer, to Richard, nephew, Ann, niece, exor., decd., Will, 1783/24 Oct.
Anthony, Brixworth, innholder, to Anne, wid., 1786/13 Oct.
James, Watford, lab., to Elizabeth Bray, Spratton, daughter, Ann, wife, decd., Will, 1789/7 Mar.
George, Wellingborough, to Hannah, wid., 1790/29 Dec.
Joseph, Kettering, staymaker, to Mary Roberts, wid., daughter, 1795/3 Apr.
Samuel, Castle Ashby, farmer, to Robert Rogers, farmer, and John Buckby, farmer, guardians of Samuel, Elizabeth, William, Thomas, Charles and Martha, minors, children, Sarah, wid., renounced, Guard., 1797/11 Feb.
Mary, Kilsby, to Robert Matthews, Yelvertoft, woolcomber, John Cattle, grazier, and Edward Wilkins, farmer, Will, 1798/2 May
Joseph, Long Buckby, lab., to Joseph, lab., son, 1799/30 Mar.
GREENOUGH, Elizabeth, Northampton, wid., to Thomas, shoemaker, 1734/3 Aug.
Rand, Northampton, to Mary, wid., 1777/10 Apr.
GREGORY, William, Everdon, Inv.only £46.0.0 1722/54A
GRENDON, Edward, Whittlebury, Inv.only £164.4.0 1713/58A

GREVILL, Francis, Mollington, Oxon., Account of Francis, son, admin., £30.0.0 1678/141
GRIEVE, Elizabeth, Northampton, wid., to Sarah, wife of William Procter, lab., daughter, 1784/24 Mar.
GRIFFIN, Thomas, Irthlingborough, Account of Richard, brother, admin., £44.2.11 1680/6
Griffen, Anne, Irthlingborough, wid., to William, son, Inv. £225.5.0 1717/24
Griffen, John, Blisworth, tailor, Inv.only £67.15.0 1717/37a A
Simon, Welton, blacksmith, Inv.only £17.2.6 1724/41A
Elizabeth, Haselbech, spin., to Thomas, North Kilworth, co. Leic., lab., brother, 1733/17 Feb.
GRIFFITH, Thomas, Northampton, to Anne, wid., 1718/67
Thomas, Ecton, gent., to William Howkins, butcher, principal creditor, 1728/1 Feb.
Thomas, Ecton, Inv.only £15.11.6 1728/205
Griffiths, Thomas, Wollaston, gent., to Thomas, Houghton le Spring, co. Durham, clerk, son, 1759/29 June
John, Blisworth, tailor, to Anne, wid., 1781/3 Dec.
GRIMES, Grymes, Mary, Brackley, to Hill, yeo., husband, Inv. £15.0.0 1711/118
Mary, Brackley, wid., to Thomas Robinson, Buckingham, tailor, grandson, 1736/8 Nov.
GROCER, George, Earl's Barton, lab., to George, shopkeeper, son, 1778/8 Aug.
GROOCOCK, James, Kettering, to Anne, wid., Inv. £49.12.0 1723/34
Mary, Northampton, to Matthew, innholder, husband, 1779/22 May
Anne, Kettering, spin., to Mary, wife of Jacob Watson, sergemaker, sister, 1781/30 Nov.
GROOME, Mary, Ringstead, spin., to Jonathan Tilley, plumber, brother, Inv. £9.8.2 Will, 1711/152
William, Spratton, to Dorothy, wife of John Heyward, daughter, 1719/48
Groom, Martha, Rushden, wid., Inv.only £5.9.6 1721/10 A
Groom, Leonard, Irthlingborough, yeo., to Alderman, Ramsey, co. Hunts., cordwainer, Thomas, schoolmaster, and Cuthbert Scarborough, husb., guardians of Elizabeth and Ann, minors, daughters, 1759/14 Apr.
Groom, William, Irthlingborough, to Matthew, farmer, son, 1773/20 Nov.
Groom, Richard, Irthlingborough, to Elizabeth, wid., 1792/16 Apr.
Groom, Daniel, Wellingborough, to Elizabeth Tilley, spin., 1799/1 June
Groom, William, Irthlingborough, to Robert, farmer, son, 1799/24 July
GROSS, Joseph, Harlestone, yeo., to Joseph, maltster, son, Will, 1748/20 Feb.
GROVE, Alice, Mears Ashby, to Elizabeth Sharman, Wellingborough, daughter, 1712/67
John, Towcester, innholder, Inv. £180.4.9 Will, 1722/132
Groves, Moses, Kettering, farmer, to Sarah, wid., 1800/5 Mar.
GRUBB, Elizabeth, Woodford cum Membris, wid., to Sarah Sharman and Mary Blunt, daughters, Inv. £29.11.0 1711/4
Grub, William, Abthorpe, to Isabell, Yardley Gobion, wid., 1716/55
Thomas, Floore, weaver, to Rebecca, wid., 1733/23 June
GRUNDON, Edward, Whittlebury, Guard.only of George, minor, son, 1719/20
GUBBINS, Elizabeth, Westhorpe, Byfield, spin., Inv.only £2.18.0 1712/28A
William, Westhorpe, Byfield, yeo., to Elizabeth, wid., Inv. £34.2.6 1730/9 Apr.
Thomas, Barby, lab., to Elizabeth, wife of William Farden, Hillmorton, co. Warwick, Amy, exor., decd., Will, 1794/2 Apr.
GUDGEON, Gudgin, Robert, Daventry, yeo., Account of Bridget, wid., now wife of Edward Fellowes, £234.4.10 1671/88
John, Daventry, to Elizabeth, Inv. £15.13.0 1714/146
William, Weedon Beck, Inv.only £7.3.2 1723/79A
Cornelius, Gayton, shoemaker, to Elizabeth, wid., 1725/17 Apr.
Gudgin, William, Weedon Beck, victualler, to Thomas, victualler, son, 1732/18 Nov.
Gudgin, William, Weedon Beck, Inv.only £52.10.0 1732/292
Richard, Gayton, to John, cordwainer and maltster, son, 1778/18 Apr.
GUESS, Gess, William, Wellingborough, to Elizabeth, wid., Inv. £29.14.8 1744/25 July
GUILFORD, Samuel, Towcester, glazier and plumber, to Dorothy, wife of Richard Winterbone, Harcot, Bucks., yeo., and Jane, wife of Stephen Adams, Swanbourne, Bucks., sisters, Inv. £30.19.6½ 1722/115

GULLIVER, Thomas, Middleton Cheney, yeo., to Anne, wid., Inv. £18.12.6 1711/90
William, West Haddon, Inv.only £119. 1716/1A
Thomas, Thornby, husb., to Mary, wid., Inv. £204.10.0 1722/126
William, West Haddon, farmer, to William, farmer, son, 1788/19 Feb.
GURDING, George, Whittlebury, to William, Passenham, yeo., uncle and guardian of John, Stephen, Richard and William, minors, sons, 1737/16 Apr.
George, Whittlebury, yeo., Inv.only £150.2.6 1737/348
GURMAN, John, Middleton Cheney, shepherd, Inv.only £6.8.6 1719/109A
GURNEY, Elizabeth, Cosgrave, wid., to William, gent., son, 1714/192
GUTTERIDGE, Bartin, Desborough, Inv.only £197.15.8 1714/52A
William, Desborough, to Elizabeth, wid., 1717/61

H

HACKLETON, John, Staverton, Account of Agnes, wid., admin., £90.4.8 1671/97
William, Staverton, to Richard, mason, brother, 1712/59
HACKNEY, John, Wellingborough, to Mary, wid., 1711/30
Henry, Wellingborough, to Mary, spin., daughter, Inv. £18.16.10 1726/22 Jan.
Fisher, Wellingborough, to Dorothy, wid., Inv. £24.0.0 1727/7 Apr.
John, Wellingborough, yeo., to Mary, wid., 1731/11 Dec.
HADLAND, Thomas, Floore, to Samuel Thompson, Daventry, feltmonger, principal creditor, Mary, wid., renounced, 1769/3 Mar.
HADDON, William, Long Buckby, baker, Inv.only £134.15.0 1715/57A
John, Floore, husb., to Elizabeth, wid., 1729/3 May
Elizabeth, Floore, to John Judkins, Crick, mercer, and Thomas Watts, Crick, yeo., guardians of John and Henry, minors, Will, 1734/16 Nov.
John, Abington, to Anne, wid., 1738/8 Apr.
HAIGH, Edward, Ashby St. Ledgers, clerk, to Joseph, Almonbury, co. York., gent., uncle and guardian of Joseph, minor, son, Inv. £410.16.6 John renounced, Will, Guard., 1712/5
HALES, Thomas, Paulerspury, to Mary, wid., Inv. £38.13.6 1724/34
Halles, Edward, Wellingborough, to Ursula, wid., Inv. £72.6.7 1724/152
HALFORD, Francis, Clipston, yeo., Account of Sarah, wid., £159.16.2 undated/114
Elizabeth, Wellingborough, to Edward, clothier, husband, 1716/129
HALL, William, Coten, Ravensthorpe, Account of Thomas Biggs, son, admin., £183.0.0 1681/78
Henry, senior, Rushden, Inv.only £451.13.6 1712/114A
William, Raunds, yeo., Inv.only £38.13.0 1713/3A
Thomas, Brackley, cordwainer, to Jane, wid., mother, Inv. £18.19.2 1713/130
Samuel, Charwelton, Inv.only £9.14.6 1714/119A
Jane, Rushden, wid., to Henry, yeo., son, 1717/69
John, Barby, husb., to Mary, wid., Inv. £36.5.0 1718/26
Thomas, Raunds, yeo., Inv.only £516.13.0 1722/58A
William, Woodford, Thrapston, to Jane, wid., Inv. £51.12.2 1723/81
William, Inv.only £51.12.2 1723/103
William, Weedon Beck, to Mary, wid., Inv. £4.13.6 1725/30 Apr.
John, East Haddon, farmer, to Anne, wid., 1725/5 June
Thomas, Brackley, to Elizabeth Murray, wid., niece, of goods not fully administered by Jane, mother, decd., 1725/29 Oct.
John, St. James End, Duston, victualler, to Anne, wid., 1731/22 July
William, Grafton Regis, lab., to Hannah, wid., 1733/31 Mar.
William, Grafton Regis, lab., Inv.only £17.0.0 1733/314
Hannah, Towcester, wid., to Hannah, spin., daughter, 1749/23 Oct.
Samuel, Barby, yeo., to Samuel, farmer, son, 1751/1 Apr.
William, Raunds, to Ann Inkersole, Spaldwick, Hunts., sister, Inv. £316.17.0 1763/15 Jan.
Richard, Watford, shepherd, to Richard, lab., son, Inv. £10.10.6 1773/4 May
Edward, Priors' Marston, co. Warwick, blacksmith, to Mary, Kilsby, spin., cousin, Elizabeth Vaus, Kilsby, wid., cousin, and Thomas Smith, Ashby St. Ledgers, cousin, yeo., 1776/25 June
Thomas, Newbottle, yeo., to Mary, wid., 1780/15 July
Mary, Asthorpe, wid., to Thomas, yeo., son, 1800/29 May

HALLAWAY, William, Thrupp Grounds, Norton, grazier, Inv.only £158.9.0 1722/33 A
HALLOADY, Richard, Moulton, to John, lab., son, 1761/2 May
HAMBIDGE, Richard, Murcott, Watford, to Elizabeth, wid., Will, 1720/119
HAMBLETON, Esau, Northampton, wheelwright, to Elizabeth, wid., 1728/4 Nov.
HAMMONS, William, Crick, to Elizabeth, wid., Inv. £12.11.6 1720/34
William, Ashby St. Ledgers, victualler, to Anne, wid., 1795/22 Aug.
HANBURY, Dorothy, Watford, wid., to John, son, Inv. £7.15.9¼ 1718/6
HANCE, Thomas, Oxenden, to William, father, 1759/23 July
HANCOCK, George, Woodford cum Membris, weaver, Inv.only £36.6.6 1713/1 A
Handcock, William, Edgecote, carpenter, Inv.only £98.5. 1714/55 A
Handcock, Jonathan, Welton, pauper, Inv.only £2.11. 1715/34 A
Thomas, West Cotton, Hardingstone, yeo., Inv.only £337.11.0 1717/56 A
John, Wootton, Inv.only £13.8.0 1727/404
Richard, Woodford cum Membris, weaver, to Job, weaver, son, 1745/12 Oct.
Thomas, Chalcombe, to Thomas, son, 1800/13 May
HANDS, John, Preston Capes, butcher, to Judith, wid., mother, 1786/10 May
Thomas, Newbold, Catesby, to Sarah, wid., 1792/9 Apr.
HANGER, Eleanor, Ringstead, wid., to John Morton, yeo., brother, Inv. £8.15.6 1711/151
HANSON, Thomas, Northampton, to Thomas, son, Inv. £17.5.0 1716/122
HANWELL, Christopher, Bozeat, to Paul, Bromham, Beds., husb., son, Inv. £18.11.0 William and Christopher, sons, exors., renounced, Will, 1718/81
William, Bozeat, to Sarah, wife of George Browne, mason, daughter, Inv. £26.13.6 1750/19 May
Thomas, Long Buckby, woolcomber, to Samuel Thompson, Daventry, fellmonger, creditor, Hannah, wid., renounced, 1769/12 June
HARBERT, Herbert, Robert, Northampton, innholder, Account of Anne, wid., admin., £204.12.7 1677/70
Herbert, Henry, Rushden, lacebuyer, to Elizabeth Palmer, principal creditor, wid., Mary, wid., renounced, Inv. £124.8.6 1713/133
Herbert, William, Dallington, to Thomas, brother, Inv. £18.7.0½ 1717/110
Herbert, William, Dallington, to John, cordwainer, brother, 1718/78
Herbert, Samuel, Navesby, yeo., to Richard, husb., brother, 1728/10 Apr.
Samuel, Navesby, yeo., Inv.only £595.14.6 1728/228
Harbord, John, Stowe Nine Churches, yeo., to Rebecca, wid., Inv. £656.13.0 1734/26 Oct.
John, Stowe Nine Churches, Inv.only £656.13.0 1734/330
John, Stowe, to John, yeo., son, of goods unadministered by Rebecca, wid., decd., 1748/25 Mar.
John, Long Buckby, joiner, to Mary, Yelvertoft, spin., sister, 1759/7 Mar.
Herbert, John, Ravensthorpe, to Samuel Shipley and Mary Shipley, wife, and Sarah, all of Kibworth Beauchamp, co. Leic., 1769/11 Dec.
Herbert, John, Stowe Nine Churches, to Rebecca, wife of John Pinkard, Farthingstone, gent., daughter, of goods not fully administered by Rebecca, wid., decd., and John, son, decd., 1780/19 Feb.
Herbert, Ann, Welford, to Samuel, butcher, husband, 1788/2 Jan.
HARDEMAN, William, Grimscote, Cold Higham, to John, farmer, brother, Hannah, mother, renounced, 1762/10 July
HARDING, Catherine, Brackley, wid., to Samuel, chandler, father and guardian of Matthew, minor, exor., Inv. £17.4.6 Will, 1714/160
Robert, Grafton Regis, clerk, to Rachel, wid., 1790/17 Aug.
HARDY, Hardey, Thomas, Braunston, to Elizabeth, wid., 1778/29 Aug.
HARGREAVES, Rev. John, Cranford St. Andrew, clerk, to Rachel, wid., Inv. £16.16.0 1761/3 July
Robert, Cranford St. Andrew, cabinet maker, to John, Bidford, co. Warwick, officer of excise, 1762/27 Sept.
HARLOCK, John, Finedon, shopkeeper, to Samuel and Joseph, labs., brothers, Anne Bates, wid., mother, renounced, 1729/24 June
HARRIOTT, Harriatt, Francis, Wellingborough, Account of Grace, wid., admin., £40.5.8 1679/43
Edward, Helmdon, gent., to Anne, wid., 1729/9 Oct.
HARRIS, Daniel, Weston Favell, Account of Sarah, wid., admin., £149.17.2 1680/3
John, Welton, Account of Elizabeth, wife of Robert Smith, sister, admin., £49.18.6 1680/28

HARRIS continued
Thomas, Pattishall, to Sarah, wid., Inv. £75.15.2 1711/61
John, Lower Heyford, to Alice, wid., Inv. £16.2.0 1711/86
John, Crick, Inv.only £16.10.0 1713/30A
George, Woodford, husb., Inv.only £87.18.6 1713/140A
George, Woodford, husb., Inv.only £87.18.6 1713/71
William, Duston, to Martha, wid., Inv. £136.3.2 1713/141
Anne, wid., Inv.only £49.5.0 1714/12A
Thomas, Duston, joiner, to Alice, wid., Will, 1714/61
John, Inv.only £334.16.0 1714/140A
John, senior, Lower Boddington, Inv.only 1714/156A
Daniel, Overstone, Inv.only £22.5.0 1715/56A
John, Harlestone, to William, Bradwell, Bucks., lab., brother, Inv. £78.9.10 1715/98
William, Great Billing, husb., to Thomas Dawson, Kettering, innholder, guardian of William Dawson, minor, son, exor., Inv. £323.6.6 Will, Guard. of William Dawson, 1717/13 and 14
James, Byfield, yeo., to Anne, wid., Inv. £323.9.0 1717/50
William, Green's Norton, to Alice, wid., 1717/122
Richard, Kislingbury, to Dorothy Folwell, wid., sister, Inv. £433.12.0 1718/21
John, Duston, to Anne, wid., Inv. £303.12.0 1718/70
William, Towcester, Guard.only of William, minor, son, 1718/101
William, Towcester, to Elizabeth, wife of Thomas Lawton, daughter, 1719/106
Sarah, Crick, wid., Inv.only £22.10.0 1720/66A
Sarah, Kislingbury, to Mary, Floore, spin., daughter, 1720/101
Richard, Preston Deanery, to Anne, wid., 1721/66
William, Weston Favell, to Elizabeth, wid., 1721/97
Anne, Harpole, wid., Inv.only £35.12.0 1722/28A
Thomas, Eydon, Inv.only £54.2.0 1724/159A
John, Yardley Gobion, Potterspury, Inv.only £7.5.0 1727/196
Christopher, Yardley Gobion, yeo., Inv.only £205.10.0 1727/197
William, Great Harrowden, husb., to Mary, wid., 1729/15 Apr.
William, Great Harrowden, Inv.only £203.1.10 undated/25
Mary, Spratton, spin., to Henry, Sibbertoft, butcher, 1729/9 May
Elizabeth, Easton Maudit, to John, lab., husband, 1729/1 Aug.
James, Duston, lab., to Mary, wid., 1729/18 Oct.
John, Great Billing, bonesetter, to Henry Lowth, Abington, gent., principal creditor, Inv. £78.11.10 1732/5 Mar.
John, Preston Deanery, farmer, to Sarah, wid., Inv. £79.6.6 1733/11 Aug.
Mary, Great Harrowden, wid., to John, yeo., 1734/23 Apr.
John, Preston, Guard.only of Anne and John, minors, children, 1734/14 Sept.
Mary, Boddington, to Elizabeth, wife of Thomas Jeffcutt, Fenny Compton, co. Oxford, sister, 1735/7 Aug.
Robert, Yardley Gobion, to Thomas, maltster, son, 1737/2 Apr.
John, Boddington, lab., to Job Woodfield, lab., of goods not fully administered by Elizabeth Wills, daughter, exor., Will, 1737/12 Nov.
Richard, Potterspury, to Mary Savage, Whittlebury, wid., daughter, of goods unadministered by Mary, wid., decd., 1739/19 Feb.
Thomas, Weston Favell, yeo., to Elizabeth, wid., 1741/8 Apr.
George, Woodford cum Membris, Will proved by Ann, wid., exor., 1744/7 Jan.
William, Blisworth, cordwainer, to Anne, wid., 1753/14 July
John, Bozenham Mill, Hartwell, miller, to Sarah, wid., Inv. £32.8.7½ 1766/12 Aug.
John, Daventry, cooper, to John, cooper, son, 1774/23 Apr.
Robert, Staverton, to Jane, wid., 1784/16 Nov.
Robert, Northampton, victualler, to Elizabeth, wid., 1787/5 May
Richard, Staverton, yeo., to Sarah, wid., mother, 1798/1 Feb.
Elizabeth, Denshanger, Passenham, Inv.only £2.2.0 undated/310
Mary, Inv.only £8.16.0 undated/411

HARRISON, Charles, Ringstead, Inv.only £8.17.6 1713/31A
Samuel, Wellingborough, Inv.only £12.7.7 1713/73A
Edward, Wellingborough, grocer, Inv.only £219.12.7¾ 1717/77A
James, Raunds, tailor, Inv.only £12.6.0 1722/45A
Robert, Great Cransley, to Elizabeth, wid., Inv. £36.9.0 1724/11
William, Northampton, innholder, to Elizabeth, wid., 1729/14 July

HARROLD, Margaret, Yardley Gobion, wid., to Charles, Cosgrave, gardener, son in law, 1736/18 Mar.
Harrald, Richard, elder, Welford, miller, to Sarah, wid., Inv. £103.15.6 1748/3 Dec.
Sarah, Welford, wid., to Richard, miller, principal creditor, Sarah, daughter, renounced, Will, 1770/26 June
Harrald, John, Welford, miller, to Mary, wid., 1793/22 May
HART, John, Brackley, blacksmith, to Dorothy, wid., Inv. £95.19.0 1711/6
Thomas, senior, Silverstone, Inv.only £51.10.0 1716/86A
John, Farndon, Woodford, to Awdrey, wid., 1723/120
John, Inv.only £111.14.10 1723/119
Anthony, Hinton, yeo., to Job, farmer, son, 1753/23 June
Samuel, Brackley, blacksmith, to William Thomas, gent., trustee of Susannah Leaper, wid., decd., principal creditor, Elizabeth, wid., renounced, 1759/15 Feb.
Thomas, Pattishall, tailor, to Thomas, miller, son, 1786/11 May
HARTOP, Hartup, Thomas, senior, Newnham, Inv.only £38.0.0 1728/257
John, Badby, carpenter, Inv.only £29.9.6 1733/321
Hartopp, Thomas, Newnham, to Thomas, grazier, and William Harding, yeo., nephews, 1780/18 Nov.
Thomas, Newnham, gent., to Elizabeth Harding, Great Horwood, Bucks., spin., niece, Will, 1783/4 Jan.
HARTSHORNE, Mary, Ravensthorpe, to John, yeo., husband, 1720/64
HASELDEN, Hasledine, Robert, Rothwell, blacksmith, to Sarah, wid., Inv. £22.2.0 1718/140
HASLEWOOD, Ann, Chalcombe, to Elizabeth, Warwick, spin., daughter, 1781/19 Nov.
Hazlewood, Nehemiah, Newnham, to John, yeo., son, 1794/31 Oct.
HASLOCK, William, Northampton, butcher, to Samuel, brother, 1784/5 Feb.
HASTINGS, Richard, Welford, gent., Inv.only 1714/193A
HAWES, Edward, Old Brackley, Inv.only £6.12.6 1718/110A
Thomas, Wellingborough, to Mary, wid., 1761/4 May
HAWGOOD, Robert, Little Harrowden, yeo., Account of Joan, wid., admin., £259.0.6 1678/84
Allgood, William, Inv.only £30.0.0 1728/237
Thomas, Silverstone, woodman, to Thomas, woodman, son, Martha, wid., renounced, 1755/11 Jan.
HAWKES, Stephen, Kingsthorpe, to Anne, wid., 1716/109
Anne, Kingsthorpe, wid., to Elizabeth, spin., daughter, 1723/37
Elizabeth, Earl's Barton, to Mary Hasledine, sister, 1735/27 Jan.
Richard, Chipping Warden, miller, to Mary, wid., Inv. £20.17.6 1736/27 Oct.
Frances, Hulcote, spin., to Joseph Lucas, lab., nephew, of goods unadministered by Anne, wife of Joseph Lucas, decd., niece, 1752/9 Apr.
Edward, Chipping Warden, miller, to Richard, miller, son, 1786/24 Mar.
HAWKINS, William, Wappenham, to Susannah, wid., Inv. £20.8.0 1714/116
William, Green's Norton, Inv.only £6.10.4 1717/148 A
Anne, Aynho, wid., to William, weaver, son, 1723/110
Anne, Aynho, wid., Inv.only £24.14.0 1723/110
Mary, Spratton, wid., to William, Great Creaton, surgeon, son, 1767/28 Aug.
William, Spratton, to William King, Northampton, grocer, principal creditor, 1773/1 Apr.
HAWLEY, John, Paulerspury, to Anne, wid., Inv. £27.4.6 1726/5 Mar.
John, Paulerspury, carpenter, to James, carpenter, son, Sarah, wid., renounced, Inv. £105.7.0 1735/22 Mar.
William, Paulerspury, to Elizabeth, wid., 1756/10 July
HAWORTH, Richard, Wellingborough, Account of Elizabeth, wid., admin., £93.13.4 1681/75
Mary, Creaton, wid., to Ann, wife of John Tarry, yeo., sister, 1723/15
HAYCOCK, Jonathan, Hellidon, to Thomas, yeo., 1714/149
HAYES, Thomas, Rothwell, to Phebe, Inv. £10.7.4 1712/15
Thomas, Rector of Old, clerk, to Elizabeth Rock, wid., sister, 1740/5 Mar.
HAYNES, Robert, Hinton, shepherd, Inv.only £11.0.0 1715/101A
Robert, Culworth, lab., to Eleanor, wid., Inv. £107.8.0 1716/49
Henry, Helmdon, husb., to Ruth, wid., 1729/24 July
Philip, Adstone, to John, farmer, son, 1770/10 Nov.
John, Norton, to Mary, 1791/11 Oct.

HAYRICK, Arthur, Denton, Inv.only £54.8.2 1715/49A
HAYWARD, Weedon Beck, yeo., Inv.only £622.12.0 1723/18A
HAYWORTH, Thomas, White Chapel, co. Middx., gent., to Elizabeth, wife of Thomas Brighting, Brighton, Kislingbury, yeo., sister, Joseph Stratford, gent., exor., renounced, Will, 1767/14 Nov.
HEALY, Nathaniel, Marston St. Lawrence, to Catherine, spin., sister, 1758/21 Aug.
HEARN, Thomas South, Brackley, maltster, to Mary, wid., 1778/24 Oct.
HEARTWELL, Hartwell, Francis, Wollaston, to Francis, Ringstead, yeo., son, 1720/44
John, Overthorpe, Middleton Cheney, to Alice, wid., 1787/19 Sept.
HEATH, Richard, Chipping Warden, Account of Isabell, wid., admin., £296.16.10 1672/103
HEATHER, John, Potterspury, to John, servant, son, 1728/10 Nov.
HEDGES, Thomas, Middleton Cheney, to John, Fawscutt, Bucks., yeo., Guard. of Elizabeth Sutton, minor, niece, 1721/98 and 99
Thomas, Gayton, to Mary, wid., 1722/6
Michael, Tiffield, to Anne, wid., 1728/27 Jan.
Michael, Tiffield, Inv.only £58.2.6 1728/203
Hedge, George, Northampton, to Samuel, cordwianer, brother, 1773/24 Dec.
Hedge, Thomas, Roade, baker, to John, baker, son, 1794/8 Nov.
HEFFORD, William, Northampton, mason, to Mary, wife of George Watkin, Wellingborough, flaxdresser, aunt and guardian of John, Charles, William, Ann, Samuel, Elizabeth and Stephen, minors, children, 1781/9 Oct.
HEMERY, Thomas, Great Houghton, Inv.only £8.6.0 1711/114A
HEMMINGS, Mary, Daventry, milliner, to Francis Zouch, Warwick, linendraper, principal creditor, Samuel, perukemaker, husband, renounced, 1763/3 Sept.
Peter, Moreton Pinkney, to Elizabeth, 1769/13 May
HENFREY, Edward, Crick, miller, to Anne, wid., Inv. £13.11.0 1711/123
HENLEY, Edward, Little Billing, to Mary, wid., Inv. £219.5.0 1713/2
HENMAN, John, Little Harrowden, to Hannah, wid., Inv. £267.16.0 1771/16 Jan.
HENSHAW, John, Roade, yeo., to Stephen Hoe, Tilsworth, co. Bedford, clerk, son, 1765/25 Apr.
HENSMAN, William, Wellingborough, Guard. of Elizabeth and Dorothy, minors, daughters, Inv. £675.19.6 1711/70 and 73
Henchman, William, Broughton, to Grace, wid., 1720/103
Henchman, Grace, Broughton, spin., to Anne, and Elizabeth, spins., sisters, Grace, wid., mother, renounced, 1722/49
Henshman, Mary, Wellingborough, spin., to Elizabeth, wife of John Worlidge, gent., sister, 1730/7 Apr.
Henchman, Henry, Wellingborough, to Ann, wife of Samuel Ward, draper, daughter, 1732/5 Oct.
William, Little Addington, to Judith, wid., now wife of Giles Abbott, husb., Inv. £9.6.4 1732/5 Oct.
Joseph, Little Houghton, to Hannah, wid., Inv. £285.8.6 1744/16 Oct.
Edmund, Earl's Barton, baker, to Anne, wid., Inv. £39.10.0 1749/4 Feb.
Joseph, Little Houghton, to Thomas, Earl's Barton, baker, son, of goods unadministered by Edmund, son, decd., 1765/24 Oct.
Hannah, Northampton, wid., to George Cliff, joiner, and Joseph Smith, butcher, guardians of George and Sarah Harris, minors, grandchildren, 1767/15 Apr.
HENSON, Thomas, Guard.only of Thomas, minor, 1712/82
John, Abthorpe, Towcester, Inv.only £127.17.6 1720/104A
Henry, Irchester, butcher, to Mary, wid., Inv. £111.6.4 1723/48
Henry, Irchester, to Mary, wid., 1724/118
William, Wappenham, to Sarah, wid., 1728/11 June
Richard, Towcester, Inv.only £13.3.11 1730/279
Robert, Pattishall, shoemaker and cordwainer, to Mary, wid., Inv. £14.7.3 1744/19 May
Andrew, Clipston, cordwainer, to Ann, wife of James Allen, weaver, and Sarah, wife of Thomas Brown, Dalscote, Pattishall, tailor, daughters, 1748/27 Aug.
Sarah, Abthorpe, to Elizabeth, wife of Edward Green, dairyman, niece, 1780/2 Nov.
George, Slapton, to Jane, wid., 1796/5 Nov.
HERBAGE, William, Chalcombe, yeo., to William, yeo., son, 1764/5 Nov.
HERBERT see HARBERT

HERITAGE, Henry, John, Chalcombe, to Hannah, wid., Inv. £208.16.0 1723/52
John, Chalcombe, to Richard Whitton, Westbury, Bucks., butcher, 1728/22 Oct.
John, Chalcombe, Inv.only £53.12.6 undated/214
als. Bennett, Hannah, Chalcombe, to John, yeo., husband, 1744/24 Mar.
HEWES see HUGHES
HERRING, Thomas, Middleton Cheney, Inv.only £33.9.4 1711/92A
John, Middleton Cheney, to Mary, wid., 1759/30 June
HEWITT, Robert, Lilbourne, butcher, to Anne, wid., Inv. £79.1.1 Will, 1721/136
Richard, Kingsthorpe, miller, to Elizabeth, wid., 1728/23 Aug.
Huit, Richard, East Haddon, husb., Inv.only £15.9.0 1737/341
Thomas, elder, Welford, to Thomas, weaver, son, Will, 1745/20 Apr.
HEWLETT, Thomas, All Saints, Northampton, to Thomas, cordwainer, son, Inv. £18.14.3 1716/11
HEWSON, Nathaniel, Kettering, draper, Inv.only £1244.3.8½ 1722/137A
HEYCOCK, John, Sulgrave, yeo., to John, yeo., son, Inv. £30.0.0 1730/15 Aug.
HEYFORD, Robert, Welford, to Mary, wid., 1776/16 Feb.
HEYRICK, Richard, Hackleton, to Christian, wid., 1723/71
Richard, Hackleton, innholder, Inv.only £31.17.0 1723/102
HEYWORTH, William, Yardley Hastings, to Elizabeth, wid., Inv. £13.8.2 1713/19
HICKMAN, Nathaniel, Newnham, to Elizabeth, wid., Will, Inv. £19.9.0 1711/88
Henry, elder, Newnham, yeo., Inv.only £935.10.0 1712/31A
Matthew, Newnham, to Sarah, wid., Inv. £30.5.0 1712/77
John, Ravensthorpe, yeo., Inv.only £234.10.4 1716/135A
Hitchman, Hichman, Henry, Upper Boddington, to Alice, wid., Inv. £124.8.0 1719/40
Henry, Newnham, turner, to Richard, shoemaker, brother, 1729/27 June
Richard, Newnham, shoemaker, to Nathaniel, tanner, principal creditor, Inv. £63.13.4 Elizabeth, wid., renounced in favour Anne Goodman or Nathaniel, 1730/2 May
Francis, Ravensthorpe, to Elizabeth, wid., and Thomas, yeo., son, 1752/4 Apr.
Francis, Inv.only £101.2.0 1752/414
Nathaniel, Newnham, to Elizabeth, wid., 1772/23 May
John, Newnham, baker, to Anne, wid., 1781/29 Sept.
Mary, Ravensthorpe, wid., to Charles Haygate, West Haddon, gent., creditor, 1790/12 Apr.
als. Checkley, Sarah, see Checkley
HICKS, als. Broome, Mary, to Richard, Warwick, cordwainer, husband, 1736/23 Mar.
William, Isham, fuller, to Elizabeth, wid., 1738/18 Nov.
HIDE see HYDE
HIGGINBOTTOM, John, Kingsthorpe, carpenter, to Sarah, wid., Inv. £18.19.2 1729/16 June
HIGGINS, Thomas, Great Houghton, Inv.only £18.2.6 1713/136A
Esther, Northampton, wid., to Elizabeth Hall, Brackley, wid., 1761/13 May
John, Wappenham, to Priscilla, wife of Joseph Reding, Redding, Chargrave, co. Bedford, innholder, sister, 1761/21 Aug.
John, Wappenham, tailor, to Priscilla, wife of Joseph Reding, Hockley, co. Bedford, innholder, sister, Will, 1763/22 Mar.
Sarah, Blakesley, wid., to Sarah, Cogenhoe, wid., daughter in law, 1774/19 Feb.
Thomas, Wellingborough, to Sarah, wid., 1789/25 Feb.
Ann, Kingsthorpe, spin., to Ren, innholder, 1797/23 Jan.
Daniel, Little Houghton, victualler, to John Pell, Cogenhoe, farmer, and Samuel Mackaness, creditors, Elizabeth, wid., renounced, 1800/20 Dec.
HIGGS, Francis, Syresham, to Elizabeth, wid., Inv. £11.9.0 1723/70
HIGHAM, Hyam, Elizabeth, Wellingborough, wid., to Thomas Robinson, turner, nephew, Inv. £31.5.5½ Anne Holyoak, wid., and Susanna Robinson, spin., sisters, renounced, 1729/25 Mar.
Hiam, William, Welford, lab., to John, lab., son, 1770/9 June
Edward, Blakesley, shepherd, to David, butcher, brother, Ann, niece, exor., decd., Will, 1771/10 June
Elizabeth, Wilby, to Mary Fisher, wid., sister, 1788/5 Nov.

HILL, John, Walgrave, yeo., Inv.only £96.14.6 1711/11 A
Hills, Joseph, Walgrave, Guard.only of Elizabeth, minor, daughter, 1713/67
John, Byfield, Inv.only £17.5.3 1713/77 A
John, Towcester, dyer, Inv.only £690.10.0 1713/144 A
John, Gayton, Inv.only £112.0.0 1714/61 A
Hills, Nathaniel, Loddington, Inv.only £434.18.8 1715/83 A
Susanna, Rothwell, spin., to Agnes, spin., sister, Susanna, wid., mother, renounced, 1715/136
Hills, John, Raunds, husb., Inv.only £37.4.0 1718/57 A
Hills, Richard, Hannington, husb., Inv.only £326.4.0 1719/59 A
Hills, William, Walgrave, Inv.only £131.13.6 1720/24 A
Elizabeth, Wellingborough, wid., to John, collarmaker, son, 1720/117
William, Wollaston, shepherd, Inv.only £1.6.0 1721/44 A
Hills, Lewis, Woodford, Inv.only £45.18.2 1724/44 A
Hills, Amy, Walgrave, wid., to Thomas, lab., son, Inv. £2.19.0 1725/19 Oct.
Mary, Inv.only £16.6.9 1727/156
Hills, Anne, Hannington, wid., to William Husb., son, 1728/18 Apr.
Hills, William, Walgrave, yeo., to John Hodgskins, Weldon, gent., husband and admin. of Jane, wife, decd., daughter and exor., Will, 1729/8 Feb.
Sarah, Rothwell, spin., to John Robinson, Cransley, and Wheeler Brooke, Great Oakley, Susan, wid., mother, renounced, Will, 1730/9 July
Joseph, Loddington, to John, gent., brother, 1732/12 May
Elizabeth, Byfield, wid., to Anne Garner, spin., sister, 1734/26 Apr.
William, Helmdon, to Jonathan, Bicester, co. Oxford, lab., brother, 1745/4 Sept.
Francis, Rothwell, to Dorothea, wid., 1745/22 Nov.
John, Helmdon, lab., Guard.only of Mary, minor, daughter, 1751/27 Apr.
Hills, John, Wollaston, shepherd, to Ann, wid., Will, 1754/23 Oct.
Elizabeth, Rothwell, wid., to Mary Umfreville, wid., daughter, Inv. £126.18.3½ Account of Mary, 1755/1 Sept.
Hills, John, Hannington, to Elizabeth, wid., 1762/5 Aug.
Anne, Northampton, to William, victualler, son, 1771/21 May
Hills, John, Moulton, victualler, to Mary, wid., 1781/3 Dec.
Hills, John, elder, Towcester, dyer, to Henry, Heathencote, Paulerspury, farmer, brother, Will, 1787/3 Jan.
Thomas, Northampton, victualler, to Elizabeth, wid., 1788/16 Sept.
Rev. John, Thorpe Malsor, clerk, to Elizabeth, wid., Inv. £706.18.6 1793/13 May
William, Hardingstone, butcher, to Mary, wid., 1797/18 July
HILLIER, Margaret, Old Stratford, to Luke Parrott, co. Surrey, chapman, 1715/92
Hillyer, Thomas, Courtenhall, to Mary, wid., 1740/31 May
HILLYARD, Jasper, Courtenhall, husb., Inv.only £236.0.0 1723/116
Hilliard, John, Courtenhall, to Ellenor, wid., 1726/27 June
William, Courtenhall, to Robert Vaux, clerk, Thomas Dunkley, hillier and plasterer, and Joseph Shaw, farmer, Will, 1763/31 July
HILTON, Joseph, Little Harrowden, shoemaker, to William, yeo., son, Inv. £38.17.0 1722/79
Thomas, clerk, Vicar of Brackley, to Kezia, wife of John Browne, clerk, daughter, 1729/6 Aug.
Mark, Helmdon, to Rebecca, wid., 1737/3 Oct.
HINCKLEY, John, Cottesbrooke, Account of Dorothy Slatyer als. Hinckley, admin., £116.5.0 1671/132
HINDE, William, Hellidon, gent., to William, Priors Hardwick, co. Warwick, son, Inv. £30.17.0 1732/1 Mar.
Elizabeth, Cold Ashby, to Richard, gent., husband, 1732/12 Apr.
Hind, William, Hartwell, blacksmith, to James Miller, Northampton, grocer, principal creditor, 1782/28 Jan.
Hind, Mary, Kirkby, Ireleth, Lancashire, wid., to Henry, Liverpool, co. Lancashire, shipwright, son, 1783/16 Aug.
Hindes, Ann, Staverton, spin., to John Reynolds, Daventry, victualler, cousin, 1786/10 Mar.
HINKES, Henry, Inv.only £38.2.0 1728/240
HINSON, William, Whittlebury, to Anne, wid., Inv. £43.14.0 1717/72
William, Towcester, victualler, Inv.only £33.16.6 1721/39 A
John, Wicken, to William, son, 1767/21 Nov.

HIPWELL, John, Kilsby, husb., to Anne, wid., Inv. £57.14.6 1717/71
HIRONS, Thomas, Eydon, to Alice, 1777/20 Jan.
HITCHCOCK, Mary, Woodford, wid., Inv.only £1.3.6 1712/27A
William, Orchard Leas, Chipping Warden, Inv.only £104.0.0 1713/124A
Thomas, Sywell, Guard.only of Martha, minor, daughter, 1714/178
John, Woodford, to Mary, wid., 1717/102
Hithccocke, John, Newton Bromswold, yeo., to Mary, wid., Inv. £750.19.6 1751/17 Sept.
Mary, Newton Bromswold, wid., to Daniel, Hail Weston, Hunts., yeo., son, Inv. £90.6.0 1755/22 July
Sarah, Byfield, wid., to Thomas, farmer, son, 1776/16 May
Hitchcox, Richard, Middleton Cheney, to Mary, daughter, 1794/19 Apr.
Elizabeth, Byfield, wid., to William Odams, son in law, Will, 1796/8 Apr.
HOARE, Thomas, senior, Green's Norton, shepherd, Inv.only £28.5.0 1714/23A
William, Green's Norton, to Thomas, husb., brother, 1714/68
Robert, Yardley Gobion, Inv.only £19.8.10 1744/397
William, Maidford, baker, to Susanna, wid., 1783/13 Oct.
HOBBS, Thomas, Wicken, farmer, to William, and Susannah Mann, 1756/28 June
Elizabeth, Wappenham, wid., to William Roberts, cordwainer, cousin, 1764/27 Jan.
James, Wellingborough, thatcher, to John Randall, shoemaker, exor. of Mary, exor., decd., Will, 1798/17 Oct.
HOBEY, Richard, Kilsby, carpenter, to Thomas, carpenter, son, Inv. £19.1.0 1711/110
Richard, Pytchley, to Ann, wid., Inv. £6.0.0 1722/131
William, Faxton Lodge, Inv.only £145.14.8 1723/86 A
Richard, Clipston, shoemaker, to Mary, wid., Inv. £26.8.6 1725/27 Feb.
Hoby, Mary, Clipston, Inv.only £11.18.11 1732/294
Hoby, Samuel, Faxton, Inv.only £206.0.0 1734/305
Hobly, Ann, Daventry, to John, innkeeper, husband, 1766/5 July
William, Spratton, to Alice, wid., 1781/9 June
HOBSON, Thomas, Wellingborough, Account of Elizabeth, wid., admin., £33.9.11 1675/55
Thomas, Sywell, Inv.only £13.10.0 1712/6 A
Mary, Cottesbrooke, spin., to Susannah, wid., mother, 1743/20 Sept.
Elizabeth, Stoke Bruerne, wid., to Eleanor, wife of John Webster, daughter, Will, 1757/4 May
George, Spratton, farmer, yeo., to Elizabeth, wid., Guard. of George, minor, son, 1788/29 Aug.
George, Spratton, farmer, to William Brown, grocer, and John Wright, yeo., guardians of George, Mary, Elizabeth and Thomas, minors, children, of goods unadministered by Elizabeth, wid., decd., Guard., 1790/28 Jan.
HOCKNELL, John, Northampton, shoemaker, to Elizabeth, wid., 1731/11 Oct.
HODGES, Thomas, Roade, lab., Inv.only £18.16.0 1714/113 A
Hodge, William, Long Buckby, weaver, Inv.only £31.8.10 1723/64 A
Hodge, William, Long Buckby, to Mary, wid., and William, yeo., son, 1739/20 Oct.
Mary, Kettering, wid., to Joseph Arnold, Burton Latimer, maltster, Will, 1746/27 Feb.
Samuel, Kettering, weaver, to John Rowlett, Geddington, grocer, principal creditor, Frances, wid., renounced in favour Mary Rogers, Oundle, wid., a principal creditor, 1755/12 Aug.
James, Northampton, to Sarah, wid., 1774/12 Dec.
HODGKIN, Hodgskin, Thomas, Hackleton, Account of Catherine, wid., admin., £46.6.2 1679/38
John, Piddington, Inv.only £19.1.0 1711/101 A
Hodgskin, Frances, Roade, wid., Inv.only £4.15.0 1715/17 A
Edward, Northampton, mason, to Anne, wid., Inv. £53.17.8 1716/22
Robert, Hackleton, yeo., to Mary, wid., Inv. £63.4.6 1716/101
HOE, Stephen, Hyde, Roade, Inv.only £37.10.0 1714/20 A
HOGG, Francis, Little Preston, gent., to Thomas Farren, Ascott, Warwick, gent., father and guardian of Thomas, minor, grandson, Inv. £27.4.0 Guard. of Thomas Farren, 1721/22 and 23
HOLDICH, Francis, East Haddon, gent., to Richard Lawrence, Northumberland Street, St. Marylebone, co. Middx., carver, and Edward Johnson, Leicester Square, St. Ann, Westminster, confectioner, exors., Elizha, St. Marylebone, victualler, son, exor., decd., Will, 1792/16 May
HOLDING, Elizabeth, Syresham, spin., to John, Brackley, bricklayer, brother, 1724/29

HOLLIDAY, James, Hollowell, servant, to Thomas Cleaver Holliday, father, farmer, 1800/18 Oct.

HOLLIS, Jane, Towcester, to Elizabeth and Mary Spilsworth, spins., 1711/147

John, West Haddon, Inv.only £93.1.10 1719/122A

Richard, Kingsthorpe, Inv.only £211.2.6 1720/148A

James, Woodford, Thrapston, to William, husb., brother, guardian of Thomas, Elizabeth, and Alice, minors, children, Inv. £143.17.6 Judith, wid., renounced, Guard., 1723/139 and 140

John, Kilsby, to Elizabeth, wid., Inv. £27.13.0 1724/76

James, Woodford, Thrapston, Account of William, brother, principal creditor, admin., £235.0.7 1724/144

William, Woodford, to Bridget, wid., Inv. £180.15.0 1727/12 July

William, Murcott, Long Buckby, husb., to Mary, wid., 1728/1 Feb.

John, Barby, yeo., shepherd, to Margaret, wid., Inv. £37.14.0 1731/18 Mar.

John, Kilsby, yeo., to Mary, wid., 1733/25 Aug.

Elizabeth, Boughton, to John, son, 1775/28 Oct.

William, Braunston, to Thomas, surgeon, brother, 1778/27 Apr.

Mary, Northampton, wid., to Catherine Hollick, Creaton, wid., sister, 1781/22 Feb.

George, Bozeat, lab., to Martha, wid., Will, 1784/27 Feb.

HOLLOWAY, Margaret, Chalcombe, wid., to Martha Heritage, daughter, Inv. £17.3.0 1712/80

George, Aston le Walls, to Elizabeth Moor, Syresham, wid., daughter, 1713/48

Thomas, Green's Norton, to Mary, wid., 1726/1 Oct.

John, Northampton, innholder, to Jane, wid., 1726/28 Dec.

Philip, Whitfield, to John, Turweston, Bucks., miller, uncle and guardian of Elizabeth, Jane, and William, minors, children, 1737/15 Apr.

HOLLOWELL, Edward, Faxton, Account of Alice, wid., admin., £149.0.0 1680/19

Francis, Faxton, Lamport, Inv.only £160.0.0 1711/98A

Mary, Bugbrooke, spin., Inv.only £8.18.6 1713/41A

William, Daventry, lab., Inv.only £56.3.0 1724/93A

James, Brafield, husb., to Anne, wid., 1727/11 Mar.

James, junior, Brafield on the Green, Inv.only £159.15.0 1727/153

William, Everdon, to Samuel, Daventry, husb., brother, 1760/29 Sept.

HOLLYOAKE, Thomas, Rushden, bachelor, to Samuel Manning, husb., 1720/33

HOLLYWELL, Thomas, Daventry, to Mary Fennell, daughter, 1714/150

HOLMAN, Richard, Brixworth, Account of Joan, wid., admin., £582.12.0 1682/74

HOLMER, William, Middleton Cheney, tailor, to Elizabeth Franklin, wid., daughter, admin. of goods unadministered by Sarah, wid., exor., Will, 1783/3 Apr.

Sarah, Middleton Cheney, wid., to Elizabeth Franklin, wid., daughter, 1783/3 Apr.

HOLMES, William, Burton Latimer, to Anne, wid., mother, 1714/131

William, Kettering, saddler, Inv.only £27.14.4 1716/71A

Anne, Burton Latimer, wid., to Richard, and John, sons, Inv. £13.8.7 1719/11

Richard, Burton Latimer, Inv.only £274.13.2 1719/98A

John, Burton Latimer, to Mary, wid., 1768/5 Aug.

HOLT, William, Whiston, Inv.only £52.10.0 1720/153A

Robert, Hackleton, innholder, to Jane, wid., 1744/1 Dec.

John, Brixworth, cordwainer, to Mary, wid., Inv. £12.12.5 1747/30 June

HOLTON, Francis, Potterspury, dealer in hogs, to Anne, wid., 1785/24 July

HOMAN, Edward, Aynho, grazier, to William Richard Lawrence, of goods unadministered by Ann Homan, exor., mother of William, Will, 1798/1 May

HONOUR, Matthew, Northampton, blacksmith, to Seth, wid., Inv. £11.12.10 1719/125

John, Stoke Bruerne, victualler, to John White, yeo., and John Campion, Shutlanger, yeo., Will, 1778/19 Sept.

HOOK, William, Little Billing, to William, innholder, son, 1737/4 June

HOOPER, Thomas, Wellingborough, to Robert, woolcomber, son, 1742/7 July

HOOTON see HOUGHTON

HOPKINS, John, Burton Latimer, Account of Richard, and Thomas Langley, exors., £1435.7.8 undated/148

HOPKINS continued
John, Norton, Account of Margery, wid., mother, principal creditor, £150.0.9 1680/39
Richard, Sibbertoft, weaver, to John, Husbands Bosworth, co. Leic., weaver, and Richard Somes, Haslebech, weaver, guardians of Richard, minor, son, Inv. £14.4.3 1713/56
Henry, Heyford, Stowe, yeo., to Elizabeth, wife of Thomas Arnold, husb., sister, Inv. £33.9.0 Will, 1714/93
Mary, Yelvertoft, wid., Inv.only £37.11.0 1721/17
Alice, Inv.only £67.17.0 1728/245
Daniel, Moreton Pinkeney, yeo., to Elizabeth Chapman, Nobottle, wid., daughter, 1732/2 Dec.
William, Stanwick, to Rose, wid., 1744/18 Apr.
Joseph, Long Buckby, to John Dagley, Daventry, soapboiler, creditor, 1752/8 Apr.
John, Silverstone, Green's Norton, lab., to Mary, wid., Robert, brother, renounced, Will, 1752/9 May
HOPPER, Hannah, Burton Latimer, wid., Inv.only £18.1.6 1716/70A
HORNBY, Joseph, Brafield, yeo., to Hannah, wid., 1745/19 Oct.
HORNE, Richard, Newnham, Inv.only £27.0.5 1715/37A
William, Weedon Beck, yeo., Inv.only £42.3.11 1715/40A
Thomas, Denshanger, Passenham, lab., to Anne, wid., 1729/17 Feb.
Martha, Wellingborough, to James, tailor, husband, 1796/2 May
HORNSEY, Elizabeth, Earl's Barton, wid., to Henry, yeo., son, 1754/25 May
HORRELL, Thomas, Walgrave, victualler, to Ann, wid., 1780/3 July
HORSFIELD, John, Kettering, weaver, Inv.only £17.17.0 1724/49A
HORTON, John, Yardley Gobion, gent., Inv.only £285.10.0 1723/126
Joseph, Ashton, gent., to Judith, spin., daughter, Mary, wid., renounced, 1726/6 Aug.
John, Yardley Gobion, gent., to Mary, wid., Inv. £73.10.0 1739/6 Mar.
Orton, Mary, Yardly, Potterspury, wid., to Thomas, yeo., uncle and guardian of John, minor, son, 1749/4 Nov.
HOSE, William, Northampton, to Eleanor, wid., 1714/107
HOUGHTON, Margaret, Wellingborough, wid., Guard.only of Margaret Walker, minor, 1711/17
Hooton, William, Bozeat, lacebuyer, to Edward, brother, Inv. £29.14.2 1717/93
Hooton, Bozeat, Guard.only of Elizabeth, Mary, Ann, Hanna and Edward, minors, 1717/113
Thomas, Kilsby, baker, Inv.only £18.18.0 1718/14A
Elizabeth, Kilsby, wid., Inv.only £15.17.6 1719/28A
Richard, senior, Mears Ashby, Inv.only £213.18.0 1721/83A
Thomas, Kilsby, Inv.only £66.0.0 1722/135A
Elizabeth, Hardingstone, wid., to Charles Kilpin, maltster, principal creditor, 1729/20 Dec.
William, Holcot, yeo., to Sibilla, wid., Inv. £615.19.7 1739/14 Apr.
Thomas, Great Houghton, to William, Mears Ashby, farmer, brother, 1752/11 Apr.
John, Hardwick, to Mary, wid., 1755/4 Feb.
William, Holcot, yeo., to Hannah, wid., mother and guardian of William, minor, nephew, Will, Guard., 1757/24 Nov. and 6 Dec.
Hooton, Daniel, Paulerspury, farmer, to Thomas Fennel, Harpole, farmer, creditor, Sarah, wid., renounced, 1785/24 Feb.
John, Hardwick, to Thomas, grazier, brother, 1785/13 Sept.
William, Overstone Lodge, farmer, to Elizabeth, wid., 1796/7 June
Thomas, Loddington, grazier, to Mary, wid., 1797/26 Oct.
HORWOOD, William, Hinton, farmer, to Matthew, yeo., brother, 1775/19 Dec.
HOW, Robert, Weston Favell, Inv.only £9.15.0 1711/131A
Anne, Weston Favell, to John, yeo., son, 1713/113
William, Cosgrave, Inv.only £481.0.6 1715/55A
Samuel, Isham, to Samuel, son, 1718/87
HOWARD, John, Spratton, victualler, to John, innholder, son, 1755/6 Dec.
William, sailor, to Martha, Duston, wid., 1761/12 Dec.
Richard, Weedon Beck, to Molly, wid., 1798/3 Feb.
HOWELL, Richard, Kettering, to Alice, wid., Inv. £35.1.6 1724/91
HOWES, William, Silverstone, to Elizabeth, wid., Inv. £17.1.0 1711/77
Maud, All Saints, Northampton, wid., Inv.only £12.10.3 1713/14A
Henry, Cold Higham, Inv.only £355.5.6 1713/68A
Howse, Joseph, Northampton, to Sarah, wid., 1714/2

HOWES continued
Henry, Cold Higham, husb., to Anne, wid., 1717/130
Howse, Richard, Aynho, to William, husb., brother, 1723/115
Howse, William, Aynho, to William, husb., son, 1723/116
William, Duncote, Green's Norton, to Susanna, wid., Inv. £48.10.0 1726/9 Feb.
Richard, Blisworth, bachelor, to Stephen, Green's Norton, lab., brother, 1742/15 Sept.
Elizabeth, Hackleton, wid., to Hatton, Northampton, cooper, son, 1742/20 Oct.
Mark, Kislingbury, yeo., to John, yeo., son, Mary, wid., renounced, 1756/22 May
John, Green's Norton, farmer, to William, Duncote, Green's Norton, farmer, brother, 1758/4 Mar.
Sarah, Eastcote, Pattishall, wid., to Thomas, farmer, son, and John Wakefield, Cold Higham, farmer and grazier, son in law, 1762/10 Apr.
Samuel, Eastcote, Pattishall, farmer, to Priscilla, wid., 1762/10 Apr.
Richard, Norton, yeo., to Thomas, yeo., son, 1766/14 Jan.
Richard, Norton, to Mary, wid., 1772/19 Mar.
Mark, Rothersthorpe, yeo., to Samuel, Chancery Lane, London, stationer, and Mark, yeo., sons, 1775/16 Feb.
Sarah, Norton, spin., to Ann Tibbs, sister, 1782/3 Apr.
John, Kislingbury, schoolmaster, to Thomas Harris, woolcomber, and Francis Linnell, yeo., creditors, Susannah, wid., renounced, 1787/31 Mar.
Thomas, Eastcote, Pattishall, gent., to Richard, Northampton, gent., son, 1793/2 Dec.
Mark, Rothersthorpe, yeo., to Sarah, wid., 1797/15 Nov.
HOWKINS, Jonathan, Clipston, shoemaker, to Hester, wid., Inv. £31.11.11 1712/141
Mary, Halse, Brackley, to Benjamin, Hinton in the Hedges, husb., uncle and guardian of John and William, minors, son, 1739/13 Dec.
William, Ecton, farmer, to Mary, wid., 1754/28 Sept.
William, Brackley, to Elizabeth, wid., 1791/29 Mar.
HOWLING, William, Quinton, to Sarah, wid., 1740/22 May
William, Quinton, Inv.only £19.15.0 1740/376
HOYTE, Anne, Wellingborough, spin., to Mary and Eliza Penwrite, spins., nieces, 1724/133
Samuel, Broughton, butcher, to Edmund Pell, yeo., guardian of Samuel, minor, son, 1743/3 Mar.
HUDSON, Daniel, Earl's Barton, Inv.only £4.5.8 1711/104A
Anne, Earl's Barton, wid., Inv.only £23.3.6 1717/132A
HUGGINS, Elizabeth, Burleigh, co. Rutland, spin., to John Clarke, Northampton, lab., cousin, Inv. £27.19.10 1712/98
HUGHES, Hewes, Robert, Silverstone, to Thomas, lab., 1718/86
John, Inv.only £18.0.0 1723/117A
Thomas, Muscott, Norton, farmer, to John and George, farmers, sons, 1792/3 May
William, Northampton, grocer, to Elizabeth, wid., mother, 1797/26 Jan.
John, Floore, farmer, to Hannah, wife of John Adams, butcher, daughter, 1797/27 May
HULL, John, Northampton, tailor, to John Jeys, mercer, principal creditor, Inv. £10.7.2 Catherine, wid., renounced, 1717/129
Benjamin, Yardley Hastings, to Mary, wid., 1724/73
William, Yardley Hastings, yeo., husb., to Sarah, wid., Inv. £689.12.1 1753/5 May
John, Mears Ashby, to Sarah, wid., 1768/7 May
Joel, Bozeat, yeo., to Mark, son, 1780/28 July
HUMPHREY, Humfrey, Edward, junior, Sulgrave, Account of Edward, father, admin., £24.3.0 1680/13
Humphreys, Robert, Rushden, to John Sanders, Higham Ferrers, miller, principal creditor, 1713/97
Richard, Rothwell, Inv.only £151.9.0 1714/39A
Humfres als. Dicker, Rebbecca, Barby, wid., Inv.only £10.19.7 1718/102A
Humfrey, Christopher, Moreton Pinkney, Inv.only £73.3.10 1725/30 Apr.
Humfrey, Susanna, Wellingborough, to Frances, wid., mother, 1726/31 Dec.
Humfrey, Thomas, Brington, husb., to Elizabeth, wid., 1728/28 Sept.
Humfrey, John, Wellingborough, butcher, to Elizabeth, wid., Inv. £4.13.4 1751/24 Apr.

HUMPHREY continued
William, Nobottle, Brington, yeo., to Margaret Cooke, Althorp, Brington, wid., creditor, 1784/13 Mar.
HUN, William, All Saints, Northampton, to Mary, wid., 1724/79
HUNT, Elizabeth, All Saints, Northampton, Inv.only £16.0.0 1715/167A
Daniel, Eydon, Inv.only £168.4.3 1723/41A
William, Thorpe Mandeville, Inv.only £311.16.3 1723/66A
John, Chalcombe, lab., to Elizabeth, wife of John Grantham, lab., daughter, 1766/19 Dec.
HURLEY, Thomas, Daventry, victualler, to Mary, wid., 1795/14 Sept.
HURST, Joseph, Denton, husb., Inv.only £83.2.0 1713/7A
HUTCHINS, William, Paulerspury, to Mary, wid., 1715/113
John, Hulcote, cordwainer, to Mary, wife of William Barford, lab., sister, 1779/15 June
HUTCHINSON, Daniel, Thornby, miller, to Abigail, wid., Inv. £29.10.0 1714/24
Daniel, Thornby, to George Linton, Harborough, co. Leic., linen draper, of goods unadministered by Abigail, wid., decd., 1715/137
Abigail, Thornby, wid., to Prudence Reddish, wife of Benjamin, Stamford, co. Linc., barber, daughter, 1715/122
HUTT, William, Paulerspury, to Sarah, wife of Stephen Howes, miller, 1772/8 Dec.
Richard, Northampton, wool stapler, to Elizabeth, spin., daughter, Mary, exor., decd., Will, 1799/15 June
HUTTON, Thomas, Grendon, to Robert, carpenter, brother, 1729/12 Nov.
HYDE, Hide, Nicholas, Harlestone, to Elizabeth, wid., Inv. £135.3.6 1729/11 Oct.
Hide, Edward, Northampton, to John, Guildford, co. Surrey, yeo., brother, 1733/5 Dec.
Samuel, Norton, to John Winrow, Newnham, tanner, and Samuel Montgomery, Daventry, ironmonger and shopkeeper, principal creditors, Mary, wid., renounced, 1770/20 May

I

IBBS, James, Kettering, to James, barber, son, Inv. £18.15.2 1724/153
IDLOT, Matthew, senior, Wellingborough, Inv.only £13.3.0 undated/409
ILETT, Thomas, Inv.only £273.19.6 1727/184
ILIFFE, Robert, Desborough, husb., yeo., Inv.only £541.18.6 1715/8A
Iley, William, Brampton, husb., to Elizabeth, wid., 1729/5 Apr.
Iliff, Eusebius, Grafton Underwood, victualler, to Thomazin Chamberlain, Cranford St. John, wid., sister, Will, Inv. £19.16.0 1781/26 Sept.
INFIELD, Thomas, Raunds, lab., to Elizabeth, wid., Inv. £4.7.0 1727/10 Oct.
INNS, John, Towcester, yeo., to Frances, wid., 1734/11 May
William, Wootton, to Mary, wid., 1778/24 Jan.
INWOOD, Charles, Blisworth, wheelwright, to Mary, wid., 1714/174
IRELAND, Thomas, Earl's Barton, to Elizabeth, wid., 1715/152
IRESON, Henry, Lilbourne, to Thomas, yeo., 1721/138
Thomas, Lilbourne, grazier, to John, grazier, son, 1788/25 Oct.
IRONMONGER, Crescent, Culworth, yeo., Inv.only £16.8.6 1724/145A
ISHAM, William, Staverton, elder, to Ann, spin., daughter, Dorothy, wid., renounced, Will, 1771/13 Feb.
IVENS, Thomas, Hackleton, victualler, to Jane, wid., 1734/4 May
IVES, Elizabeth, Northampton, wid., Inv.only £30.4.1 1719/17A
John, Kettering, Inv.only £398.15.0 1720/25A
John, Kettering, yeo., Inv.only £439.8.4 1723/17A
Thomas, Northampton, to Mary, wid., 1775/6 Dec.
IZARD, Richard, Wellingborough, victualler, to Mary, wid., Inv. £36.7.6 1757/9 Dec.
Izzard, als. Price, Elizabeth, see Price

J

JACKSON, Sampson, Thorpe Malsor, clockmaker, to Mary, wid., Inv. £84.9.0 1711/115
John, Inv.only £248.0.0 1718/56 A
Jackston, William, Claycoton, Inv.only £19.0.0 1722/76 A
Edmund, Passenham, to Judith, wife of William Tompkins, laceman, daughter, 1724/65
William, Northampton, apothecary, to Henrietta Maria, wid., 1727/31 July
Thomas, Harlestone, shepherd, to Henry, mason, 1734/14 Sept.
Frances, Green's Norton, to Thomas, Tiffield, clerk, husband, 1739/22 Jan.
Robert, Great Billing, to Robert, Bedford, carpenter, nephew, Inv. £37.16.1 1768/25 Jan.
Richard, Ashby St. Ledgers, yeo., to Naomi, wid., 1770/28 Apr.
William, Northampton, to Anne, wid., 1783/6 Jan.
Mary, Winwick, wid., to William, Eccleshall, co. Stafford, farmer, brother, 1786/10 Nov.
Anne, Northampton, wid., to Anne, wife of William Fox, Horley, co. Oxford, schoolmaster, daughter, 1791/12 Dec.
Timothy, Irchester, yeo., to John Bletsoe, farmer, nephew, Charles Bletsoe, yeo., and Anna, wife, sister, renounced, 1796/2 May
JACQUES, Richard, Addington, to John, Finedon, lab., 1792/11 July
JAKEMAN, Rev. Richard, Wootton, clerk, to Samuel Adams, clerk, 1719/63
John, Great Brington, farmer, to Elizabeth, wid., 1772/27 Oct.
JAMES, Joseph, Finedon, to Joseph, lab., son, Inv. £6.8.9 1715/125
Edmund, Little Houghton, Inv.only £631.7.0 1718/24 A
Anne, Great Houghton, spin., to Elizabeth, wid., mother, 1718/53
Henry, bachelor, Inv.only £3.3.0 1718/122 A
Thomas, Yardley Gobion, Potterspury, to Thomas and Sarah, son and daughter, Will, 1719/60
Peter, Great Doddington, Inv.only £89.16.0 1719/81A
Thomas, Irchester, to William Lovell, Grendon, weaver, father and guardian of Susanna and Mary Lovell, minors, exors., Inv. £31.2.6 Will, 1720/127
Edmund, Earl's Barton, to Anne, wid., Inv. £279.17.6 1721/86
Elizabeth, Little Houghton, wid., Inv.only £17.16.6 1722/116A
John, Harrington, pewterer, to Elinor, wid., Inv. £336.5.0 1722/125
Edmund, Earl's Barton, to John Mason, Irchester, husb., grandfather and guardian of Edmund and John, minors, children, of goods not fully administered by Ann, wid., now wife of Mark Althorpe, decd., Guard., 1725/15 Jan.
Thomas, Long Buckby, to Mary, wid., 1725/8 May
John, Burton Latimer, to Mary, wid., 1725/19 Oct.
Thomas, Oxendon, to Mary, wid., 1726/17 Nov.
Thomas, Great Oxendon, Inv.only £321.16.0 1726/175
Edmund, Earl's Barton, Guard.only of Edmund, son, 1727/13 Apr.
John, Finedon, fellmonger, to Elizabeth, wid., 1727/13 Sept.
Eleanor, Northampton, wid., to Elizabeth, wife of William Street, clerk, daughter, 1733/5 Oct.
Edward, Earl's Barton, farmer, to Goodeth, wid., Inv. £69.0.9 1747/21 Nov.
Sarah, Wellingborough, spin., to Thomas Fidgeon, weaver, guardian of John, minor, nephew, 1764/20 Sept.
Thomas, Stoke Bruerne, to Joseph, farmer, son, 1766/12 Apr.
JARMAN, Nicholas, Kelmarsh, to Job, butcher, 1721/32
JARVIS, Mary, Finedon, wid., to Humphrey Althrop, Kettering, carpenter, and Joseph James, guardians of Thomas and James, minors, children, Guard., 1723/27 and 28
Jonas, Croughton, tailor, to John, carpenter, brother, 1739/26 Jan.
Edward, Croughton, to John, carpenter, uncle and guardian of Anne, Elizabeth, Mary and Edward, minors, children, 1741/27 Nov.
Jarviss, Edward, Croughton, Inv.only £106.7.6 1741/379
Elizabeth, Middleton Cheney, wid., to James, yeo., son, Inv. £575.12.0 1742/11 Oct.
James, Middleton Cheney, yeo., to Sarah, wid., Inv. £467.16.6 1756/12 Oct.
JEFFCUTT, Mary, Northampton, spin., to Richard, grocer, brother, 1741/15 Apr.

JEFFCUTT continued
Mary, Northampton, spin., to Martha, wid. of Richard, grocer, decd., brother, 1751/1 Aug.
Elizabeth, Northampton, wid., to Thomas, Leicester, hosier, son, Thomas and Robert Peach, exors., brothers, renounced, Will, 1781/10 Apr.
Henry, Northampton, grocer, to Thomas, Leicester, hosier, son of Elizabeth, wid., exor., decd, Will, 1785/24 Feb.
JEFFERY, Ralph, Floore, shepherd, Inv.only £10.8.8 1712/60A
John, Rushden, Inv.only £231.17.4 1713/138A
Benjamin, Silverstone, to Elizabeth, wid., Inv. £3.6.0 1716/36
John, Inv.only £22.10.0 1726/161
Edward, Daventry, shepherd, to Ursula, wid., 1729/14 Nov.
Jefferyes, Edward, Inv.only £27.15.0 1729/266
Edward, Weedon Beck, to Anne, wid., 1732/4 Nov.
Moses, Stoke Bruerne, to Mary, Roade, wid., 1778/23 Sept.
John, Rothersthorpe, woolcomber, to Elizabeth, wife of Thomas Smith, Northampton, shoemaker, daughter, 1786/26 Dec.
Jane, Rothersthorpe, wid., to Elizabeth, wife of Thomas Smith, Northampton, shoemaker, daughter, 1786/26 Dec.
John, Towcester, victualler, to Esther, wid., James Hall, gent., and Samuel Sheppard, Field Burcote, Green's Norton, maltster, exors., renounced, Will, 1788/1 Nov.
John, Roade, woolcomber, to Anne, wid., 1796/22 Jan.
JEFFES, John, Aynho, Account of Elizabeth, wid., admin., 1680/9
John, yeo., Inv.only £6.17.0 1713/119A
John, Upper Boddington, yeo., Inv.only £6.17.0 1713/76
John, Northampton, harness maker, to Elizabeth, wid., Inv. £18.3.0 1715/114
William, Chalcombe, butcher, to Sarah, wid., 1738/2 Oct.
William, Wellingborough, to William Burbidge, shepherd, nephew, 1760/20 Nov.
Jeffs, John, Chalcombe, bachelor, to Ann Horseman, Tadmarton, Oxon., wid., sister, 1797/17 May
JEKYLL, Catherine, Dallington, to Joseph, husband, 1775/4 Apr.
JELLEY, Jalley, John, Oxendon, to Richard, yeo., and William, yeo., 1723/107
Richard, Oxendon, to William, Arthingworth, yeo., brother, 1725/28 June
William, Arthingworth, Inv.only £1021.16.0 1726/176
William, Oxendon, yeo., to Anne, Arthingworth, wid., mother, 1727/8 Mar.
Anne, Arthingworth, wid., to Thomas Biggs, guardian of Sarah and Elizabeth, minors, daughters, Ann, wife of Robert Wood, and Mary, daughters, renounced, 1727/28 Oct.
Samuel, Duston, maltster, to Sarah, wid., 1779/26 July
Jelly, John, Isham, husb., to Ann, wid., 1794/12 Sept.
JELLIS, William, Muscott, Norton, miller, to Elizabeth, wid., 1728/29 June
JENKINS, John, Stowe Nine Churches, husb., to Mary, wid., 1730/8 Aug.
John, Stowe, Inv.only £44.11.0 1730/273
JENNINGS, Abraham, Ashby St. Ledgers, to Anne Rastall, Will, 1718/84
JESSON, Sarah, Helmdon, spin., to Ann Harriott, wid., sister, 1765/17 May
JESSOP, Thomas, Dallington, lab., to Mary, wid., 1787/28 Sept.
JEYES, John, Brayfield on the Green, yeo., to Jane, wid., Inv. £134.14.6 1719/35
John, Sibbertoft, to Mary, Watford, wid., mother, 1721/28
Jees, Thomas, Heyford, to Joan, wid., Inv. £18.10.0 1732/27 Nov.
JOBSON, Samuel, Earl's Barton, to Elizabeth, wid., Inv. £28.3.6 1761/15 July
JOHNSON, Mary, Broughton, Account of John, brother, admin., £100.1.0 1681/67
Samuel, Broughton, Inv.only £26.15.0 1712/123A
James, Kingsthorpe, mason, to Sarah, wid., Inv. £3.7.6 1714/96
Mary, Thenford, Commission to Maximilian Bush, clerk, Rector of Thenford, and Anthony Shukburgh, clerk, Vicar of Marston St. Lawrence, to administer oath to Anne Buswell, exor., 1715/36
Anne, Earl's Barton, spin., Inv.only £8.13.2 1721/81A
Israel, Mears Ashby, Inv.only £24.2.0 1723/31A
Joseph, Broughton, gent, Inv.only £93.2.6 1724/24A
Thomas, Northampton, to Mary, wid., 1726/10 Aug.
Jane, Old, wid., to Elizabeth Cannell, wid., Inv. £277.5.0 1734/9 Mar.

JOHNSON continued
Thomas, Spratton, tailor, to Mary, wife of John Waterfield, woolcomber, daughter, 1740/19 Jan.
William, Syresham, to William, lab., son, 1746/7 Apr.
William, Maidwell, gardener, to William, gardener, son, 1747/25 Mar.
Ann, Desborough, to John Wood, Rysley, co. Bedford, brother, 1752/18 Sept.
Elizabeth, Towcester, spin., to Johnson Fretter, lab., son and admin. of Mary Fretter, decd., exor., Will, 1754/16 Jan.
Joseph, Great Houghton, to Joseph, grazier, son, 1768/26 Jan.
Solomon, Nortoft, to Elizabeth, wid., 1771/28 May
Philis, Hanslop, Bucks., wid., to Joseph, lab., son, 1782/6 July
als. Westly, Elizabeth, Northampton, to William, Lewes, co. Sussex, gent., son, 1782/10 Oct.
Solomon, Nortoft, grazier, to John Tebbett, Coton, Ravensthorpe, husb., of goods unadministerd by Elizabeth, wid., decd., 1784/8 Mar.
Mary, Nortoft, wid., to Francis, Northampton, shoemaker, son, 1786/21 July
David, Northampton, grocer, to Sarah, wid., 1791/14 Jan.
Richard, Hackleton, wheelwright, to James, wheelwright, son, 1796/10 May
Robert, Charlton, Newbottle, to Margaret, wid., 1800/10 May

JONES, Robert, Inv.only £724.6.0 1713/12A
William, Grimscote, to Judith, wid., 1713/26
Anne, Blisworth, wid., to John, gent., son, Inv. £39.9.11 1716/14
Elizabeth, Brackley, wid., to John Brassett, Preston Bissett, Bucks., husb., brother, Robert Brassett, father, renounced, 1717/28
Frances, Towcester, wid., to Woolstone, S. Sepulchre, Southwark, co. Surrey, servant, 1721/77
Henry, Moulton, husb., Inv.only £313.12.0 1721/128A
Mary, Towcester, wid., to Richard Winckles, Paulerspury, yeo., nephew, Inv. £8.14.0 1721/144
Francis, Wellingborough, clockmaker, Inv.only £22.12.2 1726/150
Joanes, Richard, Slapton, Inv.only £122.12.6 1726/165
Francis, Wellingborough, clockmaker, to Ursuala, wid., 1727/3 July
Elizabeth, Towcester, to Woolston, nephew, 1730/30 June
Anne, Blisworth, spin., to John, Tiffield, yeo., and Anna Maria, spin., brother and sister, 1736/13 Mar.
William, East Haddon, gent., to Keziah, wid., 1739/15 Jan.
Henry, Old, baker, to Esther, wid., 1741/24 Dec.
James, Cranford St. John, to Elizabeth, wid., 1757/24 Feb.
Nicholas, Paulerspury, clerk, to Sarah, wid., 1760/4 Feb.
John, Buttocks Booth, Weston Favell, to Joseph, farmer, brother, 1764/21 Jan.
John, Wollaston, yeo., to Elizabeth, wid., Inv. £355.5.6 1771/6 Feb.
John, Tiffield, to Elizabeth, spin., 1778/27 Oct.
Nicholas, Pattishall, to John, Paulerspury, lab., son, 1782/9 June

JORDAN, Thomas, Staverton, to Elizabeth, wid., 1724/22
Susanna, Irchester, to John, tailor, brother, Inv. £25.4.4 1725/17 Sept.
Thomas, Whittlebury, lab., to Mary, wid., Inv. £23.0.6 1735/3 Oct.
Jorden, John, Kettering, sergemaker, to Margaretta, wid., 1744/27 Sept.

JOSEPH, John, Passenham, lacebuyer, to Thomas, yeo., son, Inv. £23.17.5 1712/43

JOYCE, Richard, Hargrave, Account of Annie, wid., admin., now wife of Charles Peacocks, Little Catworth, Hunts., yeo., £23.10.8 1677/152
Thomas, Raunds, to Jane, wid., 1718/61
William, Kingsthorpe, Inv.only £28.11.0 1718/88A
Joyes, Richard, Passenham, Guard.only of Mary, minor, daughter, 1719/135

JUDD, Sarah, Higham Ferrers, wid., Inv.only £195.10.5 1714/97A
William, Rothwell, cordwainer, to John Peach and Robert Dexter, Market Harborough, co. Leic., 1755/24 Dec.
Frances, Northampton, wid., to Frances, daughter, 1771/1 July

JUDGE, Richard, Brington, yeo., to Thomas, Norton, servant, son, 1795/15 Dec.

JUDKINS, William, Everdon, Account of Ursula, admin., £78.1.4 1670/127
Joseph, Abington, to Elizabeth Clarke, daughter, Will, 1714/69
Mary, Inv.only £7.13.6 1716/138A
Thomas, Weedon Beck, Inv.only £1028.12.0 1724/124A

JUDKINS continued
Richard, Heyford, to Elizabeth, wid., 1724/132
Judkin, Edward, Lower Heyford, yeo., to Mary, wid., Inv. £79.12.3 1748/19 Sept.
Ann, Little Brington, wid., to Mary, wid. and exor. of Thomas Davis, cordwainer, exor., Will, 1777/27 May
George, Walgrave, yeo., to John, yeo., son, 1779/14 Dec.
John, Walgrave, yeo., to George, Puddington, Beds., lab., son, 1798/3 Mar.
JUDSON, John, Weedon Beck, to William, Floore, farmer and grazier, brother, 1795/22 Nov.
JUICE, Richard, Old Stratford, Passenham, matmaker, Inv.only £14.0.6 1719/138 A
JULIAN, Thomas, Cranford St. John, Guard.only of Thomas, minor, son, 1714/59

K

KEENE, Robert, Towcester, framework knitter, to Susanna, spin., daughter, 1796/30 July
KEEP, John, Quinton, Inv.only £3.18.0 1716/5 A
John, Kettering, to Elizabeth, wid., 1756/23 Apr.
Joseph, Wellingborough, to Sarah, wid., 1786/11 Feb.
KELLASTON, Matthew, Rushden, to Anne, wid., Inv. £106.5.0 1712/146 A
KEMMISS, Richard, Preston Capes, to William Montgomery, Fawsley, yeo., and William Allen, Fawsley, gent., principal creditors, 1743/15 Jan.
Kemmis, James, Preston Capes, butcher, to Chules Watkin, Daventry, draper, principal creditor, Elizabeth, wid., renounced, 1750/7 Dec.
Kermiss, Richard, Preston Capes, butcher, to Rachel Montgomery, Fawsley, wid., of goods unadministered by William, gent., husband, 1758/22 June
Elizabeth, Preston Capes, wid., to Betty Allen, spin., daughter in law, 1783/11 Oct.
KEMP, Robert, Broughton, victualler, Inv.only £107.19.6 1713/132A
Thomas, Dagnell, Wicken, to Anne, wid., Inv. £175.5.0 1732/27 May
William, Wicken, lab., to Mary, wid., Will, 1774/25 June
KEMSHEAD, William, Wollaston, to Mary, wid., 1717/79
Thomas, Yardley Hastings, to John, West Haddon, glover, 1722/109
John, Wollaston, matmaker, to Martha, wid., Inv. £18.2.4 1725/17 July
Henry, Rushden, maltster, to William, Knuston, Irchester, matmaker, brother, principal creditor, Mary, wid., renounced, 1764/5 Nov.
Paul, Wollaston, victualler, to Ann, wid., 1775/19 Dec.
Anne, Wollaston, wid., to William, victualler, son, 1786/1 Feb.
KENNING, Thomas, Welton, butcher, Inv.only £19.2.10 1724/86A
John, Harlestone, maltster, to William, carpenter, brother, 1729/4 Oct.
Thomas, Crick, to Mary, wid., 1767/9 July
Henry, West Haddon, shepherd, to Mary, wid., 1786/16 Oct.
William, Brington, farmer, to Elizabeth, wid., 1792/14 Aug.
KENT, Robert, Little Houghton, baker, to Lydia, wid., Inv. £23.1.6 1723/58
Nathaniel, Weston, Lois Weedon, to Elizabeth, wid., 1753/11 May
KERBY, Kirby, Thomas, Northampton, collarmaker, to Elizabeth, wid., 1746/19 June
Mary, Draughton, spin., to Mary, wife of James Francis, Scaldwell, lab., sister, 1786/12 Sept.
Anne, Northampton, wid., to John Gibson, gent., and Catherine Gibson, spin., nephew and niece, 1799/24 Apr.
KERMISS see KEMMISS
KERTON see KIRTON
KEY, John, Northampton, to Elizabeth, wid., 1720/60
Thomas, Eydon, yeo., to John, Priors Marston, co. Warwick, yeo., son, Anne, wid., renounced, 1747/28 Jan.
John, Ringstead, grocer, to Jonathan, tailor, brother, Inv. £80.19.0 1775/13 Dec.
KEYSTONE, Nicholas, Wollaston, Inv.only £95.0.6 1722/8A
KILBY, Robert, Preston Capes, lab., to Anne, wid., 1730/2 Oct.
John, Thenford, to Anne, Helmdon, wid., mother, 1757/11 Mar.
KILPIN, Charles, Hardingstone, Inv.only £357.14.6 1717/64A
Benjamin, Hardingstone, clerk, Inv.only £399.18.8 1721/3A

KILSBY, Edward, West Haddon, Account of Frances Whitehead, sister, admin., £130.3.0 1680/37

Robert, Long Buckby, Account of Priscilla, wid., admin., £68.0.0 1682/59

Killesby, Samuel, Crick, to Abraham, mason, brother, 1711/85

Thomas, Inv.only £106.17.0 1714/66A

Killesby, Francis, Broughton, to Anne, wid., 1716/115

Killsby, John, West Haddon, Inv.only £181.12.6 1722/36A

Anne, Broughton, wid., to James Pulver, husb., brother, Inv. £210.5.6 Francis, husb., son, renounced, 1727/11 Oct.

Ann, Cogenhoe, wid., to Thomas Coles, Whishton, yeo., father, and John, yeo., father in law, 1729/13 Sept.

Killsby, John, Broughton, widower, farmer, husb., to James Pulver, farmer and Bonham Norton, baker, uncles and guardians of Thomas, Mary and Elizabeth, children, Inv. £258.17.0 1754/23 Oct.

KILWORTH, Anne, Crick, spin., Inv.only £99.1.10 1717/44A

Giles, Winwick, yeo., to John Watts, Crick, yeo., guardian of Thomas, minor, son, Inv. £306.5.2 Guard., 1721/12 and 14

Elizabeth, Crick, spin., to Thomas, farmer, brother, 1763/1 Mar.

KIMBELL, William, Daventry, Account of Ephraium Satchwell, admin., £51.3.10 1676/143

Richard, Long Buckby, carpenter, to Elizabeth, wid., Inv. £9.14.0 1735/20 Oct.

KINCEY, Mary, Northampton, wid., to Elizabeth, spin., daughter, 1774/4 Apr.

KING, Robert, younger, Woodford, Account of Joyce, wid., admin., £132.2.0 1672/102

Elizabeth, Weston, to Thomas, Elizabeth, Jane and Sarah, son and daughters, 1711/105

Samuel, Lilbourne, printer, to Esther Prowett, wid., sister, Inv. £17.19.0 1713/24

Thomas, Rushton, to Hannah, wid., 1713/44

Thomas, Brackley, to Frances Middleton, Evenly, wid., sister, 1715/151

Matthew, Braybrooke, husb., Inv.only £107.6.6 1717/21A

William, West Farndon, Woodford, yeo., to Joseph, Byfield, yeo., brother, Margaret, wid., exor., decd., Inv. £28.16.2 Will, 1721/59

John, Badby, Inv.only £31.17.6 1722/18A

Richard, Woodford cum Membris, to Mary, wid., Inv. £11.0.8 1724/12

John, Rushton, St. Peter's, to John Pooley, yeo., 1724/53

John, Northampton, Guard.only of John King Barlee Lucas, minor, exor., 1726/17 Dec.

John, Badby, maltster, to Jane, wid., 1730/9 Apr.

John, Braybrooke, yeo., to James, yeo., uncle, and Sarah, spin., aunt, Inv. £202.6.9 1731/13 Feb.

John, Rushton, St. Peter's, to Mary Cooke, Loddington, spin., sister, 1742/22 Sept.

Thomas, Northampton, brazier, to Mary, wid., Will, 1743/17 Nov.

Mary, Rushton, wid., to Elizabeth, wife of John Rogers, 1751/31 Jan.

Joseph, Syresham, lab., to Mary, wid., 1751/21 Oct.

Benjamin, Charlton, butcher, to Bartholomew Churchill, Deddington, co. Oxford, gent., and Samuel Churchill, same, gent., Benjamin, St. James' Market, co. Middx., butcher, and William, Mint Street, Southworth, co. Surrey, carrier, sons, renounced, 1769/22 Mar.

Mary, Syresham, wid., to Joseph, lab., and Samson, North Newton, co. Oxford, shagweaver, 1776/28 Nov.

Matthew, Kilsby, to Prudence, wid., 1779/20 Dec.

Elizabeth, Wappenham, spin., to William, Woodend, Blakesley, lab., brother, 1790/9 Sept.

KINGSTON, Thomas, Shutlanger, Account of Mary, wid., admin., £147.18.4 1672/108

Thomas, Shutlanger, Stoke Bruerne, shepherd, to Anne, wid., Inv. £37.2.0 1714/132

Grace, Towcester, wid., to Thomas Summers, London, grandson, Will, 1716/37

William, Potterspury, yeo., to Susanna, wid., Inv. £62.4.6 1717/103

Robert, Shutlanger, Stoke Bruerne, Inv.only £11.10.10 1719/86A

Rebecca, Darlescote, wid., to Mary, wife of Thomas Hale, Stoke Bruerne, carpenter, wid., exor. of John Kingston, Hanslop, Bucks., son and exor., Will, 1719/127

John, Shutlanger, Stoke Bruerne, to John Hayles, yeo., 1721/1

Samuel, Towcester, to Mary, wid., 1724/66

KINGSTON continued
Samuel, Towcester, Inv.only £32.11.11 1724/104
Joseph, Shutlanger, Stoke Bruerne, to Elizabeth, wid., 1740/11 Sept.
William, Kislingbury, to Hannah, wid., Inv. £49.17.11 1741/7 Feb.
Thomas, Potterspury, yeo., to Martha, wid., 1747/17 Nov.
Thomas, Shutlanger, Stoke Bruerne, to Susannah, wid., 1755/15 Feb.
Thomas, Moreton Pinkney, to Mary, wid., 1755/1 Dec.
Mary, Whittlebury, to Henry Banks, Potterspury, lab., brother, 1759/1 Aug.
William, Potterspury, to Joseph Scrivaner, yeo., John Bland, shopkeeper, and Richard Campion, Paulerspury, yeo., guardians of Thomas, Martha, and William, children, 1769/7 Dec.
Elizabeth, Stowe Nine Churches, wid., to Thomas, dairyman, son, 1789/3 Jan.
John, Moreton Pinkney, to Sarah, spin., sister, 1792/3 May
Thomas, Blisworth, yeo., to Thomas Gallard, Grafton Regis, yeo., and Robert Campion, farmer, nephews, 1797/25 Mar.
KINNING, Richard, Little Houghton, miller, Inv.only £60.0.4 1711/60A
Richard, Little Houghton, miller, Inv.only £60.0.4 1711/68
KIRK, Thomas, Yardley Hastings, to Priscilla, wid., 1778/29 Oct.
KIRKHAM, Henry, Yelvertoft, to Elizabeth, wid., 1771/23 Jan.
KIRTLAND, John, Lower Boddington, yeo., Inv.only £78.15.0 1711/78A
Robert, Boughton, to Robert Tarry, London, baker, of goods unadministered by Elizabeth Tarry, sister, and Thomas Tarry, her son, decd., Will, 1773/19 Aug.
KIRTON, Kerton, Thomas, Heyford, lab., to Martha, wid., 1738/23 June
Kerton, William, Heyford, yeo., to Mary, wid., 1740/21 Feb.
KITELY, James, Piddington, to James, mason, son, 1756/23 Oct.
KNIBB, George, Boddington, to Martha, wid., 1728/14 Sept.
als. Wilson, Elizabeth, to Henry Wilson, Boddington, weaver, husband, 1728/14 Sept.
Elisha, Woodend, Blakesley, miller, to Elizabeth, wid., 1731/4 Dec.
Samuel, Middleton Cheney, yeo., to Wilkins, yeo., son, 1741/1 June
Samuel, Middleton Cheney, farmer, to John, Hinton, farmer, nephew, John, exor., decd., Will, 1789/29 July
KNIGHT, William, Orlingbury, Inv.only £31.19.0 1712/99A
Griffith, Slapton, gent., Inv.only £59.14.0 1715/18A
John, Northampton, to John, gent., son, 1715/81
John, Spratton, carpenter, Inv.only £18.16.7 1716/28A
Henry, Grafton Underwood, yeo., to John, yeo., son, Inv. £206.0.0 Catherine, wid., renounced, 1721/114
Mary, Slapton, wid., to William, Abthorpe, husb., son, Inv. £16.0.0 1722/12
William, Wilby, yeo., Inv.only £139.15.0 1723/96A
John, Orlingbury, to Elizabeth, wife of John Meade, niece, 1723/130
Thomas, Spratton, to John, yeo., 1726/14 May
William, Hannington, yeo., to Elizabeth, wid., 1727/13 Sept.
William, Pattishall, yeo., to Sarah, wid., 1730/8 Jan.
William, Thorpe Malsor, to Elizabeth Cannam, Middleton, Cottingham, sister, 1735/13 Oct.
John, Stoke Bruerne, gent., to Frances, wid., 1740/30 Sept.
Thomas, Spratton, baker, to Elizabeth, wid., 1752/29 Feb.
William, Middleton Cheney, maltster, to Samuel, maltster, son, Hannah, wid., renounced, Inv. £47.0.10½ 1754/10 May
Mary, Welford, wid., to Elizabeth, wife of Ambrose Wafforne, Lubbenham, co. Leic., grazier, and Martha Wade, daughters, 1758/29 Sept.
William, Wilby, yeo., to Elizabeth, wid., Inv. £407.3.0 1758/4 Nov.
John, Ecton, to Samuel, lab., son, 1764/17 Mar.
William, Roade, to Rebecca, wid., 1765/30 Dec.
Robert, Walgrave, to James Woolams, peruke maker, 1771/6 May
Sarah, Hannington, to John, farmer, husband, 1773/10 July
Thomas, Grafton Underwood, farmer, to Elizabeth, wife of Richard Tozeland, 1774/16 Apr.
John, Wilby, to Ann, wid., Inv. £94.9.0 1775/23 Dec.
William, Hannington, to Elizabeth, wid., 1782/26 Jan.
John, Doddington, farmer, to William, farmer, son, 1785/22 Jan.
Hannah, Thenford, to William Drury, Farnborough, co. Warwick, 1795/30 Mar.
Mary, Weston Favell, wid., to Robert, clerk, son, 1799/15 Oct.

KNIGHTLEY, Elizabeth, Bozeat, wid., Inv.only £20.15.0 1722/57A
KNIGHTON, John, Raunds, to William, brother, 1722/48
William, Brixworth, to Mary, wid., 1739/5 Mar.
William, Brixworth, Inv.only £10.6.6 1739/365
Mary, Brixworth, Inv.only £10.6.6 1739/366
KNOTT, William, Brixworth, to Joseph, Sandy, co. Bedford, grocer, son, Inv. £20.7.8 1715/48
Anne, Brixworth, wid., Inv.only £31.10.0 1715/168A
John, Northampton, victualler, to Jane, wid., and John, shoemaker, son, 1727/15 Dec.
KNOWLES, William, Holcot, to Alice, wid., 1764/24 Mar.
Jane, Irchester, spin., to Ezra Bayes, exor. of Elizabeth Hartlett, decd., Will, 1783/29 July

L

LABRUM, Thomas, Courtenhall, yeo., Inv.only £285.0.0 1723/40A
Labram, Richard, Courtenhall, yeo., to Mary, wid., 1742/21 Jan.
LACK, William, Harlestone, to Thomas, Denton, son, Inv. £5.0.2 1713/13
LACY, Lacey, John, Northampton, baker, to William, baker, son, 1731/16 Sept.
William, Northampton, baker, to William, baker, father, 1767/16 Feb.
LADBROOKE, John, Lilbourne, Inv.only £64.0.0 1717/15A
Ladbrook, William, Byfield, yeo., Inv.only £79.16.0 1724/46A
Mary, Lilbourne, wid., to Henry, watchmaker, 1728/14 Feb.
LADDS, John, Kettering, Account of Anne, wid., £291.18.10 1671/98
Ladd, Samuel, Kingsthorpe, Account of Robert Allen, Brixworth, £99.4.6 1678/32
Ladd, Judith, Weekly, Inv.only £41.8.0 1711/96A
Ladd, Mary, Yelvertoft, spin., Will, Inv. £45.0.0 1717/32
Henry, Kettering, to Elizabeth Curle, wid., sister, 1742/8 Jan.
John, Higham Ferrers, to James, Houghton, co. Hunts., lab., nephew, 1768/30 May
LADKINS, Thomas, Inv.only £13.13.0 1737/343
LAKINS, Henry, East Haddon, woolcomber, to Thomas, Ravensthorpe, yeo., brother, and William White, yeo., brother in law, 1770/23 June
LAMBE, Richard, Higham Ferrers, tailor, to Anne, wid., 1727/10 Oct.
Richard, Higham Ferrers, Inv.only £19.9.6 1727/199
Ann, Kettering, wid., to Thomas Bolney, Great Addington, farmer, guardian of Mary, minor, exor., Will, 1776/1 June
LAMBERT, Edward, Farthinghoe, weaver, Inv.only £6.19.4 1712/122A
William, Chipping Warden, to Hannah, wid., 1726/12 Aug.
Thomas, Wellingborough, costermonger, to Anne, wid., Inv. £16.11.6¼ 1733/27 Apr.
Thomas, Ecton, yeo., to John, yeo., brother, 1752/4 July
LAMLEY, Lambley, George, Kingsthorpe, to John, miller, son, Inv. £29.6.4 Will, 1717/66
LAMPREY, Thomas, Upper Boddington, Inv.only £192.2.9 1713/78
Thomas, Upper Boddington, to Anne, wid., Inv. £192.2.9 1713/95
Rachel, Overthorpe, Middleton Cheney, to Ann, wid., sister in law, 1751/20 Mar.
LAND, John, Northampton, shoemaker, to Judith, wid., 1729/9 May
LANDFORD, Francis, Wootton, yeo., to John, yeo., brother, Inv. £370.0.0 1727/18 Feb.
LANE, John, Wellingborough, to Mary, wid., Inv. £151.4.11 1735/11 Oct.
John, Rothwell, to Ann, wid., now wife of William Goodman, Stanion, 1770/16 Apr.
John, Kettering, to Matthew, Broughton, weaver, brother, Will, 1787/1 Dec.
LANGDELL, William, Earl's Barton, to Jonathan, Ecton, blacksmith, brother, Sarah, wife of William Cornfield, blacksmith, mother, renounced, 1769/18 Nov.
LANGFORD, John, Rothersthorpe, Account of Susanna, wid., admin., £149.8.0 1684/72
Alice, Milton, to Thomas, husband, 1718/69
Nicholas, Milton, to Elizabeth, spin., daughter, exor. of Margaret, wife, decd., Will, 1725/24 Apr.
Thomas, junior, Milton, yeo., to Mary, wid., mother, 1731/20 Mar.
Thomas, senior, Milton, yeo., to Mary, wid., of goods unadministered by Thomas, son, exor., decd., Will, 1731/20 Mar.

LANGFORD continued
Thomas, senior, Milton, Inv.only £57.2.0 1732/286
Thomas, Blisworth, servant, to William, Hardingstone, lab., brother, Martha, wife of Thomas Boddington, Astwood Bury, Bucks., lab., sister, and Elizabeth, wife of John Bailey, Stony Stratford, Bucks., lab., sister, Will, 1794/27 Oct.
LANGHAM, William, Braunston, to Robert, Swinford, co. Leic., son, 1772/16 June
LANGLEY, Henry, Wellingborough, to Elizabeth, wid., Inv. £333.0.0 1716/44
Henry, Little Harrowden, yeo., Inv.only £417.8.0 1718/22A
Henry, elder, Chelveston cum Caldecote, husb., Inv.only £120.11.6 1718/58
Henry, Harrowden, Guard.only of William, minor, son, 1719/91
Edward, Orlingbury, husb., to Amy, wid., Inv. £100.17.0 1727/5 July
Jonathan, Chalcombe, Inv.only £171.4.6 1728/249
William, Rothwell, to Elizabeth, wid., 1743/30 June
Susanna, Isham, wid., to Thomas, Little Harrowden, yeo., son, 1753/28 Apr.
Ann, Isham, spin., to Thomas, Little Harrowden, yeo., brother, 1753/28 Apr.
James, Orlingbury, to Hannah, wid., Inv. £66.11.6 1761/31 Jan.
Robert, to Martha, wife of Joseph Manning, Orlingbury, mother, 1770/24 May
LANSBURY, William, Northampton, lab., to John, St. Albans, Hertford, yeo., son, 1788/29 Oct.
LANTSBURY, William, Great Addington, to Sarah, wid., 1768/15 Oct.
LANUM, John, Bozeat, to Henry Hensman, Wellingborough, maltster, principal creditor, Judith, wid., renounced, 1723/42
LAPWORTH, William, West Haddon, to Edward Page, yeo., 1724/156
LATHBURY, John, Brackley, butcher, to Sarah, wid., 1788/17 Oct.
LATIMER, Edward, Old, to Edward, Faxton, son, Inv. £112.12.10 1718/126
LAUGHAM, William, Thorpe Lubenham, to John, elder, Cathorpe, co. Leic., grazier, father, Mary, wid., renounced, 1763/26 Aug.
William, Thorpe Lubenham, grazier, to Martha, wife of William Frisley, Tugby, co. Leic., grazier, aunt and guardian of William and John, minors, sons, of goods unadinistered by John, elder, father, Guard., 1778/16 Sept.
LAUGHTON see LAWTON
LAUNDON, Anne, Boughton, wid., to Samuel, yeo., son, Inv. £13.18.0 1711/21
Henry, Great Billing, husb., Inv.only £83.5.0 1717/37A
Elizabeth, Boughton, spin., to Samuel, farmer, father, 1759/4 Jan.
Elizabeth, Boughton, to Stephen, farmer, brother, of goods unadministered by Samuel, father, decd., 1763/15 Jan.
LAVASSOR, Levassor, Rev. Michael, Broughton, rector, to Elizabeth Linnell, wid., principal creditor, Inv. £165.11.10 1718/109
LAW, Thomas, Wollaston, Inv.only £75.2.0 1715/9A
John, Great Billing, to Mary, wid., Inv. £15.2.0 1717/121
Richard, Kislingbury, yeo., Inv.only £35.0.0 1719/78A
John, Rothwell, barber, to Elizabeth, wid., Inv. £12.17.6 1724/80
Thomas, Plumpton, yeo., to Sarah, wife of John Starmer, senior, Holdenby, husb., daughter, 1729/1 Mar.
Samuel, Kettering, to Anna, wid., Inv. £70.15.0 1734/5 Apr.
Mary, Kislingbury, spin., to Elizabeth, wife of William Adams, Heyford, cousin, 1753/2 June
Mary, Wappenham, spin., to John, lab., brother, 1757/25 July
Timothy, Northampton, to Elizabeth, wid., 1778/1 Sept.
Matthew, Little Bowden, to Jane, wife of Matthew, 1781/21 June
John, Rothwell, to Catherine, wid., 1784/26 Nov.
Sarah, Northampton, wid., to Catherine, wife of Hugh Higgins, Great Houghton, victualler, aunt and guardian of Sarah and Catherine, minors, daughters, Guard., 1789/12 Feb.
LAWFORD, Samuel, Walgrave, to Adam Tayler, Kettering, tailor, and Job Davenport, gent., Inv. £120.18.5 Will, 1712/17
LAWRENCE, Laurence, Simon, Clipston, Inv.only £38.14.0 1711/36A
Laurence, Thomas, Boddington, carpenter, Inv. £72.17.10 Account of Edward, Byfield, and Sarah Pitts, Thenford, exors., 1712/72
Laurence, Thomas, Boddington, carpenter, Inv.only £72.17.10 1712/112A
Martha, Syresham, wid., to Mary, wife of Thomas Wright, lab., daughter, 1747/28 Nov.

LAWRENCE continued
William, Kingsthorpe, yeo., to John Johnson, yeo., son in law, 1791/23 May
Elizabeth, Byfield, spin., to Richard, Farndon, lab., brother, 1799/6 Mar.
LAWTON, Walter, Hardingstone, to Mary, wid., 1718/28
Jonathan, Bozeat, Inv.only £28.4.0 1726/171
Laughton, William, Potterspury, yeo., to Anne, wid., 1736/18 Sept.
Thomas, Grendon, yeo., to Rebecca, wid., Inv. £536.12.0 1784/2 Jan.
LAY, Thomas, Rothwell, wheelwright, to Mary, wid., and Elizabeth, wife of Benjamin Burditt, maltster, daughter, 1799/29 Jan.
LAYNG, Rev. Peter, Everdon, clerk, to Susan, wid., 1778/30 May
LEAPER, Adam, Brackley, currier, Inv.only £16.9.0 1720/70A
John, Brackley, yeo., to Mary Williams, wid., sister, 1755/11 Dec.
LEAVER, William, Cotton End, Hardingstone, pinmaker, to Sarah, wid., 1730/21 May
LEE, Thomas, senior, Kilsby, Account of Anne, wid., £123.10.0 1672/111
Andrew, Kilsby, Inv.only £170.17.0 1720/56aA
Henry, Northampton, to Frances, wid., 1721/118
Edward, East Farndon, Inv.only £273.1.0 1724/108
Richard, Northampton, to Christian, wid., 1724/109
Hanna, Long Buckby, wid., to Elizabeth, spin., daughter, 1725/3 July
John, Kislingbury, husb., to Alice, wid., 1727/2 Dec.
John, Inv.only £129.15.0 1727/195
John, Rothwell, joiner, to Sarah, wid., now wife of William Humfreys, lab., 1749/28 Feb.
Leay, William, Rothwell, to Abigal, wid., 1765/30 Dec.
Lea, Joseph, Broughton, carpenter and maltster, to Richard Garrett, Thorpe Malsor, principal creditor, Elizabeth, wid., renounced, 1775/17 June
William, Kilsby, plasterer, to John Mason, Northampton, joiner, guardian of William, minor, son, Guard., Will, 1783/17 Dec.
Abraham, Kilsby, to Sarah, wid., Inv. £205.19.6 1784/28 July
Thomas, Long Buckby, glover, to Abraham, Spratton, weaver, cousin, 1789/20 Nov.
Elizabeth, Northampton, to Joseph, basketmaker, husband, and Thomas, basketmaker, son, 1795/29 Aug.
LEECH, John, Slapton, to George Measey, Waterpury, co. Oxon., nephew, 1724/71
LEEKE, Elizabeth, Braunston, to Thomas Baseley, yeo., and Richard Baseley, yeo., creditors, 1721/120
LEESON, Elizabeth, Welton, wid., Inv.only £12.1.3 1714/49A
Robert, Badby, to Ann, wid., 1715/166
George, Preston Capes, lab., to Elizabeth, wid., Inv. £28.10.0 1717/62
Richard, Everdon, farmer, husb., to Elizabeth, wid., Inv. £120.12.6 1748/30 Apr.
Samuel, Everdon, to Nathaniel, 1790/17 Feb.
Catherine, Green's Norton, wid., to Robert, Harpole, yeo., son, 1793/6 Dec.
LEHNO, Thomasin, All Saints, Northampton, to Sophia, wife of James Cook, Great Houghton, weaver, and Thomasin, wife of William Coulton, Nottingham, framework knitter, daughters, Inv. £38.13.6 1742/31 Aug.
LEICESTER, Anne, Hellidon, to Ann, wife of Thomas Elard, Knapton, co. Warwick, daughter, 1761/11 Apr.
LEM, Michael, Paulerspury, yeo., to Elizabeth, wid., Inv. £263.12.6 Guard. of Joseph, minor, son, 1715/11 and 12
LEMON, William, Northampton, innholder, to Anne, wid., Inv. £11.4.6 1741/11 July
LENTON, Mary, Chelveston, wid., to Edward Woodward Lenton, son, 1792/23 Apr.
LESTER, William, Brixworth, to William, husb., son, Inv. £26.15.0 1711/91
Robert, Brixworth, innholder, to Edward, innholder, son, Inv. £64.3.0 1733/17 Apr.
LETCH, Edward, Aynho, yeo., to Joan, wid., Nathaniel Stilgoe, Deddington, co. Oxford, yeo., and John Baker, baker, exors., renounced, Will, 1773/3 Mar.
LETTS, Thomas, Floore, ploughwright, to Thomas, Bugbrooke, ploughwright, son, Inv. £16.4.6 1728/10 Aug.
Richard, Holdenby, grazier, to Elizabeth, wid., 1790/20 Oct.
LEVITT, John, East Farndon, to Sarah, wid., 1724/54

LEVITT continued
Levit, John, East Farndon, Inv.only £65.16.0 1724/137
LEWIN, William, Oxendon, husb., to Mary, wid., mother, 1728/25 Sept.
LEWIS, John, Paulerspury, to Ann Butler and Elizabeth Newman, principal creditors, 1718/124
John, Paulerspury, Account, £16.18.2 1719/134
LIDDINGTON, Lidlington, John, Silverstone, Inv.only £84.18.0 1727/179
Richard, Silverstone, to Sarah, wid., 1728/31 Aug.
Lidlington, Richard, Silverstone, wheelwright, Inv.only 1728/258
Peter, Silverstone, gent., to Richard, gent., son, 1763/2 Apr.
LILLEY, Lilly, Joseph, Pytchley, Account of Elizabeth Langley als. Lillie, wid., admin., £191.4.6 1671/109
Mary, Broughton, wid., Inv.only £32.14.0 1715/6A
Mary, Broughton, Guard.only of Mary, Anne and Judith Clarke, minors, daughters of Elizabeth Clarke, wid., 1716/9
John, Orlingbury, yeo., to Richard, yeo., son, Elizabeth, wid., renounced, 1730/30 May
Lilly, John, Orlingbury, farmer, Inv.only £13.0.0 1730/281
LILLINGSTON, als. Willmott, James, Creaton, to James, yeo., nephew, 1739/17 Nov.
als. Wilmott, James, Inv.only £252.8.0 1739/368
LILLYMAN, Thomas, Ringstead, yeo., Inv.only £811.11.0 1717/92
Lilliman, Thomas, Ringstead, Inv.only undated/412
Elizabeth, Cransley, to William, Rothwell, lab., widower, 1747/17 July
LINACRE, Oliver, Wellingborough, gent., to Elizabeth, wid., 1730/7 Apr.
LINDSEY, Sarah, Northampton, spin., to Samuel Brown, victualler, nephew, 1800/8 Apr.
LINES, Thomas, Chipping Warden, to Mary Lambert, daughter, 1715/148
Lynes, Edward, Chipping Warden, to Augustine, son, 1715/150
Henry, Eydon, Inv.only £6.11.0 1719/33A
Lynn, Richard, Stanwick, to Hanna, wid., Inv. £170.9.8 1720/134
Lyne, John, Brixworth, clerk, to Elizabeth, wid., 1735/29 Apr.
Alice, Moreton Pinkney, to Francis, lab., husband, 1750/12 Oct.
LINNELL, John, Little Harrowden, to Elizabeth, wid., 1718/93
Thomas, Floore, to Anne, wid., Inv. £68.19.0 1718/117
Anne, Little Harrowden, wid., Inv.only £129.11.0 1720/76A
William, Newnham, Inv.only £25.7.0 1720/142A
William, Paulerspury, carpenter, to Mary, wid., Inv. £10.18.6 1725/30 Apr.
William, Little Harrowden, to John, husb., brother, Inv. £152.1.6 1726/22 Jan.
William, Little Harrowden, blacksmith, to Robert, yeo., brother, Inv. £108.4.8 1743/22 Jan.
Francis, Towcester, innholder, to John, fellmonger, son, Will, 1748/6 Feb.
Joseph, Holcot, lab., to Thomas, Achurch, lab., son, Hannah, wid., renounced, 1752/2 May
William, Abthorpe, victualler, to Alice, wid., 1771/10 June
William, Silverstone, victualler, to John, victualler, brother, 1773/2 Aug.
Catherine, Bugbrooke, wid., to John Turland, yeo., Will, 1774/24 Dec.
Edward, Thorpe Mandeville, to Anne, wid., 1782/16 Oct.
William, Cranford, farmer, to Mary, wid., 1784/13 Jan.
George, Astcote, Pattishall, farmer, to Anne, wid., 1788/14 Oct.
Elijah, Everdon, maltster, to Sarah, wid., mother, 1795/13 Mar.
Richard, Sulgrave, to Richard, senior, shoemaker, 1796/28 July
LINNETT, Edward, Welford, salter, to Edward, lab., son, Inv. £33.13.6 1728/13 Apr.
Thomas, East Farndon, to Lydia, wid., 1733/2 July
Thomas, East Farndon, Inv.only £15.17.6 1733/298
John, Braunston, innholder and victualler, to William Drought, Oxford, brewer, and Edward Lambe, Daventry, gent., Prudence, sister, renounced, Will, 1779/6 Mar.
LINTHWAITE, John, younger, Wellingborough, yeo., to Elizabeth, wid., 1742/28 Apr.
Elizabeth, Wellingborough, wid., to Mary Collis, wid., grandmother and guardian of John and Elizabeth, minors, children, 1742/21 June
LITCHFIELD, Vincent, elder, Inv.only £108.10.0 1712/130A
John, Teeton, Ravensthorpe, to Elizabeth, wid., 1763/8 Jan.

LITCHFIELD continued
John, Brixworth, to John, butcher, son, Will, 1765/5 Aug.
William, Overstone, lab., to Alice Rich, Moulton, wid., sister, 1789/23 May
Vincent, Kislingbury, yeo., to Vincent, farmer and baker, son, Sarah, wid., exor., decd., Will, 1793/11 May
LITTLE, Edward, Little Harrowden, to Frances, wid., Inv. £256.0.0 1718/94
LITTLEFORD, John, Denshanger, Passenham, to John, linenweaver, son, 1756/30 Aug.
John, Denshanger, Passenham, to Elizabeth, wid., 1759/7 July
LIVESEY, Charles, Wellingborough, gent., to Elizabeth, wid., Will, 1762/22 Jan.
LOAKES, Joseph, Desborough, Account of Mary, wid., £80.7.3 undated/58
Robert, Holcot, Inv.only £39.5.6 1712/55A
Loake, James, Great Oxendon, husb., Inv.only £163.14.0 1714/4A
Loake, James, Great Oxendon, shepherd, Inv.only £15.3.4 1720/72A
Loake, William, Oxendon, to William, yeo., son, 1783/17 Apr.
LOCKINGTON, Elizabeth, Daventry, wid., to Henry, hempdresser, son, 1734/14 Nov.
Henry, Daventry, victualler, to Mary, wid., 1739/9 May
Henry, Daventry, victualler, Inv.only £16.5.6 1739/354
LOCOCK, Aaron, Northampton, clerk, to Henry, apothecary, son, 1752/14 Aug.
LOLE, Margaret, Northampton, All Saints, wid., to Elizabeth, spin., daughter, Inv. £48.4.0 1712/118
Samuel, Naseby, husb., Inv.only £5.1.2 1719/13A
Lowle, John, Northampton, to Sarah, wid., 1727/14 Feb.
Joseph, Desborough, cordwainer, to Ursula, wid., Inv. £8.11.0 1728/10 Sept.
John, Culworth, carpenter, Inv.only £17.10.0 1729/243
LONGLAND, James, Yardley Hastings, yeo., to Elizabeth, wid., 1779/14 Dec.
James, Yardley Hastings, to Elizabeth, wid., mother, 1792/24 Feb.
John, Yardley Hastings, to Hannah, wid., 1792/24 Feb.
LONGSTAFFE, Edward, Piddington, maltster, to Anne, wid., 1732/15 Jan.
Longstaff, Edward, Piddington, maltster, to Edward, maltster, son, 1787/31 Mar.
LORD, Richard, Wilby, tanner, Inv.only £319.13.6 1716/103A
Thomas, Wilby, tanner, Inv.only £405.0.0 1717/88A
Mary, Wilby, wid., to Sarah, wife of James Palmer, husb., daughter, Inv. £19.16.9 1724/26
Samuel, Middleton Cheney, cooper, to Elizabeth, wid., 1798/30 Oct.
LOVE, Richard, Harpole, tailor, Inv.only £12.17.6 1726/160
LOVEDAY, Aaron, Brackley, bookseller, Inv.only £18.5.0 1721/79A
Rev. Moses, Brackley, clerk, Inv.only £27.12.0 1723/113A
William, Brackley, yeo., to Robert, yeo., brother, 1746/21 Oct.
George, Brackley, maltster, to Mary, Adderbury, co. Oxford, spin., daughter, 1756/30 Apr.
LOVELL, John, Adstone, to Richard, Farthinghoe, butcher, brother and principal creditor, Sarah, wid., renounced, 1712/76
Jane, Silverstone, Inv.only £20.8.0 1713/27A
Hugh, Boughton, to John, yeo., son, Frances, wid., renounced, 1721/42
John, Moulton, to Anne, daughter, 1721/134
John, Boughton, yeo., bachelor, to Hugh, husb., brother, Frances, wid., mother, renounced, 1722/29
Frances, Boughton, wid., to Hugh, gent., son, 1724/111
John, Yelvertoft, yeo., to Elizabeth, wid., Inv., 1727/5 Oct.
Thomas, Ecton, to Dorothy, wid., 1743/20 Apr.
Thomas, Kislingbury, shepherd, to Mary, wid., Inv. £38.10.6 1748/3 Sept.
Samuel, Charwelton, grazier, to Alice, wid., 1759/10 Feb.
Hugh, Boughton, farmer, to John Hollis, nephew, farmer, Elizabeth, wid., renounced in favour her son, 1771/15 May
Randal, Claycoton, grazier, to Mary, wid., 1773/6 Mar.
Thomas, Ecton, yeo., to Ann, wid., Will, 1776/22 June
John, Sulby Abbey, grazier, to James, grazier, brother, 1791/5 Nov.
William, Sulby Abbey, grazier, to James, grazier, brother, 1791/5 Nov.
Edith, Weston, Lois Weedon, to James, grazier, husband, 1797/21 Oct.
John, Cold Higham, yeo., to Thomas Archbold, Shoreditch, co. Middx., gent., son of Ann, wid., exor., decd., Will, 1798/31 July
Sarah, Cold Ashby, to William, grazier, husband, 1799/20 Nov.

LOYDELL, John, Brixworth, to Richard, blacksmith, brother, 1761/5 Dec.
LUCAS, John, Staverton, tailor, to Richard Horn, Newnham, husb., Inv. £15.11.10 1711/71
William, Hollowell, Guilsborough, gent., to Thomas, gent., son, 1712/82a
James, Barby, to John Blisse, Welford, shoemaker, 1712/106
Mary, Orton, Rothwell, Inv.only £22.19.0 1712/129A
William, Barby, boarder, to Ann, wife of Robert Goodman, Monk's Kirby, co. Warwick, bricklayer, daughter, Inv. £7.5.9 1712/131
Charles, Wellingborough, to Susanna, wid., Inv. £107.0.6 1713/4
Thomas, Creaton, butcher, to William Tarry, Brampton, and John, butcher, uncles and guardians of William and Elizabeth, minors, children, Guard., 1713/79
Thomas, Kilsby, freemason and husb., to Doreas, wid., Inv. £99.8.6 1713/88
John, Kettering, to Anna, wid., Inv. £7.15.0 1714/99
William, Westhorpe, Marston St. Lawrence, Inv.only £87.1.6 1716/41A
Elizabeth, Westhorpe, to John Blencow, Marston St. Lawrence, husb., 1721/102
William, Nortoft, Guilsborough, gent., to Charles, gent., brother, Inv. £125.18.6 1722/14
Anne, Kettering, wid., to Mary, spin., 1722/47
Mary, Farthinghoe, Inv.only £62.17.6 1724/37
John, West Haddon, to Richard, son, 1732/18 Apr.
William, Crick, weaver, to James Vans, weaver, Thomas Whitmell, yeo., and John Judkins, shopkeeper, principal creditors, 1732/25 Nov.
William, East Haddon, butcher, to Edward Litchfield, Northampton, surgeon, principal creditor, 1751/13 Apr.
Abraham, Barby, farmer, to Mary, wid., 1753/16 Apr.
William, Lilbourne, yeo., to Mary, wife of Nathaniel Smith, Lutterworth, co. Leic., weaver and woolcomber, daughter, Inv. £221.13.0 1754/24 June
Mary, Northampton, wid., to Samuel, Wellingborough, surgeon, son, 1756/31 May
Samuel, Moulton, to Sarah, wid., Inv. £50.14.8 1758/4 Feb.
Samuel, Wellingborough, to Elizabeth, Huntingdon, wid., 1762/20 Oct.
John, Kilsby, to Elizabeth, wid., 1763/16 Apr.
Charles, Faxton, farmer, to Martha, wid., 1768/14 May
Philip, Norton, to John Townley, blacksmith, nephew, 1774/15 Nov.
Thomas, Crick, weaver, to Thomas, Church Over, co, Warwick, weaver, son, 1780/9 Oct.
Mary, Crick, wid., to Ann, wife of Valentine Redgrave, weaver, granddaughter, Will, 1789/14 Apr.
Joseph, Daventry, to Esther, wife of John Eales, Long Buckby, yeo., sister, 1796/29 June
Sarah, Daventry, spin., to William, Claybrooke, co. Leic., grazier, brother, 1797/21 Oct.
Martha, Northampton, wid., to Martin, son, 1799/25 July
LUCK, Silvester, Overstone, Inv.only £233.13.6 1711/19A
Anne, Overstone, wid., Inv.only £189.9.0 1715/3A
Elizabeth, Northampton, wid., to Elizabeth Tyler, 1715/158
William, Overstone, Inv.only £193.0.0 1719/133A
George, Walgrave, to Mary, wid., 1727/24 Apr.
Thomas, Eydon, to Elizabeth, wid., 1787/11 June
Peter, Wootton, lab., to John, lab., son, 1791/28 Dec.
LUCY, Hugh, Wollaston, gent., Inv.only £723.16.4 1719/54A
Elizabeth, Wollaston, late of Goldinton, co. Bedford, spin., Inv.only £367.10.0 1724/72A
James, Wollaston, to Mary, wid., 1778/16 Sept.
William, Wollaston, gent., to William, London, gent., son, 1789/21 Feb.
LUDGATE, Peter, Cosgrave, Inv.only £18.17.4 1721/87A
John, Potterspury, to Mary, wid., Inv. £49.11.5 1726/11 June
LUMLEY, William, Harlestone, mason and quarryman, Inv.only £164.10.0 1720/28A
John, Northampton, Inv.only £60.14.8 1721/130A
Tubalcain, Harlestone, mason, to Elizabeth, wid., 1729/4 Oct.
Thomas, Harlestone, to Thomas, stonecutter, son, 1777/13 Dec.
John, Harlestone, quarryman, Guard.only of Frances, minor, daughter, 1785/8 Oct.

LUMMAS, James, Northampton, mason, to John, son, 1720/21
Lummis, Lomas, Richard, Broughton, to Richard, yeo., son, 1725/2 Jan.
LYNE, LYNES, LYNN see LINES
LYON, John, Northampton, to Mary, wid., mother, 1724/38
Charles, Northampton, to Frances, wid., 1735/4 Nov.
Anne, Kettering, spin., to Mary, spin., sister, 1742/20 Aug.
Daniel, Cottesbrooke, surveyor, to Elizabeth, wife of William Mundin, yeo., daughter, 1786/9 Mar.

M

MABBUTT, William, Walgrave, shoemaker, to Rebecca, wid., Inv. £39.9.6 1715/103
William, Northampton, to Thomas, father, 1717/40
Thomas, Northampton, to Elizabeth Gambell and Ann Cartwright, daughters, Deed or Gift of Will, 1717/143
Mabbott, John, Scaldwell, to Sarah, wid., Inv. £135.17.0 1723/12
Mabbott, Rebecca, Walgrave, wid., to Edward, husb., son, 1729/10 Feb.
Thomas, Long Buckby, to Elizabeth, wid., 1764/9 Oct.
William, Walgrave, to Elizabeth, wid., 1769/15 Feb.
Edward, Rothwell, to Benjamin, husb., 1777/20 June
William, Walgrave, yeo., to Richard, carpenter, brother, 1784/9 Oct.
Elizabeth, Walgrave, wid., to George, farmer, son, 1798/17 May
MACE, William, Boughton, Account of Mary, wid., admin., now wife of John Yeomans, £283.15.6 1672/106
Stephen, younger, Wellingborough, yeo., Account of Mary, wid., admin., £837.19.8 1680/17
MACKERNESS, Maccarness, John, Higham Park, Inv.only £620.19.0 1715/45A
Mackness, Joseph, Bozeat, farmer, Inv.only £120.15.0 1720/12A
Makerness, Richard, Finedon, Inv.only £48.2.6 1721/9A
Platt, Finedon, to Jane, wid., 1740/28 June
George, Great Addington, farmer, to Joseph, farmer, 1745/21 Dec.
Mackaness, Francis, Scaldwell, yeo., to Susannah, wid., 1755/30 Sept.
MACKOWEN, William, marine, to John, Moulton, butcher, brother, 1778/1 Apr.
MADDISON, John, Ashton, 1755/18 Jan.
MAHEW, Thomas, Hargrave, junior, to Mary, wid., Inv. £234.2.5 1724/18
MAIN, Robert, Piddington, Inv.only £250.10.0 1716/84A
Maine, Robert, Spratton, butcher, to Sarah, wid., 1798/10 Feb.
MAJOR, Thomas, Syresham, yeo., to Sarah, wid., 1758/20 Apr.
MAKEHAM, Robert, Wellingborough, to Elizabeth, wid., 1728/16 Oct.
Elizabeth, Wellingborough, to John Robinson, Hinckley, co. Leic., hatter, son, 1758/17 Nov.
MAKEPEACE, Richard, Braunston, yeo., Inv.only £90.8.0 1713/15A
Elizabeth, Braunston, wid., Inv.only £18.6.0 1725/143
William, Braunston, yeo., to Elizabeth, wife of Thomas Harris, yeo., daughter, 1767/25 Feb.
MALCHER, Randal, Spratton, gent., to Mary, wid., 1756/27 Dec.
Richard, Boughton, farmer, to Ann, wid., 1758/24 May
Robert, Northampton, to Mary, wid., 1763/8 Oct.
Thomas, Hanging Houghton, grazier, to Mary, wife of William Dunn, Creaton, sister, 1799/9 Sept.
MALIN, Mallin, Anne, Paulerspury, wid., Inv.only £25.8.11 1712/57A
Mallin, Anne, Paulerspury, wid., Inv.only £25.8.11 1712/73
MALL, John, Northampton, brewer, to Elizabeth, wid., 1777/9 July
MALLARD, Richard, Wootton, lab., to Richard, lab., son, 1740/18 Jan.
George, Gayton, to John, Wootton, cordwainer, son, Inv. £106.3.6 1771/27 June
MALLERY, Mary, Rushden, wid., Inv.only £112.12.0 1714/144A
Mary, Rushden, wid., Inv.only £158.2.4 1717/6A
Mallory, Robert, Rushden, bachelor, Inv.only £221.10.6 1717/136A
MALTUS, John, Farthingoe, victualler, to Mary, wid., 1782/31 Oct.
MANN, Daniel, Wellingborough, to William Barnes, guardian of Susanna and William, minors, children, exors., Will, 1715/22
Susanna, Wicken, wid., to Thomas, farmer, son, 1757/3 May
MANNING, John, Cotton End, Hardingstone, Account of Elizabeth, wid., admin., £549.11.6 1670/94
Edward, Little Brington, Account of John, admin., £71.16.8 1681/11
Anne, Little Houghton, wid., Inv.only £35.7.0 1712/8A

MANNING continued
William, Nobottle, Brington, to Sarah Rowledge als. Manning, relict, wife of Thomas Rowledge, woolcomber, Inv. £17.15.4 1712/140
Joseph, Great Brington, Inv.only £134.17.6 1713/83A
Matthew, Kettering, plumber, Inv.only £18.0.0 1715/121A
Richard, Brockhole, Inv.only £155.0.0 1716/16A
William, Irchester, Inv.only £25.12.0 1718/106A
John, Irchester, mason, to John Mason, husb., grandfather and guardian of John, William and Elizabeth, children, Inv. £250.16.4 Guard., 1720/8 and 9
John, Irchester, mason, to Catherine, wid., Inv. £40.15.2 1721/4
Joseph, Brington, grazier, to John Pooley and Thomas Walker, guardians of John Worley, minor, exor., Inv. £29.12.0 Guard., Will, 1723/22 and 23
Elizabeth, Brafield on the Green, wid., Inv.only £13.17.6 1723/62A
James, Wellingborough, to Blanch Parrett, Great Houghton, wid., mother, Inv. £8.9.4 1723/85
Joseph, Kettering, glazier and plumber, to Martha, wid., Inv. £223.12.2 1728/16 Dec.
John, Walgrave, yeo., to Thomas, Harpole, butcher, brother, 1752/21 Oct.
Elizabeth, Spratton, wid., to Mary, wife of William Brown, yeo., daughter, 1756/14 June
Elizabeth, Little Brington, wid., to Richard Claridge, Great Brington, farmer, nephew, Mary Creaton, wid., sister, renounced, 1758/19 Aug.
John, Harpole, to Mary, wid., 1761/30 Nov.
William, senior, Kingsthorpe, to William, baker, son, Inv. £119.0.6 1772/28 Mar.
Thomas, Moulton, yeo., to Richard, gent., brother, 1780/2 May
William, Kingsthorpe, miller, to Sarah, wid., Joseph, Pisford, yeo., and Richard, baker, renounced, Will, 1789/29 Aug.
William, Kingsthorpe, miller, to Richard, baker, brother, guardian of John and Stephen, minors, sons, Guard., Will, 1790/13 Mar.
George Doddington, Little Houghton, yeo., to Ann, wid., and Thomas Jones, Little Billing, farmer, and William Higgins, Whiston, yeo., 1792/12 Jan.
James, Long Buckby, victualler, to Elizabeth, wid., 1794/28 May
Thomas, Scaldwell, gent., to John, Orlingbury, farmer, brother, 1797/20 Dec.
MANSELL, Robert, Thorpe Malsor, to Catherine, wid., Inv. £127.2.0 1717/90
William, Broughton, bachelor, to Mary, wife of Joseph Norman, weaver, sister, 1724/27
MANTON, John, Great Oxendon, husb., Inv.only £505.7.6 1727/210
MAPELEY, John, Salcey Forest, to Elizabeth, wid., 1743/5 Nov.
MAPLETOFT, Nathaniel, Broughton, clerk, to Griffith Roberts, Kettering, innholder, William Rowlatt, grocer, and James Kempston, draper, creditors, Anna Maria renounced, 1782/11 Mar.
MARCH, William, Hannington, yeo., to Sarah, wid., Inv. £573.0.3 1756/30 Dec.
Sarah, Hannington, to Sarah, wife of John Knight, farmer, daughter, and Richard Sapcoat, Pilton, co. Rutland, farmer, son in law, 1771/5 Dec.
MARGETTS, Anne, Rushden, wid., Inv.only £18.19.9 1726/167
Margits, Margaretts, Edward, Rushden, to Elizabeth, wid., 1759/28 Aug.
Edward, Rushden, to Hannah, wid., 1770/2 May
John, Marston Trussell, to Hannah, wid., 1782/8 May
MARKES, John, Pattishall, to Theodore, senior, gent., father, 1711/83
Jane, wid., Inv.only £94.0.0 1712/144A
George, Pattishall, bachelor, to William Atkins, Northampton, grocer, son and exor. of Mary Atkins, sister, 1737/8 June
Markie, John, Pisford, victualler, to Martha, wid., 1784/31 July
MARLING, Joan, Raunds, to Mary Foscutt, daughter, 1719/37
John, Rothwell, weaver, to Jane, wid., Inv. £68.17.6 1750/16 Aug.
MARLOW, als. Bissell, Elizabeth, see Bissell
MARRIOTT, George, Tiffield, yeo., Inv.only £53.16.0 1711/8A
Richard, Badby, to Elizabeth, wid., Inv. £32.17.0 1711/37
Thomas, Harpole, yeo., Inv.only £291.18.2 1711/108A
Mary, Slapton, Inv.only £7.9.0 1714/8 A
Dorothy, Wellingborough, wid., Inv.only £33.6.6 1714/125A
Henry, Little Houghton, tailor, Inv.only £9.2.4 1715/64A
Marriot, John, Paulerspury, Inv.only £16.5.6 1716/17A

MARRIOTT continued
Abraham, Braunston, yeo., Inv.only £319.0.4 1716/141A
Thomas, Sywell, to Elizabeth, wid., Inv. £29.10.0 1720/62
Simon, Badby, Inv.only £15.0.0 1721/27A
John, Gayton, to Elizabeth, daughter, 1721/140
John, Daventry, innholder, to Elizabeth, wid., 1722/95
John, Little Houghton, yeo., Inv.only £301.5.0 1724/98A
Nathaniel, Kislingbury, to Sarah, wid., 1726/8 Nov.
Robert, Harpole, yeo., Inv.only £171.8.0 1726/182
Nathaniel, Kislingbury, Inv.only £18.11.0 1727/403
Richard, Hellidon, Inv.only £72.7.0 1729/270
Richard, Hellidon, farmer, to Sarah, wid., 1731/6 May
John, Wollaston, wheelwright, to Elizabeth, wid., Inv. £78.2.6 1731/12 June
Richard, Kislingbury, blacksmith, to Richard, blacksmith, son, 1731/22 Sept.
George, Northampton, schoolmaster, to Penelope, wid., 1731/27 Dec.
Thomas, Weedon Beck, yeo., to Mary, wid., 1734/20 Apr.
Mary, Potterspury, to Alice Blunt, Aston, wid., sister, 1738/4 Nov.
Isabell, Wellingborough, spin., to Susanna, wife of John Gibbs, weaver, sister, 1742/28 Apr.
John, Long Buckby, carpenter, to William, woolcomber, son, Jemima, wid., renounced, 1752/7 Mar.
Merriott, George, Northampton, gent., to George, London, cooper, nephew, of goods unadministered by Penelope, wid., decd., 1756/29 May
Mary, Lilbourne, wid., to John, Everdon, yeo., Elizabeth Goodman, Staverton, wid., cousin, renounced, 1758/5 Aug.
John, Ashton, to Susanna, wid., 1771/10 Aug.
Lucy, Everdon, spin., to Thomas, farmer, Mary, Great Wigston, co. Leic., spin., and Elizabeth, wife of John Davenport, Great Wigston, 1772/2 Dec.
Sarah, Welton, to Thomas, staymaker, son, 1774/26 Aug.
Charles, Northampton, to Sarah, wid., 1775/3 Jan.
William, Preston, to William, grazier, son, 1778/19 Sept.
Ann, Daventry, to Elizabeth, mother, 1779/5 May
John, Sywell, blacksmith, to Mary, wid., 1785/9 Aug.
John, Island of Jamaica, West Indies, to Elizabeth, Daventry, wid., 1786/13 Sept.
Thomas, Whilton, staymaker and tailor, Inv.only £2.2.6½ 1788/419

MARSHALL, Thomas, Raunds, to Susanna, spin., daughter, 1712/1
Thomas, Chipping Warden, Inv.only £322.7.9 1712/71A
Robert, Orton, Rothwell, to Jane, wid., Inv. £5.3.4 1713/54
William, senior, Towcester, Inv.only £27.18.6 1713/121A
John, Braybrooke, yeo., to Joan, wid., 1727/7 Oct.
John, Northampton, victualler, to Mary, wid., 1796/18 Feb.
William, Irchester, to Alice, wid., and Joseph, Yeldon, Beds., miller, 1797/22 Feb.

MARSTON, als. Tomlin, Catherine, East Farndon, Account of John Wright, £92.4.6 1671/92
Marson, William, Crick, Inv.only £374.0.0 1711/80A
Thomas, Wollaston, carpenter, Inv.only £41.5.10 1714/95A
Marson, John, West Haddon, gardener, to Elizabeth, wid., 1741/11 Mar.

MARTIN, Richard, Northampton, clockmaker, to Anne, wid., Inv. £122.3.6 1711/23
Mary, Scaldwell, wid., to Thomas Mabbutt, senior, yeo., and Thomas West, shoemaker, guardians of Allen Jackson, minor, Will, Inv. £90.4.0 1711/146
Elizabeth, East Farndon, wid., to William, Spratton, lab., son, Inv. £14.15.3 1712/11
William, Cottesbrooke, to John, yeo., son, Sarah, wid., renounced, 1714/182
Edward, Hartwell, husb., Inv.only 1715/155 A
Francis, Guilsborough, butcher, to Rebecca, wid., Inv. £56.1.10 1718/9
John, Spratton, tailor, Inv.only £7.18.0 1724/45 A
Thomas, Northampton, to Elizabeth, wid., mother, 1724/154
William, Brixworth, Inv.only £126.9.2 1727/158
Robert, Little Billing, husb., to Anne, wid., Inv. £300.7.0 1728/30 Oct.
Lewis, Northampton, ironmonger, to Elizabeth, wid., mother, 1732/5 Oct.
Martinne, Elizabeth, Northampton, Inv.only £25.2.2 1733/307

MARTIN continued
William, Cottesbrooke, Inv.only £400.8.0 1737/346
William, West Haddon, to William, son, 1775/30 Sept.
Edward, Rothwell, joiner, to John, shoemaker, great grandson, Thomas, exor., decd., Will, 1788/1 Sept.
James, Spratton, victualler, to Elizabeth, wid., 1796/23 Apr.
Frances, Stoke Bruerne, wid., to Mary Lambert, wid., daughter, 1797/10 Aug.
James, Brixworth, farmer, to Thomas Ekins, yeo., uncle and guardian of John, James, Elizabeth, Mary and Sarah, minors, children, Guard., 1800/29 Apr.
MASH, Thomas, Wollaston, blacksmith, to Mary, wid., 1747/25 June
Simon, Broughton, weaver, to Simon, and William, weavers, sons, 1783/6 Aug.
MASHBORNE, Edward, Brackley, Account of Matthew, £105.0.0 undated/118
Mashborn, Daniel, Radstone, to Daniel, yeo., son, 1757/11 June
Matthew, Radstone, yeo., to Daniel, Brackley, St. Peter's, yeo., brother, Inv. £581.7.2 1777/29 July
MASON, John, Irchester, Inv.only £352.0.0 1713/93A
William, senior, Irchester, to Mary, wid., Inv. £5.10.10 1716/75
William, Mary, wid., Welford, renounced execution of will in favour John, son, exor., Inv. £179.15.0 1718/128
John, Irchester, Inv.only £100.12.9 1719/61A
John, Broughton, victualler, to Ann, wid., Inv. £66.15.6 Henry Burditt and James Pulver, exors., renounced, Will, 1722/42
Charles, Preston, to Sarah, wife of Joseph Greville, Northampton, lab., sister, 1737/25 Apr.
John, Northampton, to Mary, wid., 1743/20 Sept.
Anne, Crick, wid., to John, yeo., son, 1743/26 Sept.
Edward, Daventry, to Elizabeth, wid., Inv. £62.10.3 1753/23 Nov.
Ann, Northampton, to Thomas, carpenter, son, 1774/19 Sept.
John, Northampton, carpenter, to Elizabeth, wid., 1798/23 Jan.
MASSEY, Robert, Northampton, gent., Account of Elizabeth, wid., exor., £55.9.6 1679/49
MASTERS, Richard, Wappenham, lab., Inv.only £11.18.6 1718/15A
Thomas, Daventry, wheelwright, to John Easson, tailor, principal creditor, Anne, wid., renounced, 1736/23 Dec.
MATTHEWS, Henry, Helmdon, Inv.only £103.4.6 1713/126A
Abraham, Northampton, to Mary, wid., 1728/16 Sept.
Abraham, Northampton, innholder, Inv.only £15.19.0 undated/146
Elizabeth, Elkington, wid., to Anne, wife of Thomas Castell, Yelvertoft, weaver, daughter, 1729/14 June
Edward, Everdon, yeo., Guard.only of Lydia Folwell als. Matthew, minor, niece, 1739/1 Sept.
Matthew, John, Yelvertoft, weaver, to John, weaver, son, Esther, exor., decd., 1762/20 Sept.
John, Farthinghoe, to Charles, Brackley, son, 1787/8 Jan.
John, Middleton Cheney, carpenter, to John Knibb, Hinton, husb., grandson, 1800/5 May
MATTINS, Michael, Sywell, to Jane, wid., 1718/75
Jane, Sywell, wid., to Elizabeth Mews, spin., granddaughter, Inv. £19.17.0 1722/11
MAULE, William, Weedon Beck, yeo., to John, yeo., son, Inv. £13.16.8 1729/10 May
William, Ecton, farmer, to Elizabeth, wid., 1776/26 Aug.
MAUTON, Richard, Clipston, yeo., to Mary, wid., Inv. about £300, 1727/26 May
MAWBY, Mawbey, Richard, Dallington, yeo., Inv.only £250.0.0 1711/148A
Mawbey, Richard, Guard.only of Nathan and Joseph, sons, 1716/4
Mawbey, Thomas, Northampton, lab., to Elizabeth, wid., 1717/128
William, Crick, to Joan, wid., 1725/19 Mar.
William,Crick, Inv.only £135.10.0 1725/139
Mary, Long Buckby, spin., to Anne Smith, sister, 1751/22 Oct.
Elizabeth, Cold Ashby, wid., to John Wykes, Spratton, lab., nephew, 1766/28 Jan.
Richard, Watford, to Sarah, wid., 1768/22 July
Thomas, Broughton, lab., to Thomas, lab., uncle, Mary, wid., renounced, 1775/20 Sept.

MAWBY continued
Robert, Yelvertoft, weaver, to John Linnet, weaver, son in law, Sarah, wid., renounced, 1776/11 May
Richard, Shutlanger, Stoke Bruerne, to John, lab., son, 1781/11 July
MAY, Joseph, Finedon, husb., to Mary, wid., 1731/16 Oct.
Richard, Finedon, farmer, to Anna, wid., 1753/2 June
Joseph, Rushden, yeo., to William Hooper, Wellingborough, woolstapler, brother in law, Anne Warren, wid., Elizabeth, wife of John May, Keysoe, co. Bedford, yeo., Mary Wollaston, wid., Margaret Mallery, wid., and Martha, wife of William Hooper, sisters, renounced, 1760/30 Aug.
MAYDWELL, Joseph, East Farndon, to Marcy, wid., 1715/4
Thomas, Kettering, gent., to Lewis, draper, brother, 1731/2 Nov.
MAYLE, William, Northampton, to Richard, Milton, yeo., father, 1741/14 July
MAYNARD, Jane, St. Peter's, Northampton, spin., Account of John Brafield, gent., and Richard Plowman, gent., admins., £299.18.1 1673/51
John, Syresham, farmer, to John, farmer, son, Anne, wid., renounced, 1751/21 Oct.
MAYNE, Francis, Weston, Sutton Bassett, Account of Grace, wid., £112.14.8 1685/163
MAYO, Maio, Francis, Blakesley, Inv.only £3.3.6 1712/7A
Comfort, Inv.only £97.0.0 1715/21A
Thomas, Chalcombe, to William Armistead, clerk, Vicar of Chalcombe, 1722/52
Mayoe, John, Badby, lab., to Joseph, lab., brother, 1740/24 May
Mary, Eydon, to Thomas, husband, 1785/26 May
MEACOCK, Mecock, Joseph, Newton, shopkeeper, to Jonathan Baker, Kettering, grocer, principal creditor, Will, 1759/6 June
William, Marston St. Lawrence, to Mary Buswell, daughter, 1769/27 Apr.
MEADES, Charles, Paulerspury, lab., Inv.only £14.11.6 1737/335
Mead, Mary, Weedon Beck, spin., to Felix, blacksmith, 1790/28 Oct.
MEADOWS, Thomas, Raunds, lab., to Mary, wid., Inv. £12.11.2 1720/85
Samuel, Warkton, cottager, to Elizabeth, wid., Inv. £19.5.6 1722/105
John, Kettering, to Joseph, yeo., son, Inv. £266.17.8 1732/4 July
Thomas, Desborough, to Mary, shopkeeper, wid., 1751/23 Mar.
Thomas, Wellingborough, yeo., to Elizabeth, wife of Joseph Overall, watchmaker, daughter, Mary, wid., renounced, Inv. £644.14.6 1776/8 Jan.
William, Middleton Cheney, to Mary, wid., 1785/9 July
MEDBURY, Sarah, Rushden, wid., to Edward, Wilby, tanner, son, Inv. £89.10.0 1722/62
Elizabeth, Guard.only of John Mobbs, minor, grandnephew, 1796/8 Dec.
MEDLY, John, Towcester, to Alice, wid., 1715/145
MEE, Samuel, Wellingborough, to Phillis, wid., Inv., 1716/72
Francis, Great Doddington, baker, to Sarah, wid., Inv. £36.7.2 1727/18 May
Joseph, Wellingborough, baker, to Joseph, baker, son, 1741/1 Aug.
Francis, Doddington, baker, to Elizabeth, wid., 1747/12 Dec.
Sarah, Doddington, wid., to Sarah, wife of Thomas Nutt, shepherd, daughter, 1756/22 Dec.
Thomas, Rushden, grocer, to Ann, wid., Inv. £254.15.0 1771/2 Jan.
James, Broughton, baker, to Thomas Sudborough, Burton Latimer, cordwainer, and Joseph, Wellingborough, baker, brothers, uncles, 1785/20 Jan.
MEHEW, William, Hargrave, to Thomas, husb., son, 1721/45
MENSHAW, Thomas, Middleton Cheney, framework knitter, to Joan, wid., 1747/13 Apr.
MERCER, Thomas, Hackleton, gent., to Thomas, gent., son, Elizabeth, wid., renounced, 1741/9 Feb.
MERRIFIELD, Martha, Raunds, wid., to John Drage, husb., brother, 1779/1 Sept.
MERRILL, Francis, Rothwell, weaver, to John, son, Ann, exor., wife, decd., Will, 1766/31 Mar.
MERRIOT see MARRIOTT
MERRY, Elizabeth, Croughton, wid., to Thomas, miller, son, 1799/3 Aug.
MIDDLETON, David, Harpole, to John, Drayton, servant, son, 1721/50
Thomas, Biddlesdon, Bucks., to Griffen, Syresham, lab., son, 1746/3 Feb.
Edward, Winchester, mason, to Mary, Ower, Eland, co. Hants., wid., 1779/30 Dec.
MIERS see MOYERS

MILES, Valentine, Milton, yeo., Inv.only £193.16.8 1713/64A
William, Hanley, Towcester, Inv.only £87.15.0 1717/70A
Mary, Towcester, wid., to Valentine Barford, 1719/30
John, Yelvertoft, to Edmund Bromwick, Hillmorton, co. Warwick, gent., principal creditor, 1729/7 Aug.
MILLER, Francis, Inv.only about £26. 1715/60A
William, Draughton, gent., to Elizabeth, wid., 1715/86
als. Browne, William, Great Creaton, husb., Inv.only £152.10.0 1716/143
Richard, Old, Inv.only £103.13.6 1718/3A
John, Wellingborough, to Isaac, cordwainer, brother, Inv. £18.9.6 Susannah, wid., renounced, 1725/27 Feb.
Walter, Aynho, millwright, wheelwright, to Sarah, wid., Inv. £23.15.0 1731/3 Nov.
Thomas, Northampton, to Thomas, Lyon's Inn, London, gent., son, Penelope, wid., renounced, 1737/16 Apr.
Thomas, Northampton, to Penelope, wid., 1745/3 Apr.
Benjamin, Rothwell, to Elizabeth, mother, 1754/22 Jan.
John, Wellingborough, lab., to Martha, wife of William Young, Odell, co. Bedford, lab., sister, Inv. £41.5.0 1754/20 Nov.
Richard, Hinton, to Mary, wid., 1768/19 Feb.
Henry, Brampton, to Henry, farmer, son, 1771/3 Aug.
Henry, Brampton, yeo., to James King, grazier, guardian of Bartlett, Henry, Elizabeth, John and Samuel, minors, children, Guard., 1777/9 July
John, Mears Ashby, yeo., to James, Northampton, grocer, son, 1788/8 Apr.
Anne, Northampton, to James, grocer, husband, 1800/27 June
MILLS, Elizabeth, Rushden, Inv.only £4.5.0 1714/102A
William, Isham, to William Britain, Breton, yeo., Inv. £4.16.0 Mary, wid., renounced, 1720/135
Henry, Yardley Hastings, yeo., to John, servant, brother, 1745/9 May
Henry, Northampton, maltster, to Job Castle, Chesterton, co. Warwick, farmer, nephew, William, uncle, renounced, 1749/5 Oct.
Anne, Sulgrave, wid., to Evans, victualler, son, 1781/1 Dec.
MILNER, Harrold, Daventry, clerk, Inv.only £26.14.10 1711/70
Harold, Daventry, clerk, to John, Thakeham, co. Sussex, clerk, brother, Will, 1711/132
MILWARD, Henry, Kingsthorpe, to Edward Pippin, glover, Inv. £65.11.4 1711/65
MINTON, Stephen, Braunston, yeo., to Mary, wid., 1760/26 Sept.
MITCHELL, Thomas, Hargrave, yeo., to Nathaniel, yeo., brother, 1748/21 Dec.
William, Dallington, joiner, to Mary, wid., 1756/24 Dec.
Hannah, Harlestone, wid., to Jane, Northampton, spin., and Hannah, wife of William Dunkley, Harpole, blacksmith, daughters, 1784/2 Nov.
MOBBS, Isaac, Bugbrooke, Account of Jane, wid., admin., £32.0.0 1678/136
Thomas, Inv.only £443.0.0 1714/86
John, Wollaston, lab., to Elizabeth, wid., Inv. £16.6.8 1714/183
Bartholomew, Roade, victualler, Inv.only £9.15.0 1715/24A
John, Grendon, to Elizabeth, wid., 1720/99
Robert, Bugbrooke, to Nathaniel Cory, yeo., husband and admin. of Ann, granddaughter, exor., decd., Will, 1771/7 Sept.
Peter, Northampton, mealman, to Robert Trasler, baker, principal creditor, Beatrice, wid., renounced, 1774/10 Oct.
John, Whitfield, farmer, to Anne, wid., 1797/9 Aug.
MONROE, Roree, Lamport, to Elizabeth, wid., Inv. £38.10.0 1714/85
MONTAGNE, John, Northampton, joiner, to Mary, wid., 1732/22 July
MONTGOMERY, William, Ashby St. Ledgers, grazier, to Joseph, grazier, son, John Robinson, exor., renounced, Will, 1799/20 Apr.
MOOR, John, Aston le Walls, to Elizabeth, wid., 1712/36
Moore, Thomas, Guilsborough, lab., to Anne, wid., Inv. £20.18.0 Will, 1712/128
John, Rothwell, Inv.only £17.15.0 1714/10A
Moore, William, Navesby, shopkeeper, to Elizabeth, wid., Inv. £10.4.0 1715/61
Samuel, Ashby St. Ledgers, husb., to William and Edward, brothers, Inv. £100.10.0 Sarah, wid., mother, renounced, 1715/120
James, Northampton, to Sarah, wid., 1722/91
William, Ashby St. Ledgers, Inv.only £140.5.0 1723/126A
Roger, Daventry, to Elizabeth, wid., 1724/122
Moore, Roger, Daventry, Inv.only £8.13.0 undated/109
Moore, Thomas, Kingsthorpe, to Margaret, wid., 1725/22 May

MOOR continued
Moore, Edward, Ashby St. Ledgers, husb., to Margaret, wid., 1728/19 Oct.
Moors, John, Blisworth, mason, Inv.only £14.19.6 1729/231
Moore, Moses, Doddington, to Mary, wife of William Harris, Collingtree, husb., sister, 1739/11 Jan.
Moore, John, Rushton, All Saints, to Mary, wid., mother, 1744/14 May
Moore, William, Sulgrave, to Elizabeth, wid., 1784/24 May
Morer, Andrew, Barton Seagrave, yeo., to Andrew, farmer, son, 1787/6 Nov.
William, Welford, lab., to William, Clipston, lab., son, 1788/18 Sept.
MORGAN, Edward, Preston Capes, yeo., to Hannah, wid., 1764/26 July
William, Northampton, flaxdresser, to Rebecca, wid., 1768/16 Jan.
MORRIS, John, senior, Ecton, Inv.only, 1716/73A
Isaac, Inv.only £39.0.0 1720/84A
James, Brampton, to Martha, wid., 1723/98
Judith, Cotton End, Hardingstone, wid., to John Penn, nephew, 1740/17 Mar.
John, Rushden, blacksmith, to Mary, spin., daughter, 1748/20 Apr.
William, Ecton, gent., to John Lambert, yeo., half brother, Will, 1757/5 Oct.
John, Ecton, farmer, to Elizabeth, wid., 1757/22 Dec.
William, Northampton, to Richard, maltster, father, 1767/9 Mar.
William, Stanwick, to Thomas, mason, son, 1771/23 Oct.
Sarah, Northampton, wid., to Sarah, spin., daughter, 1775/14 July
Morrice, Charles, Isham, farmer, to Edmund, farmer, son, Elizabeth, wid., renounced, 1779/23 July
Joseph, Great Creaton, baker, to Joseph, Long Buckby, baker, son of John, brother, exor., Will, 1782/9 Mar.
John, Long Buckby, baker, to Joseph, baker, son, 1782/9 Mar.
Joseph, Brampton, to Thomas, and Sarah Fellows, 1789/16 Mar.
MORRISON, John, Sulgrave, draper, to Samuel Shelton, Canons Street, London, tallow chandler, nephew, 1754/8 Jan.
MORTON, John, Weedon Beck, to Martha, wid., Inv. £19.9.6 1715/59
Martha, Weedon Beck, to Thomas, husb., son, Inv. £15.9.0 1715/140 and 141
Rev. John, junior, Curate of Stanwick, to Rev. John, clerk, Rector of Oxendon, father, Inv. £35.17.0 1724/77
Henry, Oxendon, clerk, to Anne, wid., 1738/3 Apr.
Joseph, Towcester, to Elizabeth, wid., 1738/23 Dec.
Richard, elder, Heyford, carpenter, to John, carpenter, Will, 1749/30 Sept.
MOSS, William, Abthorpe, to Thomas Eyre, Helmdon, baker, creditor, 1771/22 May
William, Cold Ashby, yeo., to William and Thomas, cordwainers, sons, 1792/12 Mar.
MOTTERSHED, Susanna, Wellingborough, Inv.only £80.6.0 1716/40A
MOULD, Thomas, Rothersthorpe, to Katherine, wid., 1742/20 Nov.
John, Northampton, carpenter, to Robert Teeken, Market Harborough, co. Leic., lab., nephew, 1798/8 Nov.
MOUNT, Thomas, Lilbourne, to Bartholomew, weaver, son, Mary, wid., exor., decd., Will, 1722/129
MOUNTAGUE, Thomas, Rector of Burton Latimer, clerk, to William West, Lacock, gent., principal creditor, Inv. £234.2.10 1719/22
MOVERLEY, Thomas, Great Brington, to Elizabeth, wid., Inv. £23.15.0 1721/82
MOYERS, Miers, John, Welford, yeo., to John, Brixworth, blacksmith, 1738/17 Nov.
John, Welford, yeo., Inv.only £583.8.0 1738/350
MUDDIMAN, John, Everdon, lab., to Elizabeth, Northampton, wid., sister, 1747/21 Mar.
MULLINER, John, Staverton, Inv.only £140.10.0 1714/90A
Rice, Northampton, farrier, to Alice, wid., Inv. £35.0.0 1723/89
MUMFORD, William, Overstone, to Elizabeth, wife of John Luck, Great Billing, husb., sister, 1727/18 Nov.
William, Overstone, Inv.only £200.18.0 1727/200
MUNDAY, Thomas, Whittlebury, yeo., to Sarah, wife of Richard Miller, lab., daughter, 1730/20 June
Thomas, Whittlebury, yeo., to Thomas, lab., son, of goods not fully administered by Sarah Miller, daughter, 1733/14 Apr.
Richard, Whittlebury, lab., Guard.only of Elizabeth, minor, daughter, 1733/20 Oct.
MUNDIN, John, Walgrave, yeo., to Mary, wid., 1753/13 Oct.
Isaac, Mears Ashby, to John, carpenter, son, 1768/4 May

MUNN, Richard, Kettering, to John, son, Inv. £42.14.3 1717/23
Mathew, Kettering, to Mary, wid., 1722/124
Matthew, Kettering, grocer, Inv.only £306.13.4 1722/106
Munns, Thomas, Northampton, cordwainer, to Elizabeth, wid., 1796/26 Apr.
MURCOTT, Valentine, Daventry, to Susanna, wid., 1715/50
Murcutt, Valentine, Daventry, Inv.only £4.15.6 1715/90
George, Floore, victualler, to Mary, wid., 1789/30 Nov.
Thomas, Floore, farmer, to Elizabeth, wid., Will, 1790/10 Aug.
MURRAY, John, Northampton, gent., to Bartholomew Higgins, Weston Underwood, Bucks., gent., and Ann Kilpin, spin., exors. of Elizabeth, wid., exor., 1777/3 Apr.
MUSCOTT, William, Long Buckby, to Joan, wid., 1713/81
William, Long Buckby, Inv.only £7.1.4 1713/74
Muscot, Thomas, Watford, shepherd, to Ann, wid., Inv. £11.4.6 1718/30
John, Daventry, servant, to Sarah, wife of Richard Smith, Stowe Nine Churches, blacksmith, sister, 1728/9 Dec.
John, Weedon Beck, blacksmith, to Ann, wife of Richard Dunkley, cobbler, daughter, 1730/2 Mar.
John, Floore, cobbler, to Hannah, wid., 1731/31 Dec.
William, Woodford, to Thomas, miller, brother, Alice, now wife of Thomas Hornsby, mother, renounced in favour Thomas, guardian of John and Mary, children of William, 1742/26 June
Elizabeth, Crick, to Abraham, brother, 1770/13 Mar.
Musket, Muskit, Thomas, Ringstead, innholder, to Alice, spin., daughter, Inv. £35.10.0 1772/26 Oct.
MUTTON, Samuel, Kelmarsh, to Samuel, pastor, son, Elizabeth, wid., renounced, 1726/26 Apr.
MUZARD, John, Scaldwell, Account of Anne, wid., admin., £163.4.2 1672/135
MYNN, Thomas, Syresham, woodman, to Sarah, spin., daughter, 1758/10 Aug.

N

NARBURY, Thomas, Bozeat, Account of Amy, wid., admin., £80.11.11 1681/68
Thomas, Grendon, Inv.only £159.6.0 1744/394
John, Grendon, to Sarah, wife of Thomas Cherry, yeo., 1747/28 Feb.
NARROWAY, Mary, Wollaston, wid., Inv.only £109.15.6 1720/132
NASBY, John, Brafield on the Green, husb., to Sarah, wid., Inv. £166.17.6 1719/93
NAYLOR, William, Farthinghoe, to Elizabeth Tims, wid., daughter, 1728/19 Oct.
John, Mears Ashby, gardener and victualler, to Elizabeth, wid., Inv. £132.6.0 1741/18 Apr.
NEALE, Christopher, Grendon, Inv.only £25.15.2 1711/100A
James, Hardingstone, shepherd, Inv.only £19.2.4 1712/4A
Neal, Fulk, Middleton Cheney, to Elizabeth, wid., Inv. £34.10.0 1716/83
Thomas, Chelveston cum Caldecott, shepherd, to Mary, wid., Inv. £19.7.0 1720/82
Thomas, Yardley Hastings, lacemaker, Inv.only £14.13.0 1720/146A
Mathew, Middleton Cheney, yeo., to Elizabeth, wid., Inv. £223.9.6 1721/89
John, Gretworth, servant, to William, Brackley, servant, 1727/14 Oct.
Sarah, Tiffield, wid., to Robert, lab., son, 1728/6 Dec.
Neal, John, Yardley, grocer, to Mary, wid., 1746/22 May
Mary, Yardley Hastings, to Ann Old, spin., 1782/22 Jan.
James, Wootton, yeo., to Mary, wife of Thomas Evans, baker, niece of Mary, wid., exor., decd., Will, 1791/13 July
NETHERCOAT, John, Sibbertoft, to Mary, relict, 1712/79
NEWBOLD, Samuel, Heyford, to Duty, wid., 1764/26 Sept.
Duty, Heyford, wid., to Mary, spin., daughter, 1766/18 Oct.
NEWCOMB, Anne, Charlton (Charwelton), 1753/11 May
NEWELL, Richard, Northampton, Inv.only £19.17.6 1722/138A
Newels, Sara, Inv.only £17.15.6 1728/239
NEWITT, Newit, Ann, Crick, wid., to Francis Gumbly, Welton, lab.,brother, 1760/26 May
Thomas, Crick, wheelwright, to Anne, wid., 1787/18 Nov.
NEWMAN, Samuel, West Haddon, Guard.only of John, minor, 1716/51
Thomas, Raunds, farmer, to Thomas, son, Inv. £248.10.0 1717/111

NEWMAN continued
Anne, Paulerspury, wid., to Elizabeth, wife of Joseph Spinall, clerk, sister, Inv. £282.16.2 1720/49
Hannah, Brixworth, wid., to Samuel Spence, Lamport, blacksmith, brother, Inv. £71.3.4 1748/29 July
John, Kettering, marine, to Sarah, wid., 1759/15 Mar.
Gabriel, Towcester, to George, Wappenham, lab., brother, 1778/11 Nov.
George, Wappenham, to Rebecca, wid., Inv. £4.14.0 1781/17 July
Elizabeth, Whittlebury, wid., to George Savage, shopkeeper, cousin, 1786/8 Mar.
NEWOLD, John, Kettering, to Martha, wid., 1714/143
NEWTON, Caleb, Harrington, clerk, Account of Richard Stone, admin., £65.19.8 1674/150
Anthony, Duston, Inv.only £16.4.0 1711/111A
Edward, Thenford, yeo., to Anne, wid., Inv. £244.17.0 1719/110
Anne, Duston, to Hannah Cranfield, wid., sister, 1721/92
Anthony, Duston, Guard.only of Elizabeth, daughter, 1722/127
John, West Haddon, to Ann, wid., Inv. £206.15.0 Guard. of George, minor, son, 1774/15 and 17 Sept.
NICHOLLS, Nichols, Thomas, Fawsley, Account of Thomas Wyment, Badby, admin., £134.13.0 1678/144
Nicolls, James, Horton, to Joan, wid., Inv. £152.2.2 1711/89
Nichols, Mathew, Earl's Barton, clerk, to William Howkins, Ecton, husb., principal creditor, 1717/42
Henry, Raunds, senior, Inv.only £41.14.0 1723/47A
Nickles, Anne, Potterspury, wid., to Mary, wife of John Godfrey, Old Stratford, daughter, 1728/18 Nov.
Nichol, Anne, Potterspury, Inv.only £4.12.11 1728/220
Richard, Guilsborough, carpenter, to Dina, wid., 1729/29 Mar.
Nicholl, Mary, Towcester, wid., to Mary, wife of John Browne, Paulerspury, gent., daughter, 1732/30 Sept.
als. Roberts, Henry, Middleton Cheney, weaver, to Ralph Wells, lab., and his wife Mary, great grandchildren, 1751/12 Mar.
William, Little Billing, to Sarah, wid., Inv. £103.0.0 1766/25 Oct.
Nichols, William, Lilbourne, to Anna, wid., 1770/8 Aug.
Clarke, Piddington, shoemaker, to Frances, wid., 1780/1 Jan.
Thomas, Bozeat, to Sarah, wid., 1785/18 Nov.
NIXON, Thomas, Boughton, to Susanna, wid., 1720/11
Richard, Boughton, stonecutter, to Thomas, stonecutter, son, Mary, wid., renounced, 1741/14 Feb.
Thomas, Boughton, to Rebecca, wid., Will, 1781/20 July
Thomas, Boughton, to Ann, wid., 1781/18 Aug.
NORBURY, Thomas, Grendon, yeo., to Sarah, wid., 1744/2 Nov.
NORCUTT, Thomas, Denton, to Sarah, wid., 1773/27 Aug.
NORMAN, John, East Farndon, yeo., Inv.only £118.8.6 1711/143A
William, Wootton, to Thomas Morton, husb., nephew, Inv. £77.13.0 1714/16
Rebecca, Wootton, wid., to Edward Waples, Towcester, brother, Inv. £60.1.9 1717/149
John, West Haddon, cordwainer, to Alice Burton, wid., daughter, Thomas Kilworth, exor., decd., Will, 1784/24 July
William, West Haddon, cordwainer, to Samuel Hughes, Northampton, ironmonger, Benjamin Bennett, Welford, currier, and Samuel Watkins, Daventry, currier, principal creditors, 1791/10 Sept.
NORRIS, William, Byfield, yeo., Inv.only £28.8.0 1711/93A
Edward, Rector of Stanwick, Inv.only £40.2.6 1717/114A
Robert, Silverstone, to Faith, wid., Inv. £26.3.6 1718/123
William, Silverstone, to Elizabeth, wid., 1730/30 June
Daniel, Paulerspury, yeo., to Anne, wid., Inv. £138.2.4 1738/27 May
John, Cotten End, Hardingstone, to John, Northampton, gent., father, 1757/11 Mar.
Robert, to Thomas, Paulerspury, lab., father, 1758/2 Dec.
Mary, Ecton, wid., to William Hall, London, currier, nephew, 1759/9 Aug.
John, Wootton, victualler, to Hannah, wife of Thomas Williams, sister, 1782/8 Nov.
NORTHORPE, James, Daventry, letter carrier, to Susanna, wid., 1775/25 Oct.
NORTON, John, Long Buckby, weaver, Inv.only £168.7.6 1711/135A

NORTON continued
Bonham, Faxton, Lamport, Inv.only £165.5.0 1716/29 A
Richard, Cransley, to Mary, wid., Inv. £38.0.0 1718/125
Mary, Cransley, maltster, to Joseph, yeo., son, Inv. £68.4.6 Richard, son, renounced, 1720/121
John, Marston Trussell, to Catherine, wid., Inv. £24.15.0 1724/94
Burnham, Broughton, to Mary, wid., 1761/1 Apr.
William, Whilton, woolcomber, to Elizabeth, wid., 1774/16 Nov.
Wykes, Yelvertoft, to Susanna, wid., 1776/28 Sept.
Elizabeth, Whilton, to Edward Hoare, Norton, lab., son in law, 1781/12 Dec.
William, Charlton, Newbottle, to Hezekiah, Brackley, tailor, son, 1784/24 Mar.
John, Marston Trussell, lab., to Ann Chapman, spin., granddaughter, Will, 1785/13 July
Ashby, Wellingborough, cornfactor, to John Carver, minister of the gospel, principal creditor, John, Joseph, and John and Ann Sloane, children, renounced, 1786/7 May
Thomas, Staverton, to Elizabeth, Inv. £150.1.0 1786/1 July
NORWICK, Ascarius, Ascinneas, Kettering, to John, pistor, brother, 1726/5 Sept.
NOTTINGHAM, John, Wellingborough, yeo., Mary, wid., renounced in favour Thomas, son and exor., 1711/45
John, Wellingborough, to Thomas, yeo., grandfather, William Harries, plumber and glazier, and Richard Lucas, yeo., guardians of Elizabeth, daughter, minor, 1750/27 Apr.
NUNNELY, William, Pytchley, Inv.only £1076.0.0 1714/172 A
Nunneley, Mary, Pytchley, to Robert, yeo., son, 1745/28 Jan.
NUNNS, John, Rushton, St. Peter's, keeper, to George, bachelor, brother, Inv. £33.18.6 1715/10
Ann, to William, Rushton, husband, 1747/22 July
William, Rushton, to Mary, wid., 1754/3 Oct.
NURSEY, William, senior, Desborough, Inv.only £6.17.0 1717/99 A
NUTT, William, Sulgrave, mercer, to Elizabeth, wid., 1731/6 May
Henry, Newnham, yeo., to Anne, wid., 1741/5 Dec.

O

OAKLEY, Thomas, Northampton, roper, to Anne, wid., 1730/30 May
ODEHILL, William, Cransley, yeo., to Alice, wid., Inv. £316.19.0 1721/125
OLD, John, Little Houghton, to Bridget, wid., Inv. £123.5.6 1720/152
William, Little Houghton, to Holden Bowker, Northampton, gent., principal creditor, 1767/6 Jan.
Richard, Wootton, gent., Guard.only of Mary, minor, niece, 1775/11 Mar.
Abraham, Little Houghton, to John, Northampton, lab., brother, 1781/7 Nov.
Richard, Preston Deanery, gent., to Francis Evans, Northampton, farmer, Mary, niece, exor., decd., Will, 1791/6 June
John Dorset, Wootton, yeo., to William, yeo., son, Sarah, wid., exor., decd., Will, 1791/29 Oct.
OLDFIELD, James, Oundle, Inv.only £304.1.10 1739/361
OLDHAM, Hannah, Towcester, wid., to Samuel, London, cheesemonger, uncle and guardian of Anne, daughter, minor, Guard. of Hannah and William, minors, children, William Henchman and John Whithorn, Northampton, exors., renounced, Will, Inv. £989.2.0 1714/46
Oadhams, Odams, Robert, Braunston, lab., to William, yeo., brother, Inv. £31.0.0 1731/16 Oct.
OLDNER, Richard, Hanging Houghton, plumber, to Richard, Market Bosworth, co. Leic., cooper, son, Mary, wid., now wife of Nathaniel Kimberlin, renounced, 1786/23 Mar.
OLIVER, Thomas, Bugbrooke, yeo., to Sara, wid., Inv. £43.2.9 1711/46
Mary, Bugbrooke, to Sarah Fisher, mother and guardian of Thomas, grandson, Inv. £56.6.6 1713/42
Elizabeth, Burton Latimer, spin., to Anne Coleman, wid., aunt, 1732/18 Jan.
Thomas, Alderton, farmer, to Richard, farmer, son, 1766/14 Jan.
Edward, Daventry, lab., to Thomas, Bugbrooke, lab., father, 1790/5 Apr.
ONELY, Richard, West Haddon, yeo., to Thomas, grazier, son, 1780/29 May

ORAM, John, Bozeat, woodman, to Mary, wid., and Edward Eaglestone, Wollaston, mason, son in law, Inv. £50.15.0 1746/29 Aug.
ORLAND, William, Creaton, miller, to Jane, wid., 1795/14 Nov.
ORME, Robert, Northampton, to Thomasin, wid., 1724/78
Orm, als. Cook, Sophia, see Cook
ORPIN, Thomas, Mears Ashby, Inv.only £498.0.0 1718/55A
Francis, Mears Ashby, Inv.only £264.6.0 1718/76 A
ORTON, John, Chipping Warden, gent., Inv.only £206.2.8 1722/60A
Henry, Byfield, to Ann, wid., 1761/28 Oct.
John, Kilsby, lab., to Alice, spin., daughter, 1766/1 Sept.
Thomas, Wellingborough, to Thomas Garret, brother in law, Inv. £23.0.0 1776/2 Mar.
OSBORN, Dorothy, Rushton, wid., to Robert, yeo., son, 1744/24 Dec.
John, Abington, tailor, to George, elder, Weston, tailor, father, Inv. £5.12.0 1748/19 Dec.
George, Everdon, victualler, to Mary, wid., 1758/20 July
Osborne, Thomas, Northampton, gent., to Henry Woolley, gent., Sarah, daughter, renounced, Will, 1771/17 May
Mary, Everdon, wid., to George, baker, son, 1776/29 Feb.
Philip, Northampton, farrier, to Elizabeth, wid., 1791/12 Dec.
Osborne, Thomas, Northampton, gent., to Richard, gent., son, Will, 1794/27 Feb.
OUTLAW, Thomas, Irthlingborough, gent., to Saint John, gent., son, Sarah, wid., exor., incapable, Will, 1783/29 July
OWEN, Francis, Isham, to Mary, wid., Inv. £86.16.6 1720/133
Samuel, Pytchley, collarmaker, Inv.only £86.0.4 1722/64A
OYNEN, Matthew, Brackley, yeo., to Elizabeth, wid., Inv. £19.2.9 1760/23 Aug.

P

PACK, Pakes, William, Castle Ashby, yeo., Inv.only £143.19.2 1712/117A
John, Wellingborough, to Christopher, butcher, 1722/41
William, Chelveston cum Caldecott, servant, to James Jackson, Irchester, yeo., next of kin, 1730/30 Sept.
Christopher, Kettering, butcher, to Sarah, wid., Inv. £37.0.0 1732/19 Apr.
John, Wellingborough, schoolmaster, to Elizabeth, Barton, wid., 1751/18 May
PACKER, Daniel, Floore, Guard.only of John, son, 1711/12
Nathaniel, Weedon Beck, Inv.only £298.10.0 1727/191
PACKWOOD, John, Cottesbrooke, to William, grazier, 1756/20 Sept.
Robert, Cottesbrooke, yeo., to Sarah, wife of John Crick, Thurnby, yeo., aunt and guardian of Sarah, Thomas, John, Michael and Mary, minors, children, Inv. £405.0.0 Guard., 1756/13 Nov.
Thomas, Cottesbrooke, farmer, to Ann, wid., 1798/3 Dec.
PADBURY, Michael, Moreton Pinkney, lab., to John, Nethorpe, co. Oxford, gardener, son, 1787/28 July
PAGE, Edward, Northampton, Inv.only £148.4.4 1711/56 A
Walter, Brixworth, to Mary, wid., 1717/5
Nicholas, Brixworth, blacksmith, to Elizabeth Martin, Northampton, principal creditor, 1717/133
James, Braybrooke, yeo., Inv.only £469.13.6 1719/69 A
Michael, elder, Wellingborough, cooper, Inv.only £10.10.0 1720/45A
Thomas, Kettering, shepherd, Inv.only £22.14.6 1721/34A
William, West Haddon, to Rachael, wid., 1721/85
William, Wellingborough, to Thomas, Kettering, innholder, son, 1725/12 Jan.
Thomas, Kettering, innholder, to Martha, wid., 1728/16 Oct.
Thomas, Inv.only £35.8.0 1728/216
Thomas, Higham Ferrers, to Elizabeth, wid., 1729/28 Apr.
William, West Haddon, cordwainer, to Alice, wife of Thomas Palmer, innholder, daughter, Ann, wid., renounced, 1752/9 Dec.
John, Wellingborough, to John, yeo., son, 1754/12 Aug.
John, Upton, grazier, to John, grazier, son, 1778/9 June
William, Upton, grazier, to John, grazier, brother, 1783/16 May
Thomas, Northampton, tailor, to Elizabeth, wid., 1793/21 May
William, Little Harrowden, weaver, to William, cordwainer, 1798/28 May
PAIN see PAYNE

PAINTER, John, Cannons Ashby, gent., Account of Christian, wid., admin., £503.1.8 1671/120
Richard, Brackley, Account of Margaret, wid., admin., £163.0.0 1680/10
William, Evenley, Account of Joseph, son, admin., £109.1.6 1681/65
Henry, Evenley, Account of Mary, wid., admin., £61.0.0 1682/73
Paynter, William, Evenley, to Joan, wid., Inv. £224.2.6 1715/146
Paynter, Elizabeth, Evenley, wid., Inv.only £63.18.6 1720/22
John, Moulton, to William, yeo., son, 1723/100
Sarah, Radstone,to William, yeo., husband, 1744/24 Mar.
PALMER, Richard, Pisford, butcher, Account of Robert Sanders and George Lucas, admins., £58.18.0 1677/149
Anthony, Stoke Doyle, to Charles, clerk, brother, Will, 1712/35
Elizabeth, Milton, Inv.only £36.14.4 1712/147A
John, Wilby, farmer, to James, husb., son, Inv. £13.3.4 1713/17
Anne, Inv.only £21.13.6 1713/111A
Samuel, Rushden, Inv.only £270.18.8 1713/117A
Joseph, Kettering, to Mary, wid., Inv. £9.3.6 1719/5
William, Scaldwell, yeo., Inv.only £131.16.0 1719/65A
Samson, Milton, yeo., to Samson, husb., son, Inv. £108.1.0 1719/117
William, Pisford, carpenter, to Jane, wid., Inv. £9.3.4 1720/139
Thomas, West Haddon, butcher, to Thomas, butcher, son, Inv. £79.10.0 1726/28 May
Jane, Wilby, spin., to Elizabeth, wife of Charles Robinson, baker, sister, Inv. £45.2.6 1728/17 Feb.
John, Northampton, to Elizabeth, wid., 1728/20 Aug.
Elizabeth, Rushden, wid., to Mary, wife of Thomas Roberts, Wellingborough, glover, daughter, 1728/16 Dec.
Edmund, Alderton, clerk, to Charles, Towcester, clerk, father, 1729/23 Apr.
William, Northampton, carrier, to Elizabeth, wid., 1729/4 Oct.
John, Milton, shepherd, to Mary, wid., 1731/10 May
Abraham, Kettering, glover, to Elizabeth, wid., Inv. £64.12.0 1731/2 June
James, Wilby, to Sarah, wid., Inv. £74.13.6 1733/22 Sept.
Edward, Scaldwell, blacksmith, to Mary, wid., 1735/22 Apr.
Thomas, Old, yeo., Inv.only £409.2.8 1738/344
Mary, Scaldwell, wid., to Hannah, wife of James Moor, Holcott, sister, Will, 1741/16 Jan.
William, Welford, to Elizabeth, wid., 1741/25 July
Pamer, William, Welford, Inv.only £135.17.6 1741/378
Mary, Draughton, wid., to Palmer Saby, Weston Favell, husb., grandson, Robert Hewitt, yeo., exor., renounced, Will, 1766/16 Apr.
William, Northampton, to Samuel, baker, son, 1778/8 Aug.
John, Duston, farmer, to Mary, wid., 1781/9 July
Mary, Duston, wid., to John Cox, Harlestone, yeo., grandfather and guardian of Thomas, Martha, Elizabeth, minors, children, Guard., 1782/2 Feb.
Mary, Kislingbury, wid., to Robert Faulkner, weaver, husband of Mary, decd., exor. of Ann Van, spin., decd., exor. of Mary, Will, 1782/28 Dec.
Anthony, Hanging Houghton, to Mary, wife of William Dickens, lab., sister, 1783/30 Dec.
Thomas, Milton, victualler, to Elizabeth, wife of John Ward, Rothersthorpe, victualler, sister, 1789/8 June
PANTHER, Thomas, Warkton, gent., to Margaret, wid., 1788/15 May
PARBURY, Thomas, Spratton, Inv.only £14.12.6 1724/68A
Sarah, Spratton, wid., to John Waterfield, weaver, cousin, 1758/28 Oct.
Richard, Bugbrooke, maltster, to Joseph Adams, farmer, and Thomas Stanton, Heyford, grazier, guardians of Beatrice, minor , daughter, Guard., 1794/13 Feb.
PARGITER, Thomas, Sulgrave, lab., to John, yeo., Inv. £14.10.0 1721/62
Samuel, Earl's Barton, clerk, to Thomas, London, gent., brother, 1729/31 Dec.
PARIS als. Taylor see Taylor
PARISH, John, Kettering, to Elizabeth, wid., Inv. £16.7.0 1733/31 Aug.
John, Towcester, to Ann, wife of Edward Jakins, Stoke Bruerne, butcher, wid., 1797/2 May
PARKE, Richard, Lilbourne, to Sarah, wid., Inv. £18.8.6 1720/68
PARKER, John, Weston Favell Mill, miller, to Mary, wid., 1715/30

PARKER continued
William, Brackley, mason, to Charles, husb., son, Inv. £9.0.6 1718/77
Francis, Northampton, to Mary, spin., daughter, 1775/23 June
John, Great Purston, Newbottle, to Avis, Inv. £429.14.0 1779/22 May
William, Overstone, yeo., to George, farmer, son, Simon Reddish, yeo., and Samuel Pell, yeo., exors., renounced, Will, 1785/13 Apr.
William, Brackley, tailor, to Bessey, spin., daughter, 1788/30 July
PARKINS see PERKINS
PARNELL, Parnel, John, Little Weldon, tailor, Inv.only £4.9.0 1728/255
Edward, West Haddon, yeo., to Thomas Webb, Kilsby, blacksmith, Thomas Usher, Kilsby, woolcomber, and Benjamin Collis, lab., 1747/15 Oct.
Thomas, West Haddon, to Richard, farmer, son, 1761/4 Mar.
PARR, Bartholomew, Wellingborough, chandler, Inv.only £369.6.1 1715/102A
PARROTT, Parrett, Thomas, Daventry, to Rebecca, wid., 1724/137
Jane, Northampton, wid., to John Chaulke, Hulcott, gent., principal creditor, Elizabeth, wife of Thomas Walmesley, daughter, renounced, 1727/18 May
PARSONS, Sarah, Drayton, Daventry, to John, tanner, husband, 1744/3 Nov.
PARTRIDGE, John, Earl's Barton, mercer, Inv.only £149.12.8 1712/124A
Wellingborough, victualler, to Mary, wid., 1794/8 Oct.
PASHAM, John, Northampton, to Elizabeth, wid., 1723/125
PATCH, Thomas, Yelvertoft, to Anne, wid., Will, 1718/137
Thomas, West Haddon, cordwainer, to Mary, wid., 1794/22 Oct.
PATCHETT, Susanna, Daventry, wid., Inv.only £47.19.4 1719/27A
PATRICK, Amon, Higham Ferrers, lab., to Elizabeth, wid., Inv. £50.2.6 1724/57
PATTISON, Mary, Wellingborough, to Ephraium, younger, yeo., husband, 1756/18 May
Epharaim, Wellingborough, farmer, to Joseph, farmer, 1788/11 July
PAXTON, Anne, Sulgrave, Account of Anthony, brother, admin., £106.3.6 1677/47
Thomas, Sulgrave, Account of Mary, wid., admin., now wife of Thomas White, £93.0.0 1683/80
Anthony, Sulgrave, yeo., to Anthony, yeo., son, Inv. £111.7.6 1732/2 Mar.
PAYBODY, Pebody, William, Marston Trussell, yeo., to Charles Buswell, yeo., and Vincent Bailey, yeo., guardians of William, Mary, Elizabeth, minors, children, Martha, wid., renounced, 1730/3 Dec.
William, Northampton, to William, London, son, 1772/24 Oct.
William, Marston Trussell, to Elizabeth, London, daughter, 1772/24 Oct.
PAYNE, Payn, Thomas, Welton, husb., to Elizabeth, wid., Inv. £199.8.3 1711/122
Paine, Payn, William, Rothersthorpe, husb., to Elizabeth, spin., sister, Inv. £200.0.0 1713/94
Payn, Thomas, Isham, yeo., Inv.only £42.16.6 1714/130A
Paine, Elizabeth, Rothersthorpe, spin., to Richard Dunckley, nephew, Inv. £179.9.0 1718/114
Randolph, Draughton, to Mary, wid., 1721/123
Pain, Susanna, Isham, wid., Inv.only £15.17.6 1722/23A
Pain, John, Caldecote, Towcester, to Ann, wid., 1723/29
Pain, John, Towcester, Inv.only £26.14.8 1723/136A
Paine, Richard, Maidford, cobbler, to Rachael, wid., 1727/11 Mar.
Paine, Richard, Maidford, Inv.only £45.2.8 1727/152
Pain, John, Great Houghton, to Anne, wid., 1732/23 Sept.
Paine, Thomas, Northampton, maltster, to Jonas, Priors Marston, co. Warwick, yeo., brother, Elizabeth, wid., mother, renounced, 1735/13 Jan.
Paine, Samuel, Kettering, to Dorothy, wid., 1735/10 Sept.
Paine, Jonathan, Northampton, gardener, to Bryan Mould, shoemaker, of goods not fully administered by Stephen Mold, exor., decd., Will, 1737/27 Aug.
Paine, Thomas, Oundle, ironmonger, Inv.only £2572.18.0 1739/373
William, Heyford, tailor, to Elizabeth, wid., 1752/15 Aug.
Paine, William, Dallington, yeo., to Mary, wid., 1755/24 Jan.
Pain, William, Daventry, butcher, to John Rainbow, Dunchurch, co. Warwick, lab., uncle and guardian of John, minor, son, 1755/17 Feb.
Pain, Jeremiah, Maidwell, gardener, to Mary, wid., 1758/5 Sept.
Pain, Thomas, Little Bowden, blacksmith, to Thomas, son, Mary, wife, decd., Will, 1765/25 Nov.

PAYNE continued
Pain, Jonas, Upper Boddington, farmer, to Elizabeth, Inv. £495.15.6 1771/16 Nov.
Paine, William, Courtenhall, to John, Rothersthorpe, farmer, brother, 1773/3 Apr.
Paine, John, Cogenhoe, farmer, to Sarah, wid., Richard Gleed, Rothersthorpe, yeo., exor., renounced, Will, 1787/11 Aug.
Paine, Robert, Little Addington, to William, son, Jane, wid., renounced, 1792/4 May
PEACH, William, Wootton, to Anne, wid., 1720/100
Sarah, Northampton, wid., to Elizabeth Harper, wid., daughter, 1736/25 June
Thomas, Brafield on the Green, shoemaker, to Elizabeth, wid., 1795/27 July
PEACOCK, Philip, Ringstead, husb., Inv.only £419.15.0 1716/57A
Robert, Denford, Inv.only £34 1716/76A
Anne, Ringstead, wid., Inv.only £28.10.0 1717/131A
Thomas, Ringstead, yeo., widower, to Thomas, yeo., son, Inv. £60.10.0 1749/18 Nov.
PEAKE, Peakes, George, Grindon, cordwainer, to Thomas Weston, Higham Ferrars, carrier, principal creditor, Inv. £13.11.0 1714/21
John, Heathencote, Paulerspury, yeo., Inv.only £870.10.0 1714/141A
William, Northampton, bachelor, to Mary, mother, 1723/43
Peak, John, Northampton, lab., to Robert Peach, gent., 1730/7 Mar.
Samuel, Rushton, yeo., to Borlass Warren, principal creditor, 1730/23 Mar.
William, Northampton, to Anne, wid., 1775/19 Dec.
PEARSIFUL see PERCIVAL
PEARSON, Thomas, Haselbech, to Alice, wid., Inv. £23.8.2 1725/20 Oct.
John, Daventry, to Thomas, Ryton upon Dunsmore, co. Warwick, husb., brother, guardian of Jane, minor, daughter, Guard., 1727/15 and 16 Oct.
Mary, Easton Maudit, to Francis Pratt, Doddington, Mary and Elizabeth Pratt, exors., minors, granddaughters, Will, 1773/1 Oct.
Thomas, Spratton, husb., to John, Creaton, farmer, brother, Will, 1780/22 Jan.
James, Northampton, mason, to Robert, Piddington, cordwainer, brother, Will, 1782/20 Apr.
Mary, Middleton Cheney, late of Banbury, wid., to John Hopkins Pearson, Banbury, co. Oxford, shag manufacturer, 1794/16 Oct.
PEASE, Peter, Wicken, brickmaker, to Anne, wid., 1735/13 Dec.
PEASNALL, Stephen, Weedon Beck, baker, to Elizabeth, wid., 1752/25 Sept.
Stephen, Moreton Pinkney, cordwainer, to William, Ashton, lab., brother, 1793/23 Oct.
PECKOVER, Nathaniel, Newbottle, tailor, Inv.only £41.12.3 1725/173
PELHAM, Samuel, Wellingborough, to Susannah, wid., 1790/5 Mar.
PELL, John, Milton Malsor, Inv.only £24.13.4 1722/119A
Susanna, Heyford, wid., to Richard Morton, yeo., nephew, 1723/74
William, Guilsborough, to Elizabeth, wid., 1728/28 Sept.
William, Guilsborough, Inv.only £157.17.0 1728/236
Elizabeth, Moulton Park, spin., to Thomas, yeo., brother, 1737/9 July
Hannah, Astcote, Pattishall, spin., to Edward, lab., brother, and Richard, Newport Pagnell, Bucks., lab., nephew, 1747/30 Dec.
John, Great Houghton, Guard.only of Thomas, Ann and Jane, minors, children, 1764/11 May
John, Overstone, to Elizabeth, wid., 1773/6 Mar.
Edward, Upton, miller, to Mary, wid., 1774/10 Dec.
PENDRED, William, Brafield on the Green, yeo., Inv.only £6.6.2 1719/73A
Benjamin, Wellingborough, hemp and rope dresser, to Samuel, hemp dresser, son, Inv. £70.9.4 1746/4 Nov.
PENN, Thomas, Middleton Cheney, mason, to John, mason, son, Inv. £15.18.0 1735/3 Oct.
Elizabeth, Little Houghton, wid., to John, son, 1740/17 Mar.
Edward, Paulerspury, yeo., to Elizabeth, wid., 1741/11 Mar.
Richard, Farthinghoe, yeo., to Mary, wife of Thomas Priest, Priors Marston, co. Warwick, yeo., sister, 1747/20 July
Humphrey, Middleton Cheney, yeo., to Elizabeth, wid., Inv. £210.13.6 1756/12 Oct.
Elizabeth, Middleton Cheney, wid., to Robert, yeo., son, 1779/14 June
Elizabeth, Middleton Cheney, spin., to Thomas, farmer, brother, 1788/9 Jan.
Thomas, Middleton Cheney, to Anne, wid., 1788/6 May

PENN continued
Timothy, Northampton, weaver, to John, weaver, and William, cordwainer, sons, 1795/17 Jan.
PENNINGTON, John, Northampton, to Rebecca, wid., mother, 1749/5 Aug.
PEPPER, Elizabeth, Kettering, to Elizabeth, 1751/28 Dec.
PERCIVAL, Percivall, William, Northampton, gardener, to Jane, wid., Inv. £6.12.11 1714/185 and 186
Percivall, Thomas, Dallington, to Samuel, Northampton, mason, 1714/191
Edward, Northampton, cooper, to Sarah, wid., Inv. £13.5.0 1715/162
James, Dallington, to Thomas Ward, brother, 1717/108
Percivall, Samuel, Northampton, mason, Inv.only £249.5.0 1718/36A
Peircivall, Samuel, Northampton, to Elizabeth, wid., mother, 1722/87
Pearsifull, Samuel, Northampton, to Thomas, Dallington, mason, uncle, of goods unadminstered by Elizabeth, decd., 1724/21
Pearsifull, Samuel, senior, Northampton, mason, to Thomas, Dallington, mason, of goods unadministered by Elizabeth, wid., exor., Will, 1724/31
Pearsifull, Samuel, Northampton, mason, to Francis Luck, Spratton, whittawer, and Cordelia Manning, wid., exors. of Elizabeth, wid., exor., decd., Will, 1732/9 Mar.
John, Northampton, lab., to Sarah, wid., 1776/20 July
PERKINS, Timothy, Hinton, husb., Will only, 1711/16
Samuel, Lilbourne, to Mary, wid., 1714/77
Parkins, Samuel, Lilbourne, gent., Inv.only £316.10.0 1714/81
Joseph, Loddington, Inv.only £14.8.0 1716/116A
John, Rector of Kislingbury, to Richard Hind, Cold Ashby, gent., principal creditor, 1729/6 Mar.
Thomas, Draughton, comber, to Hannah, wid., 1730/28 Feb.
Thomas, Towcester, innholder, to Mary, wid., 1730/9 July
Elizabeth, Higham Ferrers, spin., to Lewis, weaver, and Mary, spin., Will, 1732/30 May
Benjamin, Kettering, to Sarah, wid., Inv. £11.8.6 1733/31 Aug.
Thomas, Little Houghton, to Mary, wid., 1741/25 Mar.
Edward, Irthlingborough, farmer, to Elizabeth, spin., daughter, Inv. £470.5.0 1747/24 Mar.
Robert, Finedon, tailor, to Mary, wid. of Joseph, daughter in law, Inv. £87.14.6 1762/20 Jan.
Edward, Irthlingborough, to Robert Todd, Northampton, cutler, husband and admin. of Elizabeth, daughter, decd., 1767/17 Nov.
William, Desborough, to Elizabeth, wid., 1775/30 Sept.
Pirkins, Mary, Pattishall, to John, gent., husband, 1794/23 Aug.
Elizabeth, Lilbourne, to Thomas, gent., husband, 1796/3 Feb.
John, Northampton, gardener, to Anne, wid., 1800/17 Sept.
PERMAN, John, Kelmarsh, Account of Rebecca, wid., admin., £105.5.0 1671/95
PERRIDGE, Thomas, Green's Norton, miller, to Elizabeth, wid., 1760/19 Feb.
John, younger, Wood Burcote, Towcester, to Mary, wid., 1797/14 Jan.
Ambrose, Green's Norton, gent., to Mark Folwell, Pattishall, butcher, and John Wakefield, Farthingstone, grazier, 1797/21 Jan.
PERRIN, John, Moulton, Inv.only £127.5.0 1714/30A
Henry, Milton, yeo., to Sarah, wid., 1738/27 May
John, Sywell, victualler, to Elizabeth, wid., 1743/31 Dec.
Thomas, Cottesbrooke, farmer, grazier, to James, lab., brother, Mary Lewin, exor., decd., Will, 1795/4 Apr.
Anne, Moulton, to Edward Ward, Mears Ashby, gent., father and guardian of Elizabeth, minor, granddaughter, 1796/13 June
PETERS, John, Finedon, to Elizabeth, spin., Inv. £38.17.6 1714/126
William, Northampton, pipemaker, Inv.only £52.4.6 1715/15A
Thomas, Higham Ferrers, milliner, Inv.only £188.0.0 1716/97A
PETTIFER, Thomas, Middleton Cheney, Inv.only £71.1.6 1712/111A
Pettipher, Thomas, Middleton Cheney, husb., Inv.only £84.12.6 1715/74A
William, Hellidon, lab., to Anne, wid., 1729/15 Jan.
Pettyfer, John, Vicar of Blakesley, to Mary, wid., 1730/8 Aug.
Petifer, Richard, Sulgrave, mason, to Elizabeth, wid., Inv. £153.19.0 1744/2 June
Mary, Middleton Cheney, to John, St. Andrew, London, son, 1775/12 Jan.
Richard, Kilsby, to William, farmer, son, 1777/14 Oct.
PETTIT, Petit, John, Grendon, Account of Alice, admin., £38.15.4 undated/168

PETTIT continued
John, Wollaston, husb., Inv.only £42.0.0 1717/39 A
Richard, Bozeat, to Elizabeth Bettle and Ann Surridge, daughters, Inv. £23.13.0 1718/80
William, Northampton, gent., to John Clark, draper, guardian of William, minor, exor., Will, 1719/3
Pettitt, John, Great Doddington, Inv.only £18.16.8 1724/14 A
Pettitt, Anne, Doddington, wid., to Anne, wife of Henry Miller, daughter, 1728/17 May
Pettitt, Wilmer, Grendon, lab., to Thomas, butcher, son, Inv. £17.4.6 1730/23 Apr.
Pettitt, John, Wollaston, laceman, to William, yeo., father, 1732/5 Oct.
PEUSEY, Puzey, Roger, Clipston, yeo., Inv.only £25.0.0 1723/20 A
PHILL, Temperance, Everdon, Account of Temperance Folwell, daughter, admin., £70.0.0 1680/27 and 85
PHILLIPS, Phillipps, John, Rushton, to George, yeo., son, 1711/150
Thomas, Brackley, to John Major, cordwainer, kinsman, 1715/143
Thomas, Brackley, servant, to Samuel, Ramsey, Hunts., gent., Inv. £5.2.6 1716/68
John, Floore, to Thomas, father, 1716/94
John, Helmdon, mason, to Alice, wid., Inv. £44.13.2 1717/106
Grace, Harrington, wid., to Ann Burrow, wid., daughter, 1722/120
Thomas, Floore, grocer, to Catherine, wid., 1738/7 June
Edward, Silverstone, to Elizabeth, wid., 1740/14 June
William, Glendon, grazier, to Susanna, wid., 1750/24 Mar.
James, Great Harrowden, grazier, to Daniel, Haselbech, grazier, brother, Mary, wid., mother, renounced, Inv. £498.5.4 1765/12 Jan.
Elizabeth, Rothwell, spin., to Daniel, Great Harrowden, grazier, Elijah, brother, exor., decd., Will, 1766/5 Aug.
Daniel, Great Oxendon, to Dinah, spin., and Elizabeth, wife of Daniel Smith, Deenethorpe, yeo., sisters, 1771/5 Aug.
William, Kettering, weaver, to Grace, wid., 1780/14 July
James, Floore, farmer, to William Claridge, Whilton, shoemaker, grandfather and guardian of James, William, Thomas, Mary and Hannah, minors, children, Guard., 1787/21 July
PHIPPS, Thomas, Weedon Beck, to Sarah, wid., Inv. £114.13.8 1715/84
Thomas, Weedon Beck, Guard.only of Elizabeth, minor, daughter, 1735/8 May
Daniel, Brackley, baker, to Thomas Young, carpenter, uncle and guardian of Anne and Joyce, minors, daughters, Inv. £126.15.6 1743/15 Oct.
William, Litchborough, farmer, to Christian, wid., Joseph Winckles, Blakesley, farmer, Thomas Wright, junior, Towcester, gent., and John Cook, Paulerspury, farmer, guardians of Elizabeth, John, Sarah and William, minors, children, 1774/29 Apr.
John, Bugbrooke, farmer, to Sarah, wid., 1783/29 July
William, Litchborough, to John, Paulerspury, yeo., son, 1790/20 May
William, Litchborough, to John, Paulerspury, yeo., brother, 1790/14 Dec.
Sarah, Litchborough, to John, Paulerspury, yeo., brother, 1790/14 Dec.
PICK, Abraham, Teeton, Ravensthorpe, to Deborah, wid., 1717/75
Leonard, Kettering, gent., to Mary, wid., Inv. £102.0.11 1724/112
Thomas, Kettering, to Hephzibah, wid., 1724/128
William, West Haddon, lab., to Lydia, wid., Inv. £16.12.6 1727/28 Jan.
Lydia, Watford, wid., to Ann, wife of James Green, lab., daughter, 1756/9 Feb.
PICKERING, Richard, Bugbrooke, yeo., Inv.only £18.0.8 1711/13 A
PICKMER, Robert, Kingsthorpe, Account of Elizabeth, wid., admin., £46.17.4 1681/64
Elizabeth, Kingsthorpe, wid., Account of Elizabeth Wright, daughter, admin., £80.9.5 1684/157
PIDDINGTON, John, Badby, victualler, to Alice, wid., 1733/24 Mar.
PIGDEN, Elizabeth, Bozeat, wid., Inv.only £15.10.9 1732/293
PIKE, Matthew, Harpole, yeo., Inv.only £688.10.4 1715/65A
John, Crick, husb., to Anne, wid., Inv. £167.0.0 1718/95
James, Welford, to Elizabeth, wid., Inv. £9.13.8 1720/154
PILGRIM, Richard, Kingsthorpe, Inv.only £11.11.0 1721/98
John, Rothersthorpe, to Mary, wid., 1776/15 Aug.
PILL, Richard, Upper Boddington, yeo., Inv.only £116.15.0 1719/108A
Francis, Maidford, to Edward, St. James, co. Middx., victualler, 1726/29 Jan.
John, Boddington, to Anne, wid., 1794/25 Aug.

PINCHBACK, Robert, Finedon, fellmonger, Inv.only £25.3.0 1718/120A
Elizabeth, Finedon, Inv.only £9.8.8 1744/399
PINKARD, Pinkerd, Elizabeth, Denshanger, Passenham, wid., Inv.only £11.10.0 1714/129A
James, Drayton, Daventry, to Hannah, wid., 1715/153
James, Drayton, Daventry, yeo., to Hanna, wid., Inv. £326.6.9 1716/18
Thomas, Drayton, Daventry, yeo., Inv.only £14.12.6 1716/18A
Pinkerd, John, Woodend, Blakesley, Inv.only £124.8.0 1717/97
Pinckard, Thomas, Grimscote, to Richard, Dalscote, farmer, and Samuel, farmer, brothers, 1762/23 Oct.
Pinckard, Jane, Towcester, spin., to John, Northampton, gent., brother, 1767/28 Feb.
Pinckard, Rebecca, Farthingstone, to John, gent., husband, Will, 1782/11 Mar.
PIPPIN, William, Kingsthorpe, carpenter, to Isabella, wid., Inv. £6.6.0 1717/16
PIRKINS see PERKINS
PITHAM, Pittam, John, Blakesley, shepherd, to Alice, wid., Inv. £53.15.0 1726/1 Oct.
Susannah, Furtho, to John, farmer, husband, 1770/5 Apr.
PITTS, Thomas, Doddington, chapman, to Richard, shopkeeper, brother, 1782/29 Jan.
PLACKETT, Samuel, Northampton, sawyer, to William, son, Inv. £6.8.0 1716/87
William, Inv.only £37.6.6 1729/251
Richard, Woodend, Blakesley, lab., to Dorothy, wid., Inv. £9.3.4 1730/25 Sept.
Robert, Piddington, lab., to George Longstaffe, shopkeeper, principal creditor, Elizabeth, wid., renounced, 1786/9 Mar.
PLOWMAN, Thomas, Wellingborough, victualler, Inv.only £23.2.0 1723/122
Charles, Blisworth, yeo., to Sarah, wife of George Travell, Roade, yeo., daughter, and William, yeo., grandson, Inv. £37.16.3 1745/23 Feb.
William, Northampton, to William, fellmonger, son, 1768/21 Sept.
POINTER, Poynter, Benjamin, Paulerspury, to Ann, wid., 1793/9 Dec.
POND, Thomas, Clipston, to Ruth, wid., 1763/10 Sept.
PONTON, Samuel, Marston Trussell, miller, Inv.only £71 1715/91A
POOL, POOLE see POWELL
POOLEY, William, Little Addington, to Daniel, yeo., Inv. £90.13.10 1711/63
John, Brington (Broughton), plasterer, to Anne, wid., 1727/2 Dec.
Mary, Rothwell, to John, son, 1771/1 May
POPE, Thomas, Scaldwell, to John, father, 1717/97
PORTER, Thomas, Rothwell, miller, Inv.only £41.4.6 1718/2A
John, Abthorpe, yeo., to Mary, wid., mother, Inv. £31.10.0 1754/3 Aug.
Mary, Wicken, wid., to Robert, shopkeeper, son, 1758/13 Apr.
Rev. Thomas, Northampton, dissenting minister, to William Joseph, Deptford, co. Kent, gent., son, Sarah, wid., renounced, 1785/3 Mar.
PORTINGTON, Judith, Northampton, wid., to Henry, Little Billing, clerk, son, 1796/7 Nov.
POTTER, Edward, Cranford St. John, to Edward, son, Inv. £50.5.0 1713/34
Sarah, Northampton, spin., to Martha, wife of Thomas Cooke, hillier, sister, 1758/11 Oct.
Robert, Daventry, innholder, to Rosamond, wid., 1774/31 Dec.
John, Northampton, whipmaker, to Thomas Green, Baldock, Herts., watchmaker, cousin, Will, 1788/22 Sept.
POTTS, John, Daventry, saddler, to William, saddler, brother, Elizabeth, wid., renounced, 1797/8 Aug.
POULTON, John, Appletree, Aston le Walls, yeo., to Elizabeth, wid., 1742/23 Oct.
POUNTNEY, Kezia, Daventry, wid., to Thomas Biker, Bourton, co. Warwick, clerk, 1771/18 Dec.
William, Northampton, apothecary, to Thomas Chambers and Samuel Treslove, drapers, principal creditors, Mary, St. Thomas's Hospital, Southwark, co. Surrey, sister, renounced, 1772/9 Mar.
POVEY, Poviey, Jane, Badby, Inv.only £6.5.8 1736/337
POWELL, Samuel, Inv.only £42.16.0 1714/19A
Poole, John, Newnham, baker, to Anne, wid., Inv. £45.1.0 1718/4
Pool, Susanna, Northampton, wid., to Sarah Webb, wid., daughter, 1718/136

POWELL continued
James, Great Doddington, husb., to Elizabeth, wid., Will, 1767/4 Nov.
Pool, Samuel, Old, to Samuel, cordwainer, son, 1769/18 Mar.
Pool, Hannah, Kislingbury, to Daniel, Northampton, horsekeeper, husband, 1774/11 Apr.
Poole, John, Moulton, yeo., to Mary, wife of John Yorke, Wellingborough, cutler, and Sarah, Northampton, spin., sisters, 1782/5 Apr.
Pool, Elizabeth, Little Bowden, wid., to Thomas Palmer, Old, farmer, and Thomas Garner, Harborough, co. Leic., draper, exors. of John Taylor, gent., exor., Will, 1785/19 Sept.
Poole, Elizabeth, Brixworth, spin., to Esther, wife of William Dickins, Hanging Houghton, lab., sister, 1788/17 Dec.
Elizabeth, Helmdon, to George, Padbury, Bucks., jobber, husband, 1796/27 Sept.
Elizabeth, Ravensthorpe, wid., to Thomas, farmer, son, 1799/14 Dec.
POWERS, Elizabeth, West Haddon, wid., Inv.only £189.5.6 1712/127A
William, Welford, blacksmith, Inv.only £6.3.5 1717/124A
Samuel, Great Harrowden, innholder, Inv.only £36.17.6 1722/15A
PRATT, John, Mears Ashby, to Jane, wid., Inv. £11.10.6 1726/11 Jan.
Thomas, West Haddon, yeo., Inv.only £140.12.6 1739/355
Palmer, Mears Ashby, to Thomas, maltster, brother, 1784/3 Feb.
PRESTIDGE, John, Eydon, to Thomas, yeo., brother, 1720/122
Elizabeth, Eydon, wid., to Mary and Alice, spins., daughters, Inv. £56.14.6 1722/141
Peter, Eydon, to Mary and Alice, spins., sisters, 1722/142
Thomas, Eydon, to Mary and Alice, spins., sisters, 1722/143
Edward, Woodend, Blakesley, yeo., to Elizabeth, wid., Inv. £120.15.0 1732/23 Feb.
Thomas, Byfield, yeo., to Thomas, farmer, son, Mary, wid., renounced, 1742/23 Apr.
Thomas, Byfield, Inv.only £178.11.0 1742/384
Mary, Culworth, spin., to Susanna, wid., mother, 1751/15 Oct.
Edward, Maidford, farmer, to William, farmer, son, 1785/18 Oct.
PRESTON, Katherine, Northampton, wid., Account of Alice, daughter, admin., £47.16.2 1679/156
William, Weston Favell, Account of John, son, £135.16.8 1680/50
Samuel, Bugbrooke, to Samuel, yeo., grandson, 1720/6
Thomas, Great Everdon, Inv.only £6.9.6 1721/16A
John, Easton Maudit, glazier, to Margaret, wid., Inv. £73.9.7 1728/27 Jan.
William, Rothersthorpe, yeo., to Anne, wid., 1736/11 Sept.
Anne, Wootton, wid., to Anne, wife of John Law, weaver, daughter, 1743/20 June
Anne, Wootton, Inv.only £2.19.4 1743/386
PRICE, William, Northampton, gent., to Elizabeth, spin., daughter, 1727/6 May
Rev. Thomas, Green's Norton, clerk, to Elizabeth, spin., daughter, 1773/17 May
als. Izzard, Elizabeth, Whitfield, to Elizabeth, Beckley, co. Oxford, spin., daughter, 1785/21 Jan.
PRIEST, Eleanor, Braunston, wid., to William Chapman, husb., son in law, principal creditor, 1718/139
William, Braunston, shepherd, to Alice, wid., Inv. £40.2.6 1727/31 Mar.
PROCTOR, Thomas, Northampton, to Ann, wife of John Berry, plasterer, 1714/173
William, Whittlebury, Inv.only £20.10.3 1728/259
William, Whittlebury, lab., to Mary, wife of Joseph Cleaver, Norton, miller, daughter, Elizabeth, wid., renounced, 1760/29 Oct.
PULLEN, John, Inv.only £8.0.0 1712/134A
PULLEY, John, Wellingborough, Inv.only £17.1.10 1714/120A
PULVER, John, Broughton, to Hannah, wid., 1771/2 Jan.
PURRIER, Katherine, Weston, Lois Weedon, wid., Inv.only £25.16.0 1718/66A
PURSELL, Thomas, Wappenham, baker, to Charles Fairbrother, gent., James Jessop, yeo., and Samuel Sheppard, yeo., guardians of Thomas and William, minors, sons, Guard., 1796/13 Jan.
PURSER, James, Loddington, to James, yeo., father, 1733/18 Apr.
William, Loddington, grazier, to James, gent., father, 1739/7 July
PUSER, John, Plumpton, yeo., to Sarah, wid., Inv. £28.5.6 1712/39
Jonas, Cottesbrooke, shepherd, Inv.only £16.0.0 1719/9A

Q

QUENBY, John, Hargrave, to John, yeo., grandson, 1720/41
Simon, Hargrave, to Ann, wid., 1759/26 Dec.
QUICK, Elizabeth, Wellingborough, wid., to John Tye, nephew, 1719/88
Susanna, Hargrave, wid., to Elizabeth, spin., daughter, Inv. £13.13.9 1720/42
Thomas, Hargrave, yeo., to Thomas, yeo., son, Mary, wid., renounced, 1746/2 Oct.
QUINTON, John, Wellingborough, Account of Anne, wid., admin., £271.8.0½ 1681/79

R

RADBOURNE, John, Bozeat, yeo., to Sarah, wid., 1784/11 May
Radburn, Thomas, Norton, yeo., to Ann, wife of Simon Freeman, Whilton, gent., daughter, 1798/1 Dec.
RADHOUSE, John, Braunston, to Hannah, wid., 1783/17 July
RAGG, William, Welford, Inv.only £415.10.0 1714/7A
RAGSDALE, Richard, Kettering, to Thomas Dawson, innholder, principal creditor, 1719/71
RAGSDILL, Francis, Cransley, Inv.only £9.7.6 1716/107A
RAINER, James, Welford, to James, North Kilworth, co. Leic., cobbler, son, Will, 1713/72
RAINHOW, Elizabeth, Woodend, Blakesley, spin., to Thomas, lab., brother, 1778/17 Feb.
RAISIN, Elizabeth, Rushton, All Saints, wid., to Mary, wife of Thomas Cannon, Lamport, gardener, and Elizabeth, wife of Avery Burditt, farmer, 1798/22 June
RAMSEY, Christopher, Brington, Account of Elizabeth, wid., admin., £230.3.0 1673/83
RANDALL, Randole, John, Scaldwell, Inv.only £9.12.6 1717/10A
Matthew, Marston Trussell, to Hannah, wid., 1742/27 Sept.
Randell, Ann, Sibbertoft, to Matthew, blacksmith, husband, 1793/30 Sept.
RANDOLPH, Thomas, Astcote, Pattishall, to Catherine, wid., Inv. £65.4.0 1717/2
RANDS, Thomas, Northampton, silkweaver, Account of Elizabeth, wid., admin., £377.19.8 undated/46
Rand, James, Inv.only £108.14.6 1736/332
Rand, Thomas, Northampton, turner, to Joseph Easton, baker, and Thomas Jones, Abington, grazier, Will, 1761/26 Sept.
George, Cosgrave, yeo., to Dorothy, wid., 1777/3 May
RAPPITT, Thomas, Wellingborough, to John, gent., son, exor. of Elizabeth, wid., exor., decd., Will, 1714/29
RATCLIFF, Thomas, Potterspury, to Judith, wid., Inv. £9.0.6 1724/104
RATHBONE, George, Yelvertoft, miller, Inv.only £14.14.6 1722/53A
RATNETT, William, Woodend, Guard.only of Hannah, Joseph and Anne Johnson, minors, 1729/6 May
RATTLEY, John, Towcester, victualler, to Ann, wid., 1781/23 Apr.
RAVENS, William, East Farndon, Inv.only £433.1.4 1714/70A
RAWBONE, Richard, Hellidon, to Thomas Andrews, Daventry, tailor, of goods not fully administered by Andrew Hinde, decd., principal creditor, 1712/121
Mary, Towcester, to John Wood, Paulerspury, buthcer, brother, 1721/56
RAWLINGS, Rallings, John, Finedon, fellmonger, to Jane, wid., Inv. £143.9.3 1712/103
Nicholas, Blakesley, victualler, to Hannah, wid., Inv. £43.5.0 1728/28 Oct.
RAYNSFORD, Francis, Brixworth, to Hester, wid., 1728/27 Mar.
Henry, Brixworth, gent., to Hesther, wid., niece, principal creditor, 1731/2 July
Elizabeth, Northampton, wid., to Nicolls, Brixworth, son, 1787/12 May
READ, John, Yardley Gobion, Inv.only £70.5.0 1723/99A
William, Roade, farmer, to Anne, spin., sister, 1759/3 Mar.
READER, als. Freeman, Anne, Boughton, to William, yeo., husband, 1736/16 Aug.
REDDALL, Dixon, Wellingborough, clerk, late Rector of Simpson, Bucks., to Elinor, wid., Inv. £619.0.0 1772/30 Mar.

REEVE, Richard, Claycoton, Business of The Account, Thomas, brother, admin., 1674/165
William, Yelvertoft, Inv.only £12.6.0 1711/14 A
Thomas, elder, Watford, Inv.only £2.0.0 1711/69
William, Wellingborough, to Anne, wid., 1720/116
Reeves, Susanna, Yelvertoft, wid., to Nathaniel, yeo., son, 1724/32
Reve, John, Claycoton, senior, to John, yeo., son, Inv. £17.10.0 1725/23 Feb.
Thomas, Little Addington, to Anne, wid., Inv. £312.4.0 1739/11 Oct.
William, Thornhaugh, Inv.only 1752/415
Roger, Watford, to John Morris, farmer and grazier, 1759/6 Aug.
William, Kettering, quarter master, Queen's Regiment of Dragoon Guards, to Mary, Denford, wid., 1767/28 May
REMINGTON, William, Rothwell, schoolmaster, to Elizabeth, wid., 1746/23 Aug.
REVELL, Edward, Northampton, brazier, to George Hayes, brazier, principal creditor, 1716/38
REYNOLDS, George, Upper Boddington, Inv.only £24.7.4 1713/78 A
George, Culworth, victualler, to Elizabeth, wid., Inv. £39.13.0 1716/98
Thomas, Boddington, tailor, to Richard, husb., son, Grace, wid., renounced, 1718/111
Renals, Joseph, Kettering, Inv.only £11.14.0 1722/118 A
Simon, Lower Boddington, to Alice, wid., Inv. £16.7.6 Will, 1723/133
John, Westhorpe, Byfield, Inv.only £194.3.0 1723/112
Anne, Braybrooke, Inv.only £118.18.6 1724/5 A
Thomas, Inv.only £11.15.0 1724/140
Elizabeth, Brackley, wid., to Thomas, London, cloth worker, and Elizabeth Mays, children, Inv. £39.13.6 1725/23 Feb.
Elizabeth, Kettering, wid., to Mary, spin., daughter, Inv. £8.0.6 1726/9 Aug.
Rev. Frederick, Winwick, to Jane, wid., 1743/7 July
Renaud, Renod, Mary, Hinton , wid., to William Mayoe, Sulgrave, tailor, cousin, principal creditor, Will, Inv. £19.19.8 1750/26 Mar.
Richard, Byfield, to Jane, wid., 1759/8 May
Rev. Joseph, Marston Trussell, clerk, to Elizabeth, wid., 1771/9 Jan.
Thomas, Welton, to Thomas, weaver, son, 1784/23 Mar.
RHODES, John, Northampton, carpenter, to Mary, wid., 1792/23 June
RICE, John, Walgrave, to Sarah, wid., Inv. £38.8.4 1714/63
Thomas, lab., Inv.only £20.3.0 1735/325
William, Broughton, lab., to William, Kettering, victualler, son, 1795/9 Oct.
RICHARDS, Paul, Wollaston, victualler, to Martha Kempshead, daughter, Inv. £59.7.6 1723/45
John, Kettering, innholder, to Frances, wid., 1730/8 Jan.
Benjamin, Kettering, to Mary, wid., 1768/12 Apr.
RICHARDSON, Francis, Kingsthorpe, spin., Inv.only £26.12.7 1712/75A
Andrew, Woodford, lab., Inv.only £37.3.0 1713/77
John, Potterspury, miller, Inv.only £16.11.8 1713/122A
Andrew, Rothwell, to Jane, wid., Inv. £7.10.0 1714/137
William, Great Doddington, lab., Inv.only £1.19.8 1715/88 A
Edward, Preston Capes, clerk, to Samuel, Norton Lindsey, co. Warwick, husb., and Dorcas Cope, wid., Hatton, co. Warwick, brother and sister, Inv. £1078.10.0 Will, 1720/1
Susanna, Hardwick, wid., to William, husb., son, 1722/106
Abigail, Dallington, spin., to Robert Ash, Piddington, yeo., nephew, Inv. £7.7.0 1728/24 Aug.
William, Wellingborough, to Thomas Partridge, Wilby, uncle and guardian of Elizabeth, Mary, Edward, William, and Isabel, minors, children, Guard., 1776/19 Aug.
John, Pisford, to Martha, wife of William Cox, lab., daughter, Mary, exor., decd., Will, 1781/1 Sept.
RICKARD, William, Scaldwell, baker, to William, Faxton, yeo., father, 1737/12 Nov.
Francis, Lamport, to Susannah, spin., sister, 1740/21 June
RICKETT, James, Cotton Mills, Ringstead, miller, to Mary, wid., Inv. £7.14.0 1770/31 Mar.
RIDDELL, John, Middleton, to Mary, wife of Joseph Smith, farmer, daughter, 1800/29 Mar.
RIDDING, Thomas, Kingsthorpe, to Elizabeth, wid., 1713/22

RIGBY, John, Brampton, carpenter, to Benjamin, husb., son, Inv. £20.15.0 1729/11 Oct.
RIGHTON, Thomas, Byfield, yeo., junior, to Elizabeth, wid., Inv. £83.14.4 1725/21 Oct.
RING, Ann, Thenford, wid., to John, farmer, son, 1786/26 Apr.
RINGROSE, Agnes, Walgrave, wid., Inv.only £19.13.6 1713/60A
George, Welton, 1753/22 Oct.
RIVETT, William, Faxton, Inv.only £100.15.0 1715/53 A
ROBERTS, John, Overstone, Account of Abigall, wife of Ewstas Poole, sister, admin., £185.19.0 1672/121
Timothy, Nun Mill, Hardingstone, Inv.only £102.0.6 1711/67A
Elizabeth, Great Billing, Inv.only £19.16.4 1714/196A
Jane, Wellingborough, wid., Inv.only £124.13.4 1716/23A
Samuel, Harpole, surgeon, to Robert, brother, and Jane Timms, wid., sister, Inv. £220.10.0 1719/85
Richard, Finedon, to William, servant, son, Elizabeth, wid., renounced, Inv. £22.13.0 1720/30
Mary, Nun Mill, Hardingstone, Inv.only £20.11.0 1720/79 A
William, Kettering, to Mary, wid., 1720/136
Thomas, Daventry, gent., to Mary, wid., 1725/5 June
Timothy, Clack Mill, St. Giles, Northampton, miller, to John Gibson, pistor, guardian of Mary, Timothy, Hannah, Anne and Elizabeth, children, 1729/27 Nov.
Richard, Duston, Inv.only £1074.10.0 1738/353
als. Nicholls, Henry, Middleton Cheney, weaver, to Ralph Wells, lab., and his wife Mary, great grandchildren, 1751/12 Mar.
John, Kettering, to Joseph, Nunnely, guardian of Hannah, minor, 1756/13 Nov.
Ann, Blakesley, to Edward, Prestidge, yeo., of goods unadministered by Samuel, wheelwright, husband, decd., exor. of Richard Welch, gent., 1759/22 June
Samuel, Blakesley, gent., Guard.only of Elizabeth, Mary, Sarah, Martha and Samuel Shortland, minors, nieces and nephew, 1759/15 Dec.
Joseph, Kettering, to Mary, wid., 1767/5 Feb.
Thomas, elder, Staverton, farmer, to Elizabeth, wid., 1772/13 Aug.
Richard, Duston, to Henry, yeo., brother, 1775/25 Aug.
John, Wellingborough, to Sarah, wid., 1775/26 Oct.
Elizabeth, Staverton, to Thomas, farmer, son, 1778/25 Apr.
Joseph, Kettering, to Mary, daughter, 1779/8 June
Joseph, Northampton, to Joseph, woolcomber, son, 1780/25 Oct.
Peter, Harpole, shopkeeper, to Martha, wife of Thomas Gross, Harlestone, blacksmith, daughter, 1784/4 Nov.
ROBINS, Ambrose, Inv.only £405.5.4 1712/54 A
Mary, Middleton Cheney, wid., Inv.only £37.15.0 1718/46A
Richard, Staverton, yeo., widower, to Anne, spin., daughter, William Muscott, guardian of Elizabeth, Hester and Mary, minors, daughters, renounced admin., but they decline and appoint him, 1730/24 Jan.
John, Brington, husb., to Sarah, wid., 1731/17 July
John, Northampton, farmer, to Judith, St. Leonard's, Shoreditch, co. Middx., spin., niece, 1732/16 Nov.
Barkinsdale, Staverton, to Elizabeth, wid., 1740/16 Aug.
John, West Haddon, to Mary, wid., 1755/19 Apr.
Abraham, Woodford, to Mary Fairey, Islip, wid., sister, 1778/14 June
ROBINSON, William, Braybrooke, to Eleanor, relict, Inv. £18.16.0 1712/33
Elizabeth, Wellingborough, to John, pastor, husband, 1712/50
William, Wellingborough, to Jane als. Harvey, wid., Inv. £141.10.0 1713/20
Edward, Braybrooke, to Mary, wid., Inv. £18.5.0 1714/57
Elizabeth, Finedon, to Robert Betson, Wellingborough, gent., Will, 1715/78
Edward, Long Buckby, shepherd, Inv.only £19.4.8 1716/90A
Henry, Faxton, to Elizabeth, wid., 1717/80
Elizabeth, Hardwick, Inv.only £36.17.0 1722/66A
Joseph, Daventry, to Bridget, wid., 1722/70
Richard, Chapel Brampton, mason, to Frances, wid., Inv. £9.10.0 1724/19
Roberson, William, Middleton Cheney, Inv.only £13.14.0 1724/63A
Anne, Cranford, to Sir James, baronet, husband, 1727/4 Oct.
Edward, Guilsborough, shepherd, to Elizabeth, wid., 1736/8 May
Nehemiah, Crick, farmer, to Anne, wid., 1745/11 May

ROBINSON continued
John, Crick, yeo., to John, yeo., grandson, Thomas Farn and John Abby, yeos., renounced, Will, 1751/29 June
Thomas, Northampton, to Henry Locock, apothecary, and James Williamson, linendraper, creditors, 1753/9 Oct.
Hannah, Wellingborough, wid., to Thomas, blacksmith, son, 1760/15 Dec.
William, Wellingborough, to Elizabeth, wid., Inv. £112.0.0 1761/22 Dec.
John, Desborough, to Elizabeth, wid., 1765/27 May
Stephen, Faxton, to Stephen, blacksmith, son, 1771/8 June
Francis Wood, Burton Latimer, farmer, to Henry, farmer, and Samuel Wallis, Barton Seagrave, grazier, Will, 1778/20 Feb.
William, Cransley, to John, Manchaster, Lancashire, brother, 1781/7 Sept.
John, elder, Crick, to John, Kilsby, woolcomber, and John Killworth, farmer, of goods unadministered by Robert, son, exor., Will, 1782/22 Apr.
John, Crick, weaver, to Sarah, spin., sister, 1786/27 June
Thomas, Wellingborough, farmer, to James, farmer, son, 1788/22 July
ROBOTHAM, John, Towcester, Inv.only £127.17.6 1713/47A
Elizabeth, Towcester, wid., to George Smith, Great Harold, Bucks., husb., father, 1714/142
ROCK, John, Wellingborough, yeo., to James, yeo., son, Inv. £29.6.8 1751/19 Feb.
RODDIS, William, Lower Heyford, farmer, yeo., to Elizabeth, wid., Inv. £581.11.5 1783/12 May
Roddiss, William, Floore, farmer, to Hannah, wid., William Lucas Rose, Daventry, clerk, James Morris, clerk, and Henry Sharp, exors., renounced, Will, 1788/19 Nov.
Rodiss, Samuel, Floore, butcher, Guard.only of Samuel, minor, son, 1800/13 Feb.
Sarah, Guard.only of Sarah, minor, 1800/25 Aug.
John, Northampton, tailor, to Robert, basket maker, brother, 1800/17 Nov.
RODHOUSE, James, Weedon Beck, to Nathaniel Packer, gent., 1716/6
Hannah, Braunston, wid., to Mary Mawby, spin., 1800/17 Dec.
ROE see ROW
ROGERS, William, senior, Upper Heyford, Account of William, son, admin., £137.18.10 1674/140
Andrew, Daventry, innkeeper, Inv.only £430.13.5 1711/66A
Moses, Inv.only £36.13.11 1711/117A
Sarah, Newnham, wid., to George, husb., 1712/46
John, Mears Ashby, Inv.only £113.11.0 1714/51A
Samuel, Newnham, to Mary, wid., Inv. £18.18.2 1715/87
John, Daventry, baker, Inv.only £70.13.0 1716/15A
Rodgers, Samuel, Inv.only £5.18.6 1720/93A
Rodgers, Moses, Daventry, to Isabell, wid., Inv. £11.17.4 1721/5
Samuel, Desborough, yeo., Inv.only £171.14.7½ 1723/10A
Isabell, Kislingbury, spin., to William, woodman, and Ann Andrew, brother and sister, 1729/7 July
Sarah, Wellingborough, to William, farmer, husband, 1753/12 Jan.
William, Wellingborough, yeo., to William Grant, clerk, and John Rodick, clothier, Elizabeth Wells, wid., and Sarah, spin., daughters, renounced, Inv. £454.17.6 1756/24 May
William, Kislingbury, to Ann, wid., 1783/13 Dec.
Henry, Abthorpe, farmer, to Mary, wid., 1792/31 May
ROLFE, Thomas, Harpole, shepherd, to Thomas, son, 1728/17 Apr.
John, Harpole, farmer, to Ann, wid., 1798/13 Jan.
ROLT, Thomas, Northampton, to Elizabeth, wid., 1768/22 Jan.
ROME, Charles, Inv.only £27.13.8 1717/94A
ROOTE, Edward, Lilbourne, carpenter, to Anne, wid., 1729/6 Sept.
ROSE, Dorothy, Daventry, wid., to John Thompson, son in law, 1715/157
William, Wollaston, yeo., to George, cooper, son, Inv. £6.9.2 1723/103
John, Chadstone, Castle Ashby, lab., to Hannah, wid., 1737/13 June
Elizabeth, Northampton, spin., to Elizabeth, Potterspury, wid., mother, 1771/8 June
George, Wollaston, to George, son, Will, 1775/28 June
Samuel, Ecton, tailor, to Mary, wife of Thomas Howes, Hackleton, lab., daughter, 1782/28 May
James, Great Billing, lab., to William Campion, cordwainer, son in law, and Ann Campion, Abington, spin., granddaughter, Mary, wid., exor., decd., Will, 1788/1 May

ROSE continued
Zachariah, Broughton, clerk, to Frances, wid., 1790/7 Aug.
ROUGHTON, Samuel, Denford, dyer, to Francis, farmer, brother, 1787/3 May
ROW, Roe, John, Kettering, baker, Account of Elizabeth, wid., admin., £160.0.0 1671/116
Rowe, Hannah, Northampton, to Henry, son, 1716/35
George, Cogenhoe, to Anne, wid., 1718/1
William, Preston, to Jane, wid., 1718/121
Roe, Anne, Cogenhoe, wid., Inv.only £19.7.0 1722/9A
Samuel, Woodford, tailor, to Mary, wid., Inv. £25.7.0 1728/17 Oct.
Philip, Hargrave, blacksmith, to Mary, wid., 1729/18 Mar.
Roe, John, Little Houghton, formerly of Northampton, to Thomas, younger, maltster, and Mary, wife of Joshua Steevenson, Northampton, victualler, children, Thomas, grazier, exor., renounced, 1781/1 June
ROWELL, Elizabeth, Brixworth, spin., to George, Lamport, lab., father, 1742/24 Dec.
ROWLATT, William, Loddington, Account of John Wood, exor., £822.7.11 1711/139
John, Kettering, to Thomas Carr, Hanging Houghton, cooper, 1718/135
Rowlett, Benjamin, Kettering, tailor, to Elizabeth, wid., 1780/10 Nov.
ROWLIDGE, Thomas, Moulton, butcher, Inv.only £7.11.0 1717/20A
Robert, Slapton, maltster, Inv.only £35.2.8 1720/111A
Rowledge, Edward, Heyford, to Alice, wid., 1741/23 May
Rowledge, Rolledge, Ann, Northampton, spin., to Francis, West Haddon, lab., uncle, 1787/29 Dec.
ROXBURGH, Anthony, Northampton, to James Riley, Daventry, draper, principal creditor, 1770/18 Dec.
RUBY, John, Easton Maudit, lab., to Elizabeth, wid., Inv. £42.0.0 1715/73
RUDKIN, Job, East Farndon, tailor, to Deborah Treslow, wid., Will, 1721/31
Jonathan, Desborough, to Mary, wid., Inv. £17.3.6 1725/14 Dec.
RUFFE, Richard, Roade, yeo., Inv.only £236.2.4 1715/28A
RUSH, Thomas, Farthingstone, husb., Inv.only £271.11.8 1720/50A
RUSHALL, John, Charwelton, shepherd, to Mary, Dodford, spin., Hannah, Dodford, spin., and Elizabeth, Thorpe Mandeville, spin., daughters, 1730/11 Dec.
William, Braunston, woolcomber, to Samuel, carpenter, brother, 1764/7 Sept.
RUSSELL, Samuel, Badby, yeo., to Anne, wid., 1729/7 Mar.
Robert, Yardley Gobion, papermaker, to Mary, wid., 1729/11 Apr.
Robert, Yardley Gobion, Inv.only £38.11.0 1729/247
Elizabeth, Braunston, spin., to William, nephew, 1743/14 Dec.
Joseph, Badby, soapboiler, to Joseph, soapboiler, son, 1779/23 Nov.
Rudsdell, Jeremiah, Northampton, gent., woolstapler, to Jeremiah, gent., son, Ann, wid., renounced, Will, 1783/17 Dec.
William, Everdon, to Catherine, wid., 1791/10 Feb.
RUST, Jonathan, Cranford, butcher, to Mary, wid., 1740/2 Oct.
RYE, Mary, Northampton, wid., to Margaret, spin., daughter, Inv. £72.12.0 1735/1 May
Mary, Culworth, wid., to William Beauchamp Rye, 1751/22 Oct.

S

SABIN, John, Crick, tailor, Inv.only £137.6.8 1716/33A
Anne, Bradden, to William, London, cabinet maker, brother, 1725/3 Apr.
Sabine, John, Bradden, to John Herbert, Brackley, barber, guardian of John, minor, of goods unadministered by Anne, exor., decd., Will, Guard. of Elizabeth and Samuel Knight, 1725/20 Nov. and 20 Dec.
John, Bradden, Guard.only of Elizabeth, Anne and Gabriel, minors, 1726/6 Apr.
als. Tibbs, Anne, to John, Braunston, lab., husband, 1741/28 Nov.
Mary, Bugbrooke, spin., to Edward, Long Buckby, yeo., brother, 1756/30 Oct.
Elizabeth, Crick, wid., to Thomas Bucknell, glover, son in law, 1760/28 Nov.
John, Chalcombe, to Elizabeth, wid., 1765/24 May
Michael, Chalcombe, grazier, to Mary, wid., 1766/10 Oct.
SABY, Sabie, John, Higham Ferrers, husb., Account of Mary, wid., admin., £387.10.8 1671/87
Mary, Rushden, wid., to Mary, wife of Robert King, lab., daughter, 1731/3 July

SABY continued
James, Draughton, yeo., to Mary Palmer, wid., grandmother and guardian of Palmer, minor, son, 1742/21 Oct.
SAGE, Thomas, Rothwell, to Elizabeth, wid., 1752/19 Sept.
SALISBURY, John, Barby, weaver, to John, weaver, son, Inv. £19.6.8 1725/5 Mar.
Salsbury, Richard, Barby, weaver, to Sarah, wid., 1768/20 Oct.
SALMON, John, Towcester, gardener, to Elizabeth, wid., 1731/4 Feb.
Sammons, Edward, Blisworth, victualler, to Elizabeth, wid., Inv. £17.4.6 1732/15 Apr.
Nicholas, Irchester, to Elizabeth, wid., 1767/21 Feb.
SANDERS see SAUNDERS
SANDERSON, Saunderson, Thomas, Moulton, Account of Anne, wid., admin., £573.8.8 1672/76
Saunderson, John, Little Addington, Account of Margaret, wid., admin., £337.10.0 1673/145
Thomas, Little Addington, yeo., to Dorothy, wid., Inv. £350.0.0 1712/87
Elizabeth, Little Addington, wid., to John, rector, brother, Inv. £73.8.9 1766/18 Dec.
Thomas, Grendon, to Laurence, yeo., son; Eleanor, wid., renounced, 1776/5 Oct.
Robert, Hallgrove, co. Surrey, to John, Rushton, servant, 1782/28 May
SANFORD, Henry, Woodford, Inv.only £6.15.10 1714/79A
SANSOM, Sansum, Richard, Maidwell, Inv.only £306.9.10 1712/34A
Henry, Clipston, shoemaker, to Anne, wid., 1740/14 June
Sansum, Henry, Clipston, shoemaker, Inv.only £57.8.0 1740/375
Sannsome, John, Duston, to Edmund, Calverton, Bucks., 1766/10 May
SARGAN, SARGENT, SARGEANT, see SERGEANT
SATCHWELL, Joan, Little Harrowden, wid., Inv.only £145.0.0 1713/21A
Joseph, Northampton, victualler, to Mary, wid., Inv. £27.0.6 1714/181
William, Boughton, lab., Inv.only £15.9.0 1721/61A
SAUNDERS, John, Higham Ferrers, Account of Anne, wid., admin., £93.10.0 1675/34
Sanders, Robert, Radstone, to Mary, wid., 1711/35
Sarah, to Ambrose, Sibbertoft, gent., husband, 1713/35
Edward, Brixworth, to Penelope, wid., 1714/122
William, Crick, Inv.only £48.10.6 1716/19A
James, Potterspury, carpenter, Inv.only £26.6.8 1717/141A
Elizabeth, Moreton Pinkney, wid., Inv.only £66.8.6 1720/112A
Anne, Higham Ferrers, wid., to John, yeo., son, 1721/40
Thomas, Higham Ferrers, to Elizabeth, wid., Inv. £8.1.4 1722/144
Sanders, Richard, Northampton, to Mary, wid., 1724/39
Sanders, John, Northampton, currier, to Samuel, St. Leonard's, Shoreditch, London, cordwainer, Deborah Corby, Wellingborough, wid., and Francis, St. Giles, Cripplegate, London, brothers and sister, of goods not fully administered by Hannah, wid., exor., decd., Will, 1733/15 Aug.
Sanders, Henry, Yardley Gobion, carpenter, Inv.only £9.18.6 1738/352
Sanders, Thomas, Higham Ferrers, to Anne, wid., 1740/2 Oct.
Sanders, John, Northampton, butcher, to John, son, 1742/16 June
Thomas, Daventry, victualler, to Ashburnham Toll, Northampton, gent., principal creditor, Richard Slatcher, victualler, Elizabeth his wife, and Anne, spin., daughters, renounced, 1746/5 Apr.
Thomas, Badby, weaver, to Elizabeth, wid., 1747/26 Jan.
Sanders, Daniel, Northampton, butcher, to George, butcher, son, Mary, wid., renounced, 1764/24 Jan.
Jane, Higham Ferrers, wid., to George, St. Giles, co. Middx., currier, son, 1771/26 Aug.
Sanders, Mary, St. Giles, Northampton, wid., to Joseph Manning, lab., Will, 1779/1 Feb.
Sanders, William, Higham Ferrers, to Ann, wid., Inv. £487.3.4½ 1780/15 Jan.
Judith, Sywell, wid., to George Worley, gent., son, 1784/18 Sept.
Sanders, Thomas, Higham Ferrers, cutter, to Mary, wife of Richard Collier, breeches maker, sister, 1800/10 June
Sanders, Elizabeth, Higham Ferrers, spin., to Mary, wife of Richard Collier, breeches maker, sister, William, exor., decd., Will, 1800/10 June
SAUNDERSON see SANDERSON
SAVAGE, Laurence, Towcester, Inv.only £57.7.0 1716/120A
William, Daventry, victualler, Inv.only £75.2.0 1721/75A

SAVAGE continued
Matthew, Edgcote, to Susanna, wid., 1764/10 Sept.
George, Wollaston, to George, farmer, son, 1768/4 May
SAWELL, SAYWELL see SEWELL
SAWYER, James, Raunds, butcher, Inv.only £5.5.0 1717/31A
SAXBY, John, Kettering, lab., Inv.only £9.17.0 1714/194A
John, Hartwell, yeo., Inv.only £26. 1715/54A
SAYLE, Seal, James, Moreton Pinkeney, Inv.only £6.14.6 1718/48A
SCAMBLER, Robert, Northampton, maltster, Account of Mary Freer and Anne Baxter, sisters, admins., £164.18.6 1671/93
SCARBOROW, Peter, Irthlingborough, to Cuthbert, husb., 1776/20 June
SCARFE, Mary, Northampton, spin., to John Richardson, Loddington, grazier, next of kin, 1729/19 Dec.
SCATTERGOOD, John, Winwick, gent., Inv.only £362.0.0 1724/25A
SCOFIELD, James, Northampton, maltster, to Martha, wid., 1795/15 May
SCOTT, Henry, Rothwell, shoemaker, Inv.only £33.9.0 1716/24A
Sarah, Orton, wid., to William, son, 1718/72
William, Orton, Rothwell, shoemaker, to Frances Dainty, sister, Inv. £110.13.0 1720/16
Richard, Yardley Gobion, Inv.only £32.5.0 1723/121
William, Cosgrave, yeo., to Elizabeth, wid., 1743/12 Apr.
William, Silverstone, farmer, to Avis, wid., now wife of Richard Aris, 1751/21 Oct.
Edward, Yardley Gobion, farmer, to Susannah Bignel, wid., daughter, 1753/9 June
William, East Farndon, cordwainer, to Jane, wid., John, and John Naseby, exors., renounced, Will, 1777/1 Nov.
Thomas, Harrington, yeo., to Mary, wife of Moses Merrill, Rothwell, tailor, daughter, Mary, wid., exor., decd., Will, 1787/26 June
John, Ravensthorpe, maltster, to John, farmer, son, Mary, wid., exor., decd., Will, 1790/23 Dec.
William, East Farndon, cordwainer, bachelor, to Samuel, brother, 1794/11 Jan.
SCOTTON, Christopher, Towcester, baker, to Mary Gisling, wid., niece, 1758/18 Nov.
Elizabeth, Towcester, spin., to Mary Grisling, wid., niece, 1758/18 Nov.
SCRIVEN, Elizabeth, Northampton, to Richard Kilpin, Astwood, Bucks., grazier, father, guardian of William Kilpin, minor, Will, 1712/125
Samuel, Rothwell, apothecary, to Thomas, Twywell, clerk, Inv. £36.15.4 1714/1
Thomas, Northampton, Inv.only £18.11.6 1727/180
Thomas, Northampton, to Elizabeth, wid., 1771/18 Feb.
Edward, Harpole, gent., to Mary, wid., Will, 1777/7 Apr.
Elizabeth, Daventry,wid., to Elizabeth, Ann, Mary and Sarah, spins., daughters, 1785/2 Nov.
SCRIVENER, Richard, senior, Potterspury, gent., Inv.only £580.9.0 1723/55A
Thomas, Potterspury, yeo., to Jane, wid., 1750/28 Feb.
Edward, Cosgrave, to Elizabeth, wid., 1755/2 Dec.
Eleanor, Cosgrave, to Richard, yeo., 1784/23 Nov.
Mary, Potterspury, to Thomas, yeo., husband, 1787/11 May
SCULTHORPE, Samuel, Walgrave, to Anne, wid., 1724/129
Sculthorp, Samuel, Walgrave, baker, Inv.only £94.8.6 1724/131
SEABY, Palmer, Weston Favell, lab., to William, lab., son, and Sarah, wife of Robert Clements, daughter, 1796/13 Dec.
SEATON, Edward, Hinton, lab., to Thomas, Farndon, Woodford, lab., brother, 1712/51
Essex, Northampton, wid., to Bridget Penelope Hunt, spin., sister, 1742/2 Mar.
Richard, Hinton, grazier, to William, son, 1788/13 Oct.
SEAWELL see SEWELL
SECKINGTON, Anne, Brackley, wid., to Elizabeth, wife of William Saby, Wadenhoe, butcher, daughter, 1736/26 Apr.
SELBY, Sylby, John, Northampton, alderman, Inv.only £87.19.1 1715/93A
Samuel, Great Addington, to Sarah, spin., sister, 1728/28 Sept.
Thomas, Great Addington, bachelor, to William Beaby, farmer, and William Elderkin, Keystone, Hunts., farmer, brothers in law, 1776/5 Mar.
SENDALL, Robert, Blisworth, victualler, to Mary, wid., 1731/22 June

SERGEANT, John, West Cotton, Hardingstone, to John, husb., son, Inv. £60.0.0 1717/36
John, Desborough, to Francis Baker, Kettering, apothecary, 1720/94
John, Cotton End, Hardingstone, to Henry, Roade, yeo., William, Wootton, yeo., Charles, Northampton, cooper, Thomas, Hartwell, and Nicholas, yeo., brothers, 1725/22 July
Sergean, William, Walgrave, cordwainer, to William, servant, son, 1756/16 June
Sargan, William, Roade, yeo., to William, Woodend, Blakesley, grazier, son, Elizabeth, wife, decd., Will, 1761/30 Dec.
Serjeant, Edward, Thorpe Malsor, to Elizabeth, wid., 1766/7 Jan.
Sargeant, Thomas, Cotton End, Hardingstone, yeo., to Mary, wid., 1782/22 Sept.
Sargent, Thomas, Floore, baker, to Mary, wid., 1790/16 Sept.
SEWARD, William, Bozeat, Inv.only £54.15.0 1719/49A
SEWELL, Seawell, Elizabeth, Wappenham, wid., to Elizabeth Perkins, spin., granddaughter, 1722/98
William, Woodford cum Membris, to Henry, Byfield, brother, Inv. £16.6.6 1727/5 Apr.
Sawell, William, Wicken, yeo., to Mary, wid., 1737/27 Aug.
Saywell, William, Barby, to Mary, wife of Robert Brothers, Grandborow, co. Warwick, butcher, daughter, 1742/31 Dec.
Sampson, Byfield, farmer, to Mary, wid., 1745/10 May
John, Byfield, cutter, to Sarah, wid., 1749/24 Apr.
Elizabeth, Northampton, to John, baker, husband, 1752/29 Dec.
Saywell, John, Northampton, baker, to James, baker, grandfather and guardian of Elizabeth, minor, daughter, Guard., 1753/27 Apr.
Mary, Eydon, to Richard, husband, 1775/27 Feb.
William, Silverstone, woolcomber, to Martha, wid., 1783/13 Oct.
SHACKLETON, Elizabeth, Towcester, wid., Inv.only £7.15.0 1717/63A
SHARMAN, Richard, Thorpe Malsor, Inv.only £225.15.0 1711/2A
Samuel, Little Harrowden, mercer, to Sarah, wid., Inv. £93.15.0 1712/40
John, Doddington, to Thomas, brother, Inv. £4.11.11 1715/129
Richard, Stanwick, to Elizabeth, wid., 1716/43
William, Helmdon, to Elizabeth Reeve, daughter, 1717/116
Thomas, Cransley, to Moses, yeo., son, 1720/128
Matthew, Raunds, lab., to John, pastor, son, Inv. £12.10.0 1723/59
Thomas, Woodford, husb., Inv.only £73.10.0 1723/113
John, Marston Trussell, to Sarah, wid., 1736/26 Oct.
Moses, Cransley, yeo., weaver, to Joseph, Kettering, butcher, Will, Inv. £140.3.5 1747/21 Sept.
Richard, Thorpe Malsor, to Margaret, wid., 1752/24 Feb.
William, Marston Trussell, yeo., to Mary, wid., 1752/4 Apr.
William, Marston Trussell, Inv.only £41.2.6 1752/413
John, Marston Trussell, yeo., to Mary, wid., daughter in law, Mary, wid., renounced in favour Samuel Smith, Northampton, 1755/29 Mar.
Thomas, Marston Trussell, to Alice, wid., 1766/9 Dec.
Mary, Dodford, wid., to Mary Jones, wid., mother and guardian of Mary, minor, granddaughter, 1769/1 July
Thomas, Old, grazier, to Richard, grazier, son, 1779/13 Nov.
Richard, Cogenhoe, to Ann, wid., and Daniel, carpenter, son, 1783/22 Nov.
Daniel, Dodford, innholder, to Mary, wife of John Loe, grazier, granddaughter, Mary, wid., exor., decd., Will, 1784/23 Feb.
Thomas, Hardingstone, staymaker, to Richard, cordwainer, and Edward, St. George, Westminster, Middx., servant, sons, Will, 1793/17 May
SHARPE, James, Towcester,oatmealmaker, to Mary, wid., Inv. £49.8.0 1727/4 Mar.
Robert, Arthingworth, carpenter, Inv.only £41.2.0 1728/207
Sharp, Margaret, Inv.only £19.3.0 1735/319
William, Cranford St. Andrew, to Penelope, wid., 1757/4 Nov.
Stephen, Milton, yeo., to Anne, wid., Inv. £251.16.0 1759/30 June
Stephen, Northampton, baker, to Anne, Milton, wid., daughter, 1767/28 Nov.
Sharp, Elizabeth, Floore, to Henry, gent., brother, 1774/5 Feb.
Sharp, John, Floore, blacksmith, to Mary, wid., 1794/1 Mar.
Sharp, Mary, Northampton, to Hugh, perukemaker, husband, 1796/2 June
Sharp, Edmund, mariner, to John, Cranford St. Andrew, farmer, father, 1796/9 Sept.
SHARWOOD see SHERWOOD

SHAW, Mary, Braunston, to Joseph, farmer, husband, 1747/18 Nov.
Joseph, Braunston, lab., to Samuel, Dunchurch, co. Warwick, lab., and Thomas Harris, yeo., 1760/16 Apr.
Elizabeth, Daventry, wid., to Elizabeth, wife of Titus Wadsworth, schoolmaster, daughter, 1793/22 June
SHEARSBY, William, Great Billing, servant, to Mary, wid., Inv. £9.0.3 1718/23
Sheasby, William, Daventry, to Sarah, wid., Will, 1796/24 Dec.
SHEEN, Christopher, Daventry, staymaker, to Christian Whitmell, Charwelton, wid., principal creditor, Mary, wid., renounced, Will, 1772/23 Mar.
SHELSWELL, Sarah, to Thomas, Whitfield, son, 1714/154
SHENN, Richard, Daventry, Account of Anne, wid., admin., £55.6.0 1685/167
SHEPPARD, Mary, Dalscote, Pattishall, wid., Account of John, son, admin., £290.18.6 1680/12
William, Pattishall, Inv.only £21.19.4 1713/101A
John, Towcester, Inv.only £169.16.0 1714/15A
Shepeard, Richard, Woodend, Blakesley, to Anne, Cold Higham, wid., Inv. £99.0.0 1714/158
Thomas, Cold Higham, to Elinor, wid., Inv. £74.19.6 Richard Kirby and Henry Howes, exors., renounced, Will, 1715/116
Shepard, Thomas, Caldecote, Towcester, Inv.only £9.4.10 1720/27A
Shepherd, Thomas, Finedon, gent., Inv.only £58.15.0 1729/271
Thomas, Finedon, gent., to Elizabeth, wife of Richard Wallis, yeo., daughter, 1730/7 Apr.
Joshua, Kettering, to Elizabeth, wid., 1733/27 Apr.
John, Blisworth, gent., to Lucy, wid., Inv. £10.10.11 1747/11 July
Samuel, Eastcote, Pattishall, yeo., to Martha, Gayton, wid., and John, yeo., brother, 1799/23 Nov.
SHERIFF, Thomas, Slapton, to Jane, wid., 1759/15 Dec.
Sherriff, Elizabeth, Slapton, wid., to Mary, wife of Fletcher Betts, farmer, daughter, 1782/12 Nov.
SHERLEY see SHIRLEY
SHERRIDON, Dennis, Potterspury, yeo., to Thomas Horton, yeo., uncle and guardian of John Orton, minor, grandson, 1751/28 Dec.
SHERWOOD, Thomas, Byfield, yeo., Inv.only £162. 1715/95A
Sharwood, Thomas, Wollaston, lab., Inv.only £72.14.7 1716/32A
Sharwood, Robert, Irchester, to Anne, wid., 1718/79
John, Easton Maudit, to Joseph, son, 1724/64
William, Raunds, Inv.only £49.14.0 1728/241
SHINFIELD, Shenfield, Elizabeth, Hargrave, to Richard, yeo., husband, 1786/15 Nov.
SHIRLEY, Sherley, John, Little Houghton, lab., to Jane, wife of James Smith, Brampton, lab., daughter, Inv. £14.15.4 1729/23 Apr.
Joseph, Boddington, yeo., to Joseph, husb., son, 1730/26 Sept.
SHORT, John, Cotton End, Hardingstone, Account of Elizabeth, wid., admin., £268.10.6 1685/164
Edward, Preston Capes, to Edward, grandson, Thomas, London, cooper, grazier, son, renounced, 1745/23 July
SHORTGRAVE, Robert, Northampton, watchmaker, to John, ironmonger, brother, 1751/14 Jan.
SHORTLAND, Thomas, Upper Heyford, Inv.only £28.18.0 1712/12A
John, Weston, Lois Weedon, to Mary, wid., Inv. £62.10.0 1716/25
William, Rothwell, to Elizabeth, wid., and William, son, Inv. £95.16.6 1718/105
Richard, Helmdon, yeo., Inv.only £27.17.0 1729/234
Thomas, Helmdon, gent., to Anne, wid., Inv. £481.2.0 1730/30 June
John, Blisworth, husb., farmer, to William Langford, Collingtree, maltster, principal creditor, Mary, wid., renounced, Inv. £130.0.0 1767/21 Nov.
Thomas, Wootton, to Sarah, wife of Samuel Peach, cordwainer, daughter, 1772/14 Dec.
John, Milton, Guard.only of Mary, minor, granddaughter, 1775/21 Jan.
John, Milton, to Winifred Howes, Duncote, Green's Norton, spin., sister of William Howes, exor., Will, 1775/5 Apr.
William, Northampton, to William Gibson, maltster, principal creditor, 1782/12 Oct.
SHOWELL, Thomas, Teeton, servant, to William, Broxt, Monks Kirby, co. Warwick, husb., 1728/1 May

SHRIEVE, Abraham, Pytchley, to Agnes, wid., Inv. £25.5.0 1720/7
Alexander, Hartwell, Roade, yeo., to Anne, spin., guardian of John, Sarah, Elizabeth, Mary, minors, children, Inv. £115.4.6 Guard., 1721/107 and 108
SHUCKBURGH, Shukburgh, Thynn, Wellingborough, spin., to Judith, wid., mother, 1730/7 Aug.
Anne, Culworth, spin., to Richard, Lütterworth, co. Leic., joiner, brother, Will, 1758/14 Apr.
SHUTTLEWORTH, Mary, Rothwell, wid., to Henry, son, 1751/21 Oct.
SIBLEY, William, Great Oxendon, yeo., Inv.only £15.12.6 1712/61A
Silby, Anne, Raunds, Inv.only £135.19.0 1721/47A
Silby, Robert, Raunds, yeo., Inv.only £422.6.0 1722/44A
Silby, Samuel, Great Addington, farmer, Inv.only £159.5.0 1728/254
Silby, Matthew, Kingsthorpe, tailor, Inv.only £4.2.0 1730/277
Richard, Cogenhoe, gent., to Elizabeth, wid., 1735/5 July
Silby, als. Teeton, Mary, to John, Finedon, carpenter, husband, 1741/7 Mar.
Richard, Cogenhoe, yeo., to George Dodington Manning, Little Houghton, of goods unadministered by Elizabeth, wid., 1775/9 Sept.
Silby, John, senior, Finedon, victualler, to John, publican, 1782/18 Feb.
Robert, Cogenhoe, yeo., to Edward Islip, farmer, brother, 1788/5 July
William, Higham Ferrers, to Elizabeth, wid., 1790/3 June
SIMCOCK, Miriam, Irchester, wid., to Elizabeth, wife of Edward Handley, gardener, daughter, 1785/21 Apr.
SIMCOE, James, Little Houghton, blacksmith, to Elizabeth, wid., Inv. £96.11.0 1733/8 Sept.
John, Isham, yeo., to Martha, wid., 1753/9 May
Simco, James, Woodend, Blakesley, to Sarah, wid., 1760/8 Nov.
John, Little Houghton, to James, blacksmith, son, 1760/29 Nov.
SIMKINS, James, Warkworth, tailor, to Mary, Chalcombe , wid., Inv. £19.14.0 1716/63
SIMONS, Symons, George, Irchester, to Mary, wid., 1720/47
Mary, Cotton, Ravensthorpe, wid., to Anna Moore, Guilsborough, wid., sister, Inv. £38.0.0 1726/4 Feb.
Symonds, Thomas, Wellingborough, yeo., to Elizabeth, wife of John Nottingham, yeo., Sarah, wife of John Halles, saddler, and Martha, wife of Edward Hardwick, butcher, daughters, 1742/16 Aug.
John, Finedon, yeo., to Edmund, Huntingdon, tanner, son, 1748/9 Jan.
William, Cranford St. John, to Rebecca, wid., 1777/25 July
Simonds, Daniel, East Haddon, yeo., to Matthew, weaver, brother, Will, 1780/19 Feb.
Simmans, Richard, Middleton Cheney, husb., to John, farmer, son, Susanna, wid., exor., decd., Will, 1791/18 Apr.
Rebecca, Cranford St. Andrew, wid., to William, Great Oakley, farrier, son, 1795/10 Feb.
Simonds, Mary, Wellingborough, to Humphrey, salesman, husband, 1800/15 Aug.
SIMPSON, Thomas, Mears Ashby, Inv.only £4.16.6 1711/128A
William, Pytchley, carpenter, to Frances, wid., Inv. £14.3.0 1721/95
Simson, Ann, to George, Cambridge, co. Cambridge, gent., husband, 1753/9 Nov.
SINGLETON, Joseph, Rothwell, to Bethia, wid., Inv. £17.11.8 1728/5 Oct.
SKEGGS, Robert, Wellingborough, cordwainer, to Robert, shoemaker, son, Inv. £41.5.6 1746/9 Dec.
SKERRALL, Joseph, Moulton, to Mary, wid., 1774/8 Apr.
SKINNER, Robert, Raunds, Account of Mary, wid., admin., £25.0.0 1680/14
Henry, Braunston, mason, Inv.only £15.0.6 1719/120A
Thomas, Raunds, mason, to Mary, wid., Inv. £87.10.0 1768/15 July
SLATER, Slatter, John, Hullock Hills, Castle Ashby, miller, Inv.only £78.0.0 1711/138A
Slatier, John, Braunston, Inv.only £95.18.0 1716/47A
Slatier, Richard, Braunston, Inv.only £36.10.0 1719/97A
Slatier, Euseby, Braunston, to Katherine, wid., mother, 1741/22 July
Susanna, Ecton, wid., to John, grazier, son, 1786/28 Mar.
Thomas, Alderton, farmer, to William, farmer, son, 1789/23 Oct.
SLAYMAKER, William, Old Stratford, Cosgrave, lab., Inv.only £7.0.2 1739/371
SLEATH, Bridget, Guard.only of Bridget, Northampton, minor, 1789/24 Jan.
Richard, Kilsby, shoemaker, to Ann, wid., 1795/20 Jan.
SLEEFORD, Mary, Northampton, spin., to Martha Biker, wid., sister, 1719/112
SLIMM, Thomas, Crick, yeo., Inv.only £104.7.0 1722/88A

SLOW, Edward, Rothwell, Account of Anne, wid., admin., £60. 1679/40
Slough, John, Daventry, Account of Elizabeth Stanton, daughter, admin., £600.0.0 1683/19
Slowe, George, Gayton, Account of Elizabeth, wid., admin., £149.9.8 1685/33
SLY, Thomas, Watford, to Mary Bolton, Yelvertoft, wid., 1715/132
SLYNN, John, Crick, yeo., Inv.only £470.2.6 1712/136 A
Slinn, Grace, Crick, wid., to Samuel Edmunds, yeo., Inv. £18.13.6 1732/5 Mar.
Slinn, Martha, Crick, spin., to Elizabeth, wife of Samuel Edmonds, yeo., sister, 1740/21 June
SMALBONE, Thomas, Badby, Inv.only £22.10.0 1714/161 A
Smallbone, Daniel, elder, West Farndon, Woodford cum Membris, yeo., Inv.only £12.17.6 1723/101 A
Elizabeth, Woodford, spin., to Mary, wife of John Wigson, Eydon, husb., sister, 1733/8 Sept.
SMALLEY, Timothy, Dallington, lab., to Rebecca, wid., 1779/17 July
Benjamin, Loddington, farmer, to Anne, wid., 1794/2 July
SMALSHAW, William, Northampton, to Mary, wid., 1739/9 May
SMART, Simon, Stanwick, to Simon, miller, son, 1713/90
William, Bozeat, weaver, to John,weaver, son, 1730/10 Oct.
Samuel, Kelmarsh, shepherd, to Hannah, wid., 1760/1 Dec.
SMEETON, Henry, Maidwell, miller, to Joseph, yeo., father, Inv. £110.9.6 1723/56
SMITH, Anne, Hardingstone, Account of Thomas Vintner, admin., brother, £63.9.8 1670/125
Matthew, Higham Ferrers, baker, Account of Martha Saunders, wid., and Thomas, £142.16.4 1671/110
Thomas, Rushden, Account of Agnes, wid., admin., £464.11.8 1676/131
Thomas, Northampton, Rebecca, wid., renounced admon. in favour of the Ordinary of the Diocese of Peterborough, 1711/76
William, Little Addington, to John, husb., brother, Inv. £212.5.9 1712/16
William, Great Houghton, yeo., Inv.only £102.13.4 1712/22A
Jonathan, Great Houghton, yeo., Inv.only £114.13.0 1712/132A
Esau, Weston Favell, Account of Anne, wid., admin., £40.12.11 1713/6
John, Rothwell, grocer, to Mary, Inv. £208. 1713/55
John, senior, Newnham, Inv.only £19.1.0 1713/65A
Bryan, Yelvertoft, yeo., to Jane, wid., Inv. £30.16.6 Will, 1714/17
Samuel, elder, Daventry, cordwainer, to Anne, exor., Inv. £12.19.6 1714/32
William, Yardley Gobion, Potterspury, Inv.only £13.5.0 1714/87A
Thomas, Hargrave, yeo., Inv.only £39.5.4 1714/169A
Robert, Kettering, to Anne, wid., Inv. £17.6.6 1715/33
Thomas, Dodford, grazier, Inv.only £97.0.0 1715/44A
Thomas, clerk, Rector of Claycoton, Inv.only about £200. 1716/2A
Hannah, Higham Ferrers, Inv.only £10.15.0 1716/45A
Edward, Burton Latimer, Inv.only £91.13.1 1716/67A
Joseph, Brampton, miller, Inv.only £68.13.0 1716/81A
Mary, Badby, spin., Inv.only £23.10.0 1716/128A
Thomas, senior, Staverton, husb., Inv.only £45.5.0 1717/43A
John, Little Brington, yeo., Inv.only £61.1.11 1717/145A
Jane, Yelvertoft, wid., to Anne, wife of Samuel Ringrose, sister, Inv. £60.7.6 1718/13
Thomas, Grafton Regis, bachelor, to John, yeo., brother, 1718/131
William, Brafield, blacksmith, to John, blacksmith, son, 1719/96
Samuel, Brafield, to Sarah, wid., 1719/115
George, Desborough, yeo., to George, son, Inv. £7.1.0 1720/74
Edward, Boughton, Inv.only £87.0.0 1720/126A
Richard, Yelvertoft, to John, yeo., son, Inv. £9.10.0 1721/20
Thomas, Potterspury, yeo., Inv.only £193.0.0 1721/68A
Richard, Isham, to Jane, wid., 1721/105
John, Badby, Inv.only £37.11.0 1721/115A
Samuel, Kettering, Inv.only £16.5.0 1722/20A
John, Ringstead, butcher, Inv.only £87.1.6 1722/78A
Samuel, Isham, tailor, Inv.only £9.18.0 1722/92A
Jonathan, Rushton, Inv.only £483.15.0 1723/26A
John, Doddington, to Susanna, wid., and Robert, husb., son, Inv. £111.14.4 1723/135

SMITH continued
William, Great Cransley, to Elinor, wid., Inv. £77.7.6 1724/2
William, Lilbourne, to Thomas, yeo., brother, 1724/60
Thomas, Woodford, Inv.only £37.7.0 1724/120A
Abraham, Long Buckby, to Anne, wid., 1725/29 Apr. (29 July)
Joseph, Blakesley, to Anne, Seawell, Blakesley, spin., daughter, 1725/30 Apr.
Joseph, Seawell, Blakesley, yeo., Inv.only £94.16.0 1725/141
Francis, Spratton, to Jane, wid., 1725/23 Oct.
George, senior, East Farndon, yeo., Inv.only £127.1.0 1725/142
Obed, Daventry, to John, bookseller, son, Elizabeth, wid., renounced, 1726/4 Mar.
Thomas, Desborough, to Anne, wid., 1726/22 July
William, Kelmarsh, grazier, to Mary, wid., 1727/4 Nov.
William, Kelmarsh, Inv.only £172.1.0 1727/198
Mary, Braunston, wid., to John Skinner, husb., brother, 1728/3 Feb.
Robert, Rector of Great Addington, to Robert, fellow of Sidney College, Cambridge, 1728/17 May
John, Orlingbury, lab., to Thomas, lab., brother, 1728/15 June
David, Grendon, yeo., to Mary, wid., Inv. £245.7.0 1728/24 Aug.
Richard, Barby, lab., to Grace, wid., 1729/27 Sept.
Richard, Dodford, to Thomas, yeo., nephew, 1730/27 June
John, Cold Ashby, victualler, to Anne, wid., 1731/27 Mar.
Thomas, Weston Favell, lab., to Anne, wid., 1731/13 Dec.
Jane, Spratton, wid., to Martha, wid., principal creditor, 1732/4 Oct.
Mary, Cogenhoe, wid., to Elizabeth, spin., daughter, 1733/3 Feb.
Edward, Preston Capes, to William, lab., son, 1733/24 Feb.
Samuel, Isham, to Rose, wid., 1733/23 May
Charles, Isham, tailor, to Mary, wid., now wife of Richard Preston, Weston, co. Lincoln, husb., 1733/24 May
James, Walgrave, yeo., to Nazareth, wid., 1733/14 July
Thomas, Lamport, gent., to Elizabeth, wid., 1734/2 Mar.
Richard, Charwelton, grazier, to Richard Welch, Blakesley, gent., 1734/25 May
Caleb, Northampton, clerk, to Elizabeth, wid., mother, 1736/31 May
Samuel, Higham Ferrers, whittawer, to Margaret, wid., 1736/25 Oct.
Thomas, Staverton, to John Adams, Daventry, carrier, and John Lucas, Thulaston, Dunchurch, co. Warwick, grazier, principal creditors, Jacob Ward and John Lowe, guardians of Elizabeth, Anne and Mary, daughters, renounced, 1737/26 Feb.
Henry, Blakesley, yeo., to Elizabeth, wid., 1738/17 Aug.
Robert, Cosgrave, lab., Inv.only £6.12.0 1738/356
Sarah, Cosgrave, wid., to Sarah, wife of Richard Plackett, Darlescote, Pattishall, shepherd, niece, 1739/4 June
John, Cransley, to William, servant, brother, 1740/2 May
Richard, Heyford, to Frances, wid., 1741/24 Mar.
John, Bugbrooke, to Elizabeth, wid., 1742/16 Jan.
Lewis, Thurnley, gent., to John, Teigh, co. Rutland, gent., 1742/4 Mar.
John, Weedon Beck, to Elizabeth, wid., and John, yeo., son, 1743/7 May
John, Astcote, Pattishall, baker, to William Whitmell, Towcester, stocking weaver, nephew, 1743/28 Nov.
als. Garner, William, Long Buckby, to John Coleman, grocer, and John Wynn, Northampton, gent., 1745/28 Jan.
John, Wellingborough, victualler, to Silence, wid., 1746/23 Jan.
Thomas, Claycoton, butcher, to Elizabeth, wid., 1747/26 Oct.
John, Little Addington, farmer, to Dorcas, wid., Inv. £73.18.4 1748/20 Apr.
Mary, Badby, spin., to John, yeo., brother, 1751/1 Apr.
Richard, Heyford, turner, to William, heelmaker, son, of goods unadministered by Frances, wid., decd., 1751/27 June
John, Rothwell, to Thomas, brother, 1751/16 Oct.
Elizabeth, Bugbrooke, wid., to John, Great Brickhill, Bucks., shepherd, son, 1752/2 Dec.
John, Burton Latimer, yeo., to John, yeo., son, Inv. £126.0.0 1753/3 Mar.
Robert, Kettering, to Mary, wid., 1754/10 Jan.
Mary, Weedon Beck, wid., to William, yeo., son, Will, 1754/6 June
Peter, Walgrave, yeo., to Hannah, wid., 1754/5 Dec.
Richard, Barby, lab., to Thomas Gubbins, lab., of goods unadministered by Elizabeth, wid., decd., Will, 1755/5 Mar.

SMITH continued
John, Walgrave, yeo., to Mary, wid., 1755/21 July
Robert, Great Addington, clerk, to William Lambe, younger, Stanwick, gent., nephew, Ann, spin., daughter, renounced, Will, Inv. £108.15.6 1755/6 Oct.
Mary, Northampton, wid., to Sarah Clarke, spin., aunt of Elizabeth and Ann, minors, daughters, 1758/21 Feb.
John, Cranford St. John, to John, son, 1762/24 Apr.
George, (John), Burton Latimer, blacksmith, to Ann, wid., 1762/25 Oct.
Mary, Northampton, to Charles, staymaker, husband, 1767/27 Oct.
George, Burton Latimer, blacksmith, to Anne, wid., now wife of William Griffen, Thrapston, cordwainer, 1768/5 May
John, Maidford, husb., to Mary, wife of William Elliott, Green's Norton, yeo., and Ann, wife of Robert Gascoigne, Bloxham, co. Oxford, yeo., daughters, Ann, wid., and Richard Leeke, exor., renounced, Will, 1768/20 May
Elizabeth, West Haddon, wid., to Thomas, lab., son, 1770/28 Nov.
John, Duston, to Elizabeth, wife of Thomas Hall, Little Houghton, wheelwright, daughter, 1773/7 May
Ann, Northampton, to John, husband, 1774/24 Feb.
Ann, Yelvertoft, to Ann, wife of Joseph Healey, farmer, daughter, 1774/23 Apr.
William, Creaton, farmer, to Thomas, farmer, son, 1775/17 May
Edward, Northampton, gardener, to Sarah, wid., 1776/6 Dec.
Elizabeth, Wollaston, wid., to William Bluff, butcher, son in law, Ann, exor., decd., Will, 1777/4 Mar.
Robert, Moulton, farmer, to Robert, farmer, son, 1777/2 Aug.
Francis, Brixworth, wheelwright, to Anne, wid., 1778/23 May
John, Yardley Gobion, gent., to Elizabeth, spin., daughter, 1778/4 June
Francis, Brixworth, wheelwright, to Ann, wid. of Francis, wheelwright, son and exor., Will, 1779/30 Jan.
William, Floore, to Thomas, lab., brother, 1779/8 May
Mary, Brixworth, spin., to Sarah, wife of Thomas Law, weaver, sister, 1779/15 June
Peter, Byfield, yeo., to Elizabeth, wid., 1781/7 Mar.
Smyth, Barbara, Northampton, wid., to Christopher, gent., son, 1782/3 July
Thomas, Daventry, servant, to James, Thurlaston, co. Warwick, shoemaker, brother, John, same, lab., father, renounced, 1786/18 Oct.
Walpole, Roade, baker, to Mary, Oundle, wid., 1787/19 Feb.
John, Lilbourne, clerk, to John, Brinklow, co. Warwick, clerk, son, of goods unadministered by Elizabeth, wid., decd., 1788/9 Jan.
John, Rushton, to Mary, wid., 1788/18 Feb.
William, Woodford cum Membris, tailor, to Thomas Harris, farmer, cousin, John Harris, elder, exor., decd., Will, 1789/17 Aug.
John, Weedon Beck, victualler, to John, wheelwright, and Charles, collarmaker, sons, 1791/11 Feb.
John, Brafield, blacksmith, to Elizabeth, spin., daughter, 1792/20 Aug.
Samuel, Dallington, blacksmith, to Elizabeth, wid., 1792/16 Oct.
Richard, Kettering, to Ann, wife of William Wallis, farmer, daughter, 1795/4 July
Thomas, Bozeat, lab., to Hannah, wife of William Pilmuir, Northampton, carpenter, daughter, 1796/13 Apr.
Edward, Denton, cordwainer, to Jemima, wid., 1796/21 May
John, Northampton, cordwainer, to William and Joseph, gardeners, cousins, 1797/22 Apr.
James, Paulerspury, woolcomber, to Elisha, Blockley, co. Worcester, draper, son, Sarah, exor., decd., Will, 1798/21 Apr.
William, Hackleton, victualler, to Allen Lovell, Mears Ashby, yeo., nephew, John, Horton, yeo., brother, renounced, Will, 1800/14 June

SODEN, William, Lilbourne, victualler, to Eleanor, wid., 1731/17 Nov.
Sodin, William, Lilbourne, victualler, to Joan, wid., 1759/8 June

SOME, Ralph, Kettering, to David, draper, and John, sergemaker, sons, Jane, wid., renounced, 1715/110
Soame, Ralph, Rector of Braunston, to David, Kettering, gent., 1728/30 Jan.
Joseph, Abington, to James Ansell, Claybrooke, co. Leic., clerk, and William Ansell, Hanslop, Bucks., dealer in lace, uncles and guardians of William, minor, son, 1742/23 Apr.

SOUTHAM, Thomas, to Sarah, Badby, exor., 1714/80

SOUTHAM continued
Thomas, Badby, Inv.only £9.3.6 1714/85
John, Croughton, Inv.only £12.15.0 undated/288
SOUTHERNE, Mary, Ashton, wid., to Anne Drinkwater, daughter, Robert Crosley, clerk, rector of Ashton, and Thomas Cox, clerk, Hornsley, co. Middx., exors., renounced, Inv. £120.5.8 Will, 1718/5
SPARROW, Mary, Kettering, wid., to Joseph, son, Inv. £191.10.9 1720/89
Joseph, Kettering, to Anna Maria, wid., and John Carrington, 1759/7 Feb.
SPATEMAN, John, Rector of Whilton, clerk, to Elizabeth, wid., 1749/13 Oct.
SPEDDING, Robert, Grendon, to Ann, wid., 1776/16 Mar.
SPENCE, Sarah, Kettering, wid., Inv.only £35.12.1 1714/155A
John, Thorpe Malsor, weaver, to John, weaver, son, 1749/14 Feb.
William, Arthingworth, yeo., to Thomas, farmer, son, Inv. £366.12.6 1752/25 Mar.
SPENCER, Hannah, Northampton, wid., to John, shoemaker, Inv. £5.17.4 1711/69
William, elder, Braybrooke, yeo., Inv.only £279.10.8 1714/84
Henry, Brixworth, chandler, to John Butterfield, Buckingham, chandler, principal creditor, Elizabeth, wid., renounced, Inv. £200.9.11¾ 1730/15 Jan.
Henry, Braunston, farmer, to Anne, wid., Inv. £251.12.0 1742/23 Apr.
Thomas, Wellingborough, victualler, to Mary, spin., daughter, 1758/18 Sept.
William, Hellidon, to Nathaniel, grazier, Simon, farmer, grazier, and Catherine, wife of Joseph Ward, victualler, sons and daughter, 1765/27 Apr.
William, Horton, innholder, to Martha, wid., 1782/7 Nov.
John, Pisford, lab., to Thomas, cordwainer, son, 1798/15 Dec.
John, Welford, innholder, to Anne, wid., 1800/28 May
SPICER, Henry, Northampton, to Sarah, spin., daughter, 1717/74
John, Byfield, to John, collarmaker, son, 1740/3 May
SPIRES, Richard, Marston St. Lawrence, to Elizabeth, wid., Inv. £8.4.0 1713/106
Spier, Jane, Wappenham, wid., to Jane, wife of Henry Cockerill, yeo., daughter, 1787/21 Dec.
SPOKES, George, West Haddon, butcher, to John Bailey, yeo., principal creditor, 1742/22 Feb.
George, Holcot Mill, to Jane, wid., 1768/12 Nov.
SPRATLEY, Sarah, Hartwell, spin., to William Coles, elder, Slapton, tailor, nephew, Catherine, sister, spin., renounced, 1769/1 Mar.
SPRIGGS, John, Rushton, bachelor, Inv.only £48.13.6 1719/10A
SQUIRRELL, Elizabeth, Brackley, to Thomas Toy, Evenley, lab., son, 1711/40
Squerrell, Squirrills, Richard, Brackley, Inv.only £168.3.0 1720/109A
Squerell, Richard, Towcester, victualler, to Mary, wid., now wife of Cornelius Berry, victualler, 1742/20 Feb.
STACEY, James, Kettering, yeo., to Anne, wid., 1730/23 Jan.
Catherine, Middleton Cheney, to Elizabeth Jeffs, daughter, 1767/30 Oct.
STACKHOUSE, John, senior, Wellingborough, hatter, to Mary, wid., Inv. £33.0.3 1726/8 Mar.
STAFFORD, William, Oxendon, to John, Teddingworth, co. Leic., weaver, 1736/7 Feb.
George, Pisford, to Sarah, wid., 1778/18 Aug.
STAINES, William, Raunds, yeo., to Martha, wid., 1727/18 Sept.
William, Raunds, farmer, Inv.only £371.13.0 1727/405
John, Raunds, yeo., to Matthew, yeo., son, John, son, renounced, 1745/4 Jan.
STANION, Richard, Higham Ferrers, yeo., Inv.only £716.19.8 1714/133A
Stanyon, John, Northampton, butcher, to Mary, wid., 1730/21 Sept.
Stanyarne, Joseph, Rothwell, tanner, to Joseph, son, Ann, wid., renounced, 1751/22 Oct.
Stanyan, John, Northampton, butcher, to Elizabeth, wife of William Richardson, glover, daughter, of goods unadministered by Mary, wid., decd., 1756/21 June
STANLEY, John, East Haddon, to Susanna, wid., 1714/34
William, Middleton Cheney, to Sarah, wife of William Finch, Warrington, co. Warwick, shepherd, sister, 1734/14 Nov.
Mary, Moreton Pinkney, wid., to Anne, wife of Henry Feary, yeo., cousin, Inv. £7.2.0 1745/11 Oct.
William, Aynho, to Jane, wid., Will, 1784/28 Oct.
STANTON, Samuel, Duston, Account of Anne, wid., admin., £96.2.0 1685/161

STANTON continued
John, Drayton, Daventry, to Nicholas, Fawsley, husb., son, John, son, renounced, Inv. £429.3.9 Will, 1712/116
William, Marston St. Lawrence, Inv.only £28.10.0 1713/107A
John, Drayton, Daventry, to Mary, wid., Inv. £344.12.2 1715/135
Joyce, Eydon, spin., to John, husb., Anne Keck, wid., brother and sister, and James Key, husb., Inv. £59.14.4 1719/94
Moses, Daventry, to Jane, wid., 1723/108
Thomas, Woodford cum Membris, Inv.only £89.13.6 1724/107A
William, Blisworth, baker, to Catherine, wid., Inv. £115.0.0 1726/15 Mar.
John, Northampton, victualler, to John, farmer, father, 1767/24 Mar.
John, Drayton, Daventry, yeo., to John, Long Buckby, and Richard, yeos., 1773/12 Oct.
John, Eydon, mason, to Richard Daniel, Woodford, butcher, grandson in law, Joyce, wife of John Harris, Woodford, and John Harris, renounced, 1782/16 Nov.
William, Daventry, cooper, to Jane, spin., daughter, 1785/9 Dec.
Elizabeth, Kingsthorpe, wid., to Thomas, Upper Heyford, grazier, cousin and guardian of Ann, William, Martha and Samuel, minors, children, 1788/23 Feb.
Samuel, Northampton, gent., to Thomas, Upper Heyford, grazier, cousin and guardian of Ann, William, Martha and Samuel, minors, children, Guard., 1788/23 Feb.
John, Northampton, draper, to Anne, wid., 1794/22 Oct.
STARETON, Ladyman, Charlton, Newbottle, victualler, to Martha, wid., 1790/27 May
STARLING, Anne, Newbottle, spin., Inv.only £134.7.0 1715/46A
STARMER, William, Harlestone, Inv.only £106.15.0 1714/75A
Nicholas, Brampton, to Thomas, husb., son, 1721/142
Thomas, Brafield on the Green, to Anne, wid., Inv. £6.10.0 1729/13 Sept.
John, Northampton, to William, whittawer, son, Inv. £17.0.6 1742/2 Mar.
STEANS, William, Raunds, yeo., Inv.only £338.5.0 1713/69A
STEEL, John, Great Billing, victualler, to Jane, spin., daughter, 1746/2 Apr.
STEERE, Ursula, Floore, wid., to Thomas Arnold, husb., next of kin, Inv. £5.4.4 1712/10
Stear, Robert, senior, Wollaston, yeo., Inv.only £32.13.0 1719/104A
Steer, John, Easton Maudit, grazier, to Alice, wid., Inv. £694.14.3 1781/3 Apr.
STEFFE, Edmund, Wollaston, Guard.only of Mary, daughter, 1732/19 Apr.
STEPHENS, Steevens, Jeremie, Wootton, clerk, Account of Robert, clerk, admin., £269.12.8 1670/91
Bernard, Whittlebury, Inv.only £19.19.0 1716/112A
Richard, Helmdon, to Robert, Cuddington, Bucks., father and guardian of Richard, minor, Martha, wid., exor., decd., Inv. £152.10.6 Guard., Will, 1719/1
Martha, Helmdon, wid., to Sarah, wife of Thomas Smith, Moreton Pinkney, husb., niece, Robert, father and guardian of Richard, exor., renounced, Will, 1719/14
Richard, Helmdon, yeo., to Robert, son, 1719/15
John, Broughton, Inv.only £12.5.0 1721/60A
Stevens, Robert, Rushden, to Robert, yeo., son, Inv. £11.12.10 1728/9 Nov.
Stevens, Daniel, Cotten End, Hardingstone, to Joseph, yeo., son, 1781/23 Oct.
Stevens, Elizabeth, Hannington, wid., to Hannah Barker, spin., sister, 1784/29 Mar.
STEVENSON, Elizabeth, Daventry, wid., to Benjamin, saddler, son, 1746/26 July
Charles, Kingsthorpe, to Sarah, wid., 1754/6 July
Charles, Kingsthorpe, Guard.only of Charles, minor, son, 1771/16 Dec.
Steevenson, Thomas, Kingsthorpe, jersey comber, to Samuel, wheelwright, son, 1790/27 Dec.
STEWARD, Thomas, Marston St. Lawrence, to Elizabeth, wid., Inv. £342.17.6 1712/63
Charles, Pattishall, clerk, to Elizabeth, spin., sister, 1736/3 Jan.
STIFFE, Joseph, Glendon, Inv.only £36.4.0 1717/27A
William, Glendon, to Jane, wid., Will, 1724/103
Stiff, William, Glendon, Inv.only £247.12.0 1724/135

STILEMAN, Rev. John, Rector of East Farndon, Inv.only £78.10.0 1733/311
STILES, Christopher, Hinton, shepherd, to Eleanor, wid., 1753/2 Apr.
STIRKE, John, Salcey Forest, gent., Account of Jane, wid., admin., £248.8.0 1684/22
ST. JOHN, Oliver, Wilby, to Elizabeth, wid., 1728/11 Sept.
Joseph, Mears Ashby, to John, Little Billing, grazier, brother, 1741/7 Nov.
STOCKLEY, John, Helmdon, freemason, Inv.only £25.11.0 1715/41 A
John, Helmdon, to Robert, mason, brother, 1716/60
John, Chipping Warden, yeo., to John, yeo., nephew, 1731/1 Dec.
William, Chipping Warden, maltster, to John, yeo., son, Anne, wid., renounced, 1731/1 Dec.
John, Chipping Warden, farmer, yeo., to Elizabeth, wid., Inv. £458.0.4 1751/21 Oct.
John, Chipping Warden, farmer, to Thomas, Inv. £1604.2.0 1781/3 Mar.
William, Everdon, to Mary, wid., 1798/13 Aug.
STOKES, Theophilus, Inv.only £14.5.6 1712/83 A
Stoakes, William, Towcester, Inv.only £206.13.0 1721/38 A
Nicholas, Woodford, to John, blacksmith, son, 1742/3 Apr.
STONE, Mary, Inv.only £153.14.11 1711/31 A
John, Braybrooke, Inv.only £17.18.0 1720/46 A
Peter, Northampton, victualler, to Elizabeth, wife of Samuel Walton, victualler, 1729/31 May
Stones, Matthew, Syresham, to Mary Jones, wid., 1782/11 Sept.
STONHAM, Sarah, Northampton, to Emma Whitehead, Paulerspury, niece, 1717/89
STOUGHTON, Francis, Kettering, sergemaker, to Sarah and John, junior, Inv. £330.3.3 1714/47
John, Kettering, gent., to John, innholder, grandson, Will, 1730/23 Jan.
STOW, Elizabeth, Northampton, wid., to George, victualler, son, 1726/27 Apr.
STRATFORD, Nicholas, Northampton, to Frances Atterbury, wid., daughter, 1723/76
Sarah, Preston Capes, spin., to Hannah Sorril, wid., sister, 1800/16 Apr.
STRETTON, Thomas, Kettering, Inv.only £48.3.0 1722/17 A
STUCHFIELD, Elizabeth, Sulgrave, wid., to Thomas, farmer, and William, Slapton, farmer, sons, Inv. £17.15.0 1781/2 July
STURGIS, Sturges, Philip, Walgrave, Account of Elizabeth, wid., £71.1.2 1672/130
James, Ashton, Inv.only £207.10.0 1714/58 A
Abraham, Warkton, to Grace, wid., 1717/47
Edward, Burton Latimer, miller, Inv.only £225.5.6 1720/106 A
Giles, Great Oxendon, lab., to Anne, wid., Inv. £17.4.0 1720/144
Thomas, Great Oxendon, chandler, Inv.only £16.10.6 1723/104 A
Mary, Sibbertoft, wid., to Joseph Ashby, Ratley cum Chackmore, Bucks., yeo., Thomas Smalbone, Eydon, brother, renounced in favour Jane, wife of Joseph, daughter, 1724/35
Jonathan, Great Oxendon, husb., Inv.only £34.15.0 1724/52A
Grace, Warkton, wid., to Abraham, son, 1733/16 Nov.
Thomas, Great Oxendon, yeo., Inv.only £18.15.0 1733/306
Robert, Farndon, lab., to Edward Weston, East Farndon, farmer, uncle and guardian of Mary, Hannah, Martha, Sarah, Thomas, John, William and George, children, minors, 1765/3 July
Joseph, Northampton, tanner, to Elizabeth, wid., 1765/11 July
Elizabeth, Northampton, wid., to William Tompson, grocer, and William Stevenson, Stamford, co. Linc., tanner, of goods unadministered by Samuel, farmer, son, decd., Will, 1789/15 June
STURMAN, Robert, Sywell, yeo., to Sarah, wid., Will, 1723/65
Robert, Sywell, yeo., Inv.only £329.6.6 1723/124
Laurence, Little Houghton, to Sarah, spin., daughter, 1723/87
John, elder, Nortoft, Guilsborough, Inv.only £39.9.10 1723/122 A
Anne, Little Houghton, wid., to Samuel, lab., son, 1729/7 June
Mary, Little Houghton, wid., to William, Welton, baker, son, 1776/10 Aug.
Mary, Guilsborough, spin., to Stephen Dexter, yeo., husband of Ann, exor., decd., Will, 1794/8 Dec.
STUTCHFIELD, Crescent, to Elizabeth, Sulgrave, wid., Inv. £344.17.0 1764/30 May
See also Stuchfield
SUDBOROUGH, John, Cranford St. Andrew, to Elizabeth, wid., 1771/5 July
SUFFOLK, Esan, Gretworth, husb., to Joseph, Stutchbury, husb., son, Will, 1711/136

SUMMERFIELD, Sumerfield, Joseph, Northampton, grocer, to Elizabeth, wid., 1737/21 Feb.
Benjamin, Northampton, grocer, to Mary, wid., 1751/8 July
Sumerfield, Michael, Cotton End, Hardingstone, to Susannah, wid., 1772/17 Jan.
SUMMERLY, Somerly, John, Great Doddington, Inv.only £4.12.0 1718/138A
Sumerly, William, Earl's Barton, lab., to Sarah Clevely, wid., principal creditor, 1728/6 Dec.
SUMMERS, James, Rothwell, baker, Inv.only £19.14.6 1714/98A
Henry, Wellingborough, dissenting teacher, to Sarah Hatton Summers, wid., 1798/10 Sept.
SUMPTER, William, Oxendon, grazier, to Richard Bryan, Welham, co. Leic., grazier, and Joseph Manton, Arthingworth, grazier, uncles and guardians of William, minor, son, Guard., 1786/30 Oct.
SURRIDGE, Elizabeth, Bozeat, wid., to William Jeffery, Yardley Hastings, farmer, nephew, 1773/13 Mar.
SUTTON, John, Little Bowden, Account of Alice, admin., £39.0.8 1671/89
Thomas, Marston St. Lawrence, Inv.only £39.14.8 1717/57A
John, Guilsborough, shopkeeper, Inv.only £100.4.4 1720/90A
Dorothy, Guilsborough, wid., to Joseph, shopkeeper, son, 1728/21 Dec.
SWALLOW, John, Oakham, co. Rutland, gent., to John Hand als. Smith, butcher, Richard Brown, chandler, and Anthony Brooksby, saddler, Inv. £104.18.0 1711/47
SWAN, William, Kingsthorpe, to Thomas, son, 1715/130
Swayn, Mary, Wellingborough, spin., to John, Finningley, co. Warwick, yeo., and Richard, same, yeo., brothers, 1731/7 Sept.
Sarah, Blakesley, spin., to Penelope White, wid., principal creditor, 1743/1 Sept.
SWANSON, Thomas, Kettering, to Mary, wid., 1729/31 Jan.
SYMONS, SYMONDS, see SIMONS

T

TAFT, John, Wappenham, shepherd, to Elizabeth, wife of John Middleton, lab., daughter, 1751/27 July
TALBOTT, Thomas, West Haddon, to William Watkin, clerk, principal creditor, Anne, wid., renounced, 1714/56
Tawbut, Thomas, Everdon, yeo., to Horatio, Moreton Pinkney, blacksmith, brother, 1751/21 Oct.
Nicholas, Culworth, to Oratio, Moreton Pinkney, blacksmith, brother, 1756/17 Jan.
Talbot, Thomas, Irchester, to Thomas, Hartest, co. Suffolk, farmer, 1770/26 May
TALLIS, Thomas, Kingsthorpe, to Alice, Northampton, wid., 1774/18 Mar.
Alice, Northampton, to Thomas, Kingsthorpe, miller, son, 1775/25 Mar.
TAME, Joseph, Charlton, to Anne, wid., 1728/16 May
TAPP, John, Higham Ferrers, Account of Hannah, wid., admin., £587.14.0 1683/23
TARRY, Thomas, Thurnby, Account of Elizabeth, wid., £220.0.0 1672/112
Jane, Creaton, wid., to Robert, lab., son, Inv. £8.12.0 1712/20
John, Thurnby, butcher, Inv.only £122.2.0 1716/100 A
William, Thurnby, butcher, to John, yeo., and Samuel, brothers, Inv. £51.18.6 1721/43
John, Gayton, Inv.only £11.10.0 1723/97A
Elizabeth, Evenly, wid., to Alice, wife of John Basely, daughter, Inv. (i) £12.6.6, (ii) £17.5.8 1724/23
Tarrey, John, Yelvertoft, mercer, to Dorcas, wid., Inv. £35.13.4 1726/10 Feb.
Alexander, Northampton, cheesemonger, to Mary, wid., 1732/1 June
John, Crick, to Ann, wid., Thomas, Yelvertoft, grazier, and John, West Haddon, Inv. £208.3.4 1733/7 Apr.
Sarah, Thurnby, wid., to Elizabeth, wife of Roger Cave, Cold Ashby, weaver, and Anne, daughters, 1760/5 May
Elizabeth, Winwick, to Robert, London, baker, son, 1773/19 Aug.
John, Church Brampton, woolcomber, to William, woolcomber, father, 1781/17 Sept.
TATAM, Tateham, Bridget, Brackley, spin., to Samuel, Bath, co. Somerset, gunsmith, father, 1730/2 July
TATE, Katherine, Wallington, co. York., to Thomas, servant, husband, 1799/9 May

TAVERNER, John, West Haddon, to Anne, wid., 1741/11 Mar.
TAYLOR, Thomas, Claycoton, gent., Account of Agnes, wid., admin., £244.16.6 1685/166
Joseph, Wellingborough, tanner, Inv.only £372.5.0 1711/84
als. Paris, William, Middleton Cheney, yeo., to John, lab., son, 1712/69
Tayler, John, Marston Trussell, to John, son, 1714/135
Adam, Kettering, Inv.only £10.13.7 1715/25A
William, Hellidon, gent., Inv.only £310.12.8 1715/89
William, Hellidon, to Thomas Chiswell, Coventry, co. Warwick, 1715/163
Alexander, Northampton, innholder, Inv.only £15.17.0 1715/164A
als. Paris, William, Middleton Cheney, yeo., Inv.only £422.1.6 1717/51A
als. Paris, John, Middleton Cheney, to Anne, wid., 1719/45
Tayler, Mary, Marston St. Lawrence, spin., to John, yeo., and Edward, Sulgrave, brothers (nephews), Elizabeth, wid., mother, renounced, 1720/71
als. Paris, Richard, Middleton Cheney, lab., Inv.only £13.19.0 1720/87A
William, Rushton, innholder, to Mary, wid., Inv. £286.4.6 1721/63
Timothy, Wellingborough, to Joseph, son, Jane, wid., renounced, 1723/63
Alice, Brackley, Inv.only £22.13.4 1724/87A
Anne, Little Bowden, wid., to John, gent., son, 1727/13 Sept.
Thomas, Middleton Cheney, husb., to Alice, wid., Inv. £73.14.0 1728/27 Feb.
als. Parish, John, Sulgrave, yeo., to Elizabeth, wid., Inv. £134.10.0 1729/31 May
Abraham, Isham, to Elizabeth, wid., Inv. £18.2.0 1736/6 Feb.
Edward, Sulgrave, yeo., to Sarah, wid., 1748/12 Apr.
als. Paris, Ann, Middleton Cheney, wid., to Elizabeth, wife of Humphrey Penn, farmer, daughter, Inv. £527.8.0 1749/7 Apr.
Elizabeth, Sulgrave, wid., to Crescent Jeffs, Marsh Gibbon, Bucks., butcher, and Crescent Jeffs, Chalcombe, butcher, Inv. £94.8.4 1750/11 June
Elizabeth, Chalcombe, wid., to Mary, wife of Thomas Jeffs, butcher, daughter, 1751/27 Apr.
Thomas, to Jane, Charlton, Newbottle, wid., 1763/8 June
William, Middleton Cheney, to William, lab., son, 1770/5 Dec.
Edward, Marston St. Lawrence, farmer, to Elizabeth, wid., 1774/4 May
Anne, Northampton, wid., to John Freeman Taylor, currier, son, 1786/1 May
John, Northampton, victualler, to Mary, wid., 1788/11 Sept.
John, Northampton, innholder, victualler, to William, gent., son, of goods unadministered by Mary, wid., decd., 1789/3 Feb.
TEARE, William, Maidwell, to Elizabeth, wid., 1726/25 June
Samuel, Hardwick, yeo., to Elizabeth, wid., 1729/25 Oct.
TEBBUTT, Thomas, Boughton, to Mary, wid., Inv. £31.10.8 1711/44
John, junior, Rothwell, mason, Inv.only £16.7.0 1716/26 A
Sarah, Northampton, spin., to Edward, Milton, father, 1718/68
John, Great Billing, husb., to Mary, wid., Inv. £211.13.6 1718/103
John, Rothwell, mason, to Samuel, weaver, Inv. £34.0.6 1720/130
Edward, Faxton, Inv.only £18.10.0 1721/88 A
Elizabeth, Piddington, wid., to Mary Crouch, St. Sepulchre, London, niece, 1726/18 Apr.
Susanna, Rothwell, wid., to Thomas Martin, carpenter, Inv. £6.18.4 1728/15 Oct.
Tebbott, Mary, Piddington, wid., to Daniel Mayne, yeo., Daniel Plackett, shopkeeper, and George Cave, husb., guardians of William, minor, 1731/30 Oct.
Mary, Piddington, Inv.only £25.6.6 1731/285
John, Northampton, innholder, to Martha, wid., Inv. £39.7.8 1738/12 Sept.
Martha, Northampton, wid., to Elizabeth Orpin, Grafton Underwood, wid., aunt and guardian of Mary, Elizabeth, minors, daughters, 1742/6 Dec.
William, Easton Neston, to Sarah Arnne, wid., principal creditor, Edward, elder, Edward, younger, and Mary Clarke, father, brother and sister, renounced, 1745/13 May
Tebbitt, Richard, Long Buckby, to Sarah, wid., 1764/26 May
William, Daventry, to Thomas Boyes, Long Buckby, grazier, uncle, 1773/5 Oct.
Samuel, Cotton, Hardingstone, victualler, to Mary, wid., 1776/12 Sept.
Joseph, Hellidon, farmer, to Elizabeth, wid., 1782/27 Aug.

TEBBUTT continued
William, Earl's Barton, matmaker, to Joseph, matmaker, son, 1782/1 Nov.
Tebbitt, Elizabeth, Long Buckby, wid., to Mary, wife of William Robinson, farmer, 1789/24 Oct.
Tebbitt, Robert, Long Buckby, yeo., to Robert, yeo., father, Anne, wid., renounced, 1798/9 Oct.
TEETON, Samuel, Doddington, to John, Cogenhoe, grazier, son, 1766/17 Jan.
als. Silby, Mary, see Silby
TELFORD, Elizabeth, Wellingborough, to Elizabeth Keep, wid., daughter, 1778/16 Oct.
TEMPLE, Mary, Sibbertoft, wid., to Martha, spin., and Elizabeth, Old, spin., daughters, 1783/29 Mar.
TERRY, John, Northampton, to Elizabeth, wife of Samuel Evans, Brackley, hatter, niece, 1772/25 Sept.
TEW, John, Paulerspury, to Thomas, husb., son, 1713/116
William, Eydon, mason, Inv.only £262.16.10 1718/47A
Thomas, Paulerspury, to Sarah, wid., 1722/32
Thomas, Eydon, Inv.only £92.10.3 1723/51A
Mary, Northampton, to Edmund, fellow of Jesus College, Cambridge, son, 1723/83
Thomas, Whittlebury, to Susanna, wid., Inv. £101.8.6 1723/112
Margaret, Woodford, spin., to Elizabeth, wid., mother, Inv. £114.4.6 1733/6 Oct.
Edward, Woodford, lab., to Thomas Smith, tailor, next of kin, 1733/27 Dec.
Richard, Woodford cum Membris, to Thomas and Stephen, shoemakers, brothers, 1739/27 Oct.
Richard, Woodford cum Membris, Inv.only £168.1.6 1739/370
Thomas, Great Houghton, to Elizabeth, wid., 1745/21 Sept.
Susannah, Whittlebury, wid., to John Newman, farmer, Will, 1746/5 Apr.
George, Eydon, to Mary Mayo, daughter, 1783/7 June
Edward, Eydon, yeo., to Thomas Thornton, mason, son in law, Philicia, wid., renounced, 1787/28 June
THACKALL, Elizabeth, Eydon, wid., to William, son, 1787/1 May
THEEDE, Thomas, Daventry, to Elizabeth, wid., 1726/28 Apr.
THOMAS, Solomon, senior, Brington, to Solomon, Towcester, yeo., son, 1723/68
Nathaniel, Wappenham, farmer, to Elizabeth Johnson, Ravenston, Bucks., wid., sister, 1795/25 Mar.
THOMPSON, Thomason, Henry, Adstone, Inv.only £153.5.0 1716/21A
Tomson, William, Stanwick, Inv.only £10.18.0 1722/100
Mary, Ecton, wid., to Thomas Young, Stoke Albany, woolwinder, Elizabeth Young, Brixworth, spin., and William Arthur, Brixworth, cordwainer, cousins, 1746/5 Mar.
Samuel, Kilsby, carpenter, to John, yeo., brother, Inv. £102.15.0 1748/25 Mar.
Tompson, George, Kettering, woolcomber, to Mary West, daughter, 1787/15 May
Tomson, Christopher, Kettering, yeo., to John, Coppingford, co. Hunts., yeo., brother, 1796/28 Jan.
THONGER, George, Brackley, to Frances, spin., daughter, Inv. £11.7.0 1743/18 Apr.
THORNTON, John, Marston St. Lawrence, to Damaris, wid., Will, 1738/8 Sept.
John, Costow, Marston St. Lawrence, Inv.only £288.3.0 1738/362
William, Moreton Pinkney, yeo., to Anne, wid., Inv. £421.12.6 1754/8 Feb.
Elizabeth, to Thomas, Culworth, grazier, husband, of goods unadministered by Robert Kenning, grocer, father, decd., 1778/25 Apr.
Anne, Eydon, spin., to John, Byfield, lab., brother, 1784/3 May
Richard, Paulerspury, yeo., to William, Great Brickhill, co. Bucks., son, Sarah, wid., exor., decd., Will, 1784/10 Nov.
Stephen, Daventry, victualler, to William Clarke, victualler, son in law, William Rose, whipmaker, John Watson, St. John Street, Middx., distiller, and Richard, whipmaker, brother, exors., decd., Will, 1785/7 Jan.
William, Byfield, Guard.only of Robert, minor, 1786/22 Aug.
Thomas, Brockhall, to Thomas Lee Thornton, grandson, Thomas, son, exor., decd., Will, 1787/7 Feb.
George, Fulham, co. Middx., glazier, to Elizabeth, Sulgrave, wid., mother, 1799/14 Sept.
THOROUGHGOOD, Richard, Wollaston, victualler, to Silbilla, wid., 1750/10 Oct.

THORPE, William, Scaldwell, Inv.only £69.9.0 1716/88
Andrew, Desborough, yeo., to Ferdinando, weaver, son, 1736/18 Mar.
Josiah, Desborough, miller, to Elizabeth, wid., 1792/12 Mar.
THYNN, Rev. Robert, Floore, clerk, to Mary Goodday, Northampton, wid., principal creditor, 1717/18
TIBBETTS, Tibbitts, Thomas, Hinton, to Mary, wid., mother, 1767/18 Dec.
Mary, Hinton, wid., to John, Brackley, maltster, son, 1769/20 June
TIBBS, Thomas, Everdon, Inv.only £121.10.0 1717/67 A
als. Saby, Anne, see Saby
TIDMAN, Richard, Newnham, to Elizabeth, wid., Inv. £14.0.0 1721/80
Elizabeth, Newnham, wid., to Richard, cordwainer, son, 1724/47
Richard, Newnham, Inv.only £35.5.0 1724/142 A
TILLEY, Christopher, Vicar of Hellidon, to John, London, tallow chandler, 1725/6 Aug.
Tilly, William, Heyford, victualler, to Alice, wid., 1729/6 Sept.
John, Whittlebury, huntsman, Guard.only of John, minor, son, 1791/15 July
TIMMES, Nicholas, Brackley, lab., Inv.only £10.5.6 1711/38 A
Thomas, Chalcombe, Inv.only £24.0.6 1717/119 A
Tims, William, Farthinghoe, Inv.only £74.1.10 1723/120
Timms, Thomas, Chalcombe, cordwainer, to Mary, wid., 1748/22 Apr.
Mary, Farthinghoe, spin., to William, Haversham, Bucks., yeo., brother, 1751/19 Apr.
Elizabeth, Farthinghoe, wid., to William, Haversham, Bucks., yeo., son, 1751/19 Apr.
Timms, John, Farthinghoe, yeo., to Elizabeth, wid., 1751/29 Oct.
Timms, John, Mears Ashby, lab., to John Wright, Northampton, gardener, brother in law, 1796/10 Mar.
TIMSON, William, East Farndon, cordwainer, Inv.only £8.14.6 1736/331
TINGLE, Charles, Inv.only £69.10.2 1727/155
TIPLER, George, Great Houghton, lab., to Anne, wid., 1733/5 Feb.
George, Great Houghton, lab., Inv.only £12.10.0 1733/295
Elizabeth, Northampton, spin., to Henry Locock, apothecary, principal creditor, 1755/17 Oct.
Edward, Kettering, to Mary, wid., and Thomas, son, 1758/11 Dec.
TITE, William, Preston, to William, Duston, husb., son, Inv. £9.18.2 1717/140
William, Woodend, Blakesley, yeo., to Alice, wid., Inv. £91.5.6 1729/20 Sept.
Anthony, Hartwell Park, Roade, Inv.only £434.17.0 1733/300
William, Duston, miller, to Hannah, wife of William Esson, miller, daughter, Inv. £62.2.2 1756/1 Jan.
TODD, Tod, John, Paulerspury, tailor, to Stephen Preston, Yardley Gobion, Potterspury, tailor, Inv. £3.19.4 1716/58
Elizabeth, Northampton, to Robert, cutter, husband, 1767/16 Nov.
Thomas, Irthlingborough, to Susanna, wid., 1792/23 Mar.
TOLMEY, William, Northampton, victualler, to Elizabeth, wid., 1736/12 Nov.
TOLTON, Robert, elder, Braybrooke, Inv.only £63.3.10 1717/100 A
Robert, Braybrooke, to John, yeo., son, Mary, wid., renounced, 1738/7 Apr.
Robert, senior, Braybrooke, Inv.only £126.7.2 1738/342
Robert, Braybrooke, to Sarah, wid., 1774/27 Oct.
Sarah, Braybrooke, wid., to William, son, 1782/5 Apr.
TOMKINS, John, Braunston, yeo., Inv.only £209.18.0 1713/115A
Henry, Paulerspury, cordwainer, to Damaris, wid., Inv. £6.18.6 1722/101
Thomas, Kislingbury, to Alice, wid., 1728/26 Oct.
Thomas, Kislingbury, Inv.only £198.15.0 1728/238
Margaret, Milton, wid., to William Kenning, Little Brington, yeo., brother, Inv. £68.10.0 1745/9 Feb.
Elizabeth, Brafield, wid., to Thomas, lab., son, 1761/25 Mar.
John, Northampton, shopkeeper, to William, weaver, son, 1779/5 Jan.
Thomas, Kislingbury, yeo., to Jane, wid., 1787/18 June
TOMLIN, als. Marston, Catherine, East Farndon, Account of John Wright, £92.4.6 1671/92
John, Daventry, husb., Inv.only £476.17.8 1722/111A
Tomalin, Jeremiah, Woodford cum Membris, yeo., to Jeremiah, son, 1729/1 Nov.
Tomalin, Hannah, Long Buckby, to William, husband, 1755/11 Jan.
TOMLINSON, William, Adstone, innholder, to Mary, Courtenhall, wid., 1755/18 Oct.

TOMS, Tombs, John, Winwick, Inv.only £139.4.0 1720/10A
Tooms, John, Inv.only £165.0.0 1720/39 A
Tomes, Thomas, Bozeat, Inv.only £31.0.0 1726/162
Tombes, Henry, Potterspury, lab., to Elizabeth, wid., now wife of Thomas Hinds, 1732/17 Jan.
Thomas, Bozeat, victualler, to Jane, wid., Inv. £78.8.10 1763/21 Nov.
TOMSON, TOMPSON, see THOMPSON
TONGUE, Anne, Rothwell, wid., to Samuel Woodford, skinner, son, 1720/124
TOOLEY, Joan, Paulerspury, Inv.only £6.1.0 1712/3 A
Catherine, Middleton Cheney, wid., Inv.only £39.0.6 1713/45 A
TORDIFF, Rev. Joseph, Roade, clerk, to Elizabeth, wid., Inv. £209.6.0 1775/29 Dec.
TOWERS, Richard, Badby, to Mary, wife of Thomas Clarke, lab., daughter, Will, 1765/22 Apr.
TOWNDROW, Jane, to Samuel, Newark, Leic., hozier, husband, 1800/28 May
TOWNLEY, Francis, Maidwell, to Thomas, yeo., son, 1740/2 Oct.
John, Maidwell, farmer, to Elizabeth, wid., 1780/10 Nov.
TOWNSEND, Anne, Ashby St. Ledgers, wid., to Sarah Preston, Everdon, wid., sister, 1752/17 Nov.
William, Ashby St. Ledgers, servant, to Sarah Preston, Everdon, wid., sister, of goods unadministered by Ann, wid., mother, Will, 1752/9 Dec.
William, Long Buckby, to Elizabeth, wid., Inv. £76.0.0 1755/22 Mar.
John, Hardingstone, to Mary, wid., Will, 1775/21 Mar.
Mary, Hardingstone, wid., to Edward Gaudern, cordwainer, cousin, 1778/5 May
John, Yelvertoft, grazier, to Mary, wid., 1783/19 Sept.
TRAVELL, John, Roade, Inv.only £18.12.6 1722/77A
Katherine, Roade, wid., to Elizabeth, wife of William Cowley, Collingtree, weaver, daughter, 1747/7 Nov.
Mary, Hartwell, to William, yeo., husband, 1758/3 June
TRESLOVE, Thomas, Barby, to Deborah, wid., Inv. £93.18.6 1726/28 Apr.
Thomas, Harlestone, baker, to Elizabeth, wid., 1731/21 Aug.
TROTT, Elizabeth, Foscote, Towcester, wid., Inv.only £280. 1714/106 A
TROUTBECK, Ann, Wellingborough, wid., to Mary, wife of Solomon James, yeo., sister, 1767/20 Apr.
TROWMAN, William, Bozeat, lab., Inv.only £33.12.0 1736/322
TRUE, William, Kettering, Account of Isabell, wid., admin., now wife of John Marriott, £39.7.8 1680/2
Trew, John, Kettering, Inv.only £34.2.0 1722/75A
John, Kettering, to Rebecca, wid., Inv. £66.2.6 1734/12 Aug.
TRYST, John, Maidford, to Thomas, gent., brother, Thomas and Elizabeth, parents, renounced, 1720/78
Thomas, Maidford, to Andrew, Banbury, co. Oxon., M.D., brother, Will, 1722/134
TUCKER, Thomas, Loddington, to Elenor, Inv. £136.4.0 1711/57
William, Chalcombe, lab., to Sarah, wid., Inv. £18.15.6 1712/135
Sarah, Chalcombe, wid., to Mary, Wilscote, co. Oxford, spin., and Joan, Marsh Gibbon, Bucks., spin., daughters, Inv. £24.15.0 1714/124
Robert, Culworth, farmer and grazier, to Anne, wid., 1763/18 May
Anne, Culworth, wid., to Robert, farmer and grazier, son, Will, 1780/15 July
Ann, Culworth, spin., to Robert, grazier, brother, 1782/14 Oct.
Elizabeth, Culworth, spin., to Robert, grazier, brother, 1782/14 Oct.
TUCKWELL, Richard, Northampton, cutler, to Martha, wid., 1730/27 June
TURLAND, William, Hannington, to Henry, weaver, son in law, Inv. £9.10.0 1712/21
Matthew, Moulton, to Mary, wid., 1724/13
Jane, Moulton, spin., to Martha, wife of Thomas Meacock, farmer, sister, Inv. £94.5.6 1735/1 Mar.
Thomas, Hannington, to Ann, wid., 1762/14 Apr.
TURNBULL, Adam, Wellingborough, to Martha, wid., 1770/19 July
TURNER, Susanna, Newnham, to Elizabeth Watson, daughter, 1712/92
Joseph, Long Buckby, to Thomas Green, Kilsby, yeo., nephew, Sarah, wid., renounced, 1720/65
Samuel, Moreton Pinkney, blacksmith, Inv.only £54.15.0 1721/21A
Mary, Fawsley, wid., to John, pastor, son, Inv. £97.7.1½ 1722/40
Richard, Rothwell, to John, yeo., brother, 1730/3 Apr.
John, Kettering, mason, to Mary, wid., Inv. £11.18.2 1732/16 Dec.

TURNER continued
Francis, Syresham, victualler, to Sarah Liddington, wid., daughter, 1746/21 Oct.
William, Barby, lab., to William, servant, grandson, 1751/17 Dec.
John, Blisworth, cordwainer, to Samuel Meacock, Ravenstone, Bucks., butcher, uncle, 1797/14 Feb.
William, Badby, farmer, to William, farmer, son, 1798/22 Sept.
TURVEY, Thomas, Adstone, to Mary, wid., Will, 1721/112
Anthony, Northampton, St. Sepulchre, brickmaker, to Susannah, wid., Inv. £15.19.0 1743/24 Feb.
William, Cosgrave, farmer, to Alice, wid., 1754/22 July
TWETTREE, William, Raunds, joiner, to Robert, joiner, son, Inv. £45.11.0 1743/27 May
TWIGDEN, Valentine, Northampton, to Martha, wid., 1714/134
Mary, Northampton, spin., to John, elder, uncle, 1717/105
William, Irchester, shepherd, to Elizabeth, wid., Inv. £13.4.0 1729/7 Oct.
TYE, Thomas, Wellingborough, cutler, to Priscilla, wid., Inv. £28.12.6 1762/25 May
TYLER, Samuel, Northampton, to Welford Cooper, woolcomber, nephew of Sarah, wid., decd., Inv. of Sarah £11.6.3 1743/2 May
Thomas, Northampton, victualler, to Ann, wid., 1751/12 Feb.
Tiler, William, Brackley Hatch, woodman, to Elizabeth, wife of John Mason, Syresham, lab., Mary, wife of William Baylis, Syresham, lab., and Hannah, wife of Samuel Bonham, lab., daughters, Jane, wid., exor., decd., Will, 1774/1 Oct.
Anthony, Daventry, carpenter, to Rebecca, wid., 1789/19 Oct.
TYRELL, Adam, Rushton, to Alice, wid., Inv. £122.19.4 1719/87

U

ULE see YOULE
UNDERWOOD, Henry, Irthlingborough, Guard.only of John, minor, son, 1714/81
Richard, junior, Arthingworth, farmer, to Elizabeth, wid., Inv. £82.8.3 1718/99
George, Lilbourne, widower, Inv.only £24.4.6 1720/36A
John, senior, Clipston, Inv.only £188.1.0 1721/74A
Samuel, Braybrooke, Inv.only £117.10.6 1723/6A
Thomas, Everdon, Inv.only £26.4.0 1724/36A
Richard, Yardley Hastings, to William, tailor, grandson, 1724/59
John, Duston, to Anne, wid., 1727/26 June
John, to Havey Sparkes, Wellingborough, gent., guardian of John, son, of goods unadministered by Abigail, wid., decd., 1730/30 Sept.
Thomas, Clipston, yeo., to Isabell, wid., 1734/12 June
Benjamin, Yardley Hastings, to Mary, wid., 1743/17 Sept.
Thomas, Braybrooke, husb., to John West, brother in law, weaver, Sarah, wid., renounced, Inv. £251.10.0 1748/3 Dec.
John, Great Oxendon, to John Johnson, elder, and John Johnson, younger, farmers, guardians of John and Sarah, children, minors, Inv. £566.10.6 1765/6 Aug.
John, Great Oxendon, to Hannah, wife of Richard Shipley, Thorpe Lubenham, lab., daughter, 1768/3 Sept.
Jane, Guilsborough, to Edward, farmer, husband, 1776/30 Mar.
Richard, Braybrooke, husb., to William, son, Mary, wife, exor., decd., Will, 1776/27 Nov.
John, Oxendon, to Sarah, Market Harborough, co. Leic., spin., sister, 1781/6 Nov.
Samuel, Braybrooke, to Thomas West, nephew, 1783/10 Apr.
Edward, Wicken, yeo., to Mary, wid., Inv. £340.5.0 1786/11 May
Thomas, Clipston, grazier, to Ann, wid., 1790/27 Sept.
USHER, Eleanor, Kilsby, wid., to Thomas, woolcomber, son, Inv. £31.11.6 1713/62

V

VALENTINE, William, Hackleton, yeo., to Mary, wid., 1736/31 Jan.
John, Stoke Bruerne, yeo., to Joseph Smith, elder, Grafton Regis, gent., yeo., principal creditor, Elizabeth, wid., renounced, 1795/12 Dec.
VAN, Ann, Kislingbury, to Robert Faulkner, weaver, husband of Mary, sister, exor., Will, 1782/28 Dec.
VARDON, Verdon, Abraham, Wilby, victualler, gardener, to Hannah, wid., Inv. £8.18.6 1728/23 Mar.
VARNEY, Verney, Joseph, Barby, shepherd, to Margaret, wid., Inv. £14.15.0 1714/14
Robert, Braunston, yeo., to Elizabeth, wid., 1766/26 Sept.
Joseph, Barby, to Varnum, Harborough, co. Warwick, spin., daughter, of goods unadministered by Margaret, wid., 1767/17 July
Verney, John, Braunston, yeo., to John Reeve, yeo., and William Foster, yeo., guardians of Robert, minor, son, Guard., 1787/4 July
VARNHAM, William, Cogenhoe, Inv.only £484.9.0 1711/34A
Robert, Daventry, Inv.only £17.18.0 1717/65A
Robert, Hollowell, Guilsborough, lab., to Elizabeth, wife of William Wale, weaver, daughter, Martha, wid., renounced, 1783/25 Jan.
VAUGHAN, John, Syresham, to Elizabeth, wid., 1711/41
VAUS, Vaux, George, Rector of Courtenhall, to Frances, wid., Inv. £208.19.0 1715/32
Jonas, Barby, weaver, to Isabella, wid., 1728/25 Mar.
Jonas, Barby, weaver, Inv.only £87.16.6 1728/217
James, West Haddon, to Ann, wid., 1766/6 Sept.
Benjamin, Kilsby, to Elizabeth, wid., 1776/25 June
Vaux, John, Courtenhall, gent., to Catherine, wife of Thomas Dunkley, grazier, sister, 1793/7 Feb.
John, Floore, clerk, to Thomas Dunkley, Courtenhall, grazier, Will, 1798/31 July
VERNEY see VARNEY
VERNON, Richard, Cold Ashby, carpenter, to Sarah, wid., and Edward, carpenter, Inv. £56.15.6 1774/7 July
John, Northampton, dealer, to Thomas, dealer, son, 1779/10 Dec.
VIALLS, Violls, John, Orton, Account of Frances, wid., admin., £117.0.0 1673/134
Richard, Orton, Inv.only £409.13.0 1711/149 A
Joseph, Harlestone, Inv.only £174.3.0 1737/345
Joseph, Harlestone, to Mary, wid., 1738/28 Jan.
John, Rothwell, to Hannah, wid., 1743/2 Feb.
William, Rothwell, cordwainer, to Mary, wid., 1794/1 Feb.
VICE, Catherine, Yelvertoft, to William, victualler, husband, 1729/7 Mar.
VINE, Thomas, Bisbrooke, co. Rutland, Guard.only of Elizabeth and Catherine, minors, daughters, 1711/116
Vines, Molly Sheppard als. Page, Wellingborough, to William, plumber, husband, 1781/12 July
VINTER, Thomas, Hardingstone, gent., Inv.only £700.4.3 1718/39A
Thomas, Hardingstone, yeo., to Mary, wid., 1775/20 Oct.
VIRLEY, William, Great Addington, weaver, Inv.only £28.17.0 1719/89A
VORES, John, Northampton, innholder, to Mary, wid., 1745/19 Aug.
Mary, Northampton, wid., to William, victualler, son, 1774/11 Feb.
William, Northampton, to Elizabeth, wid., 1775/27 Oct.
Mary, Northampton, wid., to Elizabeth, wid. and admin. of William, son, 1776/29 Feb.

W

WADE, Thomas, senior, Clipston, Inv.only £36.0.0 1720/55A
Anne, Clipston, to Nathaniel, gent., and Joseph, Northampton, sons, 1725/20 Nov.
nee Bannister, Ann, Kilsby, to Thomas, gent., husband, 1796/23 Aug.
WADENER, Elizabeth, Irchester, to Mary Rappitt, aunt, Inv. £7.3.0 1721/58
WADLAND, Anne, Finedon, to John, gent., husband, 1754/12 Jan.
WADSWORTH, William, Long Buckby, weaver, Inv.only £37.7.6 1712/18A
Jane, Long Buckby, to Mary, spin., daughter, 1716/79
WAFFORN, John, Welton, gent., Inv.only £260.3.6 1723/2A
WAGSTAFF, Joseph, Aynho, to Sarah, wid., 1724/62

WAINWRIGHT, John, Wellingborough, watchmaker, to John, son, Inv. £54.8.5 1717/54

WAITE, Anne, Hackleton, wid., to Susanna Elliott, mother and guardian of John and Jarvis Wooding, minors, grandsons, Will, Guard., 1786/11 Feb.

Waight, John, Blakesley, grazier, to Elizabeth, spin., daughter, Inv. £528.16.0 1732/21 Oct.

WAKEFIELD, Charles, Hartwell, to Catherine Cox, spin., niece, 1719/55

WAKELYN, Francis, Croughton, to Francis, son, 1715/149

Joseph, Cranford St. John, Guard. of Mary and Hannah, minors, daughters, Inv. £82.0.0 1717/3 and 4

WALDEN, Richard, Welton, to Elizabeth, wid., Inv. £184.8.11 1711/75

William, Mears Ashby, Inv.only £37.9.0 1718/42 A

William, Long Buckby, lab., to William Goodman, woolcomber, son in law, 1728/21 Sept.

WALDING, Elizabeth, Harpole, wid., to Mary, wife of Robert Frost, yeo., daughter, 1723/16

WALDRON, Richard, Towcester, to Alice, wid., 1737/29 Oct.

John, Northampton, to Ruth Mulliner, wid., niece, 1772/16 July

WALE, Whale, Samuel, Raunds, to William, son, Inv. £17.8.2 1717/82

Thomas, Crick, baker, Inv.only £30.17.1 1724/4A

John, Thurnby, victualler, to Mary, wid., 1729/17 May

Mercy, Hellidon, wid., to Mary Hands, wid., daughter, 1742/12 June

WALESBY, Ann, Thenford, to Mary Franklin, Steeple Claydon, Bucks., wid., sister, Will, 1778/3 Oct.

WALKER, Phebe, Northampton, Inv.only £107.11.0 1713/61A

Thomas, Wappenham, Inv.only £4.4.6 1714/84

John, Sulgrave, yeo., Inv.only £134.15.0 1715/63A

Robert, Inv.only £12.14.6 1715/142A

Thomas, Mears Ashby, Inv.only £9.10.0 1718/54A

William, Wollaston, Inv.only £318.3.0 1720/59A

Garratt, Thurnby, gent., to Mary, wid., 1746/5 Dec.

Margery, Sulgrave, wid., to Richard Seawell, Wappenham, baker, nephew, Mary Seawell, wid., sister, renounced, Inv. £19.12.6 1747/26 Dec.

Samuel, Northampton, tailor, to Elizabeth, wid., 1763/18 Feb.

Benjamin, Gayton, victualler, to Elizabeth, wid., 1783/29 July

WALKMAN, Mark, Irthlingborough, to Susannah, wid., now wife of Joseph Ashton, Kettering, cordwainer, 1768/7 Oct.

WALL, Richard, Northampton, to Richard Matthias Linfoot, gent., nephew, 1768/24 Mar.

WALLIS, William, senior, Finedon, shepherd, to Margaret, spin., daughter, Inv. £36.6.6 1714/117

John, Kettering, to John Chamberlain, Hertford, co. Hertford, gent., principal creditor, Anne, wid., renounced, 1717/26

William, Northampton, innholder, Inv.only £18.3.6 1722/65A

William, Isham, to Alice, wid., 1722/130

Humphrey, Finedon, yeo., Inv.only £134.1.6 1724/3A

Thomas, Wollaston, baker, to Elizabeth, wid., 1738/13 May

Thomas, Irthlingborough, yeo., to Esther, wid., Inv. £447.13.0 1745/9 Oct.

John, Finedon, farmer, to John, Isham, yeo., nephew, 1746/26 Apr.

Robert, Finmere, co. Oxford, late of Brackley, gent., to Rebecca, Tingewick, Bucks., spin., daughter, sister of Frances, wife of John Ryman, Adderbury, co. Oxford, cordwainer, daughter, lunatic, John renounced, Will, 1752/13 May

Mary, Burton Latimer, wid., to Thomas and John Evans, Daventry, ropemakers, brothers, 1762/22 May

William, Irthlingborough, to Sarah, wid., Inv. £109.2.2 1774/26 Jan.

Thomas, Finedon, to Elizabeth, spin., daughter, 1779/6 Oct.

John, Kettering, butcher, to Elizabeth, wid., 1779/10 Dec.

Isabella, Middleton Cheney, to Humphrey, Twamlow, co. Chester, husband, 1788/2 Jan.

WALLS, Mary, to William, Stratford upon Avon, co. Warwick, gunsmith, husband, 1795/14 July

WALPOLE, Wallpoole, Edward, Clipston, Inv.only £167.15.0 1721/26A

Daniel, Ecton, yeo., to Mary, wid., Inv. £177.1.9 1735/8 Mar.

Steward, Ecton, apothecary and trussmaker, to Mary, wid., Inv. £406.13.6 1750/23 May

WALTER, Abraham, Little Bowden, yeo., Inv.only £324.0.0 1741/383

Walters, Joseph, Dolphin Inn, Northampton, to Elizabeth, wid., Inv. £113.10.10 1772/4 Aug.

WALTON, Edward, Walgrave, lab., to William Hawkes, gent., principal creditor, 1735/13 May
Thomas, Evenley, to Robert, Brackley, baker, son, 1738/15 Apr.
Sarah, Crick, to Alice Underwood, wid., aunt, Will, 1766/12 Nov.
Thomas, Ecton, farmer, to William Augustine, farmer, son, 1790/10 Apr.
WAPLES, George, Towcester, mercer, to Catherine, wid., 1716/93
Wapples, Thomas, Rushden, Inv.only £45.3.6 1720/75A
James, Brixworth, chaff cutter, to Ann, wid., mother, 1749/21 June
WARBURTON, Hannah, Northampton, wid., to Kezia Murphey, Norwich, Norfolk, daughter, 1796/23 Dec.
WARD, John, Stanwick Lodge, grazier, Inv.only £433.2.2 1712/62A
William, Eydon, to Mary, wid., Inv. £124.0.0 1716/46
Robert, Northampton, All Saints, to Rebecca, wid., Inv. £35.10.0 1716/137
Warde, Thomas, Bugbrooke, tailor, to Elizabeth Barnes, aunt, Inv. £7.6.5 1719/42
Andrew, Faxton, Inv.only £83.16.0 1723/121A
Abraham, Bozeat, husb., to Isaac, yeo., brother, 1727/8 Sept.
Abigail, Old, Inv.only £32.17.6 1727/189
Edward, Faxton, Lamport, to Alice, wid., 1728/28 Sept.
Edward, Faxton, Lamport, Inv.only £97.15.0 1728/253
Thomas, Dallington, victualler, to Susanna, wid., 1729/10 Oct.
Thomas Short, Wootton, yeo., to Thomas, Hollowell, yeo., father, 1734/27 Apr.
Richard, Denshanger, Passenham, mason, to Mary, spin., sister, 1735/6 Feb.
Henry, Faxton, yeo., to Richard, yeo., son, 1742/26 Jan.
John, Welford, lab., Inv.only £32.1.6 1744/396
Valentine, Brafield on the Green, to Elizabeth, wid., 1745/4 Mar.
Timothy, Wellingborough, to Elizabeth, wid., 1747/3 Jan.
Jacob, Daventry, barber, to Jane, wid., 1748/4 Feb.
William, Hardingstone, farmer, to Dorothy, wid., 1751/12 Nov.
Thomas, Northampton, to Thomas, butcher, son, 1760/8 Feb.
Mary, Whilton, spin., to Elizabeth, wife of Nicholas Starmer, Heyford, yeo., sister, 1763/30 July
Mary, Ravensthorpe, to Matthew Hail Ward, weaver, son, 1774/2 June
Thomas, Dallington, to Charles, Lincoln's Inn, co. Middx., gent., son, 1777/10 Oct.
John, Floore, to Mary, wid., 1782/29 July
Sarah, Charlton, wid., to John, Wroxton, co. Oxford, yeo., son, 1791/10 May
Sarah, Northampton, spin., to John, milkman, father, 1791/10 June
John, Wellingborough, wheelwright, to John Barker, Earl's Barton, wheelwright, 1792/4 July
John, Northampton, butcher, to Sarah, wid., Richard Buswell, gent., exor., renounced, Will, 1793/11 Dec.
Thomas, Northampton, butcher, to Lydia, wife of Mark Folwell, Pattishall, butcher, creditor, of goods unadministered by Thomas, son, 1800/15 Mar.
Lucy, Wisbech, to Thomas, Wisbech, Isle of Ely, grazier, husband, 1800/1 Dec.
WARDEN, John, senior, Wellingborough, plasterer, Inv.only £10.16.8 1714/128A
Mary, Little Harrowden, wid., Inv.only £30.14.8 1722/100A
Edward, Grendon, victualler, to Elizabeth, wife of John Shipley, ropemaker, daughter, Anne, wid., renounced, Will, 1757/26 July
Laurence, Wellingborough, to Mary, victualler, sister, 1776/26 Jan.
WARE, Lydia, Wellingborough, wid., to John, staymaker, son, 1789/2 Mar.
WARING, Henry, Yelvertoft, yeo., to Mary Bent, Stanford, co. Leic., wid., sister, Will, 1748/4 Feb.
WARKMAN, als. Gloucester, Mark, Inv.only £6.8.5 1721/69 A
WARNER, Thomas, Kettering, to John, husb., 1714/177
James, Kettering, Inv.only £16.17.0 1717/48 A
Thomas, Daventry, to Anne, spin., daughter, principal creditor, Inv. £126.11.9¼ 1718/134
Mary, Daventry, spin., to Ann, spin., sister, 1720/18
Francis, Paulerspury, lab., Inv.only £3.0.8 1721/103 A
Francis, Finedon, mason, Inv.only £14.10.8 1722/4 A
Henry, Middleton Cheney, to John, yeo., son, 1728/16 May

WARNER continued
Joseph, Wellingborough, schoolmaster, to Samuel, cordwainer, son, 1751/3 Aug.
WARNING, Thomas, Faxton, to Elizabeth, wid., 1724/149
WARR, Thomas, Spratton, to Robert, Northampton, woolcomber, son, 1713/40
Anne, Grafton Regis, wid., to Mary, wife of Joseph Gallard, Yardley Gobion, dairyman, niece, Richard and William Wigan, exors., renounced, Will, 1786/6 June
WARREN, Jane, West Haddon, spin., Inv.only £83.3.0 1716/131A
Thomas, Earl's Barton, to Sarah, wid., Inv. £18.1.4 1718/17
James, Mears Ashby, lab., Inv.only £16.9.0 1719/80A
John, Irthlingborough, to Mary, wid., 1720/125
John, Little Houghton, husb., Inv.only £325.14.10 1722/110A
John, Old, to William, yeo., son, Inv. £500.9.3 Mary, wid., renounced, 1724/40
Elizabeth, Syresham, wid., to William, lab., son, 1724/147
Mary, Old, wid., to William, yeo., son, Inv. £17.12.6 1725/31 Dec.
John, Earl's Barton, Inv.only £162.3.0 1729/225
Elizabeth, Weston Favell, wid., to Thomas, Castle Ashby, blacksmith, son, 1729/15 Mar.
Elizabeth, Weston Favell, Inv.only £32.8.6 1729/250
Samuel, Little Houghton, lab., to Anne, wid., 1730/14 Mar.
William, Syresham, to Richard, Northampton, brewer, brother, 1732/17 Dec.
Henry, marine, to Hannah, Kettering, wid., 1763/22 Apr.
John, Little Houghton, lab., to Samuel, Brafield, lab., son, 1767/10 Apr.
John, Earl's Barton, farmer, to Thomas, farmer, son, 1783/12 Apr.
Mary, Little Houghton, spin., to Elizabeth, Brafield, wid. and admin. of Samuel, lab., exor., decd., Will, 1784/9 Oct.
Samuel, Brafield, lab., to Elizabeth, wid., 1784/9 Oct.
Ann, West Haddon, spin., to Stephen, baker, father, 1788/2 Feb.
Mary, Daventry, wid., to John Godfree, Brockhall, gent., and Catherine Deacon, wid., exors. of William Deacon, surgeon, exor., decd., Will, 1789/23 Sept.
WARWICK, Michael, Inv.only £59.5.0 1711/126A
John, Roade, yeo., Inv.only £200.10.0 1713/92A
John, Northampton, lab., to Sarah, wife of Thomas Jones, Wootton, lab., daughter, 1729/25 Nov.
Mary, Northampton, wid. of Joseph, to Samuel Hartshorne, gent., and John Gibson, dyer, guardians of Mary, minor, daughter by former wife, and Elizabeth and Grace, minors, daughters by Mary, Guard., 1748/22 June
Michael, Northampton, goaler, to Guy, goaler, son, of goods unadministered by Mary, wid., exor., decd., Will, 1749/10 Oct.
Elizabeth, Roade, to Ann, spin., daughter, Will, 1769/30 Nov.
Esther, Blakesley, to William, Eydon, shoemaker, and John, weaver, 1770/14 Apr.
als. Chapman, Catherine, see Chapman
WATERS, Thomas, Darlescote, Pattishall, yeo., to Samuel Carter, Towcester, barber, nephew, Will, 1760/7 Oct.
WATERFIELD, Edward, Kettering, hotpresser, Inv.only £69.5.0 1717/1A
WATKIN, Edward, Crick, bachelor, Inv.only £60.19.10 1711/18A
William, Crick, Inv.only £92.12.6 1720/67A
Edward, Crick, yeo., Inv.only £136.9.0 1721/132A
William, Crick, husb., Inv.only £31.12.6 1722/123A
John, Thorpe Malsor, carpenter, to John, carpenter, son, 1732/6 June
John, Thorpe Malsor, carpenter, to Samuel, carpenter, and John, Yelvertoft, yeo., 1734/12 Mar.
Watkins, John, Inv.only £30.17.6 1734/299
Edward, Crick, victualler, to Susanna, wid., 1734/4 May
Samuel, Ringstead, yeo., to Anne, Raunds, wid., Inv. £955.14.0 1745/15 Mar.
John, Yelvertoft, clerk, to John Burton Watkin, Newport Pagnell, Bucks., clerk, and Jane, spin., son and daughter, 1772/14 Sept.
Robert, West Haddon, to Sarah, Walsall, co. Stafford, wid., daughter in law, 1777/22 Apr.
John, Yelvertoft, yeo., to Samuel, yeo., son, 1784/20 Sept.
WATSON, Thomas, Crick, Account of William, admin., £48.0.0 1681/5
William, Daventry, butcher, to Anne, wid., Inv. £9.1.6 1711/64
William, Gayton, Inv.only £94.3.0 1711/129A

WATSON continued
Thomas, Kilsby, yeo., Inv.only £117.4.0 1712/58A
William, Kettering, baker, to Elizabeth, wid., Inv. £31.15.6 1714/170
Thomas, Daventry, to Elizabeth, wid., 1717/123
George, Braunston, to Alice, wid., Inv. £73.15.0 1720/52
Jacob, Kettering, to Anne, wid., 1721/90
George, Elkington, to Edward Harrison, London, principal creditor, 1730/11 Apr.
Caleb, Cold Ashby, dealer, to John Morris, Long Buckby, baker, and Nicholas Heygate, West Haddon, apothecary, principal creditors, Will, 1760/5 Apr.
Elizabeth, Long Buckby, spin., to James Clarke, butcher, Will, 1760/16 Sept.
Robert, Winwick, miller, to John Chater, Long Buckby, woolcomber, Thomas Burnham and William, exors., renounced, Will, 1766/10 July
Mary, Winwick, wid., to John Chater, Long Buckby, woolcomber, principal creditor, brother in law, Thomas Burnham, William, exors., and Hannah, mother, renounced, Will, 1766/10 July
Robert, Staverton, seedsman, to Thomas, London, gent., 1790/12 Apr.
Robert, Blisworth, schoolmaster, to William, Green's Norton, lab., brother, 1794/15 Nov.
George, Northampton, collarmaker, to Maria, wid., 1796/13 Apr.

WATTS, Rebecca, Milton, wid., Inv.only £75.17.0 1713/112A
John, elder, Moulton, Inv.only £65.0.0 1715/13A
John, Middleton Cheney, butcher, Inv.only £10.12.0 1716/64A
Richard, Middleton Cheney, glazier, Inv.only £39.13.0 1716/65A
William, senior, Moulton, Inv.only £38.4.0 1723/8A
Matthew, Wollaston, Guard.only of Thomas, minor, son, 1724/55
Thomas, Long Buckby, comber, to Susanna, wid., 1727/17 Nov.
Jonas, Northampton, gardener, to William, gardener, son, 1728/13 Feb.
Richard, Long Buckby, yeo., to John, yeo., son, Elizabeth, wid., renounced, 1728/16 Nov.
Edward, Woodend, Blakesley, yeo., to Sarah, wid., 1730/26 Sept.
Robert, Naseby, husb., to Henry, husb., son, Alice, wid., renounced in favour Henry and Robert, sons, 1732/7 Oct.
John, Welton, yeo., to Elizabeth, wife of Matthew Pike, yeo., daughter, Sarah, wid., renounced, 1736/21 Apr.
John, Long Buckby, maltster, to Elizabeth, wid., 1741/18 Apr.
John, Long Buckby, maltster, Inv.only £284.12.9 1742/385
Elizabeth, Long Buckby, wid., to Anne Wadsworth, aunt and guardian of Elizabeth, minor, daughter, 1746/11 Oct.
Richard, Murcot, Long Buckby, yeo., to Thomas, yeo., brother, and John Andrew, younger, maltster, guardians of Richard Marriott Watts, minor, son, Sarah, wid., renounced, 1747/17 Jan.
Henry, Milton, farmer, to Elizabeth, wife of John Cockerill, Collingtree, and Mary, wife of Thomas Labram, Courtenhall, daughters, Mary, wid., renounced, 1747/19 Jan.
Sarah, Duncote, Green's Norton, wid., to William Core, shepherd, brother, Will, Inv. £43.2.10 1747/2 July
Thomas, Long Buckby, yeo., to Thomas Wadsworth, yeo., and John Andrew, yeo., guardians of Richard Marriott Watts, nephew, and Elizabeth, minor, niece, Guard., 1748/30 Jan.
William, Everdon, to William, nephew, Will, Elizabeth, wid., renounced, 1749/4 Sept.
Richard, Middleton Cheney, butcher, to Anne, wid., 1749/16 Nov.
William, Moulton, gent., to Elizabeth, wid., 1752/15 June
William, Middleton Cheney, hempdresser, to George, elder, lab., brother, Will, 1760/29 Feb.
Richard, Middleton Cheney, yeo., to Anne, wife of Thomas Williams, carpenter, daughter, Will, 1766/27 Sept.
Robert, Orlingbury, farmer, to Joseph Manning, gent., and William Brown, Little Harrowden, farmer, Sarah, wid., renounced, Will, 1771/28 Nov.
Joseph, Daventry, saddler, to Thomas, mason, 1774/9 Apr.
John, Floore, tailor, to John Folwell, farmer, and Henry Sharpe, weaver, Will, 1774/15 Nov.
William, Old, farmer and grazier, to William, Scaldwell, grazier, son, John, exor., decd., Will, 1777/5 Apr.
Sarah, Harlestone, to Thomas Lumley, stonecutter, nephew, Thomas Lumley, brother, exor., decd., Will, 1777/13 Dec.
John, Rothersthorpe, gent., to Elizabeth, wid., 1781/8 Sept.

WATTS continued
William, Pisford, yeo., to Anthony, yeo., brother, 1782/9 Feb.
William, Brington, yeo., to John Walker, grazier, and Samuel Dumbleton, grazier, 1797/11 Sept.
Thomas, Chalcombe, servant, to John, tailor, brother, Will, 1800/27 Oct.
WATWORTH, als. Arden, James, Silverstone, lab., Inv.only £22.0.0 1721/78A
WAUMAN, John, Daventry, to Mary, wid., 1772/10 Mar.
WAY, John, Northampton, victualler, to Elizabeth, wid., 1731/16 Feb.
WAYMANT, John, to Mary Austin and Hannah, sisters, 1767/27 Oct.
WAYTE, Mary, Brixworth, wid., to Edward, farmer, son, Inv. £14.10.7 1749/16 Sept.
WEATHERHEAD, Sarah, Oakham, co. Rutland, Inv.only £130.17.11½ 1743/389
WEAVER, Henry, Cranford, clerk, to Goodeth, wid., 1733/1 Aug.
WEBB, Agnes, Harpole, Account of Benjamin, son, admin., £42.9.0 1677/66
John, Bradden, Account of Mary Crosse als. Webb, wid., admin., £100.11.4 1680/42
Thomas, Sulgrave, lab., to Frances, wid., mother, 1712/56
Elizabeth, Towcester, wid., to Joan Watts, spin., Will, 1712/68
Thomas, Isham, gent., Inv.only £29.5.6 1717/147A
John, Shutlanger, Stoke Bruerne, to Mary, wid., and Thomas, yeo., son, Inv. £976.2.0 1720/123
William, Shutlanger, Stoke Bruerne, Guard.only of William, son, 1720/149
Thomas, Shutlanger, Inv.only £589.10.6 1728/218
Sarah, Grafton Regis, to Stephen, lab., husband, 1729/18 July
Stephen, Cogenhoe, to Henry Peers, Turvey, Beds., yeo., and Robert, yeo., guardians of William, minor, 1734/31 Dec.
William, Barby, farmer, to Mary, spin., sister, 1735/25 June
Sarah, Shutlanger, Stoke Bruerne, to Thomas Bass, yeo., and Daniel Bass, yeo., sons, 1741/29 Sept.
John, Courtenhall, carpenter, to Sarah, wid., Inv. £5.18.0 1743/25 Mar.
Sarah, Courtenhall, wid., to John Clarke, London, coach smith, 1746/25 Aug.
Emma, Towcester, wid., to John, brazier, son, 1759/3 Nov.
John, Ashton, to Mary, wid., 1788/27 Oct.
Thomas, Badby, victualler, to John Donne, Northampton, winemerchant, and John Gaitskell, Southwark, co. Surrey, distiller, principal creditor, 1798/24 Mar.
WEBSTER, Joseph, Northampton, hempdresser, to Elizabeth, wid., 1713/5
Thomas, Shutlanger, Stoke Bruerne, to Anne, wid., 1723/49
James, Stoke Bruerne, to John, parish clerk, son, 1784/12 Mar.
WEED, John, Great Doddington, Inv.only £18.14.4 1715/82A
WEEKLY, Anne, Irthlingborough, wid., to William Underwood, gent., and John Pooley, Little Addington, gent., guardians of Henry and Anne, minors, children, 1724/58
WEILD, Richard, Farthinghoe, cordwainer, to Richard, grazier, son, 1786/21 Oct.
WELCH, Margaret, Kislingbury, Inv.only £9.5.0 1711/55A
Welsh, John, Upper Boddington, Inv.only £142.19.10 1716/78A
Welsh, Anne, Harlestone, to Robert, mason, son, Inv. £30.5.0 1724/20
Thomas, Wellingborough, woolcomber, to Henry Hensman, gent., 1731/11 Aug.
John, Slapton, clerk, to Mary, wid., 1743/26 May
Henry, Weedon Beck, yeo., to Jane, wid., 1752/7 Oct.
Thomas Coleman, Pattishall, clerk, to Thomas, son, Mary, wid., renounced, Will, 1770/31 Mar.
Robert, Eydon, to John, Wormleighton, co. Warwick, servant, brother, 1776/10 Dec.
Susannah, Boddington, to George, Hockley, co. Bedford, horsedealer, husband, 1785/8 June
WELDON, Cornelius, Rushton, to Anne, wid., 1727/13 Apr.
Welden, Cornelius, Rushton, Inv.only £10.19.0 1727/181
WELFORD, Robert, Quinton, to Robert, yeo., son, 1721/143
John, Earl's Barton, yeo., Inv.only £92.0.0 1724/42A
Anne, Stoke Bruerne, wid., to Robert, Quinton, lab., son, 1733/23 Nov.
John, Wilby, yeo., to Frances, wid., Inv. £155.15.0 1742/8 May
William, Tiffield, shepherd, to Rebecca, Quinton, spin., sister, Will, 1756/27 Mar.
WELLS, Mary, Inv.only £20.12.6 1711/39A
Nathaniel, Stanwick, yeo., Inv.only £570.0.2 1713/52A
John, senior, Rothwell, Inv.only £114.17.8 1714/145A

WELLS continued
Jonathan, Rothwell, Inv.only £136.5.10 1711/34A
Richard, Milton, yeo., Inv.only £313.0.0 1719/21A
Sarah, Rothwell, wid. of John, senior, Inv.only £96.3.6 1719/53A
Dorothy, Rothwell, wid., Inv.only £44.9.6 1719/124A
Thomas, Rothwell, Inv.only £84.9.8 1723/123
Thomas, Northampton, to Elizabeth, Overstone, wid., 1725/13 Nov.
John, Overstone, to Anne, wid., 1726/4 July
Elizabeth, Daventry, spin., to Sarah, wid., mother, 1744/20 Apr.
John, Byfield, farmer, to Susannah, wid., 1750/4 Aug.
John, Wellingborough, yeo., to Elizabeth, wid., Inv. £162.13.0 1756/24 May
John, East Farndon, baker, to Jane, wid., 1764/24 Jan.
Hannah, Byfield, wid., to Thomas, cordwainer, son, 1776/16 May
WELSH see WELCH
WELTON, George, Welford, apothecary, to Ann, wid., Samuel Tilly, Spratton, gent., and Edward Freeman, Coventry, co. Warwick, exors., renounced, Will, 1780/21 June
John, Welford, woolcomber, to Samuel Laurence, Birmingham, co. Warwick, bookkeeper, brother in law, Inv. £280.15.0½ Anne, wife of Samuel Laurence, sister, renounced, 1798/26 June
WESON see WESTON
WEST, William, Bugbrooke, lab., Inv. £4.16.11 Account of Mercy, wife, 1712/104
Thomas, Scaldwell, Inv.only £54.7.2 1717/25A
Elizabeth, Long Buckby, wid., to Anne, Hardingstone, spin., daughter, 1726/26 Mar.
Mary, Lilbourne, to Anne Hall, wid., sister, 1740/7 May
John, Lower Boddington, yeo., to Robert, yeo., son, Anne, wid., renounced, 1749/25 Mar.
Thomas, Cotton End, Hardingstone, farmer, to Mary, wife of Matthew Morris, farmer, daughter, 1751/24 May
Robert, Brackley, currier, to Elizabeth, wid., 1769/7 Nov.
Benjamin, Northampton, to James Stables, draper, and William Cooper, draper, guardians of Rossina, minor, daughter, 1773/14 June
John, Braybrooke, to Thomas, 1774/29 Mar.
Richard, Dallington, to Agnes, Kingsthorpe, wid., 1774/9 May
Thomas, Little Bowden, farmer and grazier, to Thomas, grazier, son, Frances, wid., renounced, 1779/23 Jan.
Mary, Braybrooke, spin., to Mary, Marston Trussell, wid., mother and guardian of John, minor, Will, Guard., 1795/28 Mar.
Robert, Northampton, coachman, to Anne, wid., 1797/2 May
WESTLEY, John, Tiffield, Inv.only £20.18.10 1711/50A
Westly, Millicent, Whittlebury, wid., Inv.only £9.6.10 1713/83
Wessley, John, Charlton, carpenter, to William, Helmdon, lab., uncle and guardian of Elizabeth, minor, daughter, Inv. £12.15.6 1752/9 Apr.
John, Bugbrooke, gardener, to William Johnson, Lewes, co. Sussex, gent., son and admin. of Elizabeth Johnson, Northampton, exor., decd., Will, 1782/10 Oct.
William, Helmdon, to Elizabeth, Charlton, Newbottle, niece, 1788/8 Apr.
John, Northampton, upholsterer, to Mary, wid., 1799/22 Oct.
als. Johnson, Elizabeth, see Johnson
WESTON, Thomas, Guilsborough, gent., to Lydia, spin., daughter, Inv. £54.2.5 Mary, wid., renounced, 1721/8
James, Northampton, hillier, Inv.only £17.5.6 1716/7A
William, Boddington, to William, husb., son, 1721/137
John, Wellingborough, to Elizabeth, wid., Inv. £40.12.0 1723/101
William, Boddington, husb., to William, husb., son, Dorcas, wid., renounced, 1729/17 Apr.
Weson, William, Lower Boddington, Inv.only £146.0.6 1729/224
Weson, William, Rothwell, shoemaker, to Sarah Weedon, wid., daughter, 1744/25 June
Weson, William, Rothwell, shoemaker, Inv.only £16.14.6 1744/393
John, Brixworth, butcher, to Elizabeth, Hardingstone, wid., 1788/30 Jan.
WHALE see WALE
WHEATCROFT, Samuel, London, Guard.only of Samuel, minor, son, 1714/26 Aug.
WHEATLEY, Wheateley, John, Sulby, Rothwell, to Wentworth Briggs, Welford, innholder, 1720/110
John, Navesby, Inv.only £32.17.0 1723/24A

WHEATLEY continued
Richard, Haselbech, butcher, to Samuel, Desborough, husb., son, Inv. £15.0.0 1725/5 June
John, Grendon, victualler, to Jane, wid., Inv. £66.19.2 1730/14 Feb.
WHEELER, James, Maidwell, clerk, rector, to John Harper, Market Harborough, gent.,principal creditor, 1746/22 Feb.
WHEELOWS, William, Gayton, Account of Dorothy, wid., admin., £877.3.0 1682/57
WHITE, Thomas, Sulgrave, to Thomas, Highgate, Middx., cooper, son, Mary, wid., renounced, 1712/97
William, East Farndon, to Hannah Wells, daughter, Inv. £5.8.0 1712/102
George, Little Billing, Inv.only £163.0.0 1716/130A
Francis, Spratton, to Anne, wid., 1720/108
Robert, Stoke Bruerne, husb., to Margaret, wid., Inv. £115.18.6 1724/6
Henry, Cransley, to John, carpenter, son, Inv. £24.12.0 1724/146
George, Gayton, yeo., to Ann, wife of --- Wilson, husb., daughter, Inv. £358.4.6 1727/9 Sept.
Joseph, Little Billing, yeo., to Anne, wid., 1728/17 July
William, Blisworth, yeo., to William, butcher, son, Inv. £634.8.0 Anne, wid., renounced, 1729/27 Sept.
Anne, Old, wid., to Elizabeth, wife of William Ibbs, fellmonger, daughter, 1730/5 Jan.
Matthew, Overstone, farmer, to Mary, wid., 1731/21 Aug.
Francis, East Haddon, yeo., to Frances, wid., 1743/14 May
Elizabeth, Norton, Daventry, wid., to Valentine Clare, baker, principal creditor, 1748/8 Sept.
Jane, East Haddon, to Francis, yeo., son, 1750/26 May
Hannah, Spratton, wid., to William, mason, son, 1753/14 Apr.
Matthew, Overstone, yeo., to Alice, wid., John Manning and William Smith, exors., renounced, Will, 1757/26 Feb.
Elizabeth, East Haddon, to Francis, weaver, husband, 1770/13 Mar.
William, Kingsthorpe, to John, blacksmith, son, 1773/6 Oct.
William, East Haddon, to Francis, farmer, brother, 1774/2 July
John, Maidford, farmer, to Joanna Deele, Abbotts Langley, co. Hertford, wid., sister, 1785/4 June
Thomas, Denton, farmer, to Thomas, soldier, son, 1787/15 May
Elizabeth, Stoke Bruerne, wid., to Thomas, farmer, son, 1800/8 May
George, Stoke Bruerne, farmer, yeo., to Grace, wid., Inv. £683.17.0 1800/3 Oct.
WHITEHEAD, George, Kettering, carrier, to Anne, wid., Inv. £11.17.1 1730/24 Feb.
John, Kettering, gardener, to Joseph Booth, woolcomber, principal creditor, 1733/27 Jan.
Thomas, Kettering, to John, brother, 1762/17 Dec.
WHITFIELD, Peter, senior, Boughton, husb., Inv.only £83.4.0 1719/102A
WHITHEBED, John, Staverton, yeo., to Dorothy, wife of William Jennard, dairyman, daughter, 1787/13 Oct.
WHITING, Frances, Harlestone, wid., to James, stonecutter, son, 1714/103
James, Harlestone, freemason and quarryman, to Elizabeth, wid., Inv. £139.12.0 Guard. of Elizabeth, minor, daughter, 1718/127 and 129
Whiteing, William, Harlestone, stonecutter, to Elizabeth, wid., now wife of Joseph Sheppard, woolcomber, 1747/21 Apr.
Watkin, Harlestone, gent., to Hannah, Towcester, wid., 1759/14 Nov.
John, Great Houghton, to Sarah, wid., 1779/1 Nov.
William, Kislingbury, yeo., Guard.only of Ann, minor, daughter, 1779/27 Nov.
WHITLARKE, Jeremiah, Finedon, Inv.only £330.10.6 1714/35A
Whitlark, Abraham, Finedon, Inv.only £4.19.2 1723/124A
WHITLAY, George, Kilsby, tailor, to Hanna, wid., Inv. £17.4.0 1725/26 July
WHITLOCK, Susanna, Shutlanger, Inv.only £39.5.0 1721/36A
Thomas, Silverstone, woodman, to Ann, wid., 1767/11 Aug.
John, Silverstone, woodman, to Hannah, wid., 1778/28 July
WHITMILL, Joseph, Collingtree, carpenter, to John, Maidford, and Elizabeth Paine, Lower Heyford, wid., brother and sister, Inv. £67.18.7 1714/100
John, Maidford, Inv.only £291.11.0 1733/296
Whitmell, William, Moulton Park, to Mary, wid., 1768/13 July
Whitmell, William, Paulerspury, lab., to Mary, Northampton, spin., daughter, 1784/23 June

WHITMILL continued
William, Charwelton, gent., to Mary, wid., 1793/26 June
Whitmell, John, Foster's Booth, Pattishall, victualler, to William, victualler, son, Ann, exor., decd., Will, 1797/10 June
WHITMORE, William, Brackley, shoemaker, to William Dradge, Buckingham, tanner, principal creditor, 1729/24 June
Jonathan, Kilsby, to Alice, wid., 1743/30 Apr.
WHITMY, Richard, Yardley Hastings, Inv.only £306.19.0 1732/291
James, Northampton, plumber, to Elizabeth, wid., 1793/5 Apr.
WHITNEY, Henry, Yardley Hastings, to Thomas, yeo., father, 1717/30
Anne, Yardley Hastings, Inv.only £132.11.7 1718/7A
Robert, senior, Stoke Bruerne, to Rebecca, wid., 1720/129
Richard, Yardley Hastings, farmer, to Mary, wid., 1732/28 Oct.
John, Little Houghton, blacksmith, to Elizabeth Battison, spin., granddaughter, of goods unadministered by Martha, exor., decd., Will, 1786/25 Nov.
WHITTON, Clemence, Blakesley, wid., Inv.only £87.0.0 1714/5A
Richard, Denshanger, Passenham, to Mary, wid., 1715/144
Daniel, Helmdon, bachelor, Inv.only £12.0.0 1720/118A
Thomas, Yardley Gobion, bachelor, to Anne Salmon, Slapton, wid., sister, 1723/44
John, Lois Weedon, yeo., to Ruth, wid., 1741/1 June
Thomas, Sulgrave, yeo., to Elizabeth, spin., daughter, 1764/23 May
Richard, Marston St. Lawrence, butcher, to Mary, wid., 1794/31 July
WHITWORTH, William, Earl's Barton, gent., Inv.only £38.18.6 1714/82A
Richard, Earl's Barton, late of Lamport, clerk, to Robert, gent., brother, Inv. £80.5.0 1718/11
Elizabeth, Earl's Barton, wid., Inv.only 1722/7A
Edward, Great Doddington, yeo., Inv.only £175.13.6 1722/37A
Robert, Earl's Barton, gent., to William, gent., principal creditor, Inv. £62.5.6 1725/20 Dec.
Susanna, Earl's Barton, spin., to Miles, husb., 1727/4 Nov.
Ann, Earl's Barton, spin., Inv.only £371.14.0 1744/390
WICKENS, Elizabeth, Shutlanger, Account of John, brother, admin., £88.0.0 1681/82
William, Inv.only £37.0.0 1715/76A
Thomas, Shutlanger, to Margaret, wid., Inv. £361.16.10 1719/31
Jonathan, Towcester, victualler, to John Hodges, Banbury, co.Oxford, tallow chandler, grandson, 1745/10 May
John, Sulgrave, yeo., to Hannah, wid., 1754/13 May
WICKS, William, Welford, Account of Mary, wid., admin., £105.19.4 1674/129
John, Welford, innholder, to Elizabeth, wid., Inv. £390.0.0 1712/94
Wickes, Mary, Cold Ashby, spin., to John, farmer, father, 1791/19 Oct.
WIGGINS, Robert, Grendon, yeo., to Elizabeth, wife of Charles Norbury, sister, Inv. £18.8.0 1731/6 Mar.
Nathaniel, Maidwell, to Martha, wid., 1773/4 May
Thomas, Draughton, farmer, to John, farmer, brother, 1793/13 July
Thomas, Murcott, farmer, to Sarah, wid., 1798/2 July
WIGNALL, Thomas, Kettering, Inv.only £168.0.7 1713/105A
Elizabeth, Kettering, wid., to Thomas, Harborough, co. Leic., brazier, son, Inv. £86.3.8 1721/126
WIGSON, Thomas, Culworth, butcher, Inv.only £171.8.6 1711/62A
John, Eydon, farmer, yeo., to John, farmer, son, Inv. £151.3.0 1748/14 Apr.
WILBY, Thomas, Overstone, farmer, to Thomas Coldwell, Hulcott, tailor, nephew, and Phelicia Pratt, niece, 1750/4 Dec.
WILCOX, Willcox, Mary, Towcester, wid., to Thomas Bradshaw, fellmonger, son, Will, 1723/5
Mary, Shutlanger, Stoke Bruerne, wid., to Elizabeth Clarke, wid., sister, Will, 1755/20 Sept.
Dorothy, Towcester, to Robert, bookseller, son, 1781/23 June
WILDING, Benjamin, Helmdon, clerk, to William Glover Annison, London, pewterer, Rachel, wife of William Annison, sister, renounced, 1755/5 Aug.
Hannah, Mears Ashby, wid., to Thomas, baker, son, 1779/16 June
WILFORD, Hannah, Clipston, to Thomas, weaver, husband, 1788/18 Sept.

WILKINS, Robert, Brackley, laceman, to William Mason, gent., woollendraper, principal creditor, Alice, wid., renounced, Inv. £33.0.10 1716/117
Thomas, Middleton Cheney, yeo., to Mary, wid., 1735/20 May
Mary, Towcester, to Joseph, tallow chandler, husband, 1738/8 June
Thomas, Middleton Cheney, mason, to Elizabeth, wid., 1740/30 Sept.
Jane, Blakesley, spin., to William, Towcester, lab., 1741/20 Mar.
Rose, Blakesley, spin., to William, Towcester, lab., brother, 1741/20 Mar.
Thomas, Middleton Cheney, to Richard, mason, son, of goods unadministered by Elizabeth, wid., decd., 1755/11 Apr.
Robert, Blakesley, to Joseph, Towcester, soapboiler, 1774/10 Dec.
Joseph, Towcester, to Mary Thorp Wilkins, 1780/30 Oct.
Thomas, Appletree, Aston le Walls, yeo., to Judith, Inv. £212.8.2 1781/25 Aug.
Sarah, Towcester, to Ann Howe, wid., sister, Joseph, brother, exor., decd., Will, 1782/27 Aug.
Anne, Middleton Cheney, wid., to Samuel, mason, son, 1786/3 Jan.
Richard, Middleton Cheney, mason, to Samuel, mason, son, Anne, wid., exor., decd., Will, 1786/3 Jan.
WILKINSON, Daniel, Northampton, victualler, to Elizabeth, wid., Inv. £12.5.0 1717/92
Sarah, Weedon Beck, wid., to John Norris, yeo., Inv. £18.0.0 Will, 1719/75
John, All Saints, Northampton, to Mary, wid., 1724/88
John, Woodend, Blakesley, to Elizabeth, wid., 1744/8 Aug.
WILLAMOTT, Wilmott, als. Lillingston, James, Inv.only £252.8.0 1739/368
Willamot, Jane, Newport Pagnell, spin., to Joseph Johnson, Hanslop, Bucks., lab., cousin, 1782/6 July
Willamot, Ann, Newport Pagnell, Bucks., spin., to Joseph Johnson, Hanslop, Bucks., lab., cousin, 1782/6 July
WILLAN, Little, Higham Ferrers, wid., to William Knight, Spalding, co. Linc., gent., son, 1789/4 Apr.
WILLIAMS, Thomas, Middleton Cheney, Account of Catherine, wid., admin., £64.13.0 1682/56
Robert, Brackley, mercer, Inv.only £19.18.0 1713/29 A
Martha, Plumstead, Kent, Guard.only of Mary Chapman, 1715/75
Mary, Brackley, spin., Inv.only £161.1.0 1715/115 A
George, Middleton Cheney, to Martha, wid., Inv. £6.12.10 1727/5 Apr.
Mary, Paulerspury, wid., to John, husb., son, 1727/15 July
Thomas, Northampton, gardener, to Elizabeth, wid., 1729/25 Jan.
Mary, Northampton, wid., to Charles Rogers, gent., principal creditor, Inv. £14.6.4 1734/8 Oct.
John, Brackley, cordwainer, to Mary, wid., 1751/21 Oct.
George, Middleton Cheney, yeo., to Anne, wid., Inv. £335.0.0 1754/10 May
George, Middleton Cheney, tailor, to Sarah, wid., 1761/3 Apr.
Robert, Syresham, farmer, to Mary, wid., Inv. £73.12.0 1763/1 Aug.
John, Towcester, whipmaker, to John Gurney, victualler, exor. of Sarah, wid., exor., decd., Will, 1796/19 Jan.
WILLIAMSON, Sarah, Yardley Hastings, wid., to Ralph, farmer, son, 1756/2 Apr.
Ralph, Yardley Hastings, farmer, to Anne, wid., Inv. £60.0.0 1757/26 July
William, Northampton, grocer, to Mary, wid., 1765/17 May
WILLIS, Edward, Guard.only of Anne, daghter, 1685/162
Mary, Wellingborough, spin., to Anne Howby, Loddington, wid., Thomas, Hellidon, cutter, and James Woode, Catesby, gent., brother, sister and nephew, Inv. £197.19.8 1720/48
Rev. Richard, Vicar of Higham Ferrers, clerk, to Mary, wife of Jonathan Nicholls, gent., daughter, 1726/9 Aug.
WILLMER, William, Kislingbury, to Elizabeth, wid., Inv. £9.18.0 1719/32
WILLOUGHBY, Philip, Horton, gent., to Sarah Lane, Hanslop, Bucks., wid., sister, 1729/27 Oct.
WILLS, John, Cransley, Account of Anne, wid., admin., £105.13.4 1673/154
John, Spratton, Inv.only £78.10.0 1711/1 A
Anne, Inv.only £8.5.0 1711/10 A
John, Harlestone, yeo., Inv.only £330.4.4 1711/94 A
John, Harlestone, husb., Guard.only of Hanna, daughter, 1712/78
Jane, Great Brington, wid., Inv.only £111.0.0 1714/118 A
Bartin, East Haddon, Guard.only of Benjamin, minor, son, 1716/110
Wiles, Gilbert, Rushden, to Robert Stevens, principal creditor, 1717/86

WILLS continued
William, Towcester, innholder, Inv.only £110.2.3 1718/52 A
William, Kettering, to William, Winwick, yeo., son, 1721/29
William, Lois Weedon, to Elizabeth, wid., Inv. £286.10.0 1722/51
John, Lois Weedon, to Henry, son, of goods unadministered by Ruth, wid., decd., 1724/70
William, Boddington, husb., to Richard, Woodford cum Membris, husb., 1727/7 July
Sarah, Welton, wid., to Sarah Turner, Whilton, spin., niece, 1729/14 Jan.
Robert, Yelvertoft, grocer, to Ruth, wid., 1732/10 June
Joseph, East Haddon, grazier, to Dorothy, spin., daughter, Inv. £352.13.6 1734/20 Apr.
Willes, Margaret, wid., Inv.only £3.14.0 1734/316
William, Boddington, lab., to Richard, lab., son, 1737/25 Oct.
William, Weston, to Mary, wid., 1759/16 Apr.
William, Bugbrooke, to William Johnson, farmer, and Thomas Cosford, Upper Heyford, miller, principal creditors, 1779/27 July
Elizabeth, Spratton, wid., to Charles, farmer, 1784/23 Nov.
Charles, Inv.only £9.16.3 1784/418
Robert, Yelvertoft, gent., to James Gilbert, Welton, farmer, nephew, Will, 1789/30 Jan.
Thomas, Blisworth, farmer, to Hannah, wid., 1794/8 Nov.
Joseph, Blisworth, yeo., to Hannah, wid. of Thomas, farmer, exor., Will, 1794/8 Nov.
Daniel, Northampton, woolcomber, to Mary and Martha, spins., daughters, 1795/29 Apr.

WILSON, John, Brafield on the Green, lab., Inv.only £19.4.0 1717/60 A
William, Kettering, weaver, to Sarah, wid., Inv. £11.18.10 1721/49
Simon, Muscott Mill, Norton, to Sarah, wid., 1722/93
Thomas, Newnham, to Joyce, wid., 1726/28 Apr.
William, Cottesbrooke, shepherd, to Elizabeth, wid., 1727/20 May
als. Knibb, Elizabeth, to Henry, Boddington, weaver, husband, 1728/14 Sept.
Knightley, Aston le Walls, clerk, Inv.only £95.0.0 1733/304
Willson, Thomas, Gayton, to Ann, wid., 1761/13 July
Willson, William, Chipping Warden, carpenter, to Samuel, carpenter, son, Will, 1764/23 May
Willson, Margaret, Northampton, to Thomas, ostler, father, 1772/16 Nov.
William, Dallington, victualler, to Anne, wid., 1781/22 Nov.
Willson, Samuel, Long Buckby, to Anne, wid., 1788/25 Sept.

WIMPRESS, Elizabeth, Stanwick, wid., Inv.only £19.4.0 1715/5 A
Richard, Chelveston, tailor, to Roger, Higham, tailor, brother, guardian of Robert, son, minor, Will, 1754/8 May

WINCKLES, John, Chadstone, Castle Ashby, Account of Dorothy, wid., admin., £228.16.8 1673/35
Winkles, John, Sulby, shepherd, Inv.only £19.15.0 1711/107A
Anne, Green's Norton, wid., to Thomas, brother, Inv. £32.10.0 1717/134
Thomas, Green's Norton, Inv.only £26.6.0 1724/89 A
William, Hulcote, to Robert, gardener, son, Elizabeth, wid., renounced, 1739/3 Mar.
Richard, Paulerspury, lab., to Thomas Bennet, Whittlebury, victualler, his wife Ann, sister and exor., decd., Will, 1766/21 Jan.
Thomas, Blakesley, yeo., to Joseph, yeo., son, 1770/30 Oct.

WINE, Hannah, Pytchley, wid., to Mark Wisdish, tailor, son in law, Inv. £9.13.0 1727/25 July

WINGRAVE, Thomas, Collingtree, farmer, to Mary, wid., 1793/13 Apr.

WINMILL, John, Yardley Gobion, Potterspury, to John, son, 1719/66
John, Yardley Gobion, Potterspury, yeo., Inv.only £174.7.6 1740/377

WINN, Hugh, Horton, widower, to Elianor Bloodworth, daughter, Inv. £328.9.6 1720/86
John, Salcey Forest, yeo., Inv.only £61.16.0 1721/11A
Wynn, George, Blisworth, to Sarah, wid., 1780/6 May
Winns, John, Daventry, to Anne, wid., 1789/30 Sept.

WINTERTON, Thomas, Guilsborough, butcher, Inv.only £121.5.0 1723/1A

WISE, Daniel, Chalcombe, Inv.only £200.10.6 1726/163
Anne, Chalcombe, wid., to John Heritage, baker, grandson, 1740/23 Apr.
Thomas, Chalcombe, to John Heritage, baker, grandson, of goods unadministered by Anne, wid., decd., 1740/23 Oct.
William, Gretworth, lab., to Jane, wid., 1765/23 Nov.
John, Wellingborough, plumber, to Anne, wid., 1791/4 Apr.

WISH, Elizabeth, Irchester, to Mary, wife of William Lilley, matmaker, daughter, 1772/10 Aug.
WISHDISH, Susanna, Irchester, wid., to John, cordwainer, son, 1779/27 Oct.
WITHEBED, Withibed, Thomas, Staverton, Inv.only £18.15.0 1713/59 A
Richard, Yelvertoft, yeo., Inv.only £28.5.0 1718/32 A
Whithebed, John, Staverton, yeo., to Dorothy, wife of William Jennard, dairyman, daughter, 1787/13 Oct.
WODHULL, Jane, Hellidon, wid., to John, son, Will, 1717/55
Fulk, Thorpe Mandeville, to John, Hellidon, yeo., nephew, 1725/15 May
WODNOTH, Benjamin, Welford, gent., to Serena, Northampton, wid., mother, 1770/15 Sept.
WOOD, Thomas, Towcester, Account of Alice, wid., admin., £67.3.10 1680/31
Thomas, Heathencote, Paulerspury, to Elizabeth, wid., Inv. £36.8.0 1711/3
John, Towcester, to Thomas, grazier, father, Inv. £237.6.0 1715/104
John, Newnham, lab., to Anne, wid., Inv. £17.0.0 1716/42
John, Kingsthorpe, fuller, Inv.only £31.19.9 1717/58 A
Thomas, Towcester, Inv.only £192.11.6 1721/64 A
John, Loddington, grazier, gent., to Hannah, wife of Thomas Smith, daughter, Inv. £358.7.6 David Some, Great Bowden, co. Leic., Joseph Cooke, Oundle, and John Hills, exors., renounced, 1724/28
Edward, Burton Latimer, to Edward, husb., son, 1726/26 Apr.
Edward, Inv.only £15.18.3 1727/406
Thomas, Northampton, lab., to Roger, Steeple, co. Essex, husb., brother, 1729/8 Sept.
Elizabeth, Potterspury, wid., to John Harris, Hanslop, Bucks., blacksmith, and Thomas, grandchildren, 1730/28 Nov.
William, Hinton, lab., to Patinece, spin., sister, 1732/7 June
Edward, Burton Latimer, to Sarah, wid., 1737/20 June
Edward, Burton Latimer, yeo., to Sarah, wid., Inv. £289.11.6 1754/10 Apr.
Thomas, Welton, yeo., to Mary, wid., 1759/1 Dec.
William, Braunston, to Isaac, Walgrave, farmer, brother, 1761/9 Apr.
Jonathan, Higham Ferrers, to Elizabeth, wid., 1773/27 Jan.
George, Bugbrooke, farmer, to Mary, wid., 1786/4 Nov.
John, Towcester, gent., to Thomas, grocer, and Samuel, butcher, sons, 1792/2 June
Thomas, Yardley Gobion, farmer, to Joshua, Potterspury, farmer, exor. of Elizabeth, wid., decd., 1792/11 Sept.
John, Towcester, gent., to John, butcher, son, of goods unadministered by Thomas, son, decd., 1796/25 Oct.
Thomas, Kilsby, to Mary, wid., 1797/7 June
WOODBURNE, Elizabeth, Kirkby, Lancashire, to Henry Hind, Liverpool, Lancashire, shipwright, nephew, 1783/16 Aug.
WOODCOCK, Samuel, Snorscomb, Everdon, miller, to Mary, wid., Inv. £52.0.0 1729/1 Feb.
William, Kettering, to William, son, 1759/27 Apr.
WOODDARD, Richard, Yardley Gobion, to Sarah, wid., Inv. £26.10.0 1719/92
WOODEN, John, Yardley Hastings, carpenter, Inv.only £8.19.8 1716/40aA
Thomas, carpenter, Inv.only £23.13.0 1733/308
Woodin, Robert, Towcester, grocer, to Sarah, wid., 1765/12 Nov.
Mary, Yardley Hastings, to Mary Carter, spin., niece, Will, 1778/30 Apr.
WOODFORD, John, Broughton, Inv.only £62.15.6 1716/27A
Grace, Welford, wid., Inv.only £12.18.0 1724/43 A
Samuel, Broughton, yeo., husb., to Sarah, wid., Inv. £602.5.6 1732/15 Apr.
Samuel, Rothwell, to Ann, wid., 1756/7 Oct.
Richard, Northampton, to Elizabeth, wife of Edmund Tew, Bath, Somerset, doctor in divinity, sister, 1764/18 Dec.
Joseph, Broughton, farmer, to Samuel, Leicester, currier, brother, Elizabeth, spin., daughter, renounced, 1792/15 Feb.
Jonathan, Cold Ashby, grazier, to William, grazier, son, 1796/13 Sept.
WOODHAM, Woddams, John, Daventry, to John, son, Mary, wid., renounced, Inv. £17.3.0 1716/10
Thomas, Long Buckby, to John, yeo., brother, 1733/14 July
Woodams, William, Byfield, lab., to Susanna, wid., 1733/24 Oct.
WOODING, Robert, Irchester, mason, to Elizabeth, wid., Inv. £133.8.0 1723/80
Arthur, Piddington, yeo., to Anne, wid., 1734/3 Sept.
Thomas, Denton, cordwainer, to Alice, wid., 1780/3 June

WOODING continued
George, Denton, carpenter, to Elizabeth, wid., 1791/7 Nov.
Sarah, Bugbrooke, to William, woolcomber, husband, 1794/22 Mar.
Mary, Towcester, spin., to Catherine, wife of Richard Brown, butcher, sister, 1796/25 July
William, Weston Favell, carpenter, to Susanna, wid., and Thomas, carpenter, son, 1799/3 Aug.
WOOLLAMS, Richard, Byfield, surgeon, to Thomas Prestidge, gent., principal creditor, Inv. £28.13.6 1725/25 May
John, Walgrave, victualler, to James, Wollaston, baker, son, Elizabeth, wid., now wife of Samuel Stretton, miller, renounced, 1738/7 Apr.
WOOLLEY, Richard, All Saints, Northampton, to Mary, wid., 1723/4
Richard, Northampton, to Catherine, spin., daughter, 1768/7 Apr.
Thomas, Northampton, clerk, to Elizabeth, wid., 1797/5 June
WOOLLMAN, Charles, Desborough, to Ann, wid., 1714/165
WOOLSTON, Thomas, Walgrave, to Henry Hills, butcher, principal creditor, Inv. £30.10.0 1711/121
John, Wilby, Inv.only £236.11.6 1719/16 A
William, Rushden, Inv.only £18.17.8 1722/107 A
Elizabeth, Wellingborough, wid., to Elizabeth, spin., daughter, 1724/17
John, Northampton, hillier, to Mary, wife of Thomas Fascutt, sister, 1757/21 May
Jeffery, Irthlingborough, to Mary, wid., 1760/5 Apr.
Thomas, Higham Ferrers, to Jane, wid., Inv. £154.10.0 1766/30 July
William, Irthlingborough, to Lydia, wife of William Scroxson, cordwainer, daughter, Mary, wid., renounced, 1766/4 Oct.
Jeffery, Irthlingborough, farmer, to Hannah, spin., daughter, 1798/29 June
WOOTTON, Mary, Brackley, to John, mason, husband, 1715/80
Edward, Braunston, soapboiler, to Elizabeth, wid., Inv. £91.10.0 1728/18 Oct.
Joseph, Braunston, soapboiler, to Hannah Rodhouse, Badby, wid., sister, Elizabeth, wife, decd., Will, 1799/30 Sept.
WORKWORTH, Frances, Weedon Pinkney, wid., Inv.only £14.9.0 1715/67 A
WORLEY, George, Spratton, husb., to Sarah, wid., Inv. £195.9.6 1717/11
William, Great Everdon, to Alice, wid., Inv. £63.2.6 1722/133
William, Everdon, to Rebecca Keeble, wid., daughter, of goods unadministered by Abigail, wid., decd., 1726/27 July
George, Higham Park, to Judith, wid., 1742/12 Aug.
Simon, Staverton, blacksmith, to Mary Pitchley, wid., daughter, Mary, wid., renounced, 1751/22 Oct.
John, Moulton, grazier, to Joseph, yeo., son, 1755/13 Oct.
John, Moulton, to Sarah Barber, wid., sister, 1773/18 Sept.
Joseph, Moulton, yeo., to Richard Hanwell, elder, Long Buckby, grazier, and Margaret, Towcester, spin., Will, 1774/24 Dec.
Robert, Brington, mason, to Hannah, wid., 1783/4 Oct.
WORLIDGE, Thomas, Wellingborough, Inv.only £110.14.10 1717/41 A
William, Wellingborough, Inv.only £37.3.0 1720/140 A
Whorlidge, Stephen, Orton, husb., Inv.only £270.5.4 1728/256
John, Wilby, yeo., to Elizabeth, wid., and John Chettle, Chelveston, farmer, guardians of John, minor, Will, 1765/23 Apr.
WORRALL, Thomas, Whilton, to Elizabeth, wid., Will, 1714/94
WORTERS, John, Broughton, dealer, to Sarah, wid., 1800/30 June
WOSTER, Thomas, West Haddon, Inv.only £53.13.2 1717/49 A
WRENN, Charles, Northampton, victualler, to Timothy Rogers, gent., principal creditor, Anne, wid., renounced, 1742/27 Jan.
WRIGHT, Thomas, Inv.only £23.15.0 1711/106 A
Elizabeth, Kingsthorpe, to Samuel Pitman, brother, 1712/41
William, Northampton, gunsmith, to Martha, wid., Inv. £19.6.0 1712/65
Martha, Northampton, to William, Stanwick, son, 1713/46
William, senior, Holcot, Inv.only £226.8.8 1713/57 A
Thomas, Daventry, Inv.only £169.15.0 1714/3 A
William, Kilsby, yeo., to Mary, wid., Inv. £107.16.0 1716/30
Peter, Sibbertoft, baker, Inv.only £15.15.0 1716/89A
William, Stanwick, to Elizabeth, spin., daughter, Inv. £17.5.10 1719/116
Willmer, Denton, to Elizabeth, wid., Inv. £259.9.0 1720/53
William, Paulerspury, mercer, Inv.only £315.5.3½ 1720/113 A
Thomas, Brockhole, to Elizabeth, wid., Inv. £30.0.0 1721/53
Stephen, Daventry, draper, to Sarah, wife of Thomas Durrad, granddaughter, 1722/5

WRIGHT continued
Stephen, Daventry, to Sarah Durrad, sister, 1722/67
Thomas, St. James End, Dallington, to Mary Tarry, aunt and guardian of James and Susanna, minors, children, Inv. £18.5.1 Guard., 1722/72 and 73
Thomas, Moulton, to Isabell, wid., 1724/8
Roger, Northampton, St. Giles, to Samuel, husb., son, John, son, exor., renounced, Will, 1724/81
Thomas, Muscott, yeo., Inv.only £62.12.0 1724/125
John, Higham Ferrers, to Elizabeth, wid., 1725/27 Nov.
Margery, Piddington, spin., to Thomas, lab., brother, Inv. £15.19.10 1727/30 Dec.
John, Crick, husb., yeo., to John, husb., son, Inv. £46.7.6 1728/25 May
Richard, Northampton, comber, to Jane, wid., 1729/21 July
Henry, Gretworth, mercer, Inv.only £27.8.2 1729/223
William, Holcot, farmer, Inv.only £256.7.6 1731/282
William, Holcot, yeo., to Frances, wid., 1732/8 Jan.
Thomas, Daventry, yeo., to Jane, wid., 1734/9 Dec.
Thomas, Bozeat, farmer, Inv.only £172.4.6 1734/320
William, Braybrooke, to Hannah Cooper, spin., 1735/15 Jan.
Thomas, Bozeat, farmer, to Mary, wid., 1735/1 Nov.
Jonas, Stanwick, yeo., to Elizabeth, wid., 1736/25 Oct.
Elizabeth, Ringstead, wid., to Hannah, wife of Samuel Bett, baker, daughter, Inv. £8.4.11 1740/8 May
Robert, Bozeat, lab., to Anne, spin., daughter, 1742/24 Feb.
Samuel, Burton Latimer, grocer, to Thomas, grocer, son, Elizabeth, wid., renounced, 1742/28 Apr.
John, Northampton, draper, to Mary, wid., 1745/25 Apr.
John, Northampton, whitesmith, to Elizabeth, wife of John Wymant, Higham Ferrers, soldier in Flanders, sister, 1748/14 Nov.
Alice, Everdon, wid., to John, grazier, grandson, 1752/5 Oct.
John, East Farndon, yeo., to John, farmer, son, 1755/14 Jan.
Thomas, Burton Latimer, grocer, to Elizabeth, wid., Inv. £168.0.7 1756/23 Apr.
William, Braunston, yeo., to Anne, wid., 1756/27 Apr.
Edward, Kettering, to Elizabeth, wid., 1758/12 Apr.
Thomas, Denton, wheelwright, to Richard, wheelwright, son, 1767/17 Feb.
Edward, Daventry, to Ann, wid., 1771/9 Apr.
Margaret, Farndon, wid., to Thomas Clarke, Church Langton, co. Leic., butcher, Will, 1774/2 Apr.
John, Northampton, to Samuel, higler, father, 1776/11 Jan.
William, Tiffield, yeo., to Anne, wid., 1782/16 Nov.
Mary, Holdenby, wid., to John, farmer, son, 1784/6 Mar.
Richard, Holcot, cordwainer, to Thomas, cordwainer, brother, 1784/8 Sept.
Jonas, Irthlingborough, farmer, to William, farmer, son, 1789/14 Feb.
Richard, Holcot, cordwainer, to Dinah, wife of John Padmore, lab., niece, of goods unadministered by Thomas, brother, decd., 1790/26 Apr.
Thomas, Green's Norton, yeo., to John Malsbury Kirby, Towcester, gent., Will, 1791/1 Sept.
Edward, Brington, mason, to Hannah, wid., 1793/8 Nov.
Thomas, Higham Ferrers, farmer, to Mary, wife of Charles Richards, Wilby, farmer, daughter, 1795/8 Aug.
William, Rothersthorpe, farmer, to Martha, wid., 1796/24 Dec.
Thomas, Holdenby, farmer, to William, farmer, son, 1799/2 Apr.
WRIGHTON, Job, Byfield, to Thomas T--, yeo., principal creditor, 1711/7
Abraham, Sulgrave, to Thomas, yeo., son, 1735/31 Oct.
Daniel, Daventry, husb., to Sarah, wid., 1770/10 Feb.
Thomas, Litchborough, to Elizabeth, wid., 1778/7 Nov.
WYATT, John, Chalcombe, farrier, Inv.only £135.0.0 1723/95 A
John, Chalcombe, bachelor, yeo., to Catherine, wid., mother, Inv. £181.10.0 1724/83
John, Chalcombe, senior, to Catherine, wid. of John, son, exor., decd., Will, 1729/25 Aug.
William, Middleton Cheney, to Elizabeth, wife of John Wrighton, yeo., daughter, Inv. £43.6.0 1753/6 Sept.
Thomas, elder, Silverstone, to Elizabeth, spin., daughter, Will, 1783/13 Oct.
WYCKLEY, William, Northampton, to Henry, gent., father, 1763/20 Jan.
Mary, Northampton, wid., to Anne, wife of Henry Cook, tailor, daughter, 1790/25 Nov.

WYKES, Elizabeth, Great Harrowden, spin., to Ann, wife of John Houghton, 1719/74
William, Cold Ashby, to Ann, wid., 1773/27 Mar.
WYMAN, Daniel, Higham Ferrers, to Prudence, wid., 1796/11 Apr.
WYMENT, Thomas, Daventry, grocer, to Samuel, junior, son, 1745/17 June
Wymant, William, Great Oxendon, yeo., to Hannah, wid., Inv. £101.10.0 1748/1 Oct.
WYMOND, Edward, Northampton, to Alexander Petty, Heath, co. Oxford, cydermerchant, 1722/94
William, Rothwell, shoemaker, to John Colson, gardener, principal creditor, 1737/1 Aug.
WYNN see WINN

Y

YARDLEY, George, Byfield, weaver, to Ann, spin., daughter, Margaret, wid., exor., decd., Inv. £2.16.2½ Will, 1720/4
YATES, Edward, Brackley, husb., to Elizabeth, wid., Inv. £19.18.6 1713/18
Yate, Samuel, Middleton Cheney, gent., Inv.only £342.19.8 1718/112A
Ann, Brackley, to Hannah, spin., sister, 1763/12 Jan.
Edward, Daventry, butcher, to Frances, wid., 1765/7 Sept.
John, Long Buckby, gardener, to Joseph, schoolmaster, Mary Robins, wid., Elizabeth, wife of William Harbert, Northampton, and Lydia, wife of Thomas Dunkley, Milton, lab., children, Will, 1797/29 Mar.
YEOMANS, Thomas, Brackley, clerk, Inv.only £76.12.0 1715/147A
Thomas, Middleton Cheney, lab., Inv.only £34.19.0 1719/18A
Thomas, Brackley, victualler, to Alice, wid., Inv. £42.15.0 1721/101
Hugh, Blisworth, to Mary, wid., 1732/12 Feb.
Mary, Inv.only £12.16.0 1732/287
YORK, Thomas, Burton Latimer, to Tobias, Haselbech, brother, Anne, wid., mother, renounced, 1716/12
William, Paulerspury, Inv.only £163.9.2 1718/50A
Francis, Finedon, yeo., Inv.only £278.8.6 1720/120A
William, Walgrave, to William, yeo., son, Inv. £39.3.0 1724/110
Yorke, William, Finedon, farmer, to Mary, wid., 1748/18 Feb.
Yorke, Samuel, Old, whittawer, to Elizabeth, wid., Will, 1761/31 Oct.
Yorke, Richard, Walgrave, yeo., to Samuel, farmer, son, Sarah, wid., renounced, Inv. £338.10.2 1777/22 Mar.
YOUD, Thomas, Farthinghoe, lab., to Mary, wife of John Jefferies, lab., 1757/29 Jan.
YOULE, Yule, Richard, Old, Inv.only £35.0.0 1716/31A
Stephen, Old, husb., to Mary, wife of Charles Hensman, husb., sister, 1728/3 Feb.
Stephen, Old, Inv.only £80.4.0 1728/204
Ule, Richard, Inv.only undated/410
YOUNG, Daniel, Syresham, lab., to John French, husb., Inv. £9.17.0 Will, 1713/85
Robert, Irthlingborough, to Mary, wid., 1726/26 Apr.
Henry, Yardley Hastings, to Anne, wid., 1727/11 Oct.
Henry, Yardley Hastings, Inv.only £62.1.6 1727/193
Giles, Irthlingborough, carpenter, to John, shepherd, son, 1748/28 Dec.
YOUNGER, John, marine, Her Majesty's Ship Norfolk, to Mary, Great Billing, wid., mother, Will, 1760/19 Apr.

Miscellaneous

---din, John, Middleton Cheney, grocer, Inv.only £21.19.6 1717/96
Kilsby, Letter asking for monthy payment from Royal Aid, 1666/160
Kilsby Vicarage, Tithes and Supply of Cure 1673-79, 1681/159
Ringstead Chapel, concerning contributions to the repair of the Church, queston between Bryan Sutton and John Mason, churchwardens, and Elizabeth Baker, Ringstead, undated/169
Weedon Beck, Account of the vicarage tithes, 1671/155

INDEX OF OTHER PERSONS

An asterisk indicates more than one reference on the page.

C

R

S

T

Y

Z

INDEX OF PLACE NAMES

An asterisk indicates more than one reference on the page.

NORTHAMPTONSHIRE

BEDFORDSHIRE

BERKSHIRE

BUCKINGHAMSHIRE

INDEX OF TRADES AND CONDITIONS

An asterisk indicates more than one reference on the page.